ETHIOPIA
Empire in Revolution

by Marina and David Ottaway

AFRICANA PUBLISHING COMPANY
A division of Holmes & Meier Publishers, Inc.
New York   London

First published in the United States of America 1978 by
AFRICANA PUBLISHING COMPANY
A division of Holmes & Meier Publishers, Inc.
30 Irving Place
New York, N.Y. 10003

Great Britain:
Holmes & Meier Publishers, Ltd.
Hillview House
1, Hallswelle Parade, Finchley Road
London NW 11 ODL

Library of Congress Cataloging in Publication Data

Ottaway, Marina.
    Ethiopia: Empire in Revolution

    Includes bibliographical references and index.
    1. Ethiopia—Politics and government—1974-
I. Ottaway, David, joint author.   II. Title.
DT 387.95.087   320.9′63′06   77-28370
ISBN 0-8419-0362-X
ISBN 0-8419-0363-8 pbk.

Manufactured in the United States of America

The cover photo shows units of Ethiopia's peasant militia (*Photo courtesy Ethiopian Government Ministry of Information*)

Contents

Foreword

This book, the second we have undertaken together, was written mostly in Ethiopia, where we lived during the first three years of the revolution, Marina Ottaway as a lecturer at Addis Ababa University and David Ottaway as Africa correspondent for the *Washington Post.* Watching the revolution unfold in its various directions, some extremely positive, others just as negative, was a fascinating experience. It soon became evident that the revolution taking place in front of us was something quite different in its depth and magnitude from any other that has so far occurred in Africa. It was not a nationalist revolution, such as in Algeria, Angola, and Mozambique, although the problem of building a nation became part of the process. It was not simply a struggle for power among ethnic groups, such as the Hutus and Tutsis in Rwanda and Burundi, although ethnic conflicts played an important role. Nor was it an attempt at making a socialist revolution engineered from above by a small group of Marxist intellectuals trying to impose a concept of class conflict alien to the social conditions of the country. The conflicts which wracked Ethiopia were real and deep, reminiscent of those present in European countries during the 19th century, when class conflict and nationalism were rife. But the historical processes which unfolded in Europe over a period of decades and even centuries were compressed in Ethiopia into a very short span of time. It was only after 1941 that Emperor Haile Selassie started in earnest the process of transforming a loosely knit feudal empire into an absolute monarchical state. By 1974, Ethiopia was already experiencing the first attempt by its small bourgeoisie to seize power. Two years later, it was in the throes of socialist revolution.

Perhaps because of the extreme rapidity with which events have unfolded, the Ethiopian revolution has all too often been represented as the establishment of just another bloody African military dictatorship rather than a social upheaval of dramatic proportions. Some of the responsibility for this misunderstanding undoubtedly lies with the Military Council itself, which proved incapable of explaining to the world what was happening in Ethiopia, and was so afraid of adverse comments that it refused to show visitors even its very real accomplishments. But part of this misunderstanding is also due to the Western world's incapacity to understand and deal with revolutions. Condemned on principle by the conservatives, they all too often meet with the disapproval of liberals and even radicals, the liberals upset by the violence and the violations of human rights, the radicals irritated by the failure to bring about instant utopia. There is no doubt that the Ethiopian revolution has had its share of horrors, not all of which can be justified even as necessary means to a worthwhile goal. But it has often been forgotten that the pre-revolutionary situation also held its share of horrors. Death by starvation is no better than death in front of a firing squad, and probably more peasants died in the "hidden famine" of 1973–74 than in the first three years of the revolution. We have not unraveled all the mysteries of the Ethiopian revolution in these pages, but we hope to have made a solid contribution toward an understanding of the turmoil now engulfing this unique African country.

We owe a large debt to many European and American scholars, the Ethiopianists who have spent long years trying to shed light on this hidden empire, and whose works have been of invaluable assistance in understanding recent developments. In writing this book, we have obtained extensive help from a large number of Ethiopians whose names must be left unmentioned for their own protection and safety in this time of continuing instability and uncertainty in Ethiopia. One person who can be named, however, is Tamene Asmare, who worked almost three years with us patiently explaining both the past and the present intricacies of Ethiopian politics.

Writing this book has been at times hazardous and nerve-wracking. We collected the material for it and wrote the first draft of most chapters while still living in Ethiopia. But the practice of house-to-house searches, which became frequent in early 1977, forced us to stop writing and to send our files and incomplete chapters out of the country through various channels that are best not mentioned. Our precautions proved justified, for in late April 1977 the military government ordered all Western correspondents to leave the country within 48 hours. The book was completed in the unreal peace of Bonassola on the Italian coast, with friends sending or bringing us word of events underway in Ethiopia throughout the summer. Thus we were able to span in our analysis a little more than the first three years of the revolution. We hope our work will be of help to those who in the future will be studying the revolution in Ethiopia with the advantage of a broader time perspective.

Bonassola, Italy
August 1977

1.   Sketch of a Revolution

At the beginning of 1974—1966 on the Ethiopian calendar—the destiny of Ethiopia seemed firmly in the hands of Emperor Haile Selassie—King of the Kings, Elect of God, Conquering Lion of the Tribe of Judah, who claimed direct descendence from the biblical Solomon and Sheba. Like Louis XIV, he was the state. A handful of powerful aristocratic families and hand-picked retainers in league or intrigue with the Emperor and the Orthodox Christian Church dictated the daily lot of 27 million peasants, exploiting to their advantage the mountain kingdom's meager riches without troubled conscience. It was the way it had always been during the 50 years of the Emperor's reign and in the ancient feudal empire for centuries.

By the end of that year, the King of Kings was languishing in prison, the leading aristocrats and pillars of royal officialdom had been executed, and the destiny of the country lay with a group of unknown sergeants and majors who resolutely turned their backs on the Solomonic legend and proclaimed the advent of something called Ethiopian socialism. The changes that took place in the life of the empire in that one year were astounding, and those that were to follow even more so as the first "great revolution" in black Africa unfolded in protracted social conflict and political turmoil from one end of the country to the other.

It was the prevailing wisdom in early 1974 that Ethiopia was more than ripe for change and that this would come as soon as Haile Selassie passed from the political scene. Ever since the Emperor's 80th birthday in July 1972 and his ambiguous attitude toward his successor, speculation at home and abroad had been rife on the subject of "after Haile Selassie, what?" To be sure, the Ethiopian military figured prominently in such discussions, since it was the main organized force in a country where political associations of any kind had been systematically suppressed and where no significant underground opposition movement existed. Nobody guessed at the breadth and depth of the changes that would shortly shake the sleeping kingdom from stultifying poverty and debilitating palace politics.

The revolution began in a most unexpected manner. On January 12, rank-and-file soldiers of a small garrison in Neghelle Borana, a semi-arid region in southern Ethiopia, mutinied against their commanding officers. It was not political grievances that motivated the revolt, but vile food and shortage of drinking water. The soldiers' pump was out of order, and the officers refused to allow them to use their own. After first detaining their superiors, the soldiers had the audacity to seize the Emperor's personal envoy, Commander of the Ground Forces Lt. Gen. Deresse Dubale, and force him to eat and drink as they did. In this dramatic fashion the ordinary Ethiopian soldiers, the NCOs, and low ranking officers entered upon the stage of Ethiopian history.

The Neghelle revolt was the shot heard round the empire. News of the event—and of the Emperor's decision not to punish the rebel soldiers—spread by radio, telegram, and word of mouth to all army, air force, and police barracks throughout the country. A month later, on February 10, the technicians and NCOs at the Debre Zeit Air Force Base near Addis Ababa rose up in a similar revolt, imprisoning their officers in a mess hall and holding them hostage for three days while they pressed their demands for better pay and working conditions. Enlisted men and NCOs of the Second Division in Asmara were the next to rise up, and their revolt on February 25 finally brought to the attention of the outside world what was happening in Ethiopia. Led by seven corporals and sergeants, the mutineers took over the country's second largest city and began broadcasting their demands over the radio station for the entire world to hear. In startlingly rapid succession, uprisings inside the armed forces had spread from a small garrison in the wastelands of the empire to a key air force base near the capital and then to an entire division.

Unrest spread almost simultaneously to the civilian population in an initially unrelated outburst of general discontent. Life had become increasingly difficult for the inhabitants of Ethiopia's major towns and cities because of the effects of inflation on already meager salaries. In addition, there was a serious malaise within the educated elite over the drought in northern Wollo and Tigre provinces that the Emperor had inhumanely ignored, allowing more than 100,000 peasants to die from starvation. But the immediate causes of the explosion of discontent in the capital were more mundane.

On February 14, students at Haile Selassie University in Addis Ababa went on strike and staged a demonstration against a proposed reform of the educational system. There was nothing new about student strikes and demonstrations at the university, but this time there were differences. Many high school teachers and university professors supported the students in their rejection of the reform, and the demonstration triggered an unprecedented wave of strikes, demonstrations, and violence. Buses and cars were stoned in the streets of the capital, and police suddenly opened fire on the students, killing one of them. Other groups then joined in, rising up not so much in support of the students as in revolt against their own specific conditions. In fact, the Confederation of Ethiopian Labor Unions, the main civilian organization, refused to have anything to do with the students. On February 18, teachers went on strike for higher pay and against the proposed reform. But this time they were supported by their colleagues in the provinces, spreading the seeds of unrest throughout the empire. The same day, taxi drivers struck in protest over a 50 percent increase in gasoline prices, paralyzing life in the capital. (Taxis in Addis Ababa are everyman's form of transportation, moving people, chickens, vegetables, and furniture about the sprawling city.) At the same time, buses, private cars, and anything else still moving in the streets were stoned by students, street boys, and the city's poor. The general chaos could not be quickly suppressed at the Emperor's command, because the loyalty of the Fourth Division stationed in the city's center was suddenly in doubt.

On February 23, the Emperor gave in to some civilian demands—the first in a long series of concessions that would eventually leave him stripped of all authority. Addressing his "beloved" people on television, he announced the postponement of any changes in the educational system, a partial rollback in the price of gasoline, and price controls on key staples to check inflation. The following day, the government announced a salary increase for the armed forces and the police. But the rebellious soldiers of the Second Division in Asmara rejected the increase as insufficient, forcing the Emperor to send a high-level delegation to the provincial capital to discuss a further increment.

The political repercussions of the military and civilian uprisings were soon felt. After giving in to the mutinous soldiers and urban mobs, on February 28 the Emperor, in an attempt to reestablish his shaken authority, accepted the resignation of Aklilu Habte-Wold, who had been prime minister since 1958. Whether this move was wise or even warranted was debated long afterwards, for none of the demonstrating groups had specifically called for Aklilu's resignation. Moreover, it hinted at panic and weakness in the palace which soldiers and civilians would fully exploit in coming months. After a day of hasty consultations with loyalist generals and aristocrats, the Emperor appointed a new prime minister, Endelkachew Makonnen, an Oxford-educated scion of a leading aristocratic family who would shortly become as controversial as his predecessor. On March 5, the Emperor announced that the 1955 Constitution would be revised to make the prime minister responsible to parliament, a giant concession to reformist demands had it ever been carried out. But such was not to be the course of the revolution.

The new prime minister was faced with an impossible task: that of restoring order while not controlling the army. At the same time, he had to convince various protesting military and civilian groups that a new era had dawned in Ethiopia without really introducing any substantial reforms. Needless to say, he failed. But for a brief period it appeared that he was succeeding and that Ethiopia was returning to imperial autocratic rule, possibly disguised in the trappings of a 19th century European parliamentary democracy.

From early March to late May, the towns and cities of Ethiopia, particularly the capital, were plunged into an indescribable chaos of strikes and demonstrations. For the first time in the empire's history, the normally mild-mannered Labor Confederation managed to organize a general strike that paralyzed all economic activity from March 7 to 9. The success of this action unleashed a wave of wildcat strikes that left the government running from factory to factory and from one semi-state company to another to deal with the explosion of labor demands. Practically every group from prostitutes to lay priests went out on strike for better wages and working conditions. Even the usually subdued Parliament dominated by the conservative landed class caught the spirit of the times: a bill introduced in, of all places, the appointed Senate in late March asked for freedom of the press and the establishment of privately owned newspapers and radio stations to replace the tightly government controlled instruments of the mass media.

The armed forces, in the meantime, were still in upheaval. Although the early, spontaneous mutinies of enlisted men had subsided after two hefty salary increases, there were rumblings of much more serious trouble to come. On March 31, General Abiye Abebe, the new chief of staff and minister of defense in the Endelkachew cabinet, announced that a plot against the government by air force officers had been uncovered and foiled. This cabal had for some time been trying to politicize the unrest within the armed forces and to link the military's bread-and-butter demands to those of the civilians in order to form an overall movement for political change. Leaflets dropped by air force helicopters over crowds of demonstrators on different occasions in early March had asked for broader economic and political reforms.

In April, the soldiers finally seemed to be returning to their barracks, but civilians were still in the streets. The mayor of Addis Ababa was forced out of office by a large demonstration after he had refused to submit his resignation as suggested by city councilors. On April 20, a huge crowd of Moslems marched through the capital to demand religious equality and the separation of church and state. It was probably the largest demonstration ever held in Addis; some estimates put the number of participants as high as 100,000. Whatever the figure, it effectively exploded the myth promoted by the Emperor that Ethiopia was a Christian country in which Moslems were only a negligible minority.

Toward the end of April, the era of crowds, freedom of the press, and hopes for democracy suddenly came to an end when the old order made its last attempt at a comeback. A Coordinating Committee of the Armed Forces under the command of Colonel Alem Zewd Tessema of the elite Airborne Corps appeared on the scene. The army, it seemed, had finally been brought under control, and the government was using it to restore the status quo. It became immediately apparent that the day when concessions could be won by strikes and demonstrations was over. On April 27, the Coordinating Committee issued its first statement, announcing that the military intended to ensure order and peace in the country and that, as a first step, they had arrested some of the former ministers and officials guilty of neglecting the famine or of corruption. Nineteen officers of the imperial regime were detained.

The second step in the government's crackdown soon followed. Strong warnings were issued first by the cabinet and then directly by the ministry of defense against strikes by government officials trying to form unions. The Labor Confederation was also warned it would be closed down if it did not desist from its efforts to organize strikes. In the meantime, with the military backing the government again, Endelkachew began whittling away at the few gains won by the strikers and demonstrators. First, the government declared the March general strike illegal, and then it refused to recognize the newly-organized Telecommunications Workers Union. Endelkachew also became less conciliatory, telling parliament that reforms would be slow in coming and that a new constitution and a new parliament would have to precede any reforms.

The effect of the military's intervention in support of Endelkachew was soon felt, and order returned for a brief period. The first battle of the revolution appeared to have been won by supporters of the old regime. The only victims were a small group of hapless officials who had been arrested for crimes of which the entire imperial establishment was guilty, including many of those still in power. Emboldened by the sense of their renewed power, some stalwarts of the old order decided that even those few arrested former ministers and officials should not suffer. In late June, a group of deputies tried to negotiate for the release of the political prisoners in the custody of the Fourth Division. The military reaction was swift and unexpected. On June 28, a new Coordinating Committee of the Armed Forces, Police, and Territorial Army sent troops to occupy the radio station in Addis Ababa and made clear that the military would no longer be an instrument of the Endelkachew regime. In restrospect, June 28 marked the *de facto* end of imperial rule in Ethiopia and the beginning of the second phase of the Ethiopian revolution.

The Coordinating Committee, which later became popularly known as the *Derg,* at first proclaimed its "unswerving loyalty" to the Emperor and its determination to assure the "smooth functioning" of the civilian cabinet. At the same time, it started a much more widespread wave of arrests not only among former officials but also among those still in positions of high power—in the Emperor's Crown Council, in the army, and by the end of July, in the cabinet itself. On July 22, Prime Minister Endelkachew was forced to resign, and the Emperor appointed Lij Michael Imru to replace him. Michael, although also a member of a leading aristocratic family, had a reputation for being much more progressive than Endelkachew, who was arrested August 1.

With the establishment of the Coordinating Committee of the Armed Forces, Police, and Territorial Army in late June, the Ethiopian revolution entered a period of abrupt shifts in aims and direction. The break with the past, which had been more theoretical than real under Endelkachew, became increasingly sharp despite the military's pledges of allegiance to the Emperor. The Elect of God was quickly reduced to a figurehead who could no longer protect even his closest associates. They were arrested one by one.

What had started as a very spontaneous and widespread, if disorganized, outpouring of discontent became a movement firmly controlled and guided from the top. Interestingly, as the revolution entered this more radical phase, popular participation ceased almost completely, and strikes and demonstrations became rare. When they were held, it was most often at the inspiration of the military out to demonstrate the declining popularity of the Emperor.

Despite the demise of civilian participation in the revolution, the advent of the Coordinating Committee did not immediately lead to open military rule. Abroad, the operation of removing the Emperor became known as Ethiopia's "creeping coup." Civilian institutions were left standing, and although the prime minister was replaced and the cabinet reshuffled, the change of officials was far from complete. The new prime minister himself had been a member of the Endelkachew cabinet.

The position of the *Derg* was made known in a thirteen-point statement issued on July 9, notable above all for its moderate tone. The military pledged continuing support for the Emperor and even gave as its main goals the upholding of the Crown and the smooth functioning of civilian government. Nothing in the document suggested that the *Derg* wanted anything more radical than a constitutional monarchy. The vagueness of the military's political program was summed up in its official slogan *Ethiopia Tikdem*, "Ethiopia First."

It took months before the meaning of *Ethiopia Tikdem* became fully clear, but within a few weeks there was increasing evidence that the immediate objective of the *Derg,* pledges of loyalty notwithstanding, was the deposition of Haile Selassie and the scrapping of the imperial system of government. In a series of surgical operations performed during the month of August, the imperial institutions were cut out one by one until only the Emperor was left. Even his Jubilee Palace was nationalized from under him. The state-run media that had for decades sung his daily praises were suddenly being used to undermine his prestige and authority and published articles detailing the horrors and corruption of the imperial order. Thus, when the proclamation announcing his deposition came on September 12, there was no public outcry. The Elect of God was taken off in a small Volkswagen—without a shot being fired or a cry raised in his defense.

Yet even after disassembling the imperial system and deposing the Emperor, the military did not immediately eliminate the monarchy, primarily because of uncertainty as to whether the public was ready for such a total break with the past. Instead, it called upon Crown Prince Asfa Wossen, convalescing in Switzerland after a serious stroke, to return to Ethiopia and replace his deposed father. The Crown prince not unexpectedly declined what was almost certainly an invitation to prison pending a clearer indication of the "will of the people" regarding his return. (The *Derg* did not officially withdraw the offer until March 21, 1975, when it abolished the monarchy.) Having made this final concession to the old regime, the military announced on September 15 the establishment of a Provisional Military Administrative Council and the appointment of General Aman Michael Andom as its chairman. Although not a member of the *Derg,* General Aman was a well-known commander with a national reputation. The formation of the Provisional Military Council marked the beginning of the third phase of the Ethiopian revolution, which would see a sharp radicalization in the policies of the *Derg* and a clearer definition of its leadership and style of rule.

Who ruled the *Derg* and whither Ethiopia? Throughout the fall of 1974, little was known about the *Derg,* which went to great lengths to wrap itself in secrecy and anonymity, refusing to disclose the identity of its presumed 120 members or even of its top leaders. General Aman was known as a proud and forceful commander, enjoying enormous respect among the military rank and file, but he was an outsider to the revolutionary movement, and it was far from clear whether he had any authority over members of the *Derg*. It was equally obscure how much power the two vice-chairmen, Major Mengistu Haile Mariam and Major Atnafu Abate, wielded in the *Derg*'s councils, or how collegial the decision-making process was. The policies of the *Derg* remained as ill-defined as its leadership during the first few months after the Emperor's removal. Although the Military Council expropriated some properties of the royal family and arrested officials in piecemeal fashion, there was no immediate policy of wholesale nationalizations or even a hint that socialism would become the official ideology.

Perhaps the first thing to become relatively clear was the style of the *Derg*'s rule. In the same proclamation deposing the Emperor, the Military Council outlawed strikes and demonstrations and made clear that disorders of any kind would not be tolerated. It also quickly established that the Provisional Military Council would not be bullied by outside civilian groups into concessions or rushed into hasty policy decisions. When the Ethiopian Labor Federation met four days after the Emperor's removal and straightaway called for a "Provisional People's Government," the military responded by arresting its top leadership. When tenant farmers and agricultural workers in southern Ethiopia started seizing lands on their own, the new military government ordered the properties returned and the rights of landlords respected until the official proclamation of a land reform. And when students continued demonstrations in Addis Ababa against the new government, the military closed the university and the last two years of the high schools and ordered them into the countryside to bring the peasants the message of *Ethiopia Tikdem* rather than cause trouble in the capital. Indeed, the seeds of the conflict between urban civilian groups and the military—one that was to become a most serious problem of the revolution—were sown in the first weeks after the Emperor's overthrow.

The first months of the new military government were crucial in setting the course of the revolution in other areas as well—its leadership, its Eritrean policy, and finally its budding socialist ideology. Among the most complex problems the military inherited from the Emperor was that of Eritrea, the country's strategic Red Sea province that had once been an Italian colony and where a secessionist movement had been carrying on a guerrilla war since 1961. The *Derg* was split between hard-liners who basically agreed on continuing the Emperor's policy of military suppression of the movement and moderates who favored a negotiated settlement with the Eritrean Liberation Front. General Aman, himself an Eritrean, was soon leading the moderate faction in an attempt to negotiate with the Front, while a majority of the *Derg*'s members were increasingly leaning toward a military solution. The dispute over Eritrea became enmeshed in a power struggle within the *Derg* and eventually led to the resignation of General Aman around November 20 (the exact date is not known). Ordered to surrender, the general barricaded himself in his house and fought it out with the troops that had come to arrest him until he was killed. The same night, "Bloody Saturday" as November 23 was later called, the *Derg* met and voted for the immediate execution of the 57 most important political prisoners.

The executions changed dramatically—and somewhat unjustly—the image of the Ethiopian revolution from that of a skillful and peaceful reform movement to one of a bloody massacre. A storm of protest and a barrage of warnings against further killings came from the capitals of the West as well as a surprising number of African nations where the fate of the Emperor was still a major concern. But the revolution had reached a turning point without anyone outside the *Derg* itself being able to control the drift of events toward a far more radical course. The executions were the first sign that "radicals" within the Military Council were gaining the upper hand. More indications were shortly to follow. On December 20, less than a month after "Bloody Saturday," the *Derg* published a declaration stating that *Ethiopia Tikdem* was an unequivocal commitment to *hebrettesebawinet,* or homegrown Ethiopian socialism. As defined by the Council, it meant "equality, self-reliance, the dignity of labor, the supremacy of the common good and the indivisibility of Ethiopian unity." However, the concrete economic meaning of Ethiopian socialism would become clear only in the ensuing months, as the government issued a series of announcements and proclamations aimed at reshaping the mixed feudal and capitalist economy of the country. As for the political content of *hebrettesebawinet,* it remained confused and ill-defined for well over a year. Only after considerable debate and open strife among different factions within the *Derg,* and between it and more radical civilian groups, was Marxism-Leninism to be adopted as the basis for the revolution's ideology.

Beginning in early January 1975, the Military Council spelled out its economic policy in a series of nationalizations. On January 1, banks and insurance companies were taken over. On February 3, most industries of any size—a grand total of 72—were either nationalized or brought under state control. Owners in the latter case were forced to cede a majority interest to the government. The most radical decree came on March 4, when land reform was announced.

Few measures have been talked about as much as land reform in Ethiopia. For years it was the priority demand of students and indeed of all Ethiopian progressives. The government had long recognized the need for land reform, and even Emperor Haile Selassie, whose family had immense holdings, had paid lip service to the idea. International agencies and most embassies had pushed for the idea. Though Prime Minister Endelkachew had pledged to carry out a reform, he had been careful never to specify what form it might take. The proclamation issued by the *Derg* on March 4 was much more radical than anyone had expected, including the most radical students. It did not merely limit the size of landholdings; it did away with all private ownership of land. The reform did not simply regulate the complex relationships between landlord and tenants; it did away altogether with the system of tenancy. No private farmer was allowed to hire a laborer. The decree also set up peasant associations which would carry out the reform and take over from the landlords the running of all local affairs. The proclamation was so radical that it left even diplomats from Communist countries shaking their heads in dismay at the speed with which the military was moving Ethiopia from feudalism to socialism.

With land reform, forces that would assure the destruction of the old economic order were put into motion. In effect, the economic power of the landed aristocracy and even of much of the country's new, urban-based entrepreneurial class was dealt a devastating blow. In a kind of mopping-up operation, the *Derg* issued one last economic proclamation on August 4 nationalizing all urban lands and houses not physically occupied by the owner. The measure was a *coup de grace* to the landed class that in recent years had invested heavily in modern villas in Addis Ababa which were rented at high price to foreigners.

Despite the land reform decree the ideology of Ethiopian socialism remained unclear. Furthermore, as a result of the measure, the *Derg* soon discovered it was facing even more urgent political problems. Students and the Labor Federation continued to agitate for a "people's government," freedom of the press, and the right to demonstrate—none of which demands the military was ready to grant. Throughout the remaining months of 1974 and all of the following year, the malaise between the military and urban civilian groups worsened. Students sent to the countryside to preach socialism now had a concrete, revolutionary task to perform—the implementation of land reform. This should have satisfied even the most radical among them, but it proved one more bone of contention in the civilian-military struggle. Other civilian groups were no less hostile to the *Derg*. The opposition of the Labor Confederation slowly hardened so that by May 1975 the military government ordered the closure of its headquarters in Addis Ababa and elections for a new leadership. This maneuver failed since the new group of union leaders proved even more hostile to the military. A conference of the Labor Confederation in September produced a set of resolutions violently attacking the *Derg* and threatening a general strike if a civilian government were not installed. The direct confrontation between the military and the Confederation ended in the killing of a dozen airport workers and the imposition of martial law in the capital. After crushing the attempted general strike, the Labor Confederation was virtually disbanded.

Other underground groups joined in what amounted to a *de facto* civilian campaign to force the military from power. The most notable of these was a Marxist Ethiopian People's Revolutionary Party, which eventually became so vocal that by the spring of 1976 the *Derg* allowed the state-controlled press to express its viewpoint and courted its support. In an effort to reach a compromise with the revolution's leftist opposition, the *Derg,* on April 20, officially announced the adoption of "scientific socialism" and a program for a "National Democratic Revolution" leading eventually to the establishment of a "People's Democratic Republic." All "anti-feudal" and "anti-imperialist" parties were made legal, and a "People's Organizing Provisional Office," an embryonic political bureau, was set up to organize a workers' party that would one day lead the revolution in accordance with Marxist-Leninist dictates. But even these measures proved insufficient to quell opposition to the military leadership of the revolution. In mid-1976, the *Derg* remained just as isolated as ever.

Is it justified to consider the rush of events in Ethiopia between 1974 and 1976 as the beginning of a revolution? Was it all just a "palace coup," or the establishment of one more self-serving African military regime? In fact, the *Derg* had considerable trouble establishing its revolutionary credentials both at home and abroad. Abroad, socialist countries remained skeptical of the new Ethiopian regime, considering it either naively radical—as when it nationalized all land in one blow—or suspiciously linked to the "imperialist" camp—as when it sought and obtained arms from the United States. Inside the country, "progressives" refused to accept the idea that a junta of half-educated NCOs could carry out a revolution. After all, revolutions are made by the urban working class, the oppressed peasantry, and the vanguard intellectuals, while armies spawn fascist military dictatorships. There could be no revolution without a political party, without an ideology, and without the support of the proletariat and the intelligentsia. Yet, if one looks at the process through which change took place in this period, and at the depth of the transformation in Ethiopian society, there can be little doubt that this was a revolution.

The process itself was characterized by a rapid radicalization of the military's program and ideology, initiated by soldiers who were responsible for unleashing events but could not subsequently control them. Each reform generated new political forces. Incapable of controlling them and unwilling to allow civilian organizations formal political participation in the government, the *Derg* often reacted by adopting and implementing the demands of the opposition. Time and again the *Derg* announced radical reforms even while arresting leftists. Nowhere is this process better illustrated than in the *Derg*'s final adoption of "scientific socialism" and a "new democratic revolution," announced even as the military battled the growing strength of the Ethiopian People's Revolutionary Party. For all its confusing contradictions, the conflict between the military and civilians led to much more radical policies than either would have implemented on its own. Each side vied with the other to establish itself as the real revolutionary force in the country. Civilians radicalized the military and the military radicalized civilians.

The movement to the left was so rapid that after only two years it was difficult to remember how conservative the country, including its "progressive" elements, had been when the whole process began. In early 1974, a "radical" was most often someone who advocated western-style parliamentary democracy. Air force officers scattering pamphlets that advocated free elections and a free press were then considered "radical," and student "radicals" were striking in support of these demands. Two years later, political debate centered around two factions, one pro- and the other anti-military, both preaching "scientific socialism" and proletarian dictatorship. In early 1974, land reforms were conceived by most "progressives" as measures to limit the size of landholdings, changes in the land tax system, and legislation to provide more tenant protection. A year later, all land belonged to the state, no one could even have a tenant or hire a farm worker, and a debate was raging within the government over whether the newly formed peasant associations should be armed to overcome resistance from landlords and rich peasants.

Changes brought about in Ethiopian society by the revolutionary process were profound. The most significant and irreversible of these was the destruc-tion of the imperial, feudal system of government. That meant the destruction of the vast network of personal ties that Emperor Haile Selassie had woven over half a century to hold the country together. In its place a collegial body of more than 100 soldiers was created in which major decisions were decided by vote. The destruction of the old feudal system in the provinces meant the end of autocratic rule by local landlords and *balabbats,* village notables who ran their domains like autonomous fiefdoms. The wholesale razing of the old feudal order created a power vacuum that neither the central government nor the new peasants associations could immediately fill. As a result, many regions of rural Ethiopia became the scene of protracted social conflict as old and new groups fought for power and land. Thousands were killed. The tenant was finally freed from his shackles, and no peasant would ever again have to pay rent or feudal dues.

Another profound change was the politicalization of the masses. In the past, the overwhelming majority of Ethiopians even in the urban centers had been, and were deliberately kept, in political lethargy. The only type of association in which they were involved were the *edir,* simple mutual aid and funeral societies that flourished in larger towns and cities. Political parties were outlawed, and even the activities of the moderate Labor Confederation were closely watched. Politics was the affair of a few aristocratic families and of a group of upstarts promoted by the Emperor, and it took place mostly within the confines of the Jubilee and Menelik Palaces. Above all, politics was highly personal, even incestuous, with families of the ruling elite constantly intermarrying even as they intrigued against one another. With the revolution, there was a veritable explosion of grassroots politics. By 1976, peasants were everywhere electing the officers of their associations and were in charge of handling local affairs in place of the *balabbats.* In the cities, slum dwellers were electing officials of neighborhood associations and given charge of such things as housing problems, local security, and small local development projects. Workers in factories, employees in offices and civil servants were participating in twice weekly forums to discuss problems of the revolution, and the entire country was listening to lectures on Marxism-Leninism over the radio. Even if few people understood the new Marxist jargon and although discussion of political issues often degenerated into an airing of grievances over wages, cost of living, and management, the general level of political consciousness among Ethiopians was far higher than ever before.

A third fundamental change was in the relationship among ethnic and religious groups. Under Haile Selassie, the empire was dominated by Christian Amharas and to a lesser extent by Christian Tigreans with the backing of the powerful Orthodox Christian Church. In regions conquered by Emperor Menelik in southern Ethiopia at the end of the 19th century, the Amhara established virtually a colonial relationship over the native Galla, or Oromo, peoples, taking their lands and imposing an alien rule on them. Galla *balabbats* were incorporated into the system of Amhara domination; Amharic was the official language of local administration and the only medium of instruction in schools. The Orthodox Church was the official one, and the Emperor portrayed Ethiopia as a bastion of Christianity surrounded by hostile Moslem countries, despite the fact that Moslems were at least as numerous as the Christians inside the empire.

The revolution radically altered these relations. This was due partly to government policy: land reform in effect "liberated" Galla tenants from Amhara landlords, and the Moslem religion was put on an equal standing with Christianity. But partly, too, it was the result of the spontaneous outbreak of long pent-up resentment among colonized Galla peasants against Amhara "colonizers." In the southern half of the country, the turnabout in relations between the ethnic groups accelerated the destruction of the feudal order. But in many parts of the Amhara highlands, it had the opposite effect, strengthening feudal relations between landlord and peasant. This was because Amhara landlords were able to find support among their own tenants and small farmers, convincing them that land reform was a Moslem Galla "plot" which aimed at destroying the Amhara, Christian Ethiopian empire.

Paradoxically, the military exacerbated ethnic feelings by seeking to put all ethnic and religious groups on an equal footing. Ethnic consciousness blossomed, and the government was soon talking about the "nationalities problem" and discussing means to solve it. Ethnic "liberation movements" arose in various parts of the country with armed bands fighting against central government forces sent in to quell these revolts. Even the ideological debate under way in early 1976 was interpreted by many confused Ethiopians as camouflage for an underlying rivalry between Gallas who dominated the government and Amharas who dominated the opposition.

Finally, the Ethiopian revolution entailed a radical redistribution of wealth between the cities and the countryside in favor of the long exploited peasantry. Under Haile Selassie, government policies had favored the urban population, particularly that of Addis Ababa. Investment codes promoted the development of large urban industries; schools and hospitals were located disproportionately in towns, and the standard of living was much higher among urban residents than among the peasants. This did not mean that city dwellers lived well, because Ethiopia was and remains very underdeveloped. But their conditions were much better than those of the peasantry. In part, this resulted from low food prices, since much marketed grain was obtained by landlords as rent. The rural population, on the other hand, had little grain left after paying the landlord, and only a meager occasional surplus to sell to procure other basic necessities. Few schools, clinics, and social services existed. Half the rural population was estimated to live more than half a day's walk from a road, and only some 2 percent was reached by an agricultural extension service.

The revolution drastically changed this situation. While industrial wages remained largely stationary after 1974, inflation increased sharply with the result that purchasing power of city and town residents decreased. Unemployment remained as high as before, and probably even increased. Meanwhile, the urban upper class suffered a dramatic decline in its living standard, following its loss of land and other properties. On the other hand, the peasantry benefited doubly from land reform: directly, because it was relieved of stiff rent payment; indirectly, because the government, faced with food shortages in the cities due to the marketing disruptions, was forced to offer high prices for grain. In coffee growing regions, moreover, peasants reaped windfall profits because of high world prices in the 1975–76 period.

Because of the profound social and economic changes that took place in the first two years, the Ethiopian revolution may well rank among the world's "great revolutions." It was the first in black Africa to explode the internal contradictions of a complex feudal society through protracted armed conflict between social classes.

Perhaps the most dynamic aspect of the revolution was its open-ended character. Change was not the result of carefully guided reforms that left political and social structures intact. The initial measures decreed by the *Derg,* land reform in particular, were calculated to shake the entire society and to turn one class against the other. Despite its best efforts, the military council could not control the direction of the revolution or the outcome of the struggle. Paradoxically, the country's radicals saw in the *Derg's* attempts to guide its course a sign that it was a "fascist military dictatorship." Yet there is no doubt that the military, whatever its true character and sins, remained the prime mover of the revolution during its first three years.

2. Class and Ethnicity in Ethiopia

The complexities of the Ethiopian revolution and reactions to it among Ethiopians cannot be understood without some knowledge of the heterogeneous makeup of the sociey—in terms of both classes and ethnic groups. One unique feature of Ethiopian society was the existence of well-defined, essentially pre-capitalist social classes somewhat similar to those of the European feudal system.[1] In terms of class structure, there was no other black African country like Ethiopia with its 2,000-year-old institution of monarchy, a semi-autonomous provincial nobility, and millions of downtrodden peasants paying to their landlords in rents, taxes, and services all the "surplus" from the land beyond what was required for bare subsistence. Landlords, tenant farmers, and independent peasants were all destined to become important actors in the unfolding revolution, sometimes acting in violent conflict with each other, sometimes allying in defense of common economic or political interests.

At the same time, there were other social classes and groups in Ethiopian society just beginning to emerge under the impact of the economic changes under way since the mid-1950s, leading to the creation of a small modern agricultural sector and an even smaller industrial one. Among these nascent classes and groups were an entrepreneurial bourgeoisie made up mostly of modern farmers and some businessmen; workers in the small but expanding modern sector (blue collar laborers, office employees, and technicians); an educated elite consisting of teachers, students, and higher-level civil servants; and a small number of salaried agricultural laborers working on the large commercial farms established by foreign companies and Ethiopian entrepreneurs. The last 20 years saw a great economic transformation at least in relation to the preceding centuries of stagnation.

None of these new classes and groups was very large, but they grew steadily in size and importance as the modern sector slowly expanded. By the time the revolution got under way in 1974, a hodgepodge of old and new social classes coexisted, many of them involved in incipient conflicts with each other because of diverging economic and political interests. Almost all of them had an unspoken common interest in the demise of Emperor Haile Selassie, albeit for very different reasons. In effect, great tension developed between most of the old and new social classes and the monarch, who sought to exclude both of them from power by employing numerous astute devices. Political change did not keep pace with social and economic transformations and the resultant tension was a main wellspring of the revolution.

But the strain between a Louis XIV vintage political system and a society trying to make its way into the 20th century does not fully explain the dynamics of the revolution. There were other social cleavages running through Ethiopian society that as often as not crisscrossed those created by the old and new social classes. These divisions stemmed from the diverse and often highly antagonistic ethnic groups that had for centuries coexisted, while engaged in periodic power struggles. The principal ones were the Amharas of Shoa, Wollo, Gojjam, and Begemdir provinces; the Tigreans of Tigre and Eritrea farther to the north; and the Gallas who were spread throughout the central, southern, and western regions. Traditionally, Amharas and Tigreans had fought between themselves for domination of the empire, while Gallas were recently colonized subjects exploited by the other two. As the revolution progressed, challenging the established social hierarchy, the ethnic tensions within Ethiopian society increased tremendously. Ethnicity and class emerged as the most important factors in the social and political dynamics of the revolution. Any attempt to interpret ethnic clashes in Ethiopia as simply manifestations of class conflict, as Marxists tend to do, would be highly misleading. While it is true that the two occasionally overlapped, they often diverged sharply, even violently.

A broad overview of Ethiopian society and of social and economic changes occurring in the last 20 years is indispensable when placing the revolution in its proper social context. In the abbreviated socioeconomic analysis that follows, we have been enormously aided by, and heavily dependent on, many important and excellent studies of various aspects of Ethiopia that have been published in the past few years. However, our synthesis of this material is presented here in highly selective fashion, stressing, with all the wisdom derived from hindsight, only those developments and factors believed to be directly relevant to explaining the dynamics of the Ethiopian revolution.

The Traditional Land Tenure System

Discussion of changes under way in Ethiopian society must start with the rural sector. This is where 90 percent of the population lives and where 60 percent of the country's Gross Domestic Product originates. An understanding of the organization and functioning of rural Ethiopia is essential to grasp the different reactions in various parts of the country to the land reform instituted in early 1975.[2] As late as 20 years ago, the Ethiopian countryside remained largely untouched by change, except in the vicinity of Addis Ababa and in formerly colonized Eritrea Province. Methods of crop cultivation were ancient, and the growing surplus needed to feed the expanding urban population was obtained not by increasing productivity on modern, rationally managed farms but by squeezing more grain from the peasantry. The surplus was extracted through a variety of means, since the land tenure system varied greatly from one region to another, sometimes within the same region. The major differences in land tenure were those between the northern part of the country, essentially the Amhara-Tigrean heartland in Gojjam, Begemdir, Tigre, and parts of Wollo characterized by "communal" land tenure, and the southern part—the regions conquered by Emperor Menelik in the late 19th century—characterized by great landed estates, landlord absenteeism, and sharecropping.

There was very little "communal" about the so-called communal tenure system. Communal tenure meant that the land was subdivided among members of a descent group, i.e., descendants of a distant ancestor who had supposedly settled the land. Peasants who could establish their lineage from him had the right to use a piece of land, called *rist* land. About 10 percent of the peasants in communal tenure areas had no land of their own.[3] Although the majority of peasants were not tenants, neither were they landowners. In the first place, land did not belong to the individual peasant but to the descent group; it could not be sold by the individual using it; and it was periodically redistributed among members of the group.[4] More importantly, land was subject to feudal dues (*gult*) in addition to the taxes owed to the state. These feudal dues were owed either to private individuals or to the Church and took the form of a share of the crop, "gifts," and services. The figure of 20 percent of the crop is often cited as a typical *gult* payment, but this is documented for only a small area.[5] There are no estimates of additional work and "gifts" peasants provided. It is often said that only a small percentage of peasants in the north were tenant farmers. In fact, a recent study concluded that *gult* payments reduced a large number of the northern peasantry to the same status as tenants in other parts of the country.[6]

The situation in the south, on the other hand, was characterized by latifundia and outright tenancy. (We are excluding here the nomadic areas of the south, where land nominally belonged to the state.) About 46 percent of these peasants were tenants and a large number of landlords were absentee. Although figures are not completely reliable, it appears that in some regions, for example in Hararghe Province, absentee landlords held more than 50 percent of the land.[7] However, even in the south not all land was held in freehold: indeed, only after "internal colonization" at the time of conquest toward the end of the 19th century did private property evolve. Emperor Menelik gave those army officers and other supporters who settled in the south the right of taxation in return for administrative services in the conquered territories. Over the years, their administrative duties slowly lapsed, and these settlers began using their delegated tax powers to acquire private property. By the time of the revolution, between 1 and 1.5 million peasant families in the south had lost their land and become tenant farmers.[8] The rent they were forced to pay varied from region to region. Most peasants turned over about one-third of their crop, the amount varying with the services provided by the landlord. In addition, peasants usually paid a tithe (10 percent), even after it was formally abolished.[9]

Development of "Capitalist" Agriculture

Little changed until the early 1950s, when modern farming was begun by foreign concessions in the Awash Valley northeast of Addis Ababa. A large sugar plantation was established by a Dutch concern in the upper valley in 1951. Nine years later, a huge cotton plantation was set up in Dubte in the lower valley by a British firm in partnership with the Ethiopian government and Sultan Ali Mirah of the Afars, the seminomadic inhabitants of the region. A few other foreign concessions were started around this time.[10] Initially, the establishment of plantations had limited impact; they remained islands of development in an area of nomadic pastoralism. The Afars lost some of the best grazing land, but few cared, since the welfare of nomads was of little concern to Haile Selassie's government. In the long run, however, the success of these few large plantations had a major impact on agriculture by proving that large-scale, mechanized farming was highly profitable and by stimulating the formation of an indigenous Ethiopian entrepreneurial class. It was still not until the mid-1960s that modern agricultural farming started on the highlands on any significant scale. The development involved the creation of large mechanized farms producing cereals, pulses, and oilseeds for the urban market and for export. In the coffee growing areas of the southwest, a new trend developed away from merely harvesting wild coffee toward the development of big plantations. The development of modern farming was swift. A World Bank report in 1965 indicates that at that time the existence of large commercial farms was still largely limited to foreign concessions in the Awash Valley.[11] Studies carried out in Chilalo district around 1967 do not mention the presence of modern farms. Yet, by the time of land reform eight years later, Chilalo was a major center for mechanized cereal production.[12] Similarly, in 1969 there was practically no modern agricultural development in Ada district, only 40 kilometers from Addis Ababa; yet this was an important center of mechanized farming in 1974.[13] Government records of farm loans show that in the Setit-Humera area, in the western lowlands of Begemdir and Eritrea, significant agricultural development only started in the mid 1960s. By 1974, however, over 2,000 Ethiopian farmers had developed profitable plantations of maize, cotton, and sesame there.[14] The general picture is thus quite clear, even in the absence of records detailing the development of modern commercial farming in Ethiopia: with the exception of foreign plantations in the Awash Valley, modern farming did not precede the revolution by more than 10 years.

Although slow to start, mechanized farming in Ethiopia was in full swing by 1974. In the Awash Valley, the number of large concessions, some foreign and some Ethiopian, had grown to over 30. There were in addition several hundred smaller farms in the Awash delta around Assaita.[15] Chilalo was a major center of commercial farming, with some 30,000 hectares under tractor cultivation, mostly on large estates. Ada district was fast growing into a major farm center.[16] The lowlands along the Sudanese border were dotted with some 2,000 large farms. To the south of Addis Ababa, in the Rift Valley, mechanization rapidly spread around Shashamanne and Awassa. Pockets of large-scale mechanized cultivation had spread elsewhere, from Wollega Province in the west to the Jigjiga lowlands near the Somali border.[17] Only communal land tenure areas remained untouched by modern farming. There are no precise figures regarding the number of large mechanized farms in Ethiopia at the time of land reform. The best estimate is that there were around 5,000 modern Ethiopian farmers, with some three quarters of a million hectares under cultivation.[18] If 5,000 is a relatively small figure, it nonetheless indicates a very swift change from purely feudal and traditional systems of farming in less than ten years.

Three principal reasons may explain this development. The Emperor deliberately encouraged modern farming through multiple tax benefits—low land and income taxes, duty-free farm machinery, and tax-free fuel. It was in the landlords' interest, moreover, to change to modern agriculture, and they started doing so as soon as the few foreign plantations and development projects showed the way. Profits earned by them were much higher than those obtained by farmers using traditional methods. A study carried out in Ada district in 1970, for example, indicated that the net return per hectare of *teff*, a staple Ethiopian grain, increased from Eth$102 to Eth$220 after the use of improved seeds and fertilizer and to Eth$292 when machinery was also utilized.[19] But the reasons justifying modern farming were not exclusively economic. Various studies suggest that mechanization *per se* did not necessarily improve rentability. It did, however, allow the absentee landlord to disentangle himself from tenancy relations, which were difficult to administer *in absentia,* and to replace tenant farmers with permanent and seasonal laborers who could be more easily managed by the "weekend farmer."[20]

There is no detailed information about the new modern farmers. Available evidence suggests that they came from two groups: large absentee landlords who changed from feudal to capitalist exploitation on at least one part of their land, and merchants who reinvested business profits in farming A third category, particularly in the area around Addis Ababa, consisted of government employees who moonlighted on weekends. However, it appears likely that most "weekend farmers" came from landowning families since they could not otherwise have obtained the necessary capital.

An almost more important consideration is who the modern farmers were not: there is no indication that they included significant numbers of small, independent peasants endeavoring to modernize the family farm and expanding it into a larger enterprise. There was apparently no class of progressive yeoman farmers. The main reason was a lack of access to credit and probably to information about improved farming methods. Agricultural development credits that existed were scarce, favored the large farmers, and had strict collateral requirements virtually excluding anyone who did not have considerable tracts of land or urban property. The Agricultural and Industrial Development Bank, for example, did not grant loans smaller than Eth$5,000, and farmers had to prove title to at least 40 hectares to qualify.[21] Small peasants were thus excluded. A few loan programs were finally enacted after 1968, permitting small farmers to purchase fertilizer and improved seeds. By 1974, these projects reached less than 2 percent of the farmers.[22]

The growth of modern agriculture in Ethiopia undoubtedly played a positive role both by providing food for the growing urban population and by helping to accumulate capital for general development through exports. In a broader sense, it was instrumental in beginning to move Ethiopia out of feudal immobility and into the modern world. But like all socioeconomic transformations of historical significance, it had its victims, namely those tenant farmers who were replaced by agricultural machinery and wage workers. Because of the hard lot that befell them, the growth of modern agriculture in Ethiopia was often condemned by Ethiopian radicals as an unmitigated evil. However, such a judgment overlooks the fact that their displacement created tensions that contributed to making revolution possible. As events later demonstrated, it was those peasants directly affected by the growth of capitalist agriculture who most readily accepted and supported the revolution.

There are no reliable estimates of the number of tenant farmers displaced by mechanization, just as there is practically no information concerning what happened to them.[23] What we do know is that in some parts of the country the number of displaced tenants was high enough to cause considerable social disruption; for example, in parts of Chilalo district, as many as 15 percent of the tenants were displaced.[24] These victims of capitalist development apparently numbered in the thousands rather than the hundreds and their number rapidly increased. Another affected group was traditional farm tenants whose rents suddenly increased due to agricultural development but who did not benefit from the higher productivity that fertilizer and improved seed assured on the neighboring modern farms. In Ada district, for example, rents in the early 1970s were increasing from the customary one-third of the crop to fully half of it.[25] Moreover 93 percent of the tenants still payed the tithe, a 10 percent tax supposedly abolished in 1967.[26]

Out of the development of modern farming emerged a new social category of salaried farm laborers, both permanent and migrant. They were recruited from among displaced tenants or from overpopulated regions, primarily Wollo and Tigre provinces in the north and the Kambata region in southern Sidamo Province. They probably numbered between 30,000 and 35,000 by the early 1970s, but again there are no reliable figures.[27] Their conditions varied considerably. Although salaries were generally low, one Ethiopian dollar per day (roughtly US $.50) or less, the permanent workers on some of the largest commercial plantations had access to clinics and even schools, facilities nonexistent in most rural Ethiopia. A major exception to generally low salaries was in the Setit-Humera area along the Sudanese border where the difficulty of recruiting labor due to torrid climate and the region's isolation forced daily rates up to over Eth$2.00 per day during the short growing and harvesting season. These agricultural laborers were hardly well off, yet for many families seasonal employment on modern farms meant the difference between survival and starvation, particularly in years of famine. The burgeoning rural proletariat never presented a serious political problem before 1974, despite conditions which should have generated conflicts either with the modern farmers or the government. With few exceptions, such as on the Wonji sugar plantation near Nazareth, farm laborers were not unionized and were too isolated to act cohesively. Only in the Rift Valley area around Shashamanne and Awassa and in the Chilalo district did a concentration of these workers exist. And it was precisely in these areas that the first incidents of open conflict in rural Ethiopia took place in the spring of 1974 when a number of landlords were hacked to death by rebellious peasants and farm laborers who sought to reclaim their land.[28]

Another consequence of agricultural modernization was the beginning of a transformation of the land tenure system, particularly in the south, as traditional *gult* rights were used by landlords to gain ownership of the land. This change was accelerated by an attempted tax reform in 1966 that aimed, in theory, at abolishing *gult* rights altogether and at giving land ownership to the actual tillers. In practice, however, many of the *gultegnas,* or those with taxing rights, managed to register land in their own names, and tillers lost out. This was due to the fact that big landlords also controlled the lower levels of provincial administration where land ownership was registered. One study estimated that perhaps as much as 50 percent of all *gult* land in Ethiopia became the private property of *gultegnas* in this manner, concluding: "So in the long run, Proclamation 230 [formally abolishing *gult* rights] aided the landowners by firmly cementing their land rights as private tenure."[29] The trend was particularly pronounced in southern regions. In the north, the law reportedly went unheeded, and peasants continued to pay *gult* though they at least did not lose possession of their lands to avaricious *gultegnas.*[30]

Inevitably, the introduction of modern farming led to violent reaction. Only two of the peasant uprisings, those in Bale and Gojjam provinces during the mid-sixties, have received attention by scholars.[31] Many more instances of localized rebellions or isolated revolts resulted from tenant eviction. They occurred above all in southern parts of the country where a new class conflict emerged and was superimposed on old ethnic enmities between conquered Galla peasants and Amhara landlords. In Gojjam, the reaction took quite a different form, namely an alliance between *gultegnas* and small peasants who sought to maintain the status quo. The reason for this seemingly unlikely alliance probably lies in the fact that both *gultegnas* and tillers were Christian Amharas, that there was relatively little absenteeism (as in the Vendée during the French revolution), and that the system as practiced there allowed a degree of social mobility non-existent elsewhere.[32] In fact, the development of two antagonistic classes of landlords and peasants was in general far less accentuated in northern areas where communal land tenure prevailed than in the south, the region par excellence of sprawling latifundia, absenteeism, and sharp ethnic conflict. But even in the case of the south, one should not overrate the importance of peasant opposition to the development of capitalist agriculture, for it did not manifest itself in more than sporadic incidents and totally failed to develop into a sustained resistance movement. By and large, Ethiopia's peasantry was a passive spectator to the upheaval taking place in the capital and other urban centers. It is significant that the only active, spontaneous involvement by peasants in the early days of the revolution took place precisely in the region where modern farming was most developed: first in the spring and through the fall of 1974, tenants and agricultural laborers on big farms south of the capital tried to seize the land belonging to Ethiopia's rural gentry and to implement on their own land reform that would not become official for six months.[33]

Industrial Development and Labor Unions

Parallel to the development of a modern agricultural sector was the birth and growth of a small industrial one. Changes taking place in the countryside may have touched more people in absolute numbers, but those brought about by the first steps toward industrialization deeply affected major urban areas, particularly Addis Ababa, the nerve center of the country's political system and the place where the major upheaval triggering the revolution would take place. Formation of a new class of industrial workers was of major importance both in the society and polity of the empire. Numbering 50,000 to 60,000, this class was never very large in terms of total urban population, estimated at around 3 million in 1974 (about 10 percent of the country's 27–30 million people), or in relationship to the total labor force of the modern economic sector, which probably stood somewhere between 400,000 and 500,000 at that time.[34] But industrial workers did play an important role in the early months of the revolution by carrying out a general strike, the first in the history of Ethiopia.

Industrial development did not spring from a traditional system of cottage industries and craft production as happened in most Western countries. In fact, there is still no Ethiopian cottage industry of any significance; a 1975 government survey of cottage and handicraft "industries" throughout the country found roughly 210,000 "household enterprises;" altogether, 245,000 persons were engaged in these enterprises.[35] It is clear from these figures that there were few, if any, real cottage industries in existence and that the traditional "industrial" sector consisted almost entirely of one- or two-man enterprises operating from homes or even in the streets. The government of Haile Selassie apparently made no effort to turn the traditional mode of production into full-scale cottage industries. Its credit and tax system in fact discouraged the growth of small-scale enterprises that could have eventually spawned a class of Ethiopian industrialists capable of larger investments. Instead, government economic policy aimed at establishing large, modern factories producing textiles, cement, shoes, and other consumer goods, as well as an oil refinery at Assab. For this, it tended to rely heavily upon foreign entrepreneurs and companies, often acting in partnership with members of the royal family.[36]

The little industrial development that occurred began only after the mid-1950s. A 1955 government propaganda pamphlet that attempted to paint a glowing picture of Ethiopia's industrial development could list only a few cotton mills, the Wonji sugar refinery, a cement factory in Dire Dawa, and a few shoe and textile manufacturing concerns. In desperation, the list also included bakeries and small oil mills, hardly what one would normally cite as proof of industrial development.[37] In 1962, the manufacturing sector accounted for only 1.6 percent of the Gross Domestic Product.[38] Only in the latter half of that decade did industrialization begin to take off, so that by 1970, the sector represented 14 percent of the GDP and employed 50,000 workers.[39] Official government figures indicate that the number of manufacturing concerns employing ten or more persons in that year reached 401 and that the value of their combined fixed assets was only about Eth$370 million (less than US$180 million).[40] Even after a major government drive to establish new industries, Ethiopia's industrial sector was not very large as these figures indicate, particularly for a country of 27–30 million people.

The new class of industrial workers that grew out of the expansion of the secondary sector was from the very beginning quite apart from the rest of Ethiopian society. Concentrated almost entirely in the three cities of Addis Ababa, Asmara, and Dire Dawa, industrial workers were a small minority of the population even there. Moreover, because the new industries were unrelated to traditional crafts, and because these workers were allowed to unionize very early relative to the country's overall level of development, they tended to be set apart as a special, isolated social group. That the formation of a labor union in Ethiopia should have been allowed as early as 1963 was one of the paradoxes of Ethiopian politics at that time. In 1962, manufacturing industries employed only 27,000 people.[41] With the exception of the workers at the Wonji sugar refinery and plantation and of the railroad workers, there was little labor agitation. Furthermore, the government was generally opposed to the formation of organizations that might engage in political activities. In these circumstances, the formation of the Confederation of Ethiopian Labor Unions (CELU) can best be explained in terms of the country's foreign relations. A long-time formal adherent to the International Labor Organization's charter, Emperor Haile Selassie apparently found it increasingly difficult not to respect it in practice, particularly at a time when he was trying to establish himself as a central figure in independent Africa.

The concept of unionism accepted in Ethiopia was thus to a large extent the result of foreign influence.[42] This is not to say that workers did not have grievances or understand the need for collective action, or that the development of the CELU was not desirable or desired. But Ethiopian unionism did not grow spontaneously and was from the beginning particularly heavily influenced by American labor organizations that provided training for its first organizers. At the first meeting called to organize the confederation, interestingly enough, the CELU was envisaged by most of those present as a super *edir,* a traditional Ethiopian mutual aid association which workers had already organized in some plants. Ethiopian unionism may not have always remained at the mutual aid stage, but the sudden demands for collective agreements strongly suggest outside influence. Similarly, the leadership of the CELU by and large did not emerge from a struggle to organize, but rather from American organized and financed seminars. As a result, the CELU did not manifest any socialist leanings and remained isolated from the coterie of leftist intellectuals who managed to survive under the Haile Selassie government.

Moreover, because of the small size of the industrial sector, the confederation had to draw an unusually large proportion of its membership from among white collar workers in such organizations as banks, insurance companies, and airlines. The difference in salaries between industrial and white collar workers was enormous, varying between Eth$40 to Eth$60 for the former and Eth$400 to Eth$600 or more for the latter. That the confederation was not primarily concerned with industrial worker conditions is made clear by the fact that it did not seriously attempt before the revolution to establish a minimum wage, and many companies paid their employees less than one Ethiopian dollar (less than fifty U.S. cents) a day. Almost from the beginning, the strongest unions in the confederation were among the white collar workers. The very underdeveloped state of the modern economic sector did not provide conditions for the development of a strong working class movement. Even so, when the revolution began in 1974, the CELU membership had grown to 83,000 and as the largest organization representing any of the new social groups and classes, it was a potential force to be reckoned with.[43]

The Educated Elite

The growth of education in Ethiopia contributed greatly to changing the country's social structure and created new tensions and contradictions within it. The educated elite played a peculiarly ambiguous role. It served as the bearer of new ideas and suffered the brunt of new frustrations, but more often than not the elite submitted meekly to the status quo. Although the creation of a modern education system dates back to the immediate post-World War II era, Ethiopia probably has a smaller educated class for the size of its population than most other African states. John Markakis estimates that in 1970, there were at most seven to eight thousand persons with two or four-year university degrees in the country and by the time of the revolution, the figure must have been under 10,000.[44] The general pattern was for graduates to join the administration. Few went into the professions and even fewer into business. The Ethiopian educated elite refers primarily to high level bureaucrats, high school and university teachers, and middle and upper echelon officers in the armed forces and police. Altogether, they probably numbered no more than 20,000.[45]

The degree of class consciousness among the educated elite has been debated widely. If class consciousness is understood simply as the feeling of being different from others, then most educated Ethiopians are class conscious to the point of being overbearing.[46] If class consciousness means the capacity to organize and act together as a group, then it was found only among the students; there is no evidence of active organizing by the educated elite as a whole, and reports on relations within the administration, particularly on the quest for personal advancement, show that group consciousness, where it existed, could scarcely be converted into collective action. The elite was certainly not a class in the Marxist sense. Even if one is willing to accept the neo-Marxist concept that the "bureaucratic bourgeoisie" forms a new class in many Third World countries, or for that matter in most Eastern European socialist ones, the term is not applicable to the Ethiopia of Haile Selassie. Despite all the trappings of modern-style government administration, the Ethiopian political system remained very traditional in nature and the power of the bureaucracy quite limited. Furthermore, those of the educated elite who joined the administration had to share influence with more traditional elements who often wielded more power by virtue of their personal ties to Emperor and royal family. However, if education was not necessarily an avenue to power, it was certainly an avenue to comfortable living. University degrees guaranteed starting civil service salaries of at least Eth$500 a month in the early 1970s.[47] Compared to the prevailing wage scale, educated Ethiopians were automatically in a privileged category.

The general comportment of the first generations of educated Ethiopians—their submissiveness to the Emperor, their easy integration into the "imperial establishment"—has often been noted and discussed.[48] We are more interested here in the attitude of the educated elite and particularly of the students in more recent times. For it was the students who were widely seen abroad as the forefront of the movement for change prior to the revolution and the most vocal element of civilian opposition to military rule.

In 1965, Donald Levine was able to describe the Ethiopian educational system as a "welfare school" and the students as docile and passive.[49] Only three years later, the students were agitating on and off campus, defying government authority and even the Emperor. They had indeed established a reputation as *the* radical group of Ethiopia. By the late 1960s the university and high school students had become quite militant. It is rather difficult, on the other hand, to define exactly what their position was or how many students acted out of conviction and not simply because being "militant" was the student thing to do. The language of student publications of the period was essentially socialist—although it is hard to discern a clearly Marxist ideological line. Feudalism and capitalism were condemned, socialism in general extolled. The tone of the writings was quite elitist, however, in that students saw themselves as the only group that could save Ethiopia because of their superior education. Brought up as part of an elitist society, students showed in their publications that they had fully accepted the elitist point of view. If the downtrodden masses were the latent force that was going to change society, it was only the students who could provide the necessary leadership.[50]

A few efforts have been made, mostly by foreign professors at Haile Selassie University, to understand student attitudes. Their conclusions suggest that they were a rather confused and frustrated group, expecting typical bourgeois rewards in terms of future personal advancement, yet nagged by the feeling that as an educted group they had a public responsibility. At the same time, the overwhelming majority was quite unwilling to sacrifice personal advancement and a comfortable government career to live up to the ideals it propounded.[51] Discussions during a seminar on the "sociology of development" held at the university in 1968–69, for example, showed that students tended to excuse the reluctance of graduates to accept posts outside Addis Ababa or the other major towns.[52] There was also a feeling that political activism was a luxury in which only students could indulge, and that they should take advantage of it, since they would have to toe the government line once they entered the administration.[53] In fact, they tended to start acquiring a submissiveness their future careers required during their last year at the university, as shown by the fact that few seniors were active in the student movement.[54]

What happened once the students left the university largely supports these assertions. After ten years of student militancy, there was little agitation prior to the revolution within in the ranks of the bureaucracy which were replete with university graduates. To be sure, there were radical individuals tucked away in government offices, but certainly not the numbers one might expect if all students who considered themselves radical at the university had stuck to their ideas. The Ethiopian student movement did not produce a full-fledged political party. This is not surprising—the same has been true of radical student movements in Europe and elsewhere. We stress the point here because the part played by students in touching off the revolution has been exaggerated. Outside the campus, the only sign of political activity was the sporadic publication of clandestine pamphlets, circulated and read with great relish by educated Ethiopians. But there was no political party or underground opposition movement with a clearly articulated program. In conclusion, the educated elite was vocal and rebellious while at the university, but generally docile afterwards, particularly those elements that entered government service. Nonetheless, there remained among educated Ethiopians much latent discontent and a general conviction that things ought to and could change, making the educated potential actors in the political arena.

State and Society on the Eve of the Revolution

The question of the position and power of these emerging social classes and groups in the political system deserves detailed attention in order to understand their initial behavior toward the revolution. Even those groups which enjoyed a privileged economic position—the educated elite and the entrepreneurial bourgeoisie—were in fact, like all the others, quite politically powerless. Major economic changes were under way in Ethiopia, but the political system remained embedded in the structure of an absolute monarchy.

The Emperor, who had himself set these changes in motion, had not begun to cope with the political challenge posed by the new social classes.

Nonetheless, the political system had changed a great deal since the time Haile Selassie had taken power in 1926. The Emperor's goal had consistently been to destroy the extremely decentralized feudal system he found when he came to the throne, replacing it with a strongly centralized administration under his firm control. Most of his reign saw a process of consolidation of his power and that of the central government at the expense of the provincial gentry. This process has been studied and written about extensively by many scholars, and there is no need to discuss it again in detail here. In short, Haile Selassie was remarkably successful in consolidating the semi-autonomous provinces of the empire into one fairly unified country.

After Ethiopia's liberation from Italy in 1941, he started to organize a modern administrative system of sorts. By 1974 it still responded more to his will and whim than to impersonal codes, and the modern administrative apparatus did not reach beyond *woreda* (district) capitals. The bulk of the rural population remained under the control of traditional authorities, tax legislation was inequitably applied, and corruption and favoritism were rife. Yet, when one considers the starting point and the shortage of resources and trained personnel, the Emperor's achievement was considerable even if the process was still very incomplete.[55]

This centralization of power, however, created new problems. It resulted in the narrowing of the regime's political base, since the provincial gentry and landed class had been shunted aside but no new groups were allowed to replace them. The exclusion of both the traditional elite and the new social classes born out of a modernizing economy had led to a situation where political power became increasingly divorced from economic power and the state, such as it was, from society. Economic power resided either with the royalty and provincial gentry or was in the process of passing to the new entrepreneurial bourgeoisie. But none of these groups played a significant political role in the central government. The educated elite and the growing urban working class were also excluded. Such a situation could not possibly last indefinitely. Some kind of movement to realign the country's political structures with the emerging social classes was bound to develop. This was what the first phase of the revolution was about: an attempt was made to refashion the political system along the lines of a Western parliamentary democracy that would allow for the participation of the country's new economic and social groups. However, the forces set loose by the revolution led to a far more radical restructuring of the entire society.

At the onset of the revolution in February 1974, the new social classes were too weak to take advantage of the Emperor's waning power. Numerically, they were still small because economic development was recent. Politically, they were totally disorganized. Even the CELU, the largest modern organization in the country, was structured only to bargain for collective agreements with individual employers and had no national voice. As for the student union, it was adequate for campus politics but not for the national political arena. An even more fundamental weakness of these new social classes and groups was their total dependency on the new economic order which the Emperor promoted. They were all rooted in the small modern sector centered in a few urban areas and were thus completely divorced from the bulk of the Ethiopian population. The net result was that the new emerging social classes and groups still had too narrow a social, economic and political base to impose themselves as the dominant force when the monarchy began to collapse.

The Ethnic Problem

Ethnicity also played a major role in the Ethiopian revolution, and it is imperative to understand how ethnic divisions either intersected or overlapped with class divisions. In the dynamics of the revolution, conflicts among the major ethnic groups had a quite different configuration at national and local levels, and in the north and south. The northern highlands of Ethiopia are inhabited by two main ethnic groups, Amharas and Tigreans, who together make up roughly 40 percent of the total 27–30 million population. The two groups do not normally clash with each other at the local level, for they essentially inhabit different provinces. Amharas occupy northern Shoa, Gojjam, and parts of Wollo and Begemdir, while Tigreans occupy Tigre and most of the Eritrean highlands. Because the population is fairly homogeneous within each area and is largely Coptic Christian, ethnic clashes at the local level occur only in relation to small minorities, a problem that will not be considered here. An Amhara or Tigrean peasant usually confronts a *gultegna* (landlord) of his own ethnic group. A potential for class conflict exists within the same ethnic group in the northern region.

The situation in the south is more complex. The bulk of the peasant population consists of Gallas, who alone constitute 35 to 40 percent of the total Ethiopian population. There, landlords were either local notables of the same ethnic group as the peasants or Amhara settlers who came in the wake of Menelik's conquest. The big absentee landlords tended to be Amhara, as did government representatives and members of the rural police force. Generally speaking, landlords and local notables were considered part of the ruling Amhara elite, whatever their ethnic origin. But in the south, class conflict tended to coincide with ethnic conflict because Amharas were the governing local elite and Gallas the conquered people and exploited tenant farmers.

The three main ethnic groups worked together at the national level in the central government, though they were not placed on an equal footing. The vast majority of those working for the imperial establishment was Amhara or Tigrean; only a few Galla, primarily those assimilated and Christianized from Shoa and Wollega provinces, were included. The same was true of the educated elite. The fact that most secondary schools were located either in Shoa or Eritrea assured this bias. Hence, a high and unrepresentative percentage of senior government employees came from Amhara and Tigrean groups.

Relations between Amharas and Tigreans within the ruling elite were often tense. The former tended to consider the latter, particularly the Eritreans, to be haughty and overrepresented everywhere from the government to the university. Tigreans, for their part, were resentful of Amhara domination. The throne of the empire had historically passed back and forth between Amharas and Tigreans. Although the latter had lost out at the end of the 19th century, they had not lost their sense of pride or their hope of regaining power. Tigre Province, after all, was still ruled by a descendant of the last Tigrean Emperor, Yohannes IV, although Ras Mengesha Seyoum now carried the title of governor-general rather than king. The conflict between Amharas and Tigreans was, moreover, an element in the secessionist movement in Eritrea. Even at the national university in Addis Ababa, tension between these two proud ruling groups was evident. After the mid-1960s, Tigrean and Eritrean students refused to speak Amharic any longer, and all discussions involving the entire student body generally took place in English as a neutral *lingua franca* acceptable to all ethnic groups.

Despite the animosity that existed between Tigreans and Amharas, both were still very much part of the same ruling class who viewed other ethnic groups as hewers of wood and haulers of water. It is true that many Amharas and Tigreans can be found at the bottom of the social and economic ladder. Most, of course, were peasants, and in the capital Amharas provided a large number of street boys, beggars, and prostitutes. But at the top of the social scale, there were few other than Amharas and Tigreans. With the advent of the revolution, the heightening of ethnic tension could not be avoided, particularly since the Amhara and Tigrean dominated ruling class was overthrown by a military movement dominated by Gallas. Later, much of the opposition to the *Derg* at both political extremes came from the Amhara and Tigrean elites, while much of its support came from other ethnic groups, particularly Gallas. While opposition to, or support for, the revolution did not divide entirely along ethnic lines (many of the poorest peasants were, after all, Amharas and Tigreans), there was considerable evidence that Gallas were the main beneficiaries and the old Amhara and Tigrean elites the main losers. More important was the fact that many Ethiopians themselves interpreted the revolution in ethnic terms. But ethnicity does not explain the reaction of all the Ethiopian peoples to the revolution. It is one of the authors' main contentions that precisely because class conflicts cut across the country's main ethnic divisions, the various opposition groups never coalesced and the military reformers were able to prevail over their opponents.

3.   The Spring of Discontent

Civilian radicals who were opposed to the new military government assert that the wave of strikes and demonstrations by workers and students in early 1974 represented the beginning of a genuine popular revolution that was later brutally crushed by the army. We contend, however, that the civilian turmoil at that time was far too inchoate and undirected, and the nature of civilian demands too limited in scope, to support this contention. Rather, civilian agitation was essentially an expression of special grievances by what one might call "corporate interest groups." Without a doubt, this agitation was an important factor in undermining the Emperor's power and exposing the weakness of the monarchy. In hindsight it can be said that if there was any attempt to make a revolution in early 1974, it was led by the urban-based educated elite and entrepreneurial bourgeoisie seeking to establish a parliamentary democracy, not by workers and students trying to establish a dictatorship of the proletariat. Even this "bourgeois revolution" was aborted when the military seized power in late June.

While the most visible events of the first five months of the Ethiopian revolution were the mutinies in the armed forces and the strikes and demonstrations on the capital's main boulevards, the important political developments related to two parallel struggles. First was a confrontation of the old landed aristocracy with representatives of the new entrepreneurial bourgeoisie and educated elite to determine which group would prevail in the post-Haile Selassie era. Second was the struggle by a group of lower-ranking officers within the armed forces both to form a political movement by overcoming traditional divisions within the military and, further, to go beyond demands of a strictly corporate nature in order to impose fundamental social change. These two movements had their individual logic and dynamics, though they influenced each other and often intersected. Both took place at the time of army mutinies and civilian turmoil, which none of the principal actors approved of or could control, but which all tried to exploit to their own advantage.

This chapter examines the nature of civilian unrest and the struggle for power between the aristocracy, which was trying to stage a political comeback, and the country's emerging intelligentsia and entrepreneurial bourgeoisie, who were attempting to establish themselves as the dominant political forces. Strangely enough, the Emperor himself opened the floodgates to this struggle. He first appointed a member of the old aristocracy to head the new government and then ordered the drafting of a new constitution that would make the prime minister responsible to Parliament. Indeed, the attitude of Haile Selassie during this critical period of stress and change was extremely indecisive. He had little personal interest in the establishment of a constitutional monarchy which would limit his power and no interest in seeing his throne pass to one of his aristocratic rivals. While he made a feeble gesture to perpetuate the Solomonic line and to defend the institution of the monarchy, he was too senile to play a decisive role. "Our era is over. There is no use trying to fight the Almighty," the Emperor is reported to have told a close associate who was urging him to take a firmer stand.[1] It was obvious to all social classes and political groups that Haile Selassie's power and prestige were fast waning, and this served to fuel the civil unrest and the struggle for power in early 1974.

The Aristocracy's Return to Power

The spate of mutinies within the armed forces beginning in mid-January and the week of turmoil in the capital starting on February 14 triggered the power struggle. The subsequent display of weakness on the part of the Emperor and the Aklilu government was completely unexpected. The old regime appeared suddenly to collapse under its own weight. In an unprecedented move, the Emperor announced on February 23 a series of concessions to the various protesting groups: a rollback in fuel prices to placate taxi drivers; the indefinite postponement of proposed educational reforms which had angered students and teachers; and the imposition of price controls on basic commodities demanded by practically all groups. The next day, salary increases for the armed forces and police were announced. On February 27–28, Prime Minister Aklilu Habte-Wold resigned and was replaced by Endelkachew Makonnen. It was the first time that an Ethiopian prime minister had fallen because of public pressure. As a result, a long period followed in which emboldened civilian and military groups kept on pressing ever-escalating demands, while the government tried to placate them by uttering promises and promulgating minor reforms.

Endelkachew's appointment spelled a fundamental change in the existing balance of power between the Emperor and the old landed aristocracy, which had been longing to return to power. Many other leading aristocrats were included in the new cabinet. In 1969, while only one of the major aristocratic families was represented in the Aklilu cabinet, all had a member in the new government or were once again dominant figures on the political scene.[2] The most important of these families was that of *Ras* Kassa, who was related to several, including the Shoan, royal families, and whose right to the throne was equal to that of the Emperor. By 1974, *Ras* Kassa had died, but his son, *Ras*

Asrate Kassa, although not officially a member of the Endelkachew cabinet, was probably the most influential figure behind it.[3] Another was the Tigrean family of *Ras* Seyoum, a descendant of Emperor Yohannes, *Ras* Mengesha Seyoum. Seyoum's son was still governor of Tigre and one of the few provincial rulers the Emperor had not dared to remove. *Dejazmatch* Zewdie Gebre Selassie, a nephew of *Ras* Mengesha, became minister of interior in the Endelkachew cabinet. *Lij* Michael Imru, the son of *Ras* Imru, a cousin of the Emperor, became minister of commerce and industry. Also represented were the two powerful Amhara clans of Beza and Adisge: Lt. Gen. Abiye Abebe, minister of defense and chief of staff, and Endelkachew himself belonged to this group. Of these new cabinet officers only Endelkachew had occupied a ministerial post in the previous cabinet. Among them ideological differences certainly existed. Asrate Kassa was known as an uncompromising conservative, as was Abiye Abebe. Michael Imru, like his father, was known to have socialist leanings.[4] Endelkachew and Zewdie were considered "progressive," which in Ethiopia denotes an interest in modernization, but not necessarily liberalization. It appears that these men were chosen as much for their family connections as for their personal convictions.

The reappearance of so many aristocrats in the government was crucial at this point. At stake was not only the immediate problem of reestablishing order in the country but also the question of who would eventually control, or at least have the dominant influence, over the royal succession. Since the monarch was over 80 years old and Crown Prince Asfa Wossen seriously ill in Geneva, succession did not promise to be smooth, and a number of contenders was likely to emerge. Succession was apparently the major concern of Asrate Kassa.[5] The Emperor's weakened grip over the country offered new possibilities not only for those aristocratic families who had been shunted aside in previous years, but also for representatives of the new classes that had never previously been allowed to play a political role. Members of the entrepreneurial bourgeoisie and the educated elite, though never formally organized, worked quietly to influence policy directions, primarily through a constitutional committee set up to establish a new political system but also through Parliament, which had emerged as a counterforce to the throne. The bourgeois reformist faction had no leaders as prominent as those of the aristocrats. There was nonetheless a relatively well-known group of educated persons, mostly university professors, who spearheaded the struggle inside the constitutional committee for the adoption of a parliamentary democracy.[6] Ethiopia's educated elite and entrepreneurial bourgeoisie had origins similar to the landed class but, as the debate over the new constitution demonstrated, they became increasingly opposed to the economic and political interests of the aristocracy. Michael Imru, who later served as a political adviser to the *Derg,* was a rare exception since he was closer to liberal bourgeois elements than to the old aristocracy. But on the whole, there were distinct conflicting interests between conservative aristocratic and reformist bourgeois forces in the new government.

Endelkachew faced three major problems when he came to power: how to handle the armed forces, how to respond to civilian unrest, and how to deal with the struggle between conservative aristocratic and reformist bourgeois elements in his own government. His wavering attitude toward the latter two problems and his misjudgement of the situation developing within the army brought about his eventual demise.

The Civilian Challenge

Had the strikes and demonstrations that took place in early 1974 happened over a long period, their impact would not have been so very great. But the occurrence of so many within three months paralyzed the economy and nearly overwhelmed the government. Some demonstrations were expressions of long-suppressed grievances suddenly put forward when it became clear that the government was too weak or unwilling to respond with force. Such was the huge demonstration in April by the Moslem population of Addis Ababa. Others involved new grievances prompted by recent price increases, such as the strike by taxi drivers over a 50 percent rise in the price of gasoline. Most strikes, however, resulted from long-standing complaints exacerbated by inflation or new government policies. Those having the greatest political significance involved the country's few organized groups, namely, the Confederation of Ethiopian Labor Unions (CELU), the Ethiopian Teachers' Association (ETA), and the students. The position and demands of these groups deserves further attention, first because of the impact they had on the Endelkachew government and also because of claims made later by the civilian left that they marked the beginning of a socialist revolution.

The famine in Wollo and Tigre provinces has often been cited as a major factor behind the civilian uprisings in early 1974. It is true that the famine's devastating proportions were becoming known at the time, and that Ethiopians were appalled by what they heard and by the government's indifference. It is also true that eight students were killed the previous year protesting in the Wollo provincial capital of Dessie over the government's failure to help drought victims. However, famine-stricken peasants themselves never initiated or participated in any demonstrations. Those who drifted into Addis Ababa were too busy begging to storm the palace. Those who remained in Wollo and Tigre were extremely passive. Relief workers told of private grain stores remaining untouched, while nearby peasants starved.[7] Some groups demonstrated in Addis demanding government relief, but the famine was not the primary reason for their protests. Rather, it provided a convincing argument for radicals to discredit both the old government and the Emperor. More important causes stemmed from long-time grievances felt by the urban population. Most civilian complaints did not reflect national concerns at all, but the special problems of individual groups. In fact, many of their demands conflicted with the interests of the vast majority of the Ethiopian population, serving only to accentuate the differences between urban groups and the peasantry.

Agitation among the 16,000 government primary and secondary school teachers in early 1974 focused on two issues: the longstanding problem of salary increases and parity with civil service scales, and the newly-published Educational Sector Review, a proposal of far-reaching changes in the Ethiopian educational system, which teachers saw as a serious menace to both their income and status. Salary increases for teachers had been under discussion at least since 1968, when the Teachers' Association first asked for an upgraded salary scale.[8] By September 1973, the new scale had not yet been worked out, and the ETA set forth its own request for a 10 percent increase in basic salary and a 50 percent increase in annual increments. Moreover, the association threatened to call a teachers' strike unless the request was met by December 1973. The Ministry of Education failed to meet the deadline, and to make matters worse, it published a proposal for a radical reform of the educational system, known as the Educational Sector Review. This document had been prepared by a group of experts, many of them foreigners, who failed to consult teachers or students. The international agencies backing the study, such as UNESCO and the World Bank, considered the proposal a model educational system for a developing country. It would replace the urban-oriented, elitist, and excessively academic Western style of education that had been typically imposed by colonial powers on the Third World with one aimed at satisfying the needs of the long-forgotten rural population.

The Educational Sector Review proposed that the government should in the future concentrate on the expansion of primary education, while limiting enrollment in high schools and the university according to the manpower needs of the country.[9] Given the extremely low national literacy rate, 5 to 10 percent, the small enrollment in elementary schools (860,000 in 1972), the growing problem of unemployment among high school graduates, and the probable surplus of university graduates, the proposal made sense. But like all far-reaching reforms, it impinged on many vested interests, particularly those of the teachers and of the urban middle class from which were drawn the bulk of the students in higher education. The review did not suggest that salaries for teachers be formally reduced, but that the existing qualifications for teaching in elementary and junior high schools be relaxed and the less qualified teachers paid at a lower rate.[10] Actually, many school teachers did not have the required qualifications and were in fact being paid at lower rates. They resented it and fought for salary parity with those having the full formal qualifications of their rank. The review would have confirmed this existing practice. It further proposed that all new teachers of primary and junior high school grades be paid at the lower rate. This would have reduced the overall per pupil cost of education, which was far higher in Ethiopia than in other East African countries.[11]

At the same time, the status of teachers was threatened by another proposal that aimed at emphasizing practical and vocational education in the primary grades. In a country like Ethiopia, where long fingernails are displayed with pride by many teachers as indicating they do not engage in manual labor, the idea that they should cultivate vegetable gardens with their pupils was not popular. At higher educational levels, it was students rather than teachers who would have been affected. A slowdown in the expansion of secondary and higher education would have meant more rigorous entrance examinations for students entering high schools and the university. The review also revived an old proposal abolishing free university education in view of its high costs to the country and high benefits to the recipients. Instead, students would be given educational loans, repayable after graduation, with scholarships reserved only for the exceptionally needy or deserving students.[12]

On February 11, representatives of the Ethiopian Teachers' Association, bypassing the Ministry of Education, presented the Emperor with a petition asking for higher salaries and rejection of the controversial Educational Sector Review. By February 18, they struck with the support of most students, parents, and a large segment of the urban population. For many lower-class Ethiopians, the proposal appeared to downgrade education, making it impossible to improve their and their children's fortunes, and to perpetuate the domination of a small wealthy class and its foreign-educated youth. Since few had actually read the review, this distorted interpretation was readily believed. On February 23, the Emperor capitulated and announced the indefinite postponement of the new program. The teachers' strike, however, continued until mid-March when some salary increases were granted. Even then, the ETA declared that the increases would be accepted only on a temporary basis because teachers still had not been given parity with civil servants. The confrontation over the Educational Sector Review demonstrated the corporate nature of the teachers' and the students' concerns. Their demands had no "revolutionary" content; they merely reflected the concern of the urban petty bourgeoisie to safeguard its status and to keep open the channels of upward mobility.

As for the Confederation of Ethiopian Labor Unions, longstanding grievances erupted in a three-day general strike beginning on March 7. The strike was not the result of a last-minute decision, but had been planned for some time.[13] The timing was nonetheless affected by the popular unrest breaking out across the country, the increased militancy among workers affected by inflation and military agitation, and the government's apparent willingness to make concessions. On March 1, the day following the appointment of Endelkachew as prime minister, the CELU submitted a list of 16 demands and warned the government that it would call a general strike on March 7 if their demands were not satisfied. Fully two-thirds of the demands, including those that would later become the subject of intense negotiations, concerned only union issues and the status of workers. They included: 1) the right to strike; 2) a minimum daily wage of around Eth$3.00; 3) the right to form unions among the employees of parastatal companies like the Telecommunications Board and the Light and Power Authority; 4) prohibiting government labor advisors from serving on company boards; 5) the establishment of a social security system; 6) exemption of pension funds from income tax; 7) increased job security through laws regulating the hiring and firing of workers; 8) the right of the CELU to print its own publications without censorship; 9) the Ethiopianization of jobs held by foreigners; 10) a cost-of-living adjustment in salaries; and 11) legislation governing temporary employment. Only five of the CELU's demands were of a broad economic or political nature. They endorsed the shelving of the Educational Sector Review, free education for needy children, a system of price controls, and acceptance of the teachers' salary requests.[14] There was also a vague declaration in support of land reform. But CELU officials made clear at the time that political demands were secondary to their specifically corporate concerns.[15]

The new government at first did not take the general strike threat seriously, probably because similar ones in the past had failed to materialize. The Endelkachew cabinet waited until March 6 before considering the CELU demands, and then simply announced that each point would be answered, after appropriate study, within the next three to six months. To its surprise, the general strike began the very next day. With 85,000 to 100,000 workers participating, the country's main cities, particularly Addis Ababa, were paralyzed. But the CELU had no funds to sustain an unlimited strike, though they had promised one, and workers had no savings to fall back upon. By the third day, many were back on their jobs. The strike lasted long enough to force the Endelkachew government to sign an agreement, but not long enough to extract significant concessions. The prime minister hid behind a constitutional facade, claiming that all new laws affecting the confederation had to be approved by Parliament or studied by appropriate government agencies. He skillfully avoided making major concessions and promised that bills concerning strikes and firing of workers would be presented to Parliament within a month and that a minimum wage, still to be determined, would be established after a two-month cooling-off period. An answer to the teachers' demand for higher salaries was delayed until March 19. The government appeared to permit the formation of labor unions among employees in parastatal agencies and to promise that confederation members involved in the strike would not be punished or have their salaries cut—unless approved by the Labor Relations Board.[16] On April 20, the board condemned the strike as illegal and voted to deduct days lost from workers' pay. It now even refused to allow the unionization of employees of the parastatal Board of Telecommunications.[17]

The students' role in initiating or promoting the revolution was clearly secondary to that played by the military and workers. As with teachers and soldiers, they were first motivated by their own particular interests. The proposed reform of the educational system triggered a wave of student strikes and demonstrations and led eventually to the closing of the university and to a general breakdown in high schools. Yet, these events cannot be described as a general student uprising. Students never acted in a united fashion, partly because the government forbade them to reestablish their dissolved union or to publish a newspaper until March 17, and partly because the majority remained either apolitical or opposed to the political agitation. Student demonstrations in Addis Ababa usually involved from 1,000 to 2,000 persons, and on many occasions substantially fewer numbers. There were at the time about 5,000 university students and around 20,000 high school students in the city.[18]

Even after the government formally permitted the student union to function again, it never rallied the entire student body. Instead, a relatively small group of activists, supported by 500 to 2,000 students at any one time, kept the capital's university and high schools in almost continual turmoil while they agitated on campus and in the streets for reforms.[19] However, among various groups involved in strikes and demonstrations between February and June, it can be said that student activists demonstrated by far the greatest interest in the broader political issues. They were the first and most vocal opponents of the new Endelkachew government, and they, more than any other group, kept the issue of past government corruption and indifference to famine victims before the public. In a demonstration on March 11 that ended with the police invading one of the university campuses, students waved the first banners calling for a "people's government" and "land to the tillers" and issued a five-point statement demanding the election of a caretaker government and the trial of former ministers before a "people's court." They also asked for peasant and worker participation in the drafting of a new constitution. In early April, they held hunger strikes in sympathy with famine victims and collected food for those hungry peasants who had managed to reach Addis in search of help. They even asked the government to declare a state of emergency in order to deal with the famine then affecting southern Ethiopia. In addition, practically every demonstration by striking CELU workers or government employees had its student contingent, both in the capital and in smaller towns like Jimma in the southwest, Dire Dawa in the east, or Mekele in the north. There was also evidence some student activists were involved in the March peasant uprisings on the big farms south of Addis Ababa during which several dozen landlords were murdered and widespread crop destruction occurred.[20] Only after weeks of agitation on and off campus did the government close down the university on April 26, a decision bitterly opposed by fourth-year students and others anxious to graduate.

Yet students did not spearhead the general uprising in Addis Ababa; workers, taxi drivers, soldiers, and teachers all went on strike in pursuit of their separate demands, only secondarily concerned with broader issues raised by student radicals. At best, they served to raise the larger political issues of government corruption and need for fundamental reforms. Students could not do much more, for they had no organized links to the "broad masses," though they habitually claimed to speak for them. There was little evidence that student radicals had any influence with the CELU or contacts with the clandestine junior officers' committee which in June seized power from the Endelkachew government. In summary, the student protest movement during these early months of the revolution was overshadowed by labor strikes and discontent within the armed forces.

Endelkachew's Alliance with the Military and
Suppression of Civilian Disorder

Throughout March and April, the prime minister sought to bring labor unrest to an end. April saw the peak of strikes by all kinds of civilian groups in Addis

Ababa—municipal workers, bus drivers, students, railway workers, hospital employees, garbage collectors, street cleaners, civil servants in half a dozen ministries, Moslems, Christians, army veterans, priests, university staff, prostitutes, imperial palace staff, industrial workers, and, toward the end of the month, telecommunications workers. The prime minister at first tried to pacify striking workers by engaging in negotiations of a sort. The way in which he handled the general strike was typical of this early strategy: no government action unless absolutely necessary; when forced, a minimum of concessions; then postponement of implementation in the expectation that the decisions could be reversed, as in fact most were. Except for salary increases for the military and teachers, the strategy paid off and practically no concessions were made or reforms undertaken. Still, he failed to restore law and order in Addis or to consolidate his own shaky position. Military intervention toward the end of April ended this chaotic period, when Endelkachew struck a bargain with a faction of the army which insisted that concrete action be taken against former ministers and corrupt practices. Actually, the military's demand well suited the purposes of Endelkachew and Asrate Kassa, who had no more sympathy for Aklilu and members of the former cabinet than they had for civilian agitators. But by acquiescing—all too willingly—to the demand that officials in the Aklilu cabinet be arrested, Endelkachew came into a direct confrontation with the Emperor, who was not yet prepared to abandon his former protegees and supporters.

On April 18, the prime minister went to the headquarters of the Fourth Division in Addis Ababa (some reports say he was ordered to appear) and appealed to 2,000 soldiers and officers from various units of the armed forces for help in restoring order. After hearing his appeal, the military made it clear that their support was contingent on the immediate arrest of certain former ministers and top officials in the past government. They even threatened to take action on their own if he did not. Apparently Endelkachew gave orders on the spot to the security forces to put 16 ministers, his own former colleagues, under house arrest. However, the order was not carried out because of the veto of the Emperor, who ever offered shelter in the palace to many of the wanted men. Pressure for their arrest nonetheless continued to mount. When Endelkachew on the following day asked for the support of the police force in reestablishing order in Addis, he was again told that he would get it only if the former ministers were arrested and brought to trial. On the same day, Parliament passed a motion demanding the same thing. It seems certain that at this point Endelkachew fully agreed with these terms, but preferred to let the military press the issue with the Emperor.[21] On April 22, a military delegation went to the palace and asked Haile Selassie to allow the arrest of the former ministers. He again refused, but neither the military nor Endelkachew gave up.

The faction now supporting Endelkachew formed an official "coordinating committee," and on April 24, Endelkachew authorized it, together with the Defense and Interior ministries, to take all measures necessary to restore law and order. He warned the public that illegal strikes (which meant in effect all strikes) would be dealt with severely. On April 26, troops and police under the command of the coordinating committee moved into Addis Ababa, and in an open challenge to the Emperor arrested 19 ministers and former high officials as well as several generals and imprisoned them at the Fourth Division headquarters. On its part, the military kept its bargain. Speaking at a press conference the next day, Colonel Alem Zewd Tessema, head of the coordinating committee, declared that the armed forces "firmly oppose unlawful strikes and demonstrations" and made it clear that they would no longer be tolerated. "If these unlawful demonstrations continue, they can create bloodshed, chaos, looting, religious and tribal clashes, and foreign intervention. The armed forces under the government policy will not sit idly by. The change which started peacefully must continue peacefully without any bloodshed."[22] The coordinating committee, he added, had arrested the former ministers to give the country a "sense of relief," and they would soon be put on trial before a joint military-civilian board of inquiry.

Endelkachew had scored a major victory. He had managed to remove his former political rivals, had further weakened the Emperor's power, and had obtained the muscle needed to put down the strikes. This latter task was facilitated by the creation on April 30 of a National Security Commission under the leadership of General Abiye Abebe, minister of defense and a leading member of the aristocratic faction.[23] Throughout May, this joint military-civilian National Security Commission and the labor confederation engaged in a bitter fight as the Endelkachew government pressed its campaign not only to end the wave of strikes but also to break the back of the whole union movement. A statement from the Ministry of National Defense on April 30 bluntly warned the CELU that if the strikes did not immediately cease the government would ban the confederation. In response, CELU leaders announced that if the government tried to destroy the organization they would call for another general strike. But by the end of May, the only remaining center of labor resistance was among telecommunications workers, who were still agitating for their own union by holding sitdown and hunger strikes. The use of brute force—military occupation of the telecommunications center and arrests—broke up this last stronghold. Peace, though uneasy, had returned to Addis.

Is there any basis for arguing that the strikes and demonstrations occurring between February and June were the beginnings of a popular revolution which the military nipped in the bud? We believe not, principally for two reasons: the low level of political consciousness among the vast majority of participants and the complete lack of any political organization behind even the radical minority. Only a small number of students, workers, and soldiers either perceived or raised larger political issues during this spring of discontent. Moreover, there is evidence suggesting that many of those who saw these issues failed to see them in terms of a radical socialist revolution. Most student activists, for example, demanded elections and Western-style civil liberties, as did many "radical" officers. Participants in the CELU general strike who perceived their actions in political terms tended to be those who were employed in the higher status and income occupations or to come from the dominant Amhara and Tigrean ethnic groups. These were hardly sections of the population most likely to support a radical revolution.[24] Furthermore, there was no organization capable of turning the country's spontaneous agitation toward political action.

Perhaps the most striking characteristic of civilian unrest was its parochial character. Each protesting group sought to promote its own narrow demands and tried to secure as much as possible for itself without considering the overall economic or social effect. There were good reasons for this. The labor movement was still in its infancy, and its leaders had been trained in a strictly Western, indeed, American, style of unionism. Furthermore, the general population had had no experience in political organization for the past half-century. Therefore, the claims made later by radicals that military intervention snuffed out a revolutionary workers' movement remain unconvincing. From the radicals' viewpoint, the spontaneous civilian agitation in early 1974 came too soon, before they had the capacity to channel popular discontent into a political movement. As one former radical student leader said, "None of us really believed a revolution would come in our lifetime."[25]

Aristocratic Reaction and Bourgeois Revolution

While the most dramatic problems Endelkachew confronted were military mutinies and civilian strikes, there was an equally important, if less visible, conflict under way over drafting a new constitution. Here, the old aristocracy was pitted against the new educated elite and the entrepreneurial bourgeoisie. Although both factions were interested in eliminating royal absolutism, they were in sharp competition over which would control the government upon the departure of Haile Selassie. At the heart of this struggle, in a larger sense, was whether an aristocratic reaction or a bourgeois revolution would end royal absolutism.

The struggle came to a head in the constitutional committee, where the two factions faced each other across the table. The conflict also involved those close to the Emperor and in Parliament. The aristocratic faction sought to secure its position not only through Endelkachew but also by persuading the Emperor to assure an orderly succession to the throne. Even before Crown Prince Asfa Wossen suffered a stroke in January 1972, the aristocrats around the Emperor were urging him to make an unequivocal statement on the line of succession, and it was generally expected that he would do so on his 80th birthday in July 1973. However, he did not, and the issue was still undecided when the political crisis developed the following February. In April the aristocratic faction finally prevailed upon the Emperor, and in an Easter message he reconfirmed his half-paralyzed son as crown prince and his grandson, Prince Zara Yacob, then a student at Oxford, as second in line. A weak and sick successor perfectly suited the purposes of court aristocrats since their influence was almost certain to be enhanced. There was even talk of creating a regency for 20-year-old Zara Yacob, and bypassing Asfa Wossen altogether.

While the aristocratic faction under Asrate Kassa maneuvered behind the scenes, reformist bourgeois elements discovered they had an unexpected ally in the Parliament. Normally a stronghold of the conservative landed class, this institution took on new life in the wake of the Aklilu government's collapse and attempted to assert its authority by challenging Endelkachew on his nominees for important government offices and on his main statement of policy. Attempts were made to get ministers to come before the body to answer questions, and resolutions were passed demanding the resignation of governors suspected of corruption and an investigation into the alleged misconduct of past and present ministers. Parliament's assertion of power peaked on April 10, when it refused to allow Endelkachew to speak on the "White Paper" outlining his policies and appointed a seven-member committee to prepare a list of questions the prime minister would be required to answer when he eventually did appear. In effect, Parliament attempted to assume new responsibilities and powers even before the new constitution was drafted.[26]

It was never clear what the Emperor had in mind when he called for a new constitution that promised to substantially weaken the monarch's authority. In a speech delivered on March 5, he charged the newly installed Endelkachew government with drawing up a charter that would make the prime minister responsible to Parliament. Under the existing constitution, the prime minister and cabinet were appointed by the Emperor, Parliament having no control over either. Whether Haile Selassie intended to relinquish this much power to Parliament is unknown, because subsequent events made irrelevant the issue of a new constitution. It is clear that Endelkachew preferred not to see the prime minister responsible to Parliament. Commenting in mid-March on the principles that should underlie the new constitution, he talked cautiously about the need for better cooperation between Parliament and the cabinet but gave no indication that he supported the crucial point of ministerial responsibility.[27] The question of what kind of constitution Ethiopia would have was thus undecided when the constitutional committee started its work.

The committee appointed on March 21 was broader based than those that had drafted previous constitutions, but it was still very restricted and all 30 of its members were appointed. They came predominantly from the Crown Council, Parliament, the Orthodox Church, the Moslem community, and the professions. The three estates of pre-revolutionary France could be said to have been reconstituted. Representatives of the nobility and traditional landed class were drawn from the Crown Council and Parliament; those of the clergy from the Orthodox Church hierarchy, with only token representation for the Moslems; and those of the third estate were primarily from the university.[28] Notably excluded from the committee was any group then mobilized and agitating in the streets—soldiers, workers, teachers, and students.

The constitutional committee worked behind closed doors. Some of its members said later that the debates were marked by an acute division between liberal and conservative wings. The liberals pushed for election of the prime minister by Parliament, separation of church and state, elimination of an appointed Senate, and a bill of rights guaranteeing civil liberties. The conservative wing supported many fewer changes.[29] Endelkachew, with the arch-conservative Asrate Kassa behind him (either pushing or simply supporting the prime minister, according to varying reports), took the conservative side on most issues. The liberal wing was in the minority, but according to one committee member it managed to consistently outvote the conservatives simply by manipulating Robert's Rules of Order and outwitting them in procedural matters.

By the time the draft was completed, events had completely overtaken the constitutional process, but the new constitution represented the triumph of the liberal faction. The conservatives had been routed, particularly those supporting strong monarchy. The Emperor was demoted from "Elect of God" to simple head of state, church and state were completely separated, the executive was made responsible to Parliament, an independent judiciary was established, and the citizens were guaranteed the right to form political parties and enjoy Western-style civil liberties. It was, in effect, a modern democratic constitutional monarchy similar in substance to the British model.[30]

The constitution was years ahead of its time in terms of Ethiopia's social and political development, even if the military had not intervened. The most likely outcome, had the constitution ever been promulgated, would have been the creation of a political system dominated by Ethiopia's urban classes, notably the educated elite and the entrepreneurial bourgeoisie. These groups were in the best position to take advantage of civil liberties provided in the new constitution. To the vast majority of rural peasants, these opportunities would have been largely meaningless. As it was, the constitutional process never got beyond the publication of a first draft in early August. Still, the aborted constituion remains an eloquent testimonial to the changing balance of forces between traditional and modern social elements and to the effort of new classes and social groups to gain political power commensurate with their growing economic and social position.

The Failure of Reform

There was every indication in early 1974 that even moderate reforms would probably have quelled popular discontent. Instead, Endelkachew, who was known as a skillful politician, succeeded in setting loose a revolution. The reason for this may be laid to four main factors: 1) the very nature of the Ethiopian political system; 2) the personality and mentality of Endelkachew; 3) the overconfidence of the aristocrats; and 4) the ineffectualness of civilian groups.

The notion that government response to unrest should be reform rather than repression was foreign to Ethiopia. The underlying principle of the French Revolution—that the population is composed of *citoyens* and not *sujets*—was not accepted in Ethiopia, even as late as 1974. Haile Selassie always made it clear that whatever he did was of his own free will and not in response to public pressure, although as a consumate politician he of course took account of such pressure. This is why his decision to accede to the military rebels' demands with respect to Prime Minister Aklilu was totally unexpected. The aristocrats around him were furious for his having given in so easily. For Endelkachew to try and resolve the crisis through even moderate reforms would have been unprecedented.

Endelkachew's main concern was to enhance traditional aristocratic authority rather than to introduce innovations in the Ethiopian political tradition. He was no more a reformer in economic and social matters than in politics. While the Ethiopian media talked headily about momentous changes taking place under Endelkachew, there was no substance to these claims. Even the new-found freedom of the press was greatly exaggerated. Political news continued to be carefully censored, and newspapers often remained silent for long periods about important events. The Endelkachew government was characteristically facade and no substance. Nowhere was this better illustrated than in the case of the "White Paper." This major policy statement, issued on April 8, promised to give highest priority to the problems of famine victims, without giving any indication as to where the funds would come from.[31] It pledged a major effort to solve the government's growing financial problems, but without mentioning the need of fiscal reform. It advocated limiting the size of landholdings to what an individual could "develop" and the distribution of excess acreage as a basis for land reform, but in such vague outline that the program was open to widely differing interpretation. The government also promised, once again, new legislation affecting landlord-tenant relations, an issue that had been before Parliament for nearly a decade without any law having been voted. Otherwise, it pledged in general terms a wide variety of reforms without specifying detail and substance of any of them.[32] Equally revealing of his attitude toward reform was his handling of strikes. Endelkachew retracted the concessions he was forced to make as soon as he felt strong enough.

Endelkachew's personal inclinations were only encouraged by the advice and support he received from leading aristocrats. They saw the crisis as little more than a new opportunity to regain lost influence and to engage in traditional court intrigue. At no point did they seem to consider the popular turmoil in Addis as anything more than troublesome disorders that should be suppressed by force, the customary solution. An innate sense of superiority made them overconfident about their strength and caused them to dismiss the need for fundamental reforms and to ignore the maneuverings of mere NCOs and junior officers. To the bitter end, aristocrats like Asrate Kassa would accept arrest without resistance because they never doubted that the military rebellion would quickly pass. This was their fatal flaw.

Finally, protesting civilian groups must also bear part of the responsibility for the failure of reform in this period. The CELU, in particular, might have parlayed its burgeoning power into a reformist movement of some kind. To the contrary, its leadership continued to deny the "political" character of their strikes and insisted that its main aim was the redress of specific grievances, primarily salary increases to match the rate of inflation and government recognition of workers' rights to strike and organize. In an interview in May, CELU President Solomon Beyene stated emphatically that the strike was "definitely pre-planned and completely independent of any other events in the country." When asked whether the CELU had become a political force, he replied: "We hope that when the constitutional conference now in session finishes its job and there is a new constitution, we may be able to form a political party."[33] Clearly, the CELU leadership was not yet interested in launching a revolutionary workers' movement. However militant some rank-and-file CELU members, particularly employees of semi-governmental agencies like the power and telecommunications authorities, the labor confederation was unprepared to depart from its cautious unionist stance. The Ethiopian Teachers' Association similarly denied that their strike had political overtones. The ETA also denied that their opposition to the politically significant Educational Sector Review was a central issue, stressing rather the importance of salary increments.[34] Likewise, students too proved ineffectual and disorganized.

Thus despite all the tremendous agitation and turmoil lasting more than three months, there had been no significant reforms carried out in Ethiopia by June and no sign that any were on the way. But to understand why Ethiopia was about to plunge into a radical revolution rather than move cautiously toward bourgeois reformism or even to slip backwards into aristocratic rule, one must understand the developments taking place during this period inside the military.

4. From Barrack Revolt to Revolution

If the military had not so decisively intervened, there would never have been a revolution in Ethiopia. Rebellious officers had first, however, to overcome the divisions and suspicions among various branches of the armed forces, which the Emperor had skillfully encouraged. Only when military ranks became reasonably unified was the army able to bring about a profound revolution in the country's society and polity. This was accomplished not by military elements initially thought radical, but by a group of "moderate" captains and majors who actually feared their own "radicals" and were determined to hold in check the "leftist opposition" to the reform movement. The transformation of the military's political orientation, which eventually led to revolution, took place in three phases over a time span of less than a year. The first lasted from January to late June 1974, when a broadly based committee of all the military services was organized. The second lasted only ten weeks, from early July to the deposition of the Emperor on September 12. The third, from the Emperor's deposition to the proclamation of "Ethiopian Socialism" in December 1974, saw the emergence within the military of a majority favoring revolutionary change.

The Rebels Unite

Haile Selassie learned from the nearly successful coup d'etat in 1960 that the armed forces were not to be trusted, not even his own Imperial Bodyguard, whose commander, Brigadier General Mengistu Neway, led the military's first abortive attempt to overthrow him. The military establishment was carefully divided into separate commands, not only each branch of the armed forces but also each division of the army. While a defense ministry and a general staff office existed, the Emperor kept these central institutions weak and the ties between himself and individual commanders of the various units direct and strong. The U.S. Army Area Handbook for Ethiopia notes that the Emperor even provided each service with training and weapons from different foreign sources "to assure reliability and retention of power."[1] His task was further facilitated by the dispersal of the army's four divisions between Asmara (the Second), Harar (the Third) and Addis Ababa (the First and Fourth). Two of the divisions were preoccupied with a secessionist movement in northern Eritrea Province and a perennial threat from neighboring Somalia. Finally, the Emperor played one unit against the other, in particular the Bodyguard (First Division, 8,000 men) against the territorial army (5,000) and the police (28,000), and these three against the 40,000-man army. The divisions within the military proved a major obstacle to the coordination of the local uprisings by separate units and to their transformation into a broader movement. The units distrusted each other's intentions, and the Emperor and government did their best to exploit this distrust. In addition, the rebel soldiers who launched what became known as the February movement suffered from another major handicap, namely that they received little support from any officer above the rank of colonel. This explains not only why the movement started clandestinely, but also why junior officers and NCOs who shared the same basic grievances and demands acted in small, separate groups and failed for many months to coordinate their actions.

The three seminal revolts within the armed forces during January and February 1974 were similar in origin and in publicized demands, but there is no evidence that there was any coordination among them or that they were part of a larger plot to overthrow the Aklilu government. The Neghelle revolt of enlisted men and NCOs on January 12 was a spontaneous outburst of disgust at living conditions in the wasteland of Sidamo Province in southern Ethiopia, near the Kenyan border. There was nothing new about discontent among soldiers serving in the desolate regions of southern Ethiopia and the Ogaden. In fact, within the army it was considered a little bit like being "sent to Siberia" so terrible were the conditions in these far-flung garrisons. The heat was unbearable, the food barely edible, and water was bad or in short supply; still worse, there are relatively little troop rotation. (Enlisted men and NCOs were complaining about these conditions two years after the revolution began.) The immediate complaints of the soldiers of the Fourth Brigade at the Neghelle garrison concerned poor food and the fact that they were refused the use of their officers' well after the pump on their own broke down. They imprisoned their officers and petitioned the Emperor for a redress of their grievances. When he sent the commander of the territorial army, Lieutenant-General Deresse Dubale, to investigate the matter, the mutineers forced him to eat and drink as they did. They then tied him up and put him under a tree for eight hours while they negotiated with the defense ministry. The Emperor was furious both with the rebel soldiers and with the minister of defense who had failed to handle the situation himself, and he ordered two bombers to overfly the garrison to intimidate the rebels into releasing General Deresse. But he also promised the soldiers an improvement in their conditions and decided not to punish the Fourth Brigade for its flagrant insubordination. The entire incident was hushed up.

All the elements of the larger impending drama were present in the Neghelle revolt; the involvement of enlisted men, NCOs, and junior officers; the wide gap in communication between officers and soldiers; the limited scope of the initial demands; and the failure of the Emperor to punish the rebels. The revolt of technicians and NCOs at the Debre Zeit Air Force Base February 10–13 all but repeated the Neghelle incident. For three days, the mutineers held their superiors hostage inside a mess hall while they negotiated demands for better wages and working conditions. Again the Emperor tried to appease the rebel soldiers by promising to attend to their grievances, and again he sought to cover up the mutiny in the hope of avoiding further trouble in other units. His strategy failed. No sooner had the government announced an Eth$18.00 increase in the monthly salary of privates than a major rebellion broke out in Asmara. This revolt was far more serious than the previous ones, since it involved an entire division and came at the time of student demonstrations, strikes by taxi drivers, and general widespread disorders in Addis Ababa.

The mutiny of enlisted men and NCOs in the Second Division in Asmara began during the night of February 25, and by the following morning the rebels had confined their senior officers in the fortress-like garrison overlooking the city, taken control of vital installations, including the radio station, and closed the international airport and all roads leading into the city. The revolt was led by a group of seven middle-aged sergeants and corporals whose list of 22 demands revealed the very limited scope of their concern at this point. After the ritual pledge of allegiance to the Emperor, the soldiers put forth the following demands and complaints:

1. A minimum monthly salary of Eth$150.00 (about US$75.00) for privates
2. Ministers have too many Mercedes automobiles
3. Officers have too many privileges
4. A basic monthly pension of Eth$85.00 (about US$43.00) for privates
5. Special bonus for soldiers serving in a war zone or dealing with civil disorders
6. Pension rights for those serving less than six months in case of death [combat death?]
7. Free medical treatment for privates
8. Precedence to children of the military for schooling and jobs
9. Rejection of the Eth$18.00 salary increase offered by the government
10. Free food
11. The equal application of the law to all classes
12. Payment of salaries on time
13. Return of a private's body to his home village in case of death [as was done already for officers]
14. No reduction in pay in case of punishment
15. Equal medical treatment for all military personnel whether they be officers, NCOs, or privates

16. Rotation in areas of hazardous duty and transfer to other units every two years
17. The right to attend and participate in sporting events
18. Special bonus of Eth$30.00 (about US$15.00) for technicians
19. Transfer orders should be carried out immediately when soldiers are serving in hazardous areas
20. Family allowances
21. Free medical care for military families
22. The transfer of the chief medical officer to another unit because of his illegal sale of medicines

The rebels' statement was read over the Asmara radio, and the messages of support for which the mutineers appealed started pouring in immediately from units all over the country, most notably the Third and Fourth Divisions, the Royal Navy, and the Air Force Base at Debre Zeit.[2] Some units not only sent messages of support, but also mutinied in turn and arrested their own senior officers. Even the commander of the Royal Navy, Rear Admiral Iskander Desta, grandson of the Emperor, had to flee from the main naval base at Massawa and seek refuge in Djibouti. It was no longer possible to hush up these incidents. But despite their dramatic impact—Prime Minister Aklilu resigned within 48 hours of the beginning of the Asmara mutiny after approving another salary raise for the soldiers—there was still no organized movement within the military.[3] Deep divisions existed everywhere. The Second Division did not act in conjunction with air force and police units stationed in Eritrea, fearing that they would be used by the Emperor to crush its revolt. (In fact, the Emperor did sound out various units to see if they would participate in a counterattack against the Asmara rebels.) Even when other units declared support for the rebel troops, they limited themselves to arresting their own officers and did not try to form a united movement. In fact, after the second sizeable salary increase was announced, the rebel soldiers quickly released their officers, returned to their barracks, and ignored the continued agitation by civilians in the capital. In Asmara, roads and airport were soon reopened. In Addis Ababa, the Fourth Division rebels released the dozen minsiters and high officials they were holding in return for a guarantee of no reprisals, and began to patrol the streets in an effort to restore order. No complaint came from the mutineers about the appointment of Endelkachew as prime minister, although he was very much part of the old order.

What prevented the military movement from collapsing altogether was, paradoxically, its effect on the civilian population. In early March, students, teachers, and workers were busy expressing their various individual grievances. Suddenly, their anger was directed against the military rebels who so docilely returned to their barracks once their demands were satisfied. Moreover, after two increases in less than ten days military salaries were higher than those of many industrial workers and government employees. "Everywhere they went, in bars, *tej bets,* and restaurants, the soldiers were hissed and attacked," recalled one Ethiopian journalist. "They just did not dare to go anywhere."[4] The reaction of the Addis Ababa civilian population was important because it encouraged a small group of more politicized soldiers and middle-echelon officers (majors and captains) to express their views; through their actions, the entire military was eventually pushed to the forefront of the struggle for political change. The first sign of this development came when a flurry of leaflets was let loose from air force and army aviation helicopters over Addis Ababa in the first days of March. Typical of them was one dropped by a group of air force "radicals" on March 4, signed "The Armed Forces," and clearly aimed at making amends and bridging the gap between the military and civilians:

To All Ethiopian People

On the basis of the movement made by the students, teachers, taxi drivers, armed forces and workers, we hereby submit the following demands to the Emperor:

1. A free press
2. Freedom of assembly and demonstration
3. A land reform
4. Establishment of a political party and free elections
5. A review of the labor-management relationship
6. All political detainees must be released
7. Free education for everybody
8. Strict price controls
9. Former ministers must be put on trial
10. Salary increases should be given to the workers as well as to the military and should be related to current market prices
11. A committee composed of the armed forces and civil servants should be set up to investigate whether the above mentioned demands are promptly met. The ministry of information, journalists and radio reporters have time and again misrepresented [our position] by not stating correctly the democratic demands set forth by the armed forces. Consequently, they have diverted public opinion and created misunderstanding between the armed forces and the Ethiopian people.

The armed forces want the Ethiopian people to know that these demands will be promptly met in accordance with the directives given by the Emperor. Moreover, we request the new government to publicize through the media all the demands set forth by the Ethiopian people and the armed forces. Unless all the demands are met, we will be forced to take the necessary action. In addition, we would like to inform pressmen not to create misunderstandings between the armed forces and the public by releasing distorted news.

The Armed Forces

As was clear from other leaflets dropped by the military in this period and by the reaction of other units to them, there was no committee representing "the armed forces" at this time, but only small politicized factions within the Air Force, the Airborne Corps, the 29th Brigade of the Fourth Division, and the Engineers and Signals Corps. After a few months, these factions would meet with much success, but in early March they received little support from their colleagues. The Second Division in Asmara, the Police, and the Imperial Bodyguard all disassociated themselves from, or indicated their reservation about, the more political demands set forth by these groups. Despite this initial failure, however, the agitation of the more politicized elements in the military had a permanent impact through the small committees established in various units by more radical NCOs, junior officers, and enlisted men. Many were disbanded in early March, but several continued to function, especially at the Debre Zeit Air Force Base, within the Second Division in Asmara, and inside the Army Aviation unit and the Corps of Engineers in Addis Ababa. These committees provoked a new series of incidents a few weeks later.

The events of late March were different in two respects. Since they were less widespread, Endelkachew was able to use some military units to crush others. They also revealed a higher degree of organization and politicization. The events began at the Debre Zeit Air Force Base, where a committee of about 20 NCOs and officers plotted to buzz the capital with jets in order to show their dissatisfaction with the slow pace of reform and the failure of the Endelkachew government to arrest former ministers and officials of the previous cabinet. However, the government learned of the plot, and on the night of March 24–25, it arrested about 25 NCOs and junior officers, most of them in the Air Force, accusing them of planning to bomb the capital and overthrow the prime minister.[5] Whether the plotters actually intended to bomb the capital rather than buzz it remains unclear.[6] While Endelkachew quickly quashed this incipient revolt, his troubles were not over.

A day after the arrest of the Air Force rebels, a group of NCOs, which this time included representatives of all units serving in Eritrea—the Second Division, the police, and the navy—arrested some 50 senior officers, seized the radio station, and broadcast a new series of distinctly political demands. The rebels wanted the arrest and immediate trial of a long list of senior government officials and higher officers they deemed corrupt; the release of the Debre Zeit NCOs and junior officers arrested the previous day; and perhaps most significantly, a repeal of all measures taken by the government to prevent communication among rebellious soldiers, namely the cancellation of orders transferring to other units the leaders of the February revolt and the reestablishment of radio communications between Asmara and Debre Zeit. The immediate cause of the Second Division's new revolt was the arrest of the 25 rebel leaders in Addis Ababa the previous day. Yet there was considerable organization behind it, suggesting that some form of action was already being planned. However, the rebels now faced a government that controlled most military units and was in a position to use force against them.

Prime Minister Endelkachew's reaction to the late March military revolts was far different from that of Aklilu to the February ones. A skillful manipulator and politician, he made use of the situation to strengthen his position, first by threatening to resign and then by appealing to all protestors to give him a chance to prove himself. This tactic rallied practically all military units to his side, except for the Air Force base at Debre Zeit and the Second Division. He was thus able to send the Airborne Corps to surround the Debre

Zeit base, leaving the rebels in Asmara completely isolated. As a result, they sent a delegation to Addis Ababa on March 28 to begin negotiations. The concessions they won fell far short of their initial demands: the government promised only to establish a commission to investigate allegations of corruption by former government officials and to release two of the four Air Force pilots arrested in the Debre Zeit plot. Having obtained these face-saving concessions, the "Armed Forces of the North," as the Asmara rebels called themselves this time, pledged their allegiance to the government and the Emperor and returned to the barracks. Endelkachew won this confrontation by gaining the support of most military units and isolating the rebels. The government's siege of the Debre Zeit base was finally lifted on April 3.

It was after this that the prime minister became sufficiently confident of his position vis-à-vis the military to use some of the rebel officers against striking civilians and even against the Emperor in an effort to consolidate his position. Developments within the military in the period from mid-April to the end of June saw first the creation of a coordinating committee willing to cooperate with him and then its transformation into a broadly based organization which became increasingly alienated from the government.

By April 1974, the armed forces were apparently split in three factions: the old high command, which by this time controlled little more than the Imperial Bodyguard; the "radical" junior officers, momentarily defeated; and a growing body of army and police officers led by the Airborne Corps commander, Colonel Alem Zewd Tessema, who supported Endelkachew and was willing to disobey both the Emperor and the high command. The initiative of the movement belonged first to Colonel Alem Zewd and his group and then passed to the radical junior officers after they reorganized themselves following the late March events. Colonel Alem Zewd was a rebel in the sense that, by all evidence, he acted on his own rather than on orders from the high command. He had not been a leader of any of the early uprisings by junior officers and NCOs. In fact, his paratroopers quelled the revolt within the Air Force in late March. Precisely what the colonel sought to accomplish or to gain for himself remains unclear, although he undoubtedly had hopes for a higher appointment. Moreover, Endelkachew was a distant cousin and the blood relationship may have been the single most important factor in determinig his politics at this time.

The group around Colonel Alem Zewd had formally organized itself by April 24 into a coordinating committee. Among its leaders—in fact, its coordinator—was an officer who played a major role in organizing more radical elements in the military and who became one of the *Derg*'s top men: Major Atnafu Abate. At this time he was an unknown figure in the Fourth Division in Addis Ababa. Another member of the committee was Junior Aircraftsman Girma Fisseha, who a few months later became a member of the second coordinating committee and participated in the occupation of the Addis Ababa radio station on June 28. While Colonel Alem Zewd's coordinating committee was given a mandate by Endelkachew to put down the strikes by whatever means necessary, it was officially disbanded on April 29 before its task had been accomplished. The very next day, creation of the 25-member National Security Commission was announced. This commission was a mixed civilian-military body under direct command of Minister of Defense Abiye Abebe and close to both the Emperor and the military high command. Its establishment may well have been part of the command's attempt to reassert its control and to take the initiative away from Endel-kachew in restoring law and order. Since the names of the military officers serving on the commission were never known, it is impossible to know for certain whether the leaders of the disbanded coordinating committee were serving on it. But it was obvious that the two organizations took the same tough law-and-order line against civilian strikes and disorders and that troops of the Fourth Division were used by the National Security Commission to restore order, just as they had been used by the coordinating committee to arrest the former ministers. Later, the National Security Commission would be bitterly criticized in the Ethiopian press as a "weapon of repression" and accused of "atrocities and inhuman deeds" by the workers. "A grim experience in our society" was the way the *Ethiopian Herald* described the activities of the commission[7] while the Military Council's sketchy official history later condemned it for "anti-revolutionary activities" which aimed at "muffling and terrorizing all the progressive elements who continued to voice their demands for the restoration of economic and social justice to the oppressed masses."[8]

During May, when calm returned to the strife-ridden capital, a significant new development occurred, namely the organization of a second military coordinating committee which came to be called the *Derg*. Its immediate origin remains obscure, and Ethiopia's military rulers have kept it so, either because of personal rivalries or an embarrassment about their early links with nonrevolutionary groups such as the first coordinating committee and the National Security Commission. Nor was it clear whether the second military committee was a completely different organization from the first or simply a further development of Colonel Alem Zewd's organization. However, the aims of the officers who organized the second committee and engineered the take-over of vital communication installations in the capital in late June were so different from those of the first committee that it seems warranted to speak of two separate bodies.

From published evidence and from unofficial military accounts, the *Derg* was apparently formed as follows.[9] Throughout the month of May, unease mounted among the more politicized officers because Endelkachew refused to keep his pledge to bring the arrested ministers to justice. Only on June 15 did he finally set up a 15-member commission to investigate their alleged misdoings. Ten days later, he placed a ban on all ministers, civil servants, members of Parliament, and top officials of parastatal companies traveling abroad pending the outcome of the inquiry. His delayed actions did not prevent the military from taking their own initiatives.

Around mid-June (the exact date is unknown) a group of young officers in the Fourth Division headquarters began sounding out other units of the armed forces and police stationed in or near the capital about the need for further intervention.[10] A leader of this group was Major Atnafu. This time the rebel officers decided to disassociate themselves from Colonel Alem Zewd, whose paratroopers were once again quelling unrest at the Debre Zeit Air Force Base.[11] According to one source, the colonel and several of his close associates were excluded simply by barring all officers of the rank of colonel or above. This would explain why no one above the rank of major was allowed membership in the second coordinating committee. Besides Atnafu, some principal organizers were Major Tafara Teklaeb of the Army Corps of Engineers, Major Fisseha Desta of the Imperial Bodyguard, Girma Fisseha of the Army Aviation, and Captain Sisay Hapte of the Air Force. Major Mengistu Haile Mariam did not emerge as the strongman of the *Derg* until at least late June, when he became the representative of the Third Division. Apparently he had not been formally elected to the committee, but simply appointed as liaison between the Third and Fourth Division because of his frequent missions to Addis Ababa as head of the Third Division's Ordnance Company. From practically all accounts the authors could obtain about the formation of the *Derg,* the central figure was Major Atnafu, who at the outset acted as provisional chairman reportedly because no other officer wanted to assume the responsibility at such an early and uncertain stage.

On June 25, the wives and relatives of the 25 detained officials of the Aklilu government formally petitioned the Emperor, the Parliament, and the cabinet to set bail for the detainees and allow them to return home pending the outcome of the special inquiry commission's investigation. The following day, a delegation of eight deputies led by the supposedly progressive Major Admassie Zeleke went to the Fourth Division headquarters and appealed to a gathering of 2,000 soldiers to release the ministers and officials. His appeal not only incensed the restless radicals in the military but even the conservative Parliament, which on June 27 passed a resolution condemning the action of the eight deputies and disassociating itself from their request. The military radicals interpreted this attempt to free the revolution's first political prisoners as a plot to restore the pre-February political order. They decided to act immediately. On June 28, they officially established the Coordinating Committee of the Armed Forces, Police, and Territorial Army, a decision so hastily made that many units of the armed forces did not have time to send representatives before action was taken. Not even a formal election of the new committee's leaders was held. The total number of members, later to reach around 120, was far less at this time. Early in the evening of the same day, troops under the command of Major Tafara and Junior Aircraftsman Girma Fisseha occupied the government radio and television stations and began a round-up of aristocrats, high officials, and generals thought to be behind the conspiracy. It soon became clear that the new military committee was not under Endelkachew's authority and that it intended to take on the high and mighty of the whole imperial regime, not just a few officials deemed particularly corrupt. Colonel Alem Zewd's flight to the countryside also underlined the break with the previous coordinating committee.

The Rebels in Command

Nobody knew who the rebel officers were, what they intended to do, or whether they had taken over the government. Even after the election of Major Mengistu and Atnafu as chairman and vice chairman of the *Derg,* their names were not made public for months.[12] Western news agency reports of a military coup were immediately denied. None of the ministers was arrested immediately, although one, Minister of Defense Abiye Abebe, went into hiding. The demands the Coordinating Committee submitted to the Emperor and Endelkachew on July 2 suggested that it intended to influence government decisions without formally seizing power. They included: an amnesty for all political prisoners except those charged with "crimes against the unity and welfare of the nation;" the right of political exiles to return home; the rapid drafting of a new constitution; the immediate review of the draft by Parliament, which was ordered to remain in session specifically for that purpose; the appointment of General Aman Michael Andom as chief of staff; and the right of the Coordinating Committee to remain in contact with the cabinet.

The aim of the military was to clear the way for the "smooth functioning of the new cabinet," the committee said, and it even refused an offer of six posts in the government. Also wanted by the military was the arrest of officials who had misused their authority or had been involved in the cover-up of the famine in Wollo and Tigre provinces. Even as it arrested aristocratic figures like *Ras* Asrate and Rear Admiral Iskander Desta the committee pledged loyalty to the Emperor and promised to deal fairly with the arrested officials. "There is no need to fear because we do not believe in the biblical saying an eye for an eye. The military forces are pledged to bring to trial all those who misused their influence, and they want to avoid bloodshed," said a statement read over the seized radio station on July 3.

Yet it was clear that a profound change had taken place inside the military. The *Derg*'s motto, *Ethiopia Tikdem,* showed a determination to move away from strictly corporate military demands. Instead of issuing the usual list of demands and complaints, the new Coordinating Committee talked about a "movement" to bring about "lasting changes." A declaration of July 9, better than any other published at that time, expressed the spirit and hopes of the reformers: "The *Derg* believes that this movement will achieve lasting changes without any bloodshed. The culture and history of Ethiopia are unique, and so are the nature and course of this movement." But the initial reforms sought by the military were hardly radical. The same statement stressed the *Derg*'s desire for close cooperation with the civilian government and for the speedy establishment of a constitutional monarchy. However, the moderation of these statements should not obscure the great difference between the demands of the military rebels in February and those in July. This time one could seriously talk of a military reform movement.

In line with its cautions and moderate tone, the *Derg* did not order mass arrests. During the first 18 days, a carefully chosen group of 61 persons was

taken into custody. Many carried the traditional military titles of the Ethiopian nobility—*ras, dejazmatch, fitawari, kegnazmatch*—while others were
ministers, vice ministers, provincial governors, top-ranking police officers,
and army generals. The most extraordinary aspect of these arrests was the
way in which those wanted, whose names were made public in the press and
over the radio, voluntarily gave themselves up, simply appearing at the gates
of the Fourth Division headquarters in Addis Ababa for incarceration. The
paradoxical parade of the Ethiopian aristocracy to the revolutionary gallows
is difficult to account for fully. It was due partly to the superior attitude of the
aristocrats, who thought that no sergeant or major would dare touch a *ras* or
dejazmatch; there was also the conviction that the new military committee
was a passing phenomenon and would collapse shortly. Anď most aristocrats
were confident that a court of inquiry would not find them guilty. Perhaps most
important was the attitude of the Emperor, who refused to come to their aid
and sat as if in a stupor while his throne and its traditional pillars were
destroyed.

Ras Asrate Kassa and *Ras* Mesfin Sileshi, two leading figures in this
group, gave themselves up without any attempt to organize an armed resistance. This was done at the Emperor's express request. The only serious plan
to crush the military movement was also vetoed by the Emperor. It called for
an attack on the Fourth Division headquarters to wipe out the Coordinating
Committee and was to have been organized by the commander of the
Bodyguard, Major General Tafesse Lemma.[13] With most of the 8,000-man
Bodyguard still loyal to the Emperor, the plan should have succeeded, since
the committee had few troops at its immediate disposal. But it was never
implemented, and in mid-August the countercoup leaders were arrested.

The Creeping Coup

There are two views of the events leading to the removal of Haile Selassie and
the assumption of power by the military. One version is that it was a pre-
planned operation skillfully executed in deliberate stages. Another, which is
also the authors' view, is that the revolution unfolded in an unplanned series of
incidents, which began with the military's desire to help Endelkachew carry
out much-needed reforms. Among the rebel officers was a radical minority
which pushed for the Emperor's deposition from the beginning.

The official version of the Coordinating Committee's deliberations in late
June and early July states that as regards its future actions seven different
alternatives were proposed and thoroughly discussed:

1. Reforming the existing cabinet and removing all obstacles within and
outside it while retaining the throne of His Imperial Majesty.

2. Replacing entirely the existing cabinet with a new one while retaining the
throne of His Imperial Majesty.

3. Replacing the civilian administration with a military government while retaining the throne of His Imperial Majesty.

4. Setting up a civilian-military coalition government, which is independent of the Crown while retaining the throne of His Imperial Majesty.

5. Abolishing the monarchy, reforming the existing cabinet under a provisional military government to prepare the people for an eventual transfer of power to a representative popular government.

6. Setting up a military government by abolishing the Crown and Cabinet altogether.

7. Setting up a representative popular government by abolishing the Crown and the Cabinet altogether.

The version goes on to explain that the committee decided upon a three-phase approach beginning with the plan of action outlined in the first alternative, passing then to that detailed in the fifth option and ending with the fulfillment of the seventh one. That such a line was formally adopted at this early stage is doubtful. It seems more likely that the official version was written *ex post facto* to fit the evolution of events. At best it represents the initial intention of a small minority of the Coordinating Committee. Indeed, the seventh option, the establishment of a "representative popular government," had not been implemented as of early 1977, its proponents having lost out shortly after the Emperor was deposed.[15] In the beginning, there was no way for rebel officers to gauge the strength of possible resistance from the Emperor and the aristocracy. That they would have spelled out a future course of action and final political objectives when they could not have been sure of their survival seems unlikely. As things turned out, they chipped away at the foundations of an institution that was already rotten; even the slightest blow would cause it to collapse.

The first steps taken by the military committee did not foreshadow the final outcome. The *Derg* moved to establish a more liberal civilian government. On July 22, Prime Minister Endelkachew was forced to resign and was subsequently arrested. In his place, the *Derg* appointed *Lij* Michael Imru, the scion of yet another aristocratic family. His selection was indicative of the still limited goals of the *Derg* at this time.[16] In its statement of July 9, the *Derg* had pledged that "the revised constitution now being drafted is being implemented on a priority basis." They forced Parliament to postpone its summer vacation and to continue in session so that the constitution could be rapidly approved. It appeared that the *Derg* accepted the idea, shared by all major political groups at this time, that a new constitution should reduce the monarchy to representative functions and thrust parliament into the central role.

Not until early August did the majority within the *Derg* begin to change its position toward the monarchy and parliamentary institutions. When the long-awaited draft constitution was finally ready—the members of the constitutional committee had continued their work quietly in the midst of turmoil—a majority of *Derg* members moved to block steps that would lead to a return of civilian government. Many military officers did not even want the draft constitution made public, but members of the constitutional committee insisted, and the document was published in the local newspapers on August 10. Unable to stop its publication, the *Derg* took advantage of the event in a skillful and unexpected manner by promoting a debate in the state-controlled media on the whole issue of the Ethiopian monarchy. At the same time, it set about cutting out all the institutions of monarchy. On August 16, the Crown Council, the *chilot,* and the office of chief of staff in the Emperor's personal cabinet were disbanded.[17] On August 17, Imperial Bodyguard Commander General Tafesse was arrested, neutralizing the main force protecting the Emperor. On August 24, the *bejirond* office, the Emperor's private exchequer fed by the public treasury, was in effect closed. And on August 25, the Jubilee Palace, the Emperor's residence, was nationalized and renamed the National Palace.

In the meantime, the state-run newspapers, radio station, and television unleashed a barrage of attacks on the monarchy and the Emperor. The first devastating critique appeared in a discussion of the proposed constitution in *Addis Zemen* on August 16.[18] The attack came from the most unexpected quarter, a Coptic priest. He pointed out the basic contradiction between the principle of legal equality and the concept embedded in the draft constitution that the Emperor was above the law. He also questioned the myth that Haile Selassie was a direct descendant of Solomon and Sheba and, therefore, his right to the throne. Public attacks on the Emperor intensified. In the following days the press published interviews with Ethiopians who expressed the view that the Emperor squandered the country's meager resources on expensive trips abroad to boost his personal prestige and questioned whether the people could afford a monarchy any longer.[19] A national hero of the war against the Italian invasion in 1936 accused the Emperor in effect of treason, saying he was responsible for allowing the invaders to reach Addis Ababa with relatively little resistance.[20] A writer in the Asmara weekly *Ethiopia* accused the Emperor of "defecating on the Ethiopian people" and bluntly asserted it was time to abolish the monarchy altogether.[21] This last attack was more than even the *Derg* was prepared to accept, and it issued a statement calling for a halt to "slanderous personal attacks" on the Emperor. The campaign continued nonetheless. On August 28, Haile Selassie was accused of being directly involved in the cover-up of the famine in Wollo Province.[22] By the end of August, the public was psychologically prepared for his removal. When several hundred ragged youths and students paraded through the streets of the capital on September 2 to cries of "hang the Emperor" and "the Emperor is a thief," there was no adverse public reaction. But the *Derg* still hesitated to take the final step. The night of the street boys' demonstration it issued a sharp warning against any further public protests.

According to the military's own account, it was not until after a four-day secret meeting September 6–9 that the *Derg* voted to dethrone the Emperor.[23] The length of time it took to reach a consensus on this momentous action indicates how controversial it was even at this late date. When it occurred his deposition came as something of an anticlimax. On the eve of the historic occasion, the state television showed the film by British journalist Jonathan Dimbleby called "The Hidden Famine," a great exposé of how thousands of children, women, and men had been allowed to starve in Wollo Province. The film was spliced with scenes showing the Emperor and his entourage drinking champagne, eating caviar, and feeding meat to his dogs from a silver tray. The Emperor himself was forced to watch the film. Early the following morning, September 12, a group of officers went to the National Palace and summoned him to the library where the proclamation deposing him was read out by an unknown police officer. By that time, the first proclamation of the Provisional Military Government had been broadcast over the radio, and the public knew before Haile Selassie that he had been deposed.[24]

ETHIOPIA TIKDEM

Considering that, although the people of Ethiopia look in good faith upon the Crown, which has persisted for a long period in Ethiopian history as a symbol of unity, Haile Selassie I, who has ruled this country for more than fifty years ever since he assumed power as Crown Prince, has not only left the country in its present crisis by abusing at various times the high and dignified authority conferred on him by the Ethiopian people but also, being over 82 years of age and due to the consequent physical and mental exhaustion, is no more able to shoulder the high responsibilities of leadership;

Recognizing that the present system of parliamentary election is undemocratic; that Parliament heretofore has been serving not the people but its members and the ruling and aristocratic classes; that as a consequence it has refrained from legislating on land reform which is the basic problem of the country while passing laws at various times intended to raise the living standard of its members, thereby using the high authority conferred on it by the people to further the personal interests of its members and aggravating the misery of the people; and that its existence is contrary to the motto "Ethiopia *Tikdem*";

Realizing that the Constitution of 1955 was prepared to confer on the Emperor absolute powers; that it does not safeguard democratic rights but merely serves as a democratic facade for the benefit of world public opinion; that it was not conceived to serve the interests of the Ethiopian people; that it was designed to give the baseless impression that fundamental natural rights are gifts from the Emperor to his people; and that, above all, it is inconsistent with the popular movement in progress under the motto "Ethiopia *Tikdem*" and with the fostering of economic, political and social development; and

Believing that the ill effects of the past aristocratic rule have thrown the country into an abyss of economic social and political problems; that it has become necessary to establish a strong provisional administration dedicated to serve the public good and capable of developing Ethiopia and coping with the various security problems prevailing at this transitional period; It is hereby proclaimed as follows:

. . .

Haile Selassie I is hereby deposed as of today, September 12, 1974.

It is said that the police officer's hands shook uncontrollably while he read the proclamation and that some of the soldiers in the room wept so profusely that they had to leave. The Emperor refused at first to leave the palace. But then *Ras* Imru walked up to him, kissed him on the cheek, and said, "Go." The Emperor, dazed and apparently still uncomprehending, walked with the *Ras* to the palace steps looking for one of his six different-colored Mercedes limousines. Instead, he was driven in a small blue Volkswagen the short distance to the Fourth Division Headquarters and imprisoned in a small wattle-and-mud building.

The proclamation that deposed the Emperor declared that Crown Prince Asfa Wossen "shall be King of Ethiopia" and that the coronation ceremony would be held as soon as he returned. It also stated "the King shall be head of state with no power in the country's administrative and political affairs." The proclamation suspended the 1955 constitution, dissolved Parliament, postponed the implementation of the new constitution, and announced that the "armed forces, the police and territorial army have hereby assumed full government power until a legally constituted people's assembly approves a new constitution and a government is duly established." Strikes, unauthorized demonstrations, and any other kind of public assembly were outlawed. It prohibited any conspiracy against the military's official motto, *Ethiopia Tikdem*. Finally, a Provisional Military Administrative Council (PMAC) was established to govern the country and direct the course of the revolution. Without a drop of blood being spilled, the Emperor was deposed and a mysterious group of soldiers, not one of whose names was known to the public, took power in Ethiopia.

Kedem Ethiopia Tikdem[25]

The bloodless deposition of Haile Selassie was a remarkable achievement for the *Derg*. Not only had it managed to convince the country of the need to overthrow The Emperor, but it had also succeeded in maintaining the unity of the military reform movement despite sharply differing views among its leaders with regard to the aged monarch. Yet the capacity of the military reformers to resolve internal disputes without irrevocably splitting the movement had yet to meet its severest test.

The Council was at first uncertain about its own role in government. It issued a statement on September 15 saying that the "military should not be involved in politics," and it left the civilian cabinet virtually intact except for replacing Michael Imru with General Aman. In a proclamation on September 12, however, the PMAC declared that it was "assuming full government power," and ministers did not dare take decisions without the military's approval. The *Derg* quickly found itself under considerable pressure from civilian groups—particularly from students and the labor confederation—to step down and turn power over to a "people's government." These groups meant by this term not just the presence of hand-picked civilian ministers but also direct representation by various national organizations in the government.[26] On September 16, four days after the Emperor's removal, two thousand students staged a demonstration outside the main Addis Ababa university campus, chanting "down with the military government" and "we want a people's government." The same day, the Confederation of Ethiopian Labor Unions (CELU) issued a communique containing similar demands. When its three top leaders were arrested on September 24, it threatened a new general strike.

Their demands found an echo within the *Derg* itself, for groups within the Bodyguard, the Army Engineers Corps, the Air Force, and the Army Aviation all endorsed the idea of a people's government. Another faction favored the continuation of military rule but wanted to dissolve the unwieldy 120-man Council and replace it with a 10- to 15-member junta. The debate over this issue came to a head on October 1. After a meeting lasting the entire day, a majority of *Derg* members voted to maintain the ruling body in its existing form and role. The defeated minority did not submit to this decision, however, and began circulating leaflets insisting on the immediate establishment of a civilian government. Pamphlets emanating from the Army Aviation in particular openly supported civilian demands for freedom to strike and demonstrate, a free press, and a people's government. On October 7, the *Derg* finally sent troops and armored cars to the Addis Ababa headquarters of the Engineers Corps and Army Aviation to arrest the dissidents. In a shootout at the compound of the Engineers Corps, five NCOs and six other soldiers were wounded. Thirty-four dissidents in the two corps were arrested, effectively quelling the idea of a civilian government within the military movement for some time.

A second issue dividing the *Derg* was what to do with the some 200 political prisoners then being held on suspicion of corruption, abuse of office, or complicity in the famine cover-up. The original plan called for the prisoners to go on trial before special military courts after the civilian inquiry commission completed its investigation.[27] The courts were set up in late October, and on November 13 the commission released its first report on the Wollo cover-up, returning indictments against 87 persons, including all 26 members of the Aklilu cabinet and two former Wollo Province governors. Three days later, a special penal code was issued providing the death penalty even for those found guilty of failing to take action in the case of a famine in the country.[28] Until mid-November it appeared that the political prisoners would be formally put on trial and that some would be executed. But their fate, like all other issues pending before the *Derg*, suddenly became intertwined with the struggle between General Aman and other members of the Council, and the outcome was very different from the orderly one originally anticipated.

No one dominated the political scene of Ethiopia during the fall of 1974 more than General Aman Michael Andom, the 51-year-old outsider brought in to serve in multiple capacities, first as chief of staff and then as chairman of the Provisional Military Administrative Council. Aman's role in the early period of the military reform movement remains obscure, but some accounts maintain he had contacts with the young officers as far back as February and March. At that time, he was serving in the Senate as a "political exile" after having been dismissed by the Emperor in 1964 from his post as commander of the Third Division for overzealous pursuit of the border war against Somalia.[29] The "Desert Lion" was enormously popular within the armed forces and a kind of national hero after Ethiopia won the war. In fact, he proved too strong, ambitious, and popular for the Emperor and the *Derg* alike. Having been made chief of staff at the specific request of the rebel officers in early July, General Aman emerged at the time of the Emperor's deposition as the apparent strongman, holding the titles chief of staff, minister of defense, chairman of the council of ministers, and chairman of the Military Council. From that day onward, the general found himself at odds with a majority of the *Derg*'s members over most major issues, including whether he was "chairman" of the ruling military body or simply its "spokesman."

By all accounts, Aman fought the Council membership over three central issues: the size of the ruling body and his position in it; the policy to be pursued toward the Eritrean Liberation Front; and what punishment to mete out to political prisoners. Supported by a minority within the *Derg*, Aman argued that with 120 members the Council was too unwieldy and should be reduced to a junta of ten to fifteen members chosen from among higher-ranking officers of the movement. For this reason, he was later accused of plotting to "consolidate his power."[30] Given his ambitious nature, this was undoubtedly so. The second issue, that of Eritrea, found Aman once again pitted against the majority over what strategy to pursue in ending the 13-year-old dispute. Aman, himself an Eritrean, wanted to negotiate a peaceful settlement, talking directly to the Eritrean Liberation Front if necessary, while most of the Council's members hoped to crush the secessionist movement by force, just as the Emperor had attempted in the past. Aman was actively promoting his "new deal" policy when the *Derg* decided in early November to dispatch 5,000 troops to Eritrea to reinforce the war-weary Second Division. Realizing this move would spell the end of any peace-making diplomacy, Aman refused to sign the order.

The third issue, relating to the punishment of arrested aristocrats and former government officials, proved far more explosive. Aman opposed execution in principle, both because he believed in bloodless change and because many of those awaiting execution were personal friends or belonged to the same upper class. He tried to block publication of the special penal code prepared for the trial of the political prisoners that legalized both their arrests and the death sentence for their crimes. The *Derg*, on the other hand, accepted the principle of capital punishment for political crimes.

By mid-November, Aman had reached a deadlock with a majority of the *Derg*'s members on all these issues. He tried to rally the army rank and file to his side, counting on his popularity among them. He wrote a letter of resignation and sent it to all units of the armed forces, rather than the *Derg*, hoping to arouse a groundswell of support. But the letter was blocked, and Aman retired to his home on November 15. It was at this time that the name of the *Derg*'s first vice-chairman, Major Mengistu Haile Mariam, was first made public as he was touring various bases and barracks pleading for the support of the armed forces.[31] Significantly, the day after Aman retreated to his home, the special penal code and the decree officially setting up the courts-martial were published—without his signature.

Although the details are unclear, General Aman, with the support of two *Derg* members, died in a battle with troops sent to arrest them at the general's home on the outskirts of Addis Ababa in the early evening of November 23. At about 9:30, according to eyewitness reports, those political prisoners marked for execution were taken from Menelik Palace, where they were being held, to the Akaki Central Prison, where they were executed in pairs during the night and later buried in a single mass grave. It is uncertain how much support there was for these actions. It appears that the *Derg* members agreed to Aman's arrest, since the survival of the Council as a collective body appeared at stake. But it is not clear how many members supported the idea of summarily executing political prisoners, and even less certain who participated in the actual selection of the victims.[32] It also seems that the hard-line faction of the *Derg* did not have the full support of military units stationed outside the capital, and that it even feared the intervention of the Second and Third Divisions.[33] The Council's own statement, issued on the morning after the executions, threw no light on what happened. It tersely announced that the executed aristocrats, generals, and officials had been "found guilty" of gross abuse of authority, had committed injustices against the Ethiopian people, incited civil war, created divisions among the armed forces, or attempted to divide the military movement. Though most probably would have been found guilty by military courts that were then being set up, no formal trial was ever held.

The executions shattered the image of a "revolution without bloodshed" and shocked the outside world. It provoked a loud outcry not only in Europe and the United States, where it was to be expected, but also in Africa, where it was unexpected. Among African countries that protested and expressed deep concern for the fate of the Emperor were Nigeria, Tanzania, Zambia, Uganda, and many West African francophone nations. Most Western nations, led by Britain and the United States, warned the Military Council against further executions. At home, the *Derg* at first anticipated a sharp reaction from the Third and Second Divisions, possibly an attack on Addis Ababa, but none came.

Under the pressure of events and by the will of a small group of hard-liners who successfully swayed the majority of *Derg* members, Ethiopia's revolution entered a new phase. Its leaders were now united in a "blood pact" and forced to move forward quickly to maintain the initiative and their own base of power. The executions established certain basic principles, namely the collegial nature of the revolution's leadership and the use, if necessary, of ruthless and bloody means. The Military Council's policy toward Eritrea was also fixed. Within two days of the executions, a 5,000-man contingent of the Imperial Bodyguard left the capital for Asmara in preparation for a new government offensive against the Eritrean Liberation Front. On November 28, the Council elected a new chairman, 53-year-old Lt. General Teferi Bante, who was then serving as commander of the Second Division in Eritrea Province. This time the officers were careful to pick a less ambitious and dynamic figure, one who would be content to serve as a ceremonial figurehead.

Having resolved, at least for the time being, the issues of the form of government, the kind of leadership, and the policy to be followed in Eritrea, the PMAC was free to begin considering radical economic and social reforms. After nearly a month of debate, the Council issued on December 20 its first socialist proclamation and announced a policy of *hebrettesebawinet,* or Ethiopian socialism. Although vague in content, the statement nonetheless enunciated the guiding principle of "public ownership of the nation's economic resources" including land, where a sweeping reform was promised. While the declaration marked a decided shift to the left in economic policy, it could hardly be considered a radical socialist document. There was no mention of Marx or Lenin, and the authors went out of their way to use Amharic words, like *hebrettesebawinet,* to explain to Ethiopians the nature of the anticipated economic and social changes. In political philosophy, the revolution was still in its infancy, and the Military Council's hard-liners remained remarkably soft and uncertain. The soldiers had nonetheless come a long way from the Neghelle barracks revolt only eleven months earlier. The *Derg* no longer saw itself merely as representing the armed forces, but also the millions who had suffered exploitation under the *ancien régime.* Having resolved internal problems of unity, purpose, and direction, Ethiopia's new military rulers were ready to tackle the enormous social problems of Ethiopia.

5. Ethiopian Socialism

"*Ethiopia Tikdem,*" the Provisional Military Administrative Council declared on December 20, "means *hebrettesebawinet* (Ethiopian socialism); and *hebrettesebawinet* means equality; self-reliance; the dignity of labor; the supremacy of the common good; and the indivisibility of Ethiopian unity."[1] Such was the first official explanation of Ethiopian socialism, a homespun ideology made to fit the special conditions and needs of Ethiopian society. While this explanation may appear vague, it was in fact addressing itself to important problems in traditional Ethiopian social relations. The notion of equality was as revolutionary in deeply class- and status-conscious Ethiopia as it had been in 18th and 19th century revolutionary Europe. Self-reliance was also a singular innovation in a society where begging is pervasive and carries little stigma, and where the patron-client relation is central to social relations. The dignity of labor was foreign to a long tradition of disdaining manual activity to the point where craftsmen were members of despised castes. The unification of the empire had been a problem throughout its long history, and the threat of the Eritrean secessionist movement made it central to the contemporary situation. But perhaps the most important new idea of Ethiopian socialism was that the common good was to take precedence over individual, ethnic, or regional interest. *Ethiopia Tikdem* meant in effect the rejection of a pluralistic parliamentary system in which various interest groups were represented in a struggle to determine national policy. It implied that only some higher body, namely the *Derg,* could interpret the common good and steer Ethiopia in the right direction. It meant finally the rejection of the ideals that stood behind the civilian agitation of early 1974, ideals that were corporate, individualistic, and libertarian in nature. Significantly, when the military's slogan *Ethiopia Tikdem* was first heard, practically no Ethiopian understood what message the reformers were attempting to convey.

Because of the low level of political consciousness among Ethiopians, the country's statist traditions, and the corporate nature of the few civilian organizations, revolution, if it were to come at all in 1974, had to be imposed from the top. In adopting a socialist policy, the *Derg*'s hand had not been forced by a revolutionary groundswell among workers or peasants. The CELU was more concerned with organizational survival than with national economic policy. In many parts of the country, particularly the south, peasants expected land reform and in a few areas even began to take over holdings or crops on their own.[2] But by and large, there was no mass uprising. In those few instances where they tried to seize land and crops in the fall of 1974, the PMAC reacted sharply, warning peasants that all laws concerning tenancy and land use would remain in effect until an official land reform proclamation.[3] Until its announcement on socialism, the government pursued a cautious economic policy. It declared a rent freeze in August in order to curb inflation in urban areas. In September, it issued statements guaranteeing the safety of foreign economic interests. After the deposition of the Emperor, it nationalized through a variety of means several businesses controlled by the royal family.[4] The bus company in Addis Ababa, a macaroni and biscuit factory, and a brewery were brought under control in this way. But there was no systematic policy of nationalizing businesses or land owned by former officials now under arrest.

The path of economic reform followed by the *Derg* was classical in some respects, radical in others, but also pragmatic. It began with the nationalization of major financial institutions, progressed to key industries, and climaxed in a sweeping land reform. While its land reform was radical beyond all expectations, the government's policy toward the industrial and commercial sectors was characterized by caution, even moderation. On January 1, 1975, banks and insurance companies were seized. Nationalization of the banks was not a radical step, since the government already controlled the major financial institutions. But nationalization of the 13 insurance companies brought the government into an area that had hitherto been reserved for private enterprise. Nationalization was accompanied by an announcement that owners and stockholders would be compensated, but it was not specified when or on what basis this would be done.

The next major step came on February 3, when the PMAC nationalized 72 industrial and commercial companies and took majority control in 29 others.[5] In so doing, the government seized control of practically every important company in the country. They were few. The list of nationalized properties underlined the country's industrial underdevelopment. It included 14 textile companies; 13 food processing companies, most of them flour or oil mills; 9 leather and shoe factories; 8 beverage manufacturers; 8 chemical industries (e.g., a match producer, a small drug concern, a paint factory, and plants producing tennis shoes and plastic sandals); 5 small iron-and-steel works; 4 job printing plants; and 2 non-metal industries (a cement plant and a bottle and jar manufacturing concern). Also nationalized were several small transportation companies and building supply manufacturers. The companies in which the government assumed majority control were the large food manufacturers, such as the Wonji sugar plantation and refinery, and the Elaberet estate in Eritrea, which included a dairy industry and a cannery; all fuel distribution companies (the country's only refinery at Assab was already state owned); a large Japanese-built textile company; and several small woodworks, chemical, and metal-works industries.

Shortly after these nationalizations, the PMAC issued a "Declaration on Economic Policy of Socialist Ethiopia." The major and immediate economic goal of Ethiopia, the paper declared, was to eliminate poverty and exploitation. "This . . . can be achieved only when the government, as the representative of the people and in the interest of the mass of Ethiopian workers and peasants, directly owns and controls the natural resources and key industrial, commercial and financial sectors of the country."[6] The statement further specified the activities reserved for the government and for private enterprise. The position taken by the PMAC in this regard was highly pragmatic, almost to the point of inconsistency. Despite its stated intention to control key commercial enterprises, it left in private hands not only retail trade, but also the wholesale and import-export sectors. Yet having nationalized all the major food processors just a few days before, it declared that the food industry, including grain and flour mills, should be left to private enterprise. In practice, if not in theory, the economic policy of the *Derg* seemed one aimed at nationalizing all public activities it thought it could easily manage, while leaving to private enterprise anything it did not think it could handle at the time. For example, the policy statement singled out education as an area reserved for the government, but that ". . . until such time . . . as basic structural changes in the economy are realized, these schools [church, mission, and private] will continue to function as they are."[7] Another example was the government's decision to denationalize foreign-owned fuel distribution companies when it discovered it could not run them on its own.

The government's pragmatism sometimes caused more problems than it solved. This was above all true in the commercial sector, where such policy greatly complicated efforts at price control. The *Derg* was determined to impose controls on food staples in order to curb inflation—a major cause of the civilian agitation in February 1974—and to reduce the risk of further discontent in urban areas. However, the decision to leave wholesale and retail trade in the private sector made controls impossible. A price list for grain, meat, poultry, and eggs was issued in January, but the government had no enforcement mechanism. The predictable result was that basic commodities disappeared from the open market, a black market flourished, and prices dramatically increased. Eggs and chickens, usually sold all over Addis Ababa from the baskets and cages hanging from peddlers' shoulders, vanished. Grains could be bought only on the black market at exorbitant prices. On February 5, the government recognized its failure and revised prices upward. At the same time, a number of officials involved in setting prices, all civilians, were arrested in an attempt to save face.[8] They were accused of "sabotaging the economy" by fixing unrealistically low prices. In reality, the fault was not theirs but the *Derg*'s, which naively assumed it could control prices when it had no means to do so.

However, the nationalization of industry did not result in major economic dislocation. The government had some problems finding qualified managers and occasionally resorted to employing former owners or top management personnel, usually at very high salaries. Probably because the number of nationalized enterprises was so small the shortage of cadres did not reach critical proportions, and despite acute labor-management problems later in 1975, production in the new state sector did not significantly decline. While the government had released no figures as of early 1977, most Western economists estimated that excluding Eritrea the drop in the first year was no more than 5 percent. No figures were available for Eritrea, which contains some 35 percent of the country's industries, but the decrease in production was certainly much higher there due to the war.

While nationalization of industry did not create serious economic disruptions, it did result in renewed tension between the government and workers over the management of nationalized enterprises. The government's economic policy statement was silent on this point. There was only passing reference to the fact that "those who work in these [nationalized] enterprises will have a say in the actual running and management of these enterprises."[9] In practice, the unions, without being eliminated officially from the nationalized companies, were often prevented from functioning by state-appointed managers who had support from the military. The existing "work councils" were simply grievance committees with no real management functions. The issue of management in nationalized enterprises would later become a major dispute between civilians and the military.[10]

Land Reform

Without a doubt, the key economic reform in Ethiopia was land reform. It was a measure fraught with profound social and political consequences, because land was still the major source of power in the countryside and of status and wealth in the cities. By 1974, there was widespread agreement as to the necessity of land reform, but tremendous differences of opinion as to its content. The prevailing notion, generally supported by international agencies and even "progressive" Ethiopian officials, was distinctly moderate. It aimed essentially at creating conditions in which productivity could be greatly increased rather than at rendering social justice to the long-exploited peasantry. The measures most often suggested sought to place a limit on the size of landholdings and to regulate landlord-tenant relations.[11] As a result, it was generally thought, idle land on big estates would be brought under intensive cultivation while the security of tenant-farmers would so increase that they, too, would invest in modern farming supplies, fertilizer in particular. It was also believed that this would move Ethiopia out of its feudal stagnation into modern development. Even a majority of students who clamored for "land to the tiller" accepted this moderate approach. Rare were the voices calling for total abolition of private property and establishment of state or communal farms; most of these were students educated in the United States or Western Europe.

Various projects were submitted to the PMAC beginning in the fall of 1974, notably by the Ministry of Land Reform, the Chilalo Agricultural Development Unit (CADU), and the Ministry of Agriculture. These drafts were largely variations on the land limitation theme. Some proposed that reform be only applied at the initial stage to land owned by the royal family and arrested officials; others would have exempted the large, highly productive modern farms; and still others suggested generous upper limits on private holdings of 40 hectares and even more. Every proposal demonstrated a major concern for maintaining and increasing the level of production.

The choice was not easy. There was the very real danger that any land reform would severely disrupt production, a particularly sensitive issue in the wake of the famine; nor had the country any grain reserves. Land reform was also a highly divisive issue within the military because of the Emperor's land distribution policy which usually allotted a *gasha* (about 40 hectares) to all soldiers and officers who had completed five years of service. As a result, there were many small landlords in the military, about 35,000 according to one estimate.[12] Moreover, there were strong pressures on the PMAC from within both the bureaucracy and the private sector to keep land reform relatively moderate. From accounts given us, the *Derg* received much advice, including that from the Soviet, Yugoslav, and Chinese embassies, which urged moderation in the initial phase to avoid a sharp drop in production and excessive strife in rural areas, particularly between small and large peasants. But it disregarded such counsel and adopted a far more sweeping reform than even the most radical proponents had urged.

There were two main reasons for this radicalism. Foremost was an ideological commitment by some influential *Derg* members, notably Major Mengistu, the first vice-chairman, and Captain Mogus Wolde-Michael, chairman of the economic subcommittee, who were supported by many lower-ranking Galla NCOs from the south, where tenancy and exploitation were key issues. In addition, the government simply did not have the technical or administrative personnel capable of measuring, limiting, and redistributing land in an orderly fashion. Furthermore, local government officials who would administer these measures came mostly from the very class against which land reform was directed. *Balabbats* could hardly be expected to dispossess themselves, and consequently a moderate reform seriously risked being blocked on the local level.

The land reform proclamation issued on March 4 was unequivocally radical, even in Soviet and Chinese terms; it nationalized all rural land, abolished tenancy, and put peasants in charge of enforcing the whole scheme.[13] Each farm family was to be given a plot no larger than ten hectares. (This was still a very large amount for a peasant using traditional farm implements.) The land could be transmitted to children. However, peasants would only have the use of land, not full ownership, and they could not employ other people to work on it for them.[14] In order to implement the program, farmers were expected to organize "peasant associations," one for each 800 hectares or more of land. Membership in the associations would be open to former tenants, laborers, and owners of less than ten hectares and extended to larger landowners only after land distribution had been carried out and only if they were willing to cultivate the land personally. The associations would be headed by an elected executive committee, and they would also form a judiciary committee.

The proclamation spelled out in some detail the functions of peasant associations:[15]

1. to distribute, with solicited assistance of the Government when necessary, land forming the area mentioned in Article 8 as much as possible equally, and in the following order:

   a. to former tenants and former landlords residing within the area;
   b. to evicted tenants;
   c. to persons who reside within the area but do not have work or sufficient means of livelihood;
   d. to farmers coming from outside the area;
   e. to pensioned persons who are willing to undertake personal cultivation;
   f. to organizations needing land for their upkeep;

2. to follow land use directives issued by the Government;

3. to administer and conserve public property within the area, especially the soil, water and forest;

4. to establish judicial tribunals to hear land disputes arising within the area;

5. to establish marketing and credit co-operatives and other associations like *debo* [mutual aid] which would help the farmers cooperate in manual and other work;

6. to build with the cooperation of the government schools, clinics and similar institutions necessary for the area;

7. to cultivate the holdings of persons who, by reason of old age, youth or illness, or even in the case of her husband's death, cannot cultivate their holdings;

8. to undertake villagization programs; and

9. to exclude from distribution mining and forest lands and places of historical or antiquarian significance.

Despite this long list, there was a certain amount of ambiguity concerning how much autonomy peasant associations would be given. Their functions were numerous, though carefully specified, suggesting that the government wished to keep the associations under its thumb. In reality, the associations would operate at the village level where no government presence existed, so that they could easily become self-governing units. The local peasant associations were to send representatives to form *woreda* (district) councils, and in turn the *woredas* would send representatives to form larger *awraja* councils.[16] The latter councils, or peasant associations, would coordinate distribution of land among their members and solve disputes that might arise. There was, however, no indication of how these councils would relate to the *woreda* and *awraja* government administrations. Finally, the fate of the large commercial farms was left in doubt since the proclamation stated that they could become either state farms, cooperative farms, or be divided into small holdings and distributed among tenants. The decision would be up to the Ministry of Land Reform.

Rist, or communal tenure, areas were treated somewhat differently. Tenancy was also forbidden here, and farmers were given the use but not ownership of land; however, it would not be redistributed, so that each family would retain the fields it was already cultivating. The main function of the peasant associations in *rist* areas, then, would simply be to encourage their members to form cooperatives and to increase production. The nomadic populations were given use of their customary grazing lands, the government thereby dropping a longstanding claim, and they were relieved of traditional obligations and the payment of tribute to *balabbats.* The *Derg* obviously considered these payments equivalent to rent.[17]

The military government had few resources at hand to help implement the announced reform. By clearly establishing the principle that all land belonged to the state and that redistribution would be carried out by the peasants themselves, it eliminated the problem of having landowning local officials enforce a measure of which they would be the principal victims. In fact, land reform caused the local administration to collapse virtually overnight, because it wiped out the network of unpaid local landlords and their clients on whom the government had relied in the past below the *woreda* level. However, no one else could fill the vacuum. The Ministry of Interior did its best to appoint new, more radical administrators both at the *awraja* and *woreda* levels, and by March 4 it had replaced all 102 *awraja* administrators and 313 of the 556 at the *woreda* level.[18] But this personnel was mostly new to the job and often to the area—most appointments were made just days before the land reform proclamation—and they still had the same small, untrained staff and meager budgets that precluded them from playing an active role. The Ministry of Land Reform was barely able to place one officer in each *woreda.* The net result was that while the local administration was hardly able to prevent land reform from being carried out, it was also scarcely able to promote it. Thus, implementation was left in the hands of peasants and depended heavily on their ability to organize themselves. For this reason, the government immediately launched a campaign to set up the associations.

The Student *Zemacha*

One of the most important factors in determining how land reform would actually be implemented and how the peasantry would react to it was the student *zemacha,* or "Development through Cooperation Campaign," destined to become the government's main instrument for organizing peasant associations. Beginning in early 1975, the PMAC dispatched more than 50,000 high school and university students to 437 locations in the countryside to set up the associations, teach reading and writing, and carry out small local development projects. But the students did not limit themselves to government directives. They also tried to mobilize and politicize peasants and turn them against the military government. The way in which this was done was often naive, hardly surprising given the fact that the bulk of students were in the 11th and 12th grades of high school. In fact, the *zemacha* led eventually to much strife not only with the government but also with the peasants whom the students sincerely wanted to help.

The antagonism between the students and military reformers needs some explanation. Historically, it dated to the first months of civilian agitation. While some students admired and voiced support for the "radical" Air Force officers arrested by the Endelkachew government in April 1974, the vast majority were reserved toward or suspicious of the military, particularly after the first coordinating committee and the National Security Council began to break up strikes and stop demonstrations. Later, they hailed the deposition of the Emperor but at the same time decried the advent of military rule under the *Derg,* demanding instead a "people's government." They disliked the authoritarian tendency of the PMAC, its immediate banning of strikes and demonstrations, and curbs on freedom of expression. Furthermore, they remained highly dubious that the military would carry out any real land reform.

In early September, students drifted back into the capital in preparation for the new academic year. Everyone, including the government and the *Derg,* assumed that there would be further demonstrations and strikes. It was widely rumored at the time that they were planning a massive demonstration when the university opened in mid-September. Under such pressure, the *Derg* announced on September 3 that the university and the last two years of high school would not re-open and that students would instead be sent out to rural areas to help the peasantry.[19] Interestingly enough, it was the students themselves who had first proposed such a plan: in early April, they had suggested that the university be closed down for a year in order to allow students to assist in famine relief, teach peasants how to read and write, and contribute in other ways to rural development. Participation in their suggested campaign, however, would be strictly voluntary.

The *Derg*'s proposal was similar, but its political meaning for the students was drastically different. What had originally been a scheme proposed in a fit of revolutionary fervor was now turned into an obligation. As a result, the students' response became quite hostile. The government's registration forms issued to prospective campaign participants were defiantly torn up. In turn, the government announced that those who refused to participate in the campaign would not be eligible to continue studies in Ethiopia or abroad, or to get a job in the public or private sector. The measure put an end to their open defiance of the military government, though they remained resentful.

The campaign inevitably started slowly, since no preparations had been made before September. It was officially launched on December 21, and by early January the first groups departed for their assigned posts. Campaign goals were ambitious: students were to teach reading, writing, hygiene, and basic agriculture; instill the principle of self-reliance; rid Ethiopians of the spirit of individualism and teach them to strive for the common good; conduct research and gather data; and explain and help implement the forthcoming land reform.[20] Organization for carrying out these objectives was scant, and initially there was little for the students to do. The announcement of land reform on March 4 dramatically changed the situation. The radical students, probably a minority but politically important, were highly enthusiastic. During a massive demonstration in Addis Ababa immediately following the announcement, a group of students broke through police and army barriers, climbed the wall and escarpment around Menelik Palace, and embraced Major Mengistu as the hero of the reform and true representative of revolutionary Ethiopia. The reform gave concrete meaning to the *zemacha,* and the more radical students saw themselves as the bearers of revolution throughout the country. Yet, within three months, they had irrevocably decided that the *Derg* was "fascist." They came to this view after some students were arrested, others accused of being "anarchists" who sabotaged the land reform program, and after a few *zemacha* camps had been closed.

The dissension between the students and the *Derg* grew out of a profoundly different perception of what land reform was all about. To the PMAC, it was organizing peasant associations, helping them to carry out land redistribution, and establishing cooperatives. But for radical students, land reform meant the beginning of a true revolution in which peasants would become decision-makers while they moved quickly from feudal modes of farming into a modern Chinese system of "communes." If these peasant communes defied the government, that was in complete accordance with their views. The situation was well summed up by one official in the Ministry of Land Reform, who told the authors that the problem was that "the government refused to let land reform follow its own logic because, if the peasants are organized, politicized, and armed, the government becomes afraid of them."[21] In fact, for a long time the government refused to allow peasants to arm themselves in order to fight reactionary landlords, and it quite naturally reacted sharply to student attempts to turn the peasantry against them.

Implementation of Land Reform

In the more ethnically homogeneous "communal" land tenure areas of the north, land reform was initially received with great suspicion by small and large peasants who both tended to resist it. For tenants there, particularly Moslem outsiders, it was a curse. The reform's ban on the use of hired labor allowed landlords to force tenants off the land. Since the tenants were in a minority, this was easily done. Within two months of the proclamation, the government was obliged to set up "refugee camps" for Moslem tenants in Gojjam and had unexpectedly to resettle them elsewhere.[22] Generally speaking, little real land reform proceeded in the north for some time, and the process of setting up peasant associations was painfully slow. Although there was a good deal of agitation in the rural areas, it had more to do with the conservative opposition to the new military government than with land reform *per se.*[23]

The most important problem in implementing land reform in the south was the presence of the *zemacha* students and the complex relations that developed between them, the *Derg,* and peasants. A further difficulty stemmed from armed resistance offered by landlords in many parts of the country, often complicated by the emergence of ethnic movements and foreign interference.[24] At first, relations between students and peasants were generally excellent, with the peasantry looking to the *zemacha* for guidance and moral and material support in organizing their associations. There was a fair amount of violence as peasants, encouraged and sometimes even led by students, turned against not only the large landlords and their agents but also against the rich peasants and the local police. In such instances, peasants and students stood together as allies. Later, however, relations between them considerably soured. Many peasants began to doubt the students' sincerity and questioned their authority and objectives. Frequent student strikes, the fact that the *zemacha* headquarters sometimes closed down camps in troubled areas, and the high rate of desertion among the campaigners, both for political reasons and because they could not endure the rigors of rural life, convinced many peasants that students could not be counted upon to help them.

During the first few weeks after the proclamation, there was a feeling of euphoria among tenants and little resistance from the easily dispossessed landlords, who fled to Addis Ababa and provincial towns rather than attempt to fight the reform. Galla tenants in particular were elated and aggressive, and in many areas they chased out not only their landlords but also every representative of Amhara colonization they could find—police officers, civil servants, traders, and in at least one case malaria eradication personnel. Their response can be seen as an attempt to settle the historic account between Amhara conquerors and Galla subjects. However, before long tenants began to encounter resistance as landlords, rich peasants, and local police all tried in various ways to impede reform.

Outnumbered by their tenants, large landlords could not prevent them from seizing their land, though they tried to undermine the popularity of reform by spreading rumors. They circulated reports at planting time that the proclamation did not authorize peasants to begin cultivation until further notice. Actually, the government had specified that during the first year, each peasant should work the same plot of land as in the previous year and that redistribution would start only after the 1975 fall harvest. Later, when the crops were growing, landlords began a rumor that the government intended to requisition the entire crop. Such efforts failed to upset the traditional planting and harvesting cycle and had little long-term effect.

More serious was the problem of armed resistance. After first fleeing, many landlords returned home and organized small armed bands to terrorize peasants and prevent cultivation. Both Galla and Amhara landlords participated in this resistance. It created serious problems in numerous localities, often forcing the government to dispatch police or army reinforcements. Most of these rebellions had only local significance; at most they slowed down rather than halted application of reform. Nevertheless, it seems probable that the number of deaths resulting from such rural strife mounted into the thousands in the year following reform. These rebellions became a problem of national significance only when they overlapped and reinforced ethnic and regional resistance movements, particularly in Bale, Hararghe, and most of the northern provinces.

The problem created by the rich peasants—those who cultivated some land personally and rented out the rest—was probably the most pervasive. Not having any place to go, they fought their battles inside the peasant associations, often attempting to dominate them. While they relinquished excess land to their tenants, they were armed and determined to hold onto the rest. One of the first battles was over oxen. The proclamation required landlords who had traditionally provided oxen to now surrender them to their tenants. Inevitably, rich peasants hoped either to keep their oxen or sell them. The problem became particularly acute because reform was inaugurated at the beginning of the plowing season. In some instances, the shortage of oxen, as a result of these conflicts, became so serious that the government had to provide tractors and undertake emergency plowing for tenants.[25]

Another problem involved the local police, who were often small landowners themselves or at least had defended the interests of the landlords dominating the local government. The police often felt directly menaced by these reform measures, and student hostility did nothing to assuage their fears. The police's sympathy with the landlords was evidenced in a tendency to enforce the reform only minimally, if at all. For example, in frequent conflicts over the small estate flour mills—machinery which landlords wanted to remove but peasants wanted for themselves—the police often took the position that the reform proclamation did not nationalize flour mills. In other cases, the police sided with the landlords or refused to intervene even in disputes over land and oxen distribution. When faced with these difficulties, the students usually took an uncompromising line. All problems had to be instantly solved, and the peasants had to be organized to oppose any counter-maneuvers by the rich peasants and landlords. They believed policemen should be considered "class enemies," not law enforcement agents, and peasants should not rely upon them, but take matters into their own hands. With the support of some of the most radical, younger elements in the Ministry of Land Reform, they even demanded that peasants be given arms.

The first open confrontation between students and the military government, a turning point in the history of land reform, occurred in mid-April at Jimma, the capital of southwestern Kaffa Province. The exact course of events is not clear; on a visit to Jimma at the time, the authors received contradictory accounts. What is certain is that the conflict started in the rural areas around the town when students and their peasant followers arrested and jailed some small landlords, rich peasants, and members of the local police force. Some peasants were killed in these incidents. Subsequently, unrest spread to Jimma itself and led to a series of anti-government demonstrations. The situation became sufficiently serious for the *Derg* to send a special delegation, which at one point in its tour found itself surrounded by hostile students. Not surprisingly, the delegation and the *Derg* both came out against the radical students' position. The *Derg* favored a gradualist approach to land reform and made it clear that the rural police, whatever its faults, was an arm of the government. Civilians would not be allowed to arrest policemen. But further violent incidents occurred in the town, leading to the death of 24 students, the arrest of many more, and the withdrawal of others from *zemacha* camps in the area. The government's position was crystalized in May after a seminar on land reform attended by officials of the *zemacha* and a number of interested ministries. Directives were issued to the campaigners that they should avoid needless strife and confrontation and, in particular, that they should stop pressing for the immediate establishment of collectives. Students did not easily accept this gradualist, law-and-order approach, and considerable violence ensued.

Not all incidents were as dramatic as the one at Jimma or at Wollamo Soddo, where a less violent but nonetheless notable incident also occurred.[26] The Jimma pattern was repeated in dozens of other, smaller clashes throughout the country: students incited the peasants to class struggle and violence, the government tried to restore order, and the campaigners turned against the *Derg* and vice-versa. Whenever the PMAC stood for moderation, the students concluded it was not sincere about land reform. In fact, the *Derg,* far from going back on its reform decision, worked hard to see that it was implemented. Delegations, and occasionally troops, were sent into each province to explain the measure and oversee its application.[27] In this, the *Derg* showed concern for maintaining control over the reform process in order to avoid anarchy in the countryside. In the long run, the radical students' intransigence made them enemies not only of the PMAC but also of many peasants.

Student revolutionaries had their own vision of the new rural order, which included immediate implementation of collective farming, equality of the sexes, elimination of traditional authorities, and suppression of the rich and moderately wealthy peasant class. Their vision, of course, blithely disregarded the fact that even China had taken decades—and numerous carefully planned campaigns—to reorganize rural society. Nevertheless, students, carrying Mao's Little Red Book, would lecture peasants on class struggle and the necessity for collective farming, while peasant association leaders kept asking where they would get the oxen urgently needed for plowing and when fertilizer would be delivered. To make matters worse, these students would speak in Amharic to an assembly of Galla peasants in a region where feeling against Amharas ran high. They took up organizing collective farming with a vengence, practically dominating embryonic "communes" and imposing collective work discipline on peasants who were unprepared.[28] In Chilalo district, they set up "Red Guards" and "people's tribunals," where they sat as judges and issued verdicts on land reform and many other issues. In the same area, they tried to turn urban "lumpens" from the town of Assela who had been resettled on a nearby state farm against the neighboring peasants, all in the name of class struggle. At another settlement of urban unemployed in Wollo, students tried to impose a whole new social order two weeks after the settlers had arrived, demanding not only collective farming but collective living. In one case, they tried to establish a virtually autonomous "red commune."[29] When the peasants balked, students concluded: ". . . this peasant response confirms the Fanonian thesis that peasants are incapable of sustained, spontaneous organization; but, instead, confirms the Leninist thesis that leadership must be brought to the peasantry because they can only be organized from outside their social structure."[30] On a less theoretical level, a great deal of contempt emerged among students for the ignorant, backward Ethiopian peasants who failed to appreciate their vision.

The peasant vision of land reform was much different. While they were prepared to turn against the landlords and rich peasants to form associations, they were not prepared to reject all traditional, particularly religious, authorities or to accept the idea of collective farming. After decades of paying rent to a landlord for cultivating land they regarded as their own, the peasants wanted above all to legalize their position. Not surprisingly, the vast majority of student-organized experiments in collective farming came to an abrupt end when the students left, and sometimes before. Another important factor that helped turn peasants against the students was an increasing confusion as to who the *zemacha* campaigners represented. At first they accepted students as government agents. But when the campaigners tried to arouse the peasants against the government that had given them land, they began to question in whose name these students spoke.[31]

Peasant distrust increased when students started deserting their posts or were pulled out in large numbers by the government, leaving the peasants alone to face problems these outsiders had initially created. It is worth noting here that by early 1976 only about 18,000 student campaigners of the original 51,000 remained at their posts.[32] The growing antagonism was reflected in a large number of requests for withdrawal of students submitted by peasant associations to the *zemacha* headquarters.[33] On the positive side, peasant reaction against the students was a sign that their associations were beginning to function and that they were beginning to make their own decisions. The students, for all their mistakes and misguided enthusiasm, had made an important contribution to the success of land reform. They had attempted a great leap forward. They fell short of their own expectations but nonetheless contributed measurably to the radicalization of the peasantry. Furthermore, the number of experiments in collective or cooperative farming they started had great future potential.

Despite the tensions and problems in student-peasant and student-*Derg* relations, the first steps in implementing land reform were surprisingly successful, at least in the south. The countryside was far from peaceful, but the tenancy system was dead, land was effectively returned to the tillers, and the peasant associations were beginning to function. Notwithstanding a shortage of oxen, the delays in distribution of seed and fertilizer, and radical changes in farm management, the land was plowed and planted. Predictions by foreign agronomists of a major shortfall in grain production in the 1975–76 season did not come true, and the country enjoyed a remarkably good harvest.[34]

Thanks largely to the *zemacha,* peasant associations were organized and launched by the thousands. The Ministry of Land Reform estimated that by the end of the summer 18,000 associations had been registered, with total membership of some 4.5 million. The largest number of associations and members was in the south, particularly those areas where latifundia and modern farms had been concentrated. In the north, where communal farming was common, distinctly fewer associations existed.[35] The provinces with the highest registration were Sidamo, where almost one of every two persons was enrolled in an association; Arussi, with one out of every four; and Illubabor, also with one out of every four. Those with the lowest were Gojjam, where only one of every twenty-eight persons belonged, and Begemdir, with one out of nine.

Our scant information on the kind of peasants elected to association executive committees indicates that they varied considerably from region to region, from peasants with very small landholdings, women, and priests, to peasants owning more than ten hectares. It does not appear that the majority of the associations was dominated by traditional leaders or landlords. The available evidence indicates that associations tended to be controlled by those peasants who already occupied the land and who were reluctant to share any of it with landless farm laborers or evicted tenants. In the coffee growing areas of the southwest, for example, seasonal laborers who had traditionally done the picking were not given any land and often found themselves without a job when the peasants mobilized their own families to do the work. In the Chilalo district south of Addis Ababa, displaced tenants who had become drifters in Assela had to be resettled on former commercial farms because the peasant associations in the surrounding area would have nothing to do with them. In general, the "outsiders" in any given region suffered most from land reform and the organization of peasant associations. Moslem tenants in Gojjam and Christian laborers from the highlands working on farms in the lowlands were, for example, driven off the land. Since most Ethiopian peasants cultivate very small holdings, averaging perhaps 1.5 hectares, little wonder that they were unwilling to share their land with outsiders.

While land reform was generally successful, it did create some serious new problems for the government. Probably the most critical was shortage of food in the urban areas, overestimated by the Ministry of Agriculture at around 230,000 tons of grain the first year of the reform but eventually amounting to only 75,000 tons.[36] Although there was a better than average harvest—thanks largely to good rains—the pattern of rural consumption radically changed as peasants who had traditionally been obliged to relinquish one-quarter to one-half of their crops to landlords simply kept this "rent" and consumed it themselves. It is not known for sure how much grain the peasantry held back from the market during the first year of land reform. The estimate at the time was around 200,000 tons.[37] Another cause of the shortfall was a disruption in the marketing system. This can be laid to the following causes: the breakdown in the network of farmgate collection in which the landlord and his agents had played a central role, the shortage of trucks due to government requisition orders, and hoarding practices on the part of peasant asociations with the aim of driving up prices.[38]

The government attempted to overcome expected distribution and marketing difficulties by purchasing itself grain for urban areas. The newly established Agricultural Marketing Corporation set out to buy 227,000 tons of grain, or about one-third of what was needed, but succeeded in getting only about 150,000 tons, since production on the nationalized large commercial farms had dropped sharply—according to one estimate from over 400,000 tons to about 200,000 tons.[39] Part of these farm lands had been distributed to, or taken over by, peasant associations, with at least 40,000 hectares taken out of the modern farm sector.[40] In addition, farms in the Jigjiga area were severely affected by a regional drought and those in the Setit-Humera area by the war in Eritrea. Production on state farms was very good in the Rift Valley and Chilalo district, but even there it was difficult for the Agricultural Marketing Corporation to purchase grain because of the general confusion from the change in management, acts of sabotage, and sharp competition for grain from both private wholesalers and the government's own Relief and Rehabilitation Commission. The failure of government agencies to feed the cities provoked a major scandal in the spring of 1976. The *Derg* arrested the minister of national resources, Mebratu Mengeste, the minister of agriculture, Asrat Feleke, and 17 other high officials from these ministries which were responsible for state farms; they were accused of economic sabotage.

The overall impact of these problems was not famine in the cities, but sharp price increases for staples, development of a black market, and an acute shortage of the grains usually consumed by the urban population, *teff* and wheat. Within a few months, there was a substantial shift in purchasing power and consumption from the cities to the countryside. While such a shift was undoubtedly justified given the condition of the Ethiopian peasantry, it did create considerable hardship for the low income urban population. Moreover, the resulting discontent in the cities, particularly Addis Ababa, became a delicate political problem for the PMAC. There are some indications that the *Derg* had not foreseen or wanted such a sudden economic shift, but simply proved incapable of holding prices down.[41]

Land reform also left in its wake a number of unresolved issues. The first and most sensitive was land redistribution. Landless peasants and some land reform officials favored egalitarian distribution of the land. The moderates in the government urged acceptance of some inequality in landholdings, at least for the moment. Most radical students as well as other land reform officials wanted to skip redistribution altogether and immediately organize collective farms. Each course of action had its problems. Egalitarian distribution would have met with considerable resistance from middle income peasants and made civil strife in rural areas far worse. Accepting the unequal distribution of land would have left the poorest peasants, who already in the spring of 1975 were clamoring for farms, extremely dissatisfied. Meanwhile collective farming was proving unpopular with the peasants and impossible to carry out rapidly. Faced with this dilemma, the PMAC finally decided not to aim for immediate collectivization and to allow each peasant association to judge when and how to redistribute land under its jurisdiction. Only where there was no resistance from entrenched interests did the government adopt a collective farm strategy. Even then, the results were mixed, leaving the future of collectivization very much in doubt.

Another unresolved issue was the legal status of peasant associations. The March 4 proclamation failed to give them legal standing or to delineate the respective powers of their executive and judicial committees. This became a serious problem when government and international agencies tried to redirect rural development projects toward peasant associations and away from individual peasants. For example, the associations could not take out loans, become members of cooperatives, or enter into contractual agreements because they lacked legal status. Due to conflicts which arose from internal disputes about the respective powers of various committees, some of the associations fell apart barely after they were formed. Such problems were resolved after much debate in December 1975, when a new proclamation was published giving the associations a legal standing and regulating their internal functions.

Urban Land Reform

The land reform proclamation applied only to rural areas. The fate of urban land and real estate remained uncertain until July 1975, when the PMAC issued a decree that nationalized all urban land and rentable houses and apartments. Furthermore, it announced that the three million urban residents were to be organized into "cooperative societies of urban dwellers," or neighborhood associations. Membership in neighborhood associations was open to all residents, but former landlords were barred from the executive committees during the first year. The functions of these associations were:[42]

1. to follow and execute land use and building directives to be issued by the Ministry [of Public Works and Housing];

2. to establish a judicial tribunal composed of three members;

3. to set up, with the cooperation of the Government, educational, health, market, road and similar services necessary for the area;

4. to collect urban land and house rent amounting to up to Eth$100 per month per house or per piece of land using the receipt form issued by the Ministry and to undertake the administration and repair of such houses;

5. to deposit the rents it collects with a Peoples' Housing and Savings Bank in an account opened by the Ministry;

6. to preserve, by establishing a public welfare committee, all public and government property within the area and in particular to ensure, with the

cooperation of government authorities, the protection of the welfare and lives of people in the area;

7. to expend, in accordance with directives issued by the Ministry, the rents it collects and the subsidy it obtains from the Government for the building of economical houses and the improvement of the quality of life of urban dwellers in the area;

8. to draw up its internal regulations consistent with the requirements of this Proclamation, which shall be effective upon the approval of the Minister.

The same proclamation also cut rents from 15 to 50 percent, with the largest reduction in low rent housing. These cuts somewhat offset the increase in food prices, which was 28 percent in 1975.

Urban associations were given broad theoretical powers. In reality, they had no funds to carry out any but the smallest projects. All rents they collected were deposited in the central ministry account from which each association received Eth$500 a month, a sum hardly sufficient to carry out even basic repairs on homes under their jurisdiction and totally inadequate for new construction. The associations, popularly known as *kebeles,* had no other financial resources; as a result, their unpaid officials could work only part-time. Despite such limitations, the *kebeles* became quite active, particularly in Addis Ababa, in trying to assert their authority over neighborhood affairs even before their powers were clearly defined. For the first time, the urban population became organized at the neighborhood level. The associations undertook a census of people and houses, began to organize buying coopera-tives for the distribution of scarce grain and sugar, and hired night guards (paid by contributions) to stem the tide of theft and petty crime.

The nationalization of urban housing created many serious problems, most important of which was the housing shortage that developed when house-owners who had leased part of their dwellings tried to repossess them. There were many owners of two- and three-room dwellings who had survived by renting one room to another family. They now tried to retrieve their extra rooms, which no longer provided extra income. The problem became so serious after a few months that the government ordered such evictions to cease. The shortage was compounded by the machinations of those who owned several houses. These landlords tried to keep all of them by moving relatives who had all been living under the same roof into different properties. The Ministry of Public Works and Housing was overwhelmed with nearly 100,000 housing applicants within a few months of the urban proclamation. While there had been a shortage of low-rent housing before, the problem now became much more severe. Additionally, families who had survived by renting out rooms were left without income. According to the proclamation, they were entitled to monthly compensation from the government for lost income. As a result, the ministry found itself making payments to about 50,000 people in Addis Ababa alone. Inevitably, the scarcity of housing led to innumerable cases of corruption within the still poorly organized *kebeles.*

As with its rural counterpart, urban reform created new problems for which the proclamation did not provide answers. For instance, it did not define the relations between the existing municipal governments and the newly formed *kebeles.* Particularly in Addis Ababa, which had both a mayor and a city council, there arose the serious question of the respective powers of City Hall and neighborhood associations, which often became involved in conflicts over jurisdiction. The *kebeles,* like the peasant associations, had no legal status, an awkward situation when cooperatives were to be organized or houses to be built. The issue was not resolved until October 1976, when a supplementary proclamation was announced.

With the nationalization of urban land and rental properties, the first great wave of economic reforms was over. The process was on balance successful, at least from the point of view of not causing excessive economic dislocations. Yet, while the reforms affected the ownership of the means of production, they did not tackle overall problems of economic development. In a sense, the reforms were more political than economic, since they aimed at replacing the power of the old ruling class with public ownership of the means of production; but they did not create either a planned socialist economy or a strategy for development.

Land reform destroyed the land tenure system, which in the past was a major obstacle to economic development. In this sense, it was a significant step forward for Ethiopia. Yet after two years, the *Derg* was still trying to decide how land reform and peasant associations could be made into vehicles for economic growth. Land reform itself had not changed—indeed it could not change—the subsistence character of Ethiopian agriculture which was marked by extremely low productivity and a very fragile equilibrium between population and food supply. The government had for several years been faced with a growing food deficit, and the World Bank estimated that the country would need to import about 150,000 tons of grain a year at least until 1980. Yet, for political and ideological reasons, a sizeable amount of land was allowed to revert from modern farming to subsistence agriculture without considering the effect on overall development.

As for industrialization, it had in the past been linked to urban growth at the expense of the rural areas. The *Derg* now seemed committed to giving priority attention to the peasantry, but there was as yet no policy indicating what this would mean in practice or how industrialization would be related to this goal. In fact, there was no industrial policy at all. Private enterprise was neither prohibited nor encouraged. In December 1975, the PMAC established a Eth$500,000 ceiling on private investment in industry and expressed the hope that Ethiopians would invest in larger enterprises than cottage industries.[43] But it substantially failed to create a climate conducive to private investment, and practically none was forthcoming. What little public investment was made in the first year following nationalizations occurred in response to immediate market demand—for instance, doubling the capacity of the Pilsner Brewery in Addis Ababa—and was unrelated to any overall development plan. As of early 1977, there was little investment of any kind, and the country's foreign reserves were allowed to accumulate, reaching Eth$730 million by June 1976. For a country among the 20 poorest in the world, this was far too high, and reflected an unhealthy state in the economy.

Politically, however, the economic reforms were handled skillfully. The PMAC faced and surmounted difficult political pressures from civilians and army alike. Throughout March, military elements pressed hard for a revision of the land reform proclamation which would allow soldiers to obtain land from the government as they had under the Emperor. The *Derg* reportedly received somewhere between 12 and 25 petitions from various units, notably in the Second and Third divisions, calling for such a change. This debate within the *Derg* caused a six-week delay before the proclamation finally appeared in the *Negarit Gazeta,* the official journal. A strong stand by Major Mengistu and the other radicals, which prompted a two-day debate within the PMAC, resulted in the reform being upheld in its original form; it was finally published on April 19. This was a further indication that the *Derg* did not intend to yield to the narrow demands of the military or of other special interest groups.

6.   Feudal Reaction and Ethnic Revolts

The passing of the old order did not take place without an enormous amount of violence and chaos, particularly in the countryside. Hope for a "revolution without bloodshed" soon vanished before the reality of multiple conflicts. In the cities, the major sources of violence stemmed from the confrontation between civilian groups and the military and ideological differences among members of embryonic political parties; in the countryside they were the resistance of the landed class to land reform and a resurgence of ethnic conflict. Throughout 1974, however, there was surprisingly little open or violent opposition to the revolution and wanted members of the aristocracy and government continued to turn themselves in quietly to the military. Moreover, very few Ethiopians tried to escape from the country or go into hiding. One reason for their amazing passivity, according to a political prisoner who was later released, was a general conviction that the rule of the *Derg* would not last long and that the old elite would soon return to power. It was only after the November executions that even the most confident among conservative Ethiopians began to realize the ancient empire was facing more than a temporary crisis and that the days of the old order were over unless an armed opposition was organized. The land reform proclamation of March 1975 removed all remaining doubts as to the new military government's radical leanings. It proved the catalyst for the development of feudal reaction.

The course of this reaction is a revealing page in the history of the revolution, for it debunks many myths cherished by Ethiopians and foreigners alike about the old empire. During the summer of 1974, it was "common knowledge" that a peaceful military take-over was not possible because the great *rases* would mobilize their private armies in defense of the Emperor. As it turned out, no private armies existed, and the great *rases* turned themselves in as meekly as everyone else. After the Emperor's deposition, it was still

-videly believed that the *Derg* would not last long and that at least the reform-minded members of the aristocracy would stage a comeback. Land reform only served to heighten the expectation that the *Derg* would shortly be annihilated by aroused traditional forces. Not only would provincial landlords swing into opposition against the new government, but also much of the peasantry would take the side of church and provincial lord. It was rumored that Gojjam peasants were about to rise in arms, stirred by messages sent there by Crown Prince Asfa Wossen—royal words incongruously hidden inside sardine cans, according to some reports, or inscribed on cartridges with his initials, according to others. It was also widely believed that the Afars of the eastern lowlands would rise up *en masse* in defense of their sultan, Ali Mirah, and blow up every bridge on the road between Addis Ababa and the Red Sea, bringing the capital to a standstill and the *Derg* to its knees. An alliance of all dispossessed landlords from the Sudanese border to the Red Sea, supported by disaffected peasants and nomads, would sweep the central highlands and flush out the revolutionaries. Even radicals in the *Derg,* like Major Mengistu himself, were said to be convinced that their days were numbered and that they had to act quickly and ruthlessly to bring about irreversible changes before they were overthrown. None of the predictions as forecast by conservatives and widely discussed in other Ethiopian circles became reality.

Ethiopia's feudal reaction never coalesced into a unified movement. Rather, it took the form of local isolated rebellions. Many were led by the provincial nobility—local potentates bearing the titles of *kegnazmatch, grazmatch, dejazmatch* and *fitawari*—and supported by followers numbering less than a dozen to several hundred. They often degenerated into pure banditry, rarely having any other objective than to defend a particular region from the encroachment of government authority. Rebel bands held up buses and robbed passengers, sometimes even of their clothes, terrorized peasants, and occasionally attempted to take over small towns and drive out government officials. But few main roads were ever closed for long, peasants did not stop cultivating their land, and government officials usually returned after getting reinforcements. If rebels did control fairly extensive areas at times, they were in the remote backcountry and made little difference to the central government, which in most cases had scarcely controlled such areas in the past. It is impossible to know how many local rebellions occurred, how many individuals were involved or how many died in the resultant strife. Certainly thousands participated and thousands died. Accounts published in the local press between October 1975 and January 1977 acknowledged more than 250 rebels killed, 2,800 surrendered and over a thousand captured in scattered incidents from Begemdir in the northwest to Bale in the south. These accounts gave no indication of the number of deaths among peasants or security forces; they dealt basically with incidents where the government scored victories. Indeed, the Ethiopian media never revealed the hundreds of small incidents that occurred nor the few major encounters between rebels and government forces that resulted in massacres, such as at Bichena in Gojjam Province and near Dessie in Wollo Province in 1975.[1] While the cost in lives will never be precisely known, one estimate emanating from security officials and circulating in diplomatic circles in mid-1976 put the total death toll throughout the country by that time at around 10,000. This was probably not much of an exaggeration, but the worst violence was yet to come.

Not all fighting in rural Ethiopia in this period was the direct result of feudal opposition to land reform. Some was due to the revival of old feuds which had been kept in check in the past by the belief that the central government would not tolerate such fighting. After the deposition of the Emperor, however, the government was perceived as being much weaker and thus incapable of intervention in purely local feuds. As a result, tribal strife flared up again in many remote parts. Missionaries working in the extreme southwest, for example, noticed that intertribal raiding became particularly fierce in 1975, and medical personnel in Wollo Province reported treating an unusually high number of casualties after a series of cattle raids between the Afars of the lowlands and Gallas of the eastern escarpment. These incidents testified to the general relaxation of central authority in the country, but they were too localized to have any national repercussion.

There was a noticeable revival of traditional conflict among the three major ethnic groups. This, too, was a direct consequence of land reform and to some extent of the ethnic composition of the *Derg* which, rightly or wrongly, was considered predominantly Galla. Land reform benefited Galla peasants above all, while dispossessing mainly Amhara landlords. It was thus not surprising that there should be much resentment among Amharas. Nor was it surprising that there should be a heightening of nationalistic feelings among Gallas, who now felt freer to vent their hatred against the previously dominant Amharas. What is perhaps more surprising is that revived Galla nationalism should at times take the form of opposition to the very central government that had decreed land reform and ended Amhara domination in the southern provinces. This strange turn of events was principally due to the manipulation of Galla "nationalism" by Galla landlords who suffered from land reform and was particularly effective in Bale Province, where there already existed a Galla movement fueled by neighboring Somalia. The social and political upheaval underway in Addis Ababa also led to a resurgence of ethnic consciousness among the Tigrean people. Although they were hardly sorry to see the deposition of a Shoan Amhara ruler like Haile Selassie, who had treated their province without respect for its ancient history, culture, and language, many Tigreans did not welcome the new ruling military group either, considering it predominantly Galla. Profiting from the example, and later the direct help, of Eritrean nationalists, two rival "liberation fronts" were formed in Tigre Province within a year of the Emperor's overthrow.

With spreading provincial unrest, why did the feudal opposition fail to coalesce into a unified movement that could have fulfilled the oft-made predictions that the *Derg* would soon be overwhelmed by a rising tide of discontent? The three main reasons for this failure relate to the strictly local nature of landlord-peasant ties, the crisscrossing of class and ethnic divisions in many regions, and the formation of peasant associations which succeeded in enrolling a large proportion of the peasantry on the government side, against the old order.

Most of the landlords and local potentates who led the opposition did not see beyond the confines of their personal fiefdoms. In the early stages of the revolution, they neither understood nor cared for national politics and wanted to be left alone to rule "their" peasants as they had always done. Thus the main goal of most provincial rebellions was limited for some time to merely chasing out representatives of the central government rather than trying to force a change in national policy. For example, the rebel landlords hardly ever tried to cut the main roads, a move that might have turned local protests into a national problem. The few landlords with a broader perspective on the revolution failed to act for a long time because their support was limited to their fiefdoms. Even less than the landlords did the peasantry see the link between what was happening at the local level and in Addis Ababa. Under certain circumstances, peasants would agree to take the side of their landlords in defense of home territory, but their support could not necessarily be converted into a nation-wide movement to overthrow the new government in the far-away capital.

The crisscrossing of ethnic and class divisions also played a role in keeping feudal opposition fragmented and weak. Galla and Amhara landlords might have the same economic and political interest in opposing land reform, but they were generally separated by different "nationalistic" movements. Similarly, the revival of ethnic conflict as the revolution progressed made it impossible for Amhara landlords to find a following among Galla peasants. And even when landlords and peasants did belong to the same ethnic group, land reform as often divided as united them because of conflicting class interests. As a result of such cleavages, the development of a grand alliance of all dispossessed landlords against the *Derg* was enormously slowed down, and feudal opposition remained local, or at most provincial, in character. Finally, the formation of peasant associations also worked to weaken the landlords' grip over the peasantry of similar ethnic background. As the associations became stronger, the peasants' sense of class interest and solidarity increased and their willingness to follow blindly the landlords, whether from respect, tradition, or fear, steadily decreased. After June 1976, when the military government began forming a peasant militia, the feudal opposition faced increasingly stiff resistance from the peasantry, except in those regions like Bale and Begemdir provinces where strong ethnic feelings, reinforced by outside support, continued to abet peasant-landlord solidarity.

The Reaction in the North

The first sign of open aristocratic resistance to the military came in early September 1974 just before Haile Selassie's deposition. On the third of that month, *Dejazmatch* Tsehayu Enqu-Selassie, a former governor of Gojjam and Kaffa provinces, fought a pitched battle with security forces sent to arrest him. He was killed. Tsehayu had been in hiding near Fiche north of Addis Ababa since early July. When he was first notified by the military to turn himself in, he refused to do so. He sent a defiant note to the Emperor, who advised him to surrender peacefully. Tsehayu's behavior was at that time unique. All other aristocrats and officials asked to come into military custody had done so voluntarily. One official, Getachew Mahteme-Selassie, even returned from London where he was undergoing medical treatment in order to surrender.

Only one other well-known personality refused to give himself up in the entire period preceding the November executions. This was *Ras* Mengesha Seyoum, governor of Tigre, a member of the Tigrean royal family and a grandson-in-law of the Emperor. *Ras* Mengesha thus occupied a special position in the province. He was a traditional ruler and a landowner, but also, by Ethiopian standards of the period, a modern administrator. As governor, he had taken steps to develop the province. The most successful of these was the building of a rural road network, carried out by mobilizing peasants in a kind of feudal corvée system. The peasants benefited directly from their labor, since the roads linked many remote villages to the main highways. In fact, the new road network saved thousands of lives during the famine of 1973 and 1974 by making it possible to transport grain to needy villages. Other schemes promoted by *Ras* Mengesha were not so successful. An ambitious plan to integrate agricultural and industrial development totally failed, and the only part of it which materialized, the collection and export of incense, was firmly controlled by a small number of wealthy Tigrean families.

Ras Mengesha remained governor of Tigre until October 1974, when he was ordered to surrender. Rather than comply, he went into the hills and began organizing a Tigrean resistance movement. The reaction of Tsehayu Enqu-Selassie had been typical of a traditional Ethiopian concept of honor which considered death, even when futile, preferable to surrender. Mengesha's reaction was much more modern: instead of fighting alone to defend his honor, he organized an anti-government movement appealing to Tigrean ethnic pride. The name he chose for his organization, the Tigrean Liberation Front, conveyed the impression that he was not a traditional ruler in revolt, but was attempting to free a people oppressed by "external" domination. Thus parallels could be drawn to the struggle waged by the Eritrean Liberation Front just to the north. Exactly what *Ras* Mengesha himself wanted in the beginning remains unclear. Despite its name, the propaganda of the Tigrean Liberation Front did not stress Tigrean independence but simply the replacement of the "military dictatorship" in Addis Ababa with a liberal democratic state. However, many suspected the *Ras* of hoping to install himself on the throne, thereby restoring the glory of the Tigrean royal family. His national, rather than strictly provincial, ambitions were confirmed in early 1975 when he left Tigre and joined other aristocrats to form the Ethiopian Democratic Union (EDU), a nationwide movement discussed below.

The merger of the TLF with the EDU did not end Tigrean nationalism as such, since a splinter group broke off from the Front under the influence of the

Eritrean People's Liberation Forces (EPLF), the more Marxist of the Eritrean movements. Members of the Tigrean People's Liberation Forces (TPLF), as the new group was called, were mostly radical students who initially combined Marxist ideology with the concept of an independent state comprising Tigre and Eritrea. It rejected the leadership of *Ras* Mengesha, who was considered a representative of the old order and thus disliked as much as the *Derg*. The TPLF managed to survive largely because of the support and arms it received from the EPLF. The Eritrean faction found it expedient to sustain the TPLF because its existence made it more difficult for the Ethiopian army to transport military personnel and material through Tigre into Eritrea. By mid-1976, the TPLF was active in northern Tigre along the Eritrean border and had a fighting force estimated at around 1,000 guerrillas. Its main military activity was the harassment of traffic on the main road between the provincial Tigrean capital of Mekele and Asmara. The movement's heavy dependence on the Eritreans and its limited hold on Tigre province became clear in mid-1976, when it felt obliged to turn over to the EPLF for safekeeping British journalist John Swain and a British veterinarian and his family whom it had kidnapped on Tigrean roads. The leftist TPLF remained the exception to the general character of the opposition to the *Derg* in the northern provinces, usually led by aristocrats and local landlords who were predominantly conservative.

The scope of the opposition, which had started with Tsehayu Enqu-Selassie and *Ras* Mengesha, dramatically broadened after the November executions. These made abundantly clear that the *Derg* aimed to destroy the old order and that those who surrendered risked death. Typical of the kind of localized resistance that began developing in this period was the revolt of Mesfin and Merid Biru, sons of the late *Ras* Biru, one of Ethiopia's largest landowners. In January 1975, they slipped away from Addis Ababa to organize a rebellion among peasants in their home district of Manz. This region is an isolated Amhara stronghold in northern Shoa, strongly Christian, very conservative and extremely hostile to outsiders. It was not the center of the Biru family's empire, however. The two brothers owned vast expanses of land in Hararghe Province, prime property in Addis Ababa and modern mechanized farms in Chilalo. Yet, it was only in the conservative atmosphere of Manz that they could obtain peasant support. Agricultural workers and tenant farmers displaced by mechanization in Chilalo had no interest in rallying behind a wealthy landlord. In Hararghe, Galla tenants were only too happy to be rid of two absentee Amhara landlords who had done little but to exploit them. In feudal Amhara Manz, the brothers' position had more legitimacy. Moreover, because of the area's isolation they could sell to the peasants their own interpretation of events taking place in far-away Addis Ababa. Their explanation was ominous indeed: the government was dominated by Moslems who would destroy the Coptic Church and take away land from Christians. As proof, the brothers played tape recorded statements of alleged government declarations broadcast over Radio Ethiopia which stated as much. The Biru brothers managed to win enough support through such ruses to hold out for almost ten months, fighting off several police and military contingents sent to quash them. It was a doomed and sterile revolt. Their efforts to organize a broader resistance movement linking Manz to Chilalo and central Shoa, particularly the region around the town of Nazareth, came to nought; the social situation in these areas of high tenancy and wage labor did not lend itself to an alliance between landlords and peasants. In October 1975, Mesfin and Merid were finally tracked down by security forces and killed. Their bullet-shattered bodies were subsequently shown on national television.

Many other landlords in the central highlands followed their example. In Gojjam, Wollo, and parts of Shoa Province, scores of rebels took to the mountains in the months following the announcement of land reform. Most were obscure local notables who did little more than spread rumors and terrorize the peasants. A surprisingly large number of them surrendered in July and August of 1975, during the rainy season. Others acquired temporary notoriety, like *Dejazmatch* Berhane Meskal, who occupied Lalibela, the site of Ethiopia's famous rock churches and the country's major tourist attraction, and held it for nearly six months until he was routed by the army in late 1975. Similarly, a group of local landlords and their followers took over Debre Tabor in Begemdir Province in September 1975, killing the provincial governor and impartially evicting a Chinese road-building team and missionaries of the Seventh Day Adventist Church who ran a local hospital. In these Christian areas, the landlords' argument that the military government was dominated by Moslems was persuasive in gaining peasant support.

The first real test of conservative opposition strength in the central highlands did not occur until late 1975, when an attempt was made to bring together the most important local opposition groups under the umbrella of the Ethiopian Democratic Union (EDU). The Union was formed in March 1975 by *Ras* Mengesha, General Nega Tegegn, and General Iyassu Mengesha. General Nega had been commander of the Third Division and then governor of Begemdir, a post he held when he fled the country in January 1975. He was married to a granddaughter of the Emperor, whose sister was *Ras* Mengesha's wife. General Iyassu was Ethiopia's ambassador to Britain when he, too, defected about the same time as General Nega. Originally the EDU leaders sought the support of Crown Prince Asfa Wossen. Soon, however, they publicly disassociated themselves from the royal family and tried to project a more liberal, anti-monarchist image. In terms of the leadership's composition, the EDU had a strong aristocratic tinge, although many of its members favored a Western democratic form of government. Still, the choice of London as the EDU's headquarters was reminiscent of the royal family's exile there during the Italian occupation, and at least one faction of the organization was indisputably monarchist. The Union was led by a 17-member Supreme Council responsible for formulating policy and an eight-member Executive Committee in charge of its implementation.[2] In an effort to dispell the Union's image as an Amhara-Tigrean movement, its leaders stressed that the Supreme Council contained members from all regions of Ethiopia. While this was probably true, the EDU remained centered in Begemdir and Tigre provinces, the heartland of the Amhara and Tigrean peoples.

The first EDU program, published in March 1975, was extremely vague. It pledged respect for "unfettered liberty of belief, expression and association," support for civilian rule, and promised to implement "essential reforms," particularly land reform, but only after the policies had been "democratically debated and agreed, instead of the arbitrary imposition of measures upon peoples who took no part in the decision-making process."[3] The revised EDU program which appeared in September 1976 showed how far left the country had moved in 18 months. The new platform contained a strong commitment to land reform and did not mention the return of nationalized properties to former owners; instead, it promised immediate attention to such pressing economic problems as inflation and unemployment.[4] Most interesting was its new attitude toward the restoration of the monarchy. "Is the EDU in some way a 'front' for the restoration of the monarchy?" the program asked. "The answer is a resounding 'no.' The royal family is emphatically not a factor in the EDU."[5] The Union's first program had only expressed opposition "to any return to the outmoded regime of the past," but not specifically to the monarchy. In addition, the new platform presented the Union as a bridge between traditional and modern forces:

EDU's membership cannot easily be defined in terms of numerical strength, since the vast majority of men and women who lend both active and tacit support are inside Ethiopia, where their activities must for the time being remain clandestine. In its ranks are Ethiopians of the most diverse backgrounds, ethnic origins, and political points of view.

The broad base of EDU is the peasantry who have, of their own accord, established themselves in opposition to the *Derg* and have come under the EDU "umbrella." In some cases, these people have followed their traditional leaders into the EDU ranks. The EDU leadership includes traditional leaders, traditional in the historical sense, but not necessarily in outlook. At their side are ranged educated corps of modern Ethiopians: international civil servants, military officers, businessmen, diplomats, educators, and government administrators. Membership cuts across the political spectrum, and the common bond which unites them is that each and every one of them opposed the feudal system (and many of them suffered for this opposition) and rejoiced at the popular changes sparked off in 1974.[6]

The net impression conveyed by the EDU program was of a movement favoring a bourgeois-type revolution which had been unsuccessfully attempted by the educated elite in 1974: civil and political rights, a liberal democratic political system, moderate economic reforms that respected private property—the sort of government that guaranteed the domination of urban upper classes and educated groups. There is no doubt that its social base in the cities consisted of dispossessed landlords, fallen aristocratic families, businessmen, merchants, civil servants, and professionals. As the revolution turned radical, the EDU appealed to an increasingly broad spectrum of the population, including many who had been very much against the old regime. This explains the change in the character of its program between 1975 and 1976. As the Union tried to capitalize on spreading urban discontent, it liberalized its program and softened its initial royalist and aristocratic image.

The EDU could have become a serious threat to the military government. If it had succeeded in coordinating scattered opposition groups in the central highlands, bringing into its fold the movement led by the exiled Sultan of the Afars, Ali Mirah, as well as accommodating the Eritreans, the Union could have broken the central military government's authority in the northern half of the country, and could have severed the capital's crucial road link to the port of Assab. At the outset, very little came from the creation of the EDU because of its difficulty in securing money and arms through outside support. There proved at first to be little interest abroad in a movement which, for all its efforts to promote a different image, smacked of a last-ditch comeback attempt by the fallen Ethiopian aristocracy. The conservative Arab countries already supporting the Eritrean nationalists showed little enthusiasm for a movement which seemed to represent Christian Amharas and Tigreans. The EDU's limited appeal and strength became all too apparent when a general offensive planned for January 1976 failed to materialize. In the following six months, the activity of the Union primarily consisted of making publicity for its cause abroad and issuing sporadic communiques from London.

In mid-1976, however, the *Derg* suffered a major foreign policy setback which unexpectedly provided the EDU with the foreign support it so desperately sought. Sudanese President Jaafar Numeiry became convinced that Libya and Ethiopia were acting together to support his opponents, who staged a nearly successful coup in early July. In retaliation, he lent wholehearted support not only to Eritrean nationalists but also to the EDU. Thus, the Union finally gained indispensable foreign support needed to organize, train and arm a serious guerrilla force. The effect was first felt in January 1977, when the Union launched a major offensive against Ethiopian garrisons along the Sudanese border in Begemdir Province and captured the town of Humera.[7]

Galla (or Oromo) Nationalism

While it is possible to talk of a "feudal reaction" in the Amhara and Tigrean central highlands, opposition in predominantly Galla, or Oromo, regions most often took a nationalist form, even when led by dispossessed landlords and *balabbats.* Paradoxically, the military government itself established the climate in which a Galla nationalist renaissance occurred.

One of the principal themes of the *Derg*'s propaganda was that all ethnic, religious, and linguistic groups would henceforth be equal. Moslem holidays were for the first time officially recognized, Radio Ethiopia began broadcasting programs in all major languages, the Ministry of Information promoted the publication of a weekly newspaper in Gallinya called *Berissa,* and even

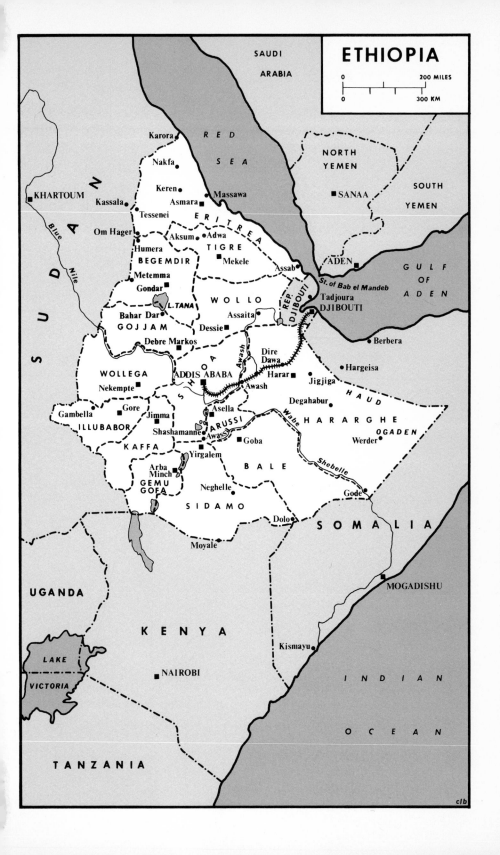

Provinces and Areas Where Main
Opposition Movements Operated, 1974-77

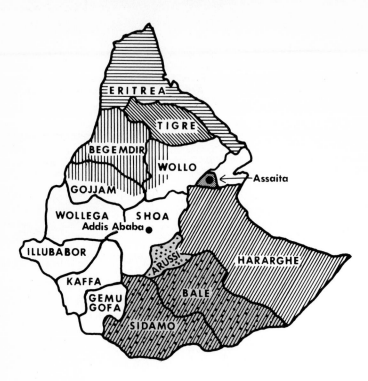

Eritrean Liberation Front and Eritrean People's Liberation Forces

Tigrean People's Liberation Front

Ethiopian Democratic Union

Afar Liberation Front

Western Somolia Liberation Front

Oromo Liberation Front

A peasant at work in the Ethiopian highlands.

Pomp and poverty were companions in the Ethiopia of Emperor Haile Selassie. In a 1960 ceremony, the Emperor accepts an offering. Crown Prince Asfa Wossen sits under an umbrella at left. Air Force General Abera Ayana is at the extreme right. (*Photo courtesy Ethiopian Government Ministry of Information*)

Ras Bitwodet Ali Mirah Anfere, sultan of the Afars, one of Ethiopia's surviving great lords.

From left to right: Michael Imru, former prime minister and special advisor to the *Derg;* Lieutenant Colonel Mengistu Haile Mariam, first vice-chairman; Brigadier General Teferi Banti, chairman; Lieutenant Colonel Atnafu Abate, second vice-chairman.

The large demonstrations following the announcement of the land reform were a rare spontaneous show of support for the *Derg* in Addis Ababa.

e of the cartoons seen in the city on Victory Day
icting reactionaries making futile plots against the
ular revolution. Depicted in the picture (clock-
e) are Nega Tegegn, Ali Mirah, Iyassu Mengesha,
konnen Makonnen, Mengesha Seyoum, Merkoreos
ile, Osman Saleh Sabeh, and Tedla Beiru.

Poster which appeared in Addis Ababa shortly before
the overthrow of Emperor Haile Selassie, depicting a
famine victim on the left and the Emperor feeding his
dogs meat presented by a servant on a silver tray.

S.-made tank on parade in Keren. The two flags are (left) the new flag of Eritrea and the old flag designed by the
N. *(Photo courtesy Dan Connell)*

An alleged Somali tank, disabled outside the airport at Dire Dawa. (*Photo courtesy Ethiopian Government Ministry of Information*)

Zemacha students breaking through police lines to embrace Mengistu and other *Derg* members during demonstrations in favor of the land reform.

Ethiopian group captured at Keren is being reviewed en masse. EPLF schools them (1,784 in all) in Afabet. (*Photo courtesy Dan Connell*)

the Ministry of Education began studying the feasibility of imparting elementary education in the main local languages rather than in Amharic as in the past. These measures greatly encouraged the revival of ethnic feelings among all groups, particularly Gallas, whose language and culture had been calculatingly suppressed under Haile Selassie. Even "assimilated" Gallas began re-identifying themselves, speaking Gallinya and sometimes even changing their Amhara names back to the original ones. There was no doubt that some top *Derg* leaders deliberately encouraged the resurgence of ethnic consciousness. Chief among them was Major Mengistu, himself a member of a minority group and resentful of the forced Amharization of Ethiopia.[8]

The new attitude was made official in April 1976 when the military government recognized the "right of nationalities to self-determination" within the context of Ethiopian unity. What the *Derg* did not sufficiently appreciate was the possibility that the revival of ethnic consciousness would lead to the growth of a separatist movement in the southern regions similar to that already under way in Eritrea, or that it would be manipulated by landlords to suit their own ends. While a genuine separatist movement did not develop among all Gallas, an incipient revolt among Somalis did grow to serious proportions. But attempts made by dissident Galla landlords, using ethnic solidarity to gain support for their opposition to land reform, proved unsuccessful because of peasant support for the central government which had given them land. As a result, Galla nationalism really only became a threat in Bale Province, where historical grudges and Somali machinations played into the hands of disgruntled *balabbats*. A comparable situation also developed among the Afars of the eastern lowlands where Sultan Ali Mirah, deposed and expelled by the *Derg*, exploited a strong sense of ethnic solidarity among Afar tribesmen. But before turning to the situation in Bale Province and to the Afar problem, it is instructive to consider first the case of one old Galla nationalist leader who attempted to revive the movement he had led during the Emperor's time but was defeated because of Galla peasant support for the government's land reform. His case well illustrates how dispossessed Galla landlords tried to use the nationalist theme in support of class interests.

General Tadesse Biru (unrelated to the Biru brothers of Manz) had been a prominent leader of an embryonic Galla nationalist movement dating back to the early 1960s.[9] At that time, he had been among the major promoters of the Mecha-Tuloma self-help association, a voluntary organization that aimed at raising money among Gallas to stimulate development projects in Galla regions. Similar associations had been formed by other ethnic groups, particularly the Gurage, and had been allowed to function freely. The Mecha-Tuloma organization was soon met with deep suspicion by the Haile Selassie government which saw it, with cause, as the beginning of a Galla nationalist movement. In late 1966, the government started taking into custody the most prominent leaders of the association. Tadesse Biru himself was arrested in November 1966, brought to trial in July 1968 and condemned to death. His sentence was subsequently commuted to life imprisonment by the Emperor. After the military came to power, General Tadesse was set free along with a number of other political prisoners. Within a few months, he again tried to organize a Galla movement in open opposition to the new government, establishing a base in the mountains near Holetta in western Shoa Province. Tadesse, himself a minor landowner, was apparently encouraged and supported by local landlords who after the November executions realized their vulnerability unless an opposition movement was organized. They hoped the name of Tadesse Biru would rally peasants to their side. But times had changed, and Tadesse failed to win many followers. The proclamation of land reform on March 4 proved fatal to his movement. Significantly, his whereabouts was revealed to security forces by peasants themselves who saw in him an exploiting landlord and only secondarily a Galla. He was captured without struggle on March 13 with only a handful of followers, among them a Galla colonel, Hailu Regassa, who only a few months earlier had been named vice president of the Special Court Martial. Tadesse and Hailu were put on trial, condemned to death, and executed on March 18.

Bale Province, where Galla nationalism became a serious problem, is a huge territory with a predominantly Moslem and largely semi-nomadic population of only 700,000. It was here that Somalia had a territorial claim to the lowland areas inhabited mostly by Somali-speaking nomads. Since the early 1960s, the Somalis had found nearly ideal conditions for stirring up opposition to the central government, even among non-Somali people.[10] Bale was a glaring example of exploitation and maladministration by the Addis Ababa government. It had few roads, hospitals, or schools, and those that existed served mainly the Amhara Christian population of the urban centers. In 1970, for example, the province had only one high-school with a total enrollment of 680 students, only 86 of whom were Moslem.[11] Discrimination against Moslems had been practiced since Emperor Menelik's conquest of the region in the late 19th century. Government officials and judges tended to be Christian and the few employed Moslem officials were paid far lower salaries.[12] In settled areas of the province's highlands, conquering Christians had seized thousands of acres of Moslem land. In short, a classic case of exploitation of a conquered people by a "colonial" power existed.

Beginning in the early 1960s, periodic clashes between Somalia and Ethiopia erupted all along the Bale border, culminating in a brief full-scale war between the two countries in 1964. The border fighting was accompanied by numerous incidents in small towns of the lowlands between armed Somali or Galla tribesmen and the police. Somalis apparently took advantage of every local conflict to fuel discontent and armed rebellion against the central government. For example, when a conflict broke out between different Galla clans in 1964 over grazing rights, the Somalis wasted no time in providing arms. Waqo Gutu, who became a major rebel leader, explained that after waiting three months for the Ethiopian government to settle the dispute, he "went to Somalia and brought back 42 rifles and two Thompson submachine guns."[13] The conflict was soon converted from one between feuding Galla clans to one between Gallas and the central government. The rebellion's reorientation was greatly facilitated by an ill-timed government effort to forcibly collect unpaid taxes from Galla peasants in the Bale highlands. At first, the government used local police to suppress the rebellion, but as soon as the police moved out of one area, the rebels reoccupied it. By the end of 1966, about three-fifths of Bale was in turmoil. Finally, in February 1967 the central government sent an expeditionary force of 4,000 soldiers and within a month had occupied the main rebel strongholds. Yet once again, as soon as the government forces moved out, the rebels moved back in. It was not until 1970, six years after the rebellion had begun, that Waqo Gutu surrendered and the movement collapsed. Many of its followers fled to Somalia.

When he gave himself up on March 27, Waqo Gutu carried a seal describing him as "General of Western Somalia," a title bestowed by the Somali government, which had created the "Western Somalia Liberation Front," grouping dissident Gallas as well as Somalis. However, Waqo seems to have been little more than a local Galla potentate who exploited Somali support. The Ethiopian author of the only detailed study of the 1963–1970 Bale revolt concludes: "The rebellion seems to have started without political objectives and came to an end without creating any."[14] The cost of the rebellion to Waqo was minimal: he was "exiled" to Addis Ababa, given a comfortable villa and treated well by the Emperor. Those who paid the price were primarily settled Galla peasants in the Bale highlands. The government confiscated tens of thousands of hectares and redistributed the land among Christian settlers who fought against the rebels.[15]

The Bale rebellion is the background to the resurgence of the Galla nationalist movement in 1975 in which Waqo Gutu again played a central role. This time there were two distinct elements in the movement. In the lowlands, the new rebels were almost all Somali and Galla refugees from the first uprising who had returned from Somalia with arms and training in guerrilla warfare tactics. The exact number of guerrillas is unknown, but they numbered at least several thousand. In the highlands, the rebellion was primarily led by Galla *balabbats* and landlords who found ready support among those peasants who had lost their land in the first uprising and were still sharing it with Christian settlers even after the land reform. The highland rebels were also provided with sophisticated arms—bazookas, mortars, and automatic rifles—by the Marxist Somali government, which showed no compunction about arming Ethiopian reactionary elements opposed to the socialist revolution. Once again, it was very doubtful that the highland Galla rebels were supportive of, or even interested in, Somalia's irredentist claims. Nor does it appear that they had any broader objective other than to reclaim their land.

It is true that in early 1976 followers of Waqo Gutu were distributing a publication in Gallinya, called *Warraaqa,* which also periodically circulated underground in Addis Ababa. But there was no evidence that the Bale group was part of a national Galla organization. Even if one assumed that *Warraaqa* represented a nation-wide Galla movement, it is still not clear what its goals were. The publication expressed a great deal of hatred for Amharas and Tigreans and urged solidarity with all oppressed "nationalities" in Ethiopia—

Oromos, or Gallas, Sidamas, Guragues, Kambattas, Afars, and all other non-Amhara or Tigrean groups. Its slogan "Organization, Struggle, Freedom" suggested a Galla intention to develop an organized movement for independence such as the one existing in Eritrea. Yet the publication ignored the issue of Oromo independence and regional autonomy. Its main pitch was that all oppressed nationalities should be watchful against a Tigrean-Amhara conspiracy to subvert the revolution. The EDU was singled out as the epitome of such a conspiracy, becoming therefore the major enemy of the Oromo people. Strangest of all was the publication's failure to make any mention of the *Derg*. Considering that *Warraaqa* was an underground pamphlet and that the Bale group was fighting against the central government, this omission was indeed surprising. Similarly, while the language of *Warraaqa* often had Marxist overtones, it contained no reference to the existence of class contradictions within the "oppressed nationalities." The stated objectives were, moreover, vague and limited:

    I) organize the Oromo youth in order to join the battle for freedom

    II) political education of the Oromo people

    III) support for the youth of other oppressed tribes in their political struggle

    IV) cooperation with other factions which support the struggle of freedom-seeking tribes

    V) refutation of false and fabricated accounts given by the oppressors and capitalists about the struggle of the oppressed tribes.[16]

The origins of the Bale movement and the involvement of landlords and *balabbats* are on the whole more suggestive of its character than the obscure pamphlets distributed by its leaders. It was by and large a movement organized by Galla notables against land reform and the central government; only marginally could it be viewed as a Somali front fighting for Somali or Galla secessionist causes. The movement's impact created serious problems for the central government in Bale, since Somali support kept landlord opposition from fizzling. However, the rebel leaders only obtained support from one segment of the Galla peasants. The government was able to organize in mid-1976 a militia of 8,000 to 10,000 men from among members of peasant associations in Bale Province and to use it not only to deal with the landlords, but also to counter incursions by Somali-trained guerrillas. In August, the media reported the surrender, capture, or killing in one week of nearly 600 insurgents by members of the peasant militia working with local security forces. In December, the government mounted an expedition of thousands of mounted militiamen which left the provincial capital of Goba in order to clear rebels from the area. In summarizing, by crisscrossing ethnic and class conflicts in the province the government blunted the ethnic appeal of landlords by counter-appealing to the economic and class interests of the peasantry, at least until that time when increased Somali involvement changed the meaning and scope of rebellions in south-eastern Ethiopia.[17]

The Afar Problem

The other important center of conservative opposition to the *Derg*, kept alive by foreign support and ethnic resentment, was in the Awash River Delta, near the border of the former French Territory of the Afars and Issas (TFAI), which upon its independence in June, 1977, became known as the Republic of Djibouti. It was led by *Ras Bitwoted* Ali Mirah Anfere, sultan of the Afars, who rallied a consideration force to his side. During the reign of Haile Selassie the sultan had ruled, as he claimed in an interview with the authors, an Afar nation of some three million tribesmen who grazed their herds from Metahara in the mid-Awash Valley to the port of Massawa in Eritrea. More sober accounts of Western and Ethiopian scholars suggest the sultan's rule only extended over the Afars in the Awash Delta, perhaps 150,000 semi-nomads concentrated around the town of Assaita, where he himself resided.[18] The Sultan's position in eastern Ethiopia was nonetheless important, and the Emperor granted him a degree of autonomy and authority that even the powerful *rases* could not match. In return, Ali Mirah promoted Ethiopia's interests in the region.

The sultan's power lay less in his personality than in the location of his fiefdom. It straddled the main highway connecting Addis Ababa to the port of Assab, where the country's only oil refinery is located, and bordered both on southern Eritrea and the former French Territory. In fact, many of Ali Mirah's "subjects" crossed regularly into the Territory, following traditional trade and grazing routes and participating in a modern lucrative smuggling network. With the TFAI due to become independent in mid-1977, the attitude of the Afars toward the Ethiopian government was crucial in determining whether the territory would maintain its independence in the face of Somali irredentism, since the Afars constituted nearly 50 percent of the population. Without their support it was unlikely Ethiopia could maintain free access to the port of Djibouti, the terminus of the only railroad linking the capital to the Red Sea. The region controlled by Sultan Ali Mirah was also becoming economically important, since it had proved suitable for irrigated agriculture. After the establishment in Dubte of the Tendaho Cotton plantation, a British-Ethiopian joint venture in which the sultan was a stockholder, Ali Mirah and many of his *balabbats* developed their own smaller cotton plantations. Once a petty Moslem ruler, he suddenly became one of Ethiopia's wealthiest landowners and businessmen, and his *balabbats* were transformed from mere traditional judges and chiefs into semi-modern entrepreneurs. The sultan thus built up a network of followers with economic and political interests in his survival.

With the advent of the new military government and the radical land reform proclamation, the Military Council was uncertain whether to negotiate or use force in its dealings with the sultan. In late April of 1975, the government opened negotiations through intermediaries first in Assaita and then in Addis Ababa. Reaching any agreement or applying land reform in his fiefdom, however, proved impossible. The sultan's position was well summed up by himself in an interview with the authors at the time: "Until now we have had no problems with the new government. So long as they do not touch our land or our religion, there will be no problems."

In fact, the sultan and his followers had already begun preparing for armed conflict and smuggled truckloads of arms, including brand new Soviet-made AK-47 automatic rifles from the TFAI. The inevitable showdown came in early June when the Military Council abandoned negotiations and dispatched a battalion of troops to capture the sultan. Conflicting accounts of the ensuing two-day battle agree a "massacre" occurred in and around Assaita. The sultan claimed the army killed as many as 1,000 Afars in the attack and alleged that airplanes and armored cars had been used. The government said that the massacre was carried out by the sultan's forces which incited the Afars to turn against non-Afar highland plantation workers at Dit Bahari, killing 221 persons. Probably the death toll lay somewhere between the two figures and the victims included both Afars and highlanders. The charge that the Afars massacred highlanders was certainly true; the Afars feared that the government would hand over land to those tilling it in accordance with the land reform proclamation. Throughout the sultan's fiefdom, it was migrant highlanders, Amharas and Gallas, who did the work on the Afar-owned plantations. Among those who escaped the army's assault on Assaita were both Ali Mirah and his sons, who made their way into the French Territory. The sultan himself was shortly afterwards asked by the French to leave, and he took up exile in Saudi Arabia. His sons remained behind to organize an Afar Liberation Front, operating from the Territory and Somalia.

Throughout the rest of 1975 and the following year, Afar guerrillas carried out sporadic hit-and-run attacks on trucks carrying gasoline and merchandise from Assab to Addis Ababa. The problem became so serious that the government set up a system of gas rationing throughout the country and organized military-guarded convoys through the sultan's old territory. Gas rationing was strict in the capital, where the normal allowance for a private car was only 15 litres (less than 4 gallons) a week. Towns dependent on fuel oil-powered generators for their electricity were sometimes blacked out, and the internal distribution system was sometimes disrupted as trucks waited days for fuel oil. For example, in late December 1975, the city of Gondar in northwest Ethiopia was operating its electric power plant for less than two hours a night and scores of trucks were idled because no fuel oil was available. But the situation measurably improved the following year as the army gained better control of the lower Awash Valley and was able to organize regular convoys from Assab to the capital. Still, the sultan's Front remained a real threat as became clear in September 1976 when the government took journalists to Assaita during celebrations marking the second anniversary of the Emperor's overthrow. Though about 3,000 soldiers were stationed in the town, they could not prevent incidents from taking place on the roads. A bus identical to the one carrying journalists was blown up on the track between Dubte and Assaita during their stay there. Elsewhere, bands of Afar guerrillas periodically raided the plantations throughout the lower Awash Valley, killing highland workers and disrupting production.

The Afar Liberation Front would probably have sputtered out like other landlord-led local rebellions were it not for the involvement of outside powers, notably socialist Somalia and conservative Saudi Arabia. Both countries were interested in supporting the Front, Somalia because it wanted to weaken in whatever way possible the central Ethiopian government and Saudi Arabia because of its general opposition to Marxism. Ideology proved no barrier to Somalia's pursuit of nationalist interest. The Marxist Somali government found no contradiction in allowing Anfere Ali Mirah, one of the Sultan's sons, to use Radio Mogadishu to attack the Ethiopian government for its land reform policy. Once again, the general rule regarding the importance of conservative opposition to the revolution obtained: only when it was linked to larger issues, such as the Somali-Ethiopian or the Arab-Ethiopian dispute, did it receive outside support and become serious.

The End of the Empire

By the summer of 1975, only a few months after the land reform proclamation, many Ethiopian observers began to think the country was close to disintegration. Visiting journalists concluded that civil war would consume the old empire. Optimists countered by arguing that numerous small isolated rebellions did not add up to a civil war. The overall picture was nonetheless disquieting. Early predictions that the demise of Haile Selassie would lead to chaos seemed correct after all; the calm that prevailed during the revolution's first few months seemed only the lull before the storm. In fact, both optimists and pessimists were partially correct. While it was an exaggeration to equate these rebellions with a civil war, they manifested a profound transformation under way in the traditional relations between center and periphery of the country. To fully appreciate what was taking place, one has to keep in mind how the empire had been structured. Its unity had been fragile at best even under Emperor Haile Selassie, despite his efforts to centralize power and establish a modern bureaucratic administration. The Emperor never managed to impose the central government's policies on the province of Gojjam, left Tigre under the control of its own royal family, accepted the semi-autonomous status of Ali Mirah's sultanate and had had to send a large expeditionary force to maintain control over Bale. He depended heavily on personal diplomacy and relationships with local potentates to keep the empire together. He dispensed titles, land and pensions, flew village and tribal chiefs to Addis Ababa to secure their allegiance, and offered amnesty and royal treatment to former enemies, like Waqo Gutu, to prevent further rebellions. The revolution ended the network of personal ties which for over half a century had linked the Emperor to the provinces. The Military Council made clear that it would not permit personal fiefdoms and semi-autonomous regions to exist. There was to be no place for the *Ras* Mengeshas or the Ali Mirahs in the new Ethiopia. The *Derg* attempted to convert a loosely knit empire into a modern, unified state. Seen in this perspective, the scattered rebellions were not so much a sign of

Ethiopia's disintegration as it was of its integration into a new, more cohesive unit. They marked the last agonies of feudal Ethiopia.

The problem of building a modern nation-state is never simple. The administrative weaknesses that forced Haile Selassie to rely on personal diplomacy also bedeviled the new military government. Civil servants or soldiers were too scarce to impose a new concept of Ethiopia overnight. Consequently, the new government was long in quelling local rebellions. Conversely, these provincial uprisings, though colorful and romantic in the best Evelyn Waugh tradition, seldom weakened or disrupted the government except in those instances when outside support was found. Berhane Maskal could occupy Lalibela or destroy an Ethiopian Airlines DC-3 airplane, but the government eventually sent troops to deal with him. The EDU could "occupy" the Semien Mountains National Park driving out a mere handful of game wardens, but the power of the *Derg* was hardly affected. Not until late 1976 did some revolts transcend a local character and coalesce into movements having provincial or national scope. Like the *Derg,* opponents of the revolution found the parochial tradition in Ethiopia a principal obstacle to their larger goals. No local rebellion could survive without joining with forces both inside and outside the country. Thus in 1976 the main conservative opposition group, the EDU, finally began bringing a number of local leaders under one umbrella and transforming feudal reaction into a national movement. Not having sufficient manpower to impose forcibly its rule throughout the country, the *Derg* had to win over enough peasants from all ethnic groups to keep Ethiopia from disintegrating. Its task was facilitated by the aristocratic composition of the opposition leadership. It became possible to appeal to peasant economic and political interests and in this manner to build a new network of ties between the center and the periphery. The links between Addis Ababa and the countryside were no longer *rases* and *balabbats* but peasant associations. The transformation of the ancient empire into a new nation-state would prove a long and painful process, and there was always the serious danger that the country would disintegrate before a new Ethiopia could consolidate itself.

7. The "Leftist" Opposition

Every major socialist revolution has its leftist opposition, and the Ethiopian revolution proved no exception. Within a few days of the Emperor's deposition, the military found itself being challenged by students and workers, who agitated for a "people's government" and accused the *Derg* of usurping power and stifling the revolution. These groups saw themselves as the true radical forces by virtue alone, it seemed, of their civilian status. In the terminology of the opposition, "left" became synonymous with "civilian" and "right" with "military," though it became increasingly questionable as the revolution progressed that civilians were left of the military.

The nature of radical civilian opposition to the *Derg* cannot be explained in terms of "left" and "right," terms which tend to confuse the fact that both sides shared the same fundamental ideology. Rather, the revolutionary opposition can best be understood in terms of several key non-ideological considerations: the civilians' alienation from power and the decision-making process and their determination to regain the initiative lost since mid-1974; the Ethiopian "political culture," characterized by an incapacity to compromise and cooperate; and, finally, a factionalism typical of all revolutionary movements which develops when political power is contested.

The revolution's leftist opposition dates to the events of April and May 1974, when the civilian groups that had early played a role in bringing down the old regime—the CELU, the Ethiopian Teachers' Association, and the students—failed to evolve an organized political movement and as a result were crushed by Endelkachew's National Security Commission. After the massive and continuous street demonstrations of February and March, the populace in Addis Ababa, unlike its counterpart in Paris during the French revolution or St. Petersburg during the Russian revolution, played a singularly unimportant role in immediately subsequent events. Nor was the populace directed by a small, disciplined revolutionary cadre. It was only after the *Derg* decreed urban and land reform that common people once again directly participated in the revolution. But the crucial decisions being made throughout the early months of the revolution remained essentially in the hands of a small civilian-military minority.

Civilian groups like the CELU, the ETA, and students initially acted and reacted to the Endelkachew government in accordance with their own corporate interests. Not until the summer of 1975 were they able to put forth a comprehensive reform program. By this time, however, the *Derg* had already initiated sweeping economic and social reforms and had thus far outdistanced the civilian left in deed if not in ideology. The main reason for this was probably that the civilian organizations were at the outset of the revolution dominated by moderate leaders closer ideologically to the *ancien régime* than to the Marxists in their ranks. Although these organizations eventually fell under the control of radicals, this happened too tardily to prevent the military from consolidating its power. It is important here to distinguish between the character of civilian opposition in 1974, when it was by and large moderate, reformist, and dedicated to the defense of corporate interests, and its posture after mid-1975, when it began espousing a Marxist ideology and calling for a revolutionary "people's government."

In organization as in programs and leadership, the civilian left began with a serious handicap. Its strongest support came from the unions which by definition could organize only special interest groups—industrial workers, teachers, and students. Such unionized bodies, however, did not even represent their full constituencies. The fact that the CELU increased its membership by one-third in the months following the general strike shows how great was its past failure to fully organize the working class. The student movement, albeit dominated by a more radical leadership than the CELU, was chronically bogged down by such organizational disputes as whether students at the agricultural college at Alemaya or the public health college at Gondar should be allowed to form autonomous unions. To be sure, their organizational weakness was not all of their own making. Haile Selassie had discouraged the formation of organizations, and the student union in particular had periodically been banned. But his policy does not explain the opposition's tendency to indulge in internal squabbles, factional disputes, and ideological nitpicking. When the military seized power in the summer of 1974 it did not wrest the leadership of the revolution from students and workers; rather, it relaunched a movement that the civilians had proven incapable of sustaining.

The civilians' exclusion from power also explains their hostility to the military, but not the particular form their opposition took. Specifically, it does not explain why civilians, while pressing for participation in the decision-making process, also demanded that the military unconditionally surrender its power to them. We believe that this extremist approach, backed by threats of general strikes and popular uprisings which the civilian organizations could not possibly engineer can probably be understood only in terms of the country's political culture. Many authors have noted the pride and fractiousness of the Ethiopian upper class, its penchant for intrigue, its inability to cooperate, and unwillingness to compromise.[1] Writing in the 1940s, Margery Perham had remarked on the problem posed by great families which, by tradition, "must be either rulers or rebels in their respective districts."[2] The revolution demonstrated that such an attitude was not limited to the aristocracy, but affected most members of the educated elite. Personal intrigue so characteristic of court life in the past seemed to pervade every organization in Ethiopia. Within the CELU, candidates who had been defeated in union elections invariably organized dissident factions within the confederation. The student movement was similarly fragmented. Not only were students studying in North America, Europe, and inside the country organized into rival factions, but each group was splintered internally and absorbed in power struggles. Neither the students' shared hatred of the regime of Haile Selassie nor the common concern of the labor confederation's leaders for working class conditions proved strong enough to prevent this fractiousness. There is, of course, nothing exclusively Ethiopian in such political behavior. It was simply rooted in Ethiopia's feudal political traditions. This political culture was very much alive in Ethiopia in 1974 and could not be expected to disappear overnight.

The tendency toward factionalism and intransigence was only reinforced by the revolution, which destroyed all concepts of legitimacy and opened up unlimited opportunities for ruthless and ambitious men to rise to positions of power. Though the formation of political factions is a typical revolutionary phenomenon, the Ethiopian situation was special in that substantial ideological or programmatic differences did not separate the various contending parties. All civilian factions as well as the military left eventually called themselves Marxist-Leninist, though without discernibly different shades of Marxism-Leninism. Attempts to define the military's policies as "Soviet-style," and those of the civilian opposition as "Chinese-style," for example, do not hold up to close scrutiny; nor can the differences among civilian groups be described in such terms.

As a result of these two factors—the feudal political culture of Ethiopia and the factionalism spawned by the revolutionary process—the inability of like-minded politicians to compromise or cooperate remained a constant impediment to the revolution. It gave rise to the civilian left's bitter hatred for the military left; it spawned some half-dozen splinter leftist civilian groups with practically identical ideological platforms; and it led eventually to fratricidal killings among former student leaders and their followers and the subsequent emergence in early 1977 of a "white terror" by royalist and conservative elements and a "red terror" by Marxist supporters, similar to those that existed in the Russian revolution. The same inability to compromise also helped undermine the effectiveness of the leftist opposition. It led the CELU to threaten the *Derg* repeatedly with general strikes it was totally incapable of organizing and to issue ultimata it could not possibly back up with action. Similarly, this attitude caused the Ethiopian People's Revolutionary Party (EPRP), the main leftist civilian group, to reject all cooperation with the military even though there was little difference between its program and that of the *Derg*. Infighting among rival ideologues reached quite ugly proportions when, in the summer of 1976, the new splinter group calling itself the Ethiopian Communist Party broke away from the EPRP and promptly published the names of all EPRP leaders in the hope of having them arrested and executed by the *Derg*. To be sure, the EPRP reciprocated by publishing the names of the Communist Party's top leaders.

CELU and the Military

The antagonism between the military and the labor confederation, which would become a major conflict in the revolution, developed after April 1974. This was the period in which the Coordinating Committee of the Armed Forces, Police, and Territorial Army was being formed in opposition to Colonel Alem Zewd's committee, and when radical junior officers revitalized the military movement in opposition to Endelkachew. The confederation, too, was trying to redefine its goals and role, but with considerable lack of success. It overestimated its capacity to oppose the government, and strikes by workers in the parastatal sector in April and May were forcibly put down. This defeat, at a time of unprecedented success in its organizational drive,[3] prompted a reexamination of the organization's goals and tactics and increased the influence of the more radical, or at least more politicized, elements. Despite its much larger size, the Confederation nevertheless soon became politically inconsequential, the implications of which were spelled out in an editorial in the CELU's monthly publication, *The Voice of Labour*, in August. The workers, the article said, could not achieve their goals unless they went beyond the purely economic struggles they had waged in the past:

> Trade unions cannot, through economic struggles alone, resolve the recurring conflicts between the workers and the capitalists. This is evidenced by the fact that strong trade unions in the developed western world, despite their strength, have not been able to find a lasting solution to inherent class contradictions. The trade union movement, therefore, is only a forum to advance economic interests within a given social framework. The resolution of the worker-capitalist conflict can be effected only with the elimination of classes. The elimination of the exploiting classes necessitates a political struggle which in turn necessitates a political party. In other words, a political party of the working class and of the oppressed classes in general is absolutely essential if a just, democratic and egalitarian society is to be brought into being. The political party of the working class and other exploited sections of the population such as peasants, soldiers, small merchants, the lumpen proletariat, etc. will join hands with other democratic political organizations in the burial ceremony of feudalism and imperialism, the twin enemies of the Ethiopian people.[4]

Whatever its official organ said, the CELU defined a politically moderate role for itself. Its officials believed in the need for organization and action within a liberal democratic framework; in fact, the same issue of *The Voice of Labour*, which stated in Marxist terminology the necessity for the labor movement to overcome the narrow boundaries of unionism, also expressed support for the liberal democratic draft constitution, which had just been published. But even as the CELU prepared to play a broader political role in the proposed new democratic system, it was suddenly faced with a military government more radical than itself and deeply suspicious of independent civilian activity. The proclamations of September 12, 1974, which announced the deposition of the Emperor and the formation of the PMAC, also banned all strikes, unauthorized demonstrations, and public meetings. Moreover, no role was offered to the existing civilian organizations such as the CELU and only limited civilian participation was permitted through an advisory committee which was granted unspecified powers.[5]

The confederation held a general meeting four days later and passed a set of resolutions taking direct issue with the government. It condemned the ban on demonstrations and strikes, demanded the immediate establishment of a "people's government," and threatened to call a general strike unless all these demands were met promptly. It declared that while the Ethiopian "toiling masses" fully supported the measures taken by the Coordinating Committee up until the Emperor's deposition, it now opposed the establishment of a provisional military administration.[6] The reasons given were that the military proclamation of September 12 failed to recognize the basic rights of assembly, strike, and peaceful demonstration. After reminding the military that the revolution was "the result of the qualitative accumulation of years of struggle by the working class, students, peasants, soldiers and all democratic forces," the document asserted that the solution to Ethiopia's problems would come only through formation of a "provisional people's government" to be composed of:[7]

1. the Ethiopian labor unions
2. the committees that were formed in various provinces during the February movement
3. the armed forces
4. The Teachers' Association
5. the University Teachers' Union and the University Teachers' Forum
6. the Civil Servants' Association
7. the Ethiopian Students' Union
8. the Ethiopian Businessmen's Association
9. the Ethiopian Women's [Welfare] Association

The CELU further demanded a constitution abolishing the Crown and guaranteeing the "right of assembly, speech, press, peaceful demonstration, including the right to form political parties." Copies of the resolution were sent not only to the new PMAC but to all existing civilian organizations, including the *edir,* the traditional mutual aid associations in urban areas.

In this document, two ideas stand out as particularly interesting. The CELU leadership officially endorsed a liberal democratic form of government that displayed few traces of Marxist thinking. At the same time, in trying to apply a model of representative government to Ethiopia it had to propose a corporate system of government because of the absence of political parties; this would have meant that most power would have been put in the hands of the urban elite to the exclusion of the rural population and with only a minimal role for workers. It is difficult to conceive of a government less representative of the whole Ethiopian population than that proposed by the CELU since the organizations called upon to form a "people's government" represented few other than the privileged professional urban groups. To be sure, the military government was not representative of the people either, but at least it was not controlled by corporate interest groups to the same extent as the political model proposed by the CELU. The organizations the CELU wanted to participate in government represented very narrow interests indeed. The labor confederation itself, for instance, only represented a relatively privileged segment of urban workers. The Women's Association was not a mass organization of Ethiopian women, but a charity oriented, paternalistic organization controlled by aristocratic families. There is no need to detail who was represented by the associations of civil servants, university teachers, and businessmen. Ideologically, the only progressive organizations in late 1974 were the student union and the University Teachers' Forum, composed of younger faculty members at Haile Selassie I University.

The military's swift response to the CELU's resolutions was to arrest the three top officials of the confederation. The attempt to organize a general strike completely failed, and the confederation was effectively silenced for the next six months. This initial confrontation merely hardened the opposition of all civilian organizations to the military government and set the tone of a relationship that was to plague the revolution in the future. Civilians refused to credit the *Derg* for the historic changes it had brought about, while the military demonstrated an exaggerated fear that civilian political activity would lead to uncontrollable and embarrassing strikes and demonstrations. Noticeably lacking in this acrimonious debate was any discussion of goals or concrete reforms.

The *Derg* nominally conceded to the demand for a people's government by forming in late September a civilian advisory board. It was a fifty-man body, whose members were, according to a government statement, to be elected by "Ethiopian nationals who believe in the aims and objectives of *Ethiopia Tikdem*, have no religious or tribal bias, be upright citizens with physical and mental capabilities to shoulder their responsibilities and be untainted by association with the previous corrupt administration."[8] In fact, sixteen of the advisers were elected by ministerial personnel, and fourteen by "individuals in all fourteen governatorates of Ethiopia." In addition, the Ethiopian Teachers' Association provided four representatives, the CELU three, and the two major agricultural development projects, CADU and WADU—renamed "farmers' cooperatives" for the occasion—sent one representative each.[9] The University Teachers' Association was allotted two representatives, while the Moslem community, the Christian community, big business, medium-sized business, the Central Statistical Office, the Public Administration Institute, the Central Personnel Agency, the Auditor General's Office, and the Pension Commission each had one representative. The difficulty of organizing a representative body in Ethiopia was pointed up in this advisory body, which was heavily slanted toward the urban population, particularly civil servants and professionals. Perhaps no committee could have been representative under the circumstances. Without political parties or an administrative apparatus enabling the rural population to cast votes, a truly representative system at this time was necessarily impossible, and it may be questioned whether the Western concept of representation made any sense at all in the Ethiopian context.

The civilian advisory board officially started functioning at the end of October. On paper, its duties appeared extensive: recommending "guidelines to the PMAC that will enable the Ethiopian People to choose the type of government they want, drafting a constitution in accordance with the provisions of the first Proclamation of the military council in line with the philosophy of *Ethiopia Tikdem,* and preparing studies for the reform of the political, economic and social systems of the country."[10] In practice, the board could do little. Shortly after its election, the more radical faction within the *Derg* came to power. General Aman was killed, 60 political prisoners executed, and the new socialist policy announced. The semi-constitutional process in which the civilian body would have played a role was superseded by a revolutionary government in which such an organization became irrelevant. Nonetheless, it produced a plan for establishing a constituent assembly to prepare for a return to civilian government. The plan was never publicized, and the advisory board, depleted of many of its members, ceased functioning in June 1976.

After the proclamation on socialism in December 1974, the military began carrying out reforms the civilian left advocated. Its thunder stolen and no longer able to portray itself as the voice of progress in the face of a "reactionary" military regime, the civilian opposition needed to reassess its program and tactics. This was a difficult and delicate task since the Marxist left felt it had to welcome the government's general economic reform policies while at the same time opposing its policy against the independence of political organizations and labor unions. The CELU was the first to come to grips with the new situation. Wracked by internal dissension, its leaders were unable to choose between a Western concept of unionism, which meant freedom from government control, and a Soviet socialist unionism in which unions were government-controlled. At least one faction seemed ready to abandon Western-style unionism by April 1975, as indicated in that month's issue of *The Voice of Labour.* It depicted the duties of labor unions in a socialist country as raising productivity, acting as a bridge between government and workers, and educating the workers.[11] But another faction complained bitterly in the same period that the working class was losing rather than benefiting from the government's reforms and noted that salaries were unchanged, state-appointed managers of nationalized enterprises were proving as dictatorial as former bosses, and, worse, union chapters were being quietly shut down.[12] In May 1975 this latter disgruntled faction came to power after an intense organizational struggle.

Politics within the CELU were complicated by the imposition of new ideological conflicts on old factional disputes and personal rivalries. In late

1973, personal conflicts among the top leaders had become particularly serious, but these internal fissures were temporarily healed by the success of the general strike and the membership drive that followed. When on September 24 the PMAC ordered the arrest of the confederation's top leaders, political infighting resumed. Though the details are obscure, it seems that the newly-elected officers were not only controversial but also incompetent. This situation strengthened the dissident factions. Thus, at the time of the nationalizations, when the CELU most needed to rethink its role, it continued to be riddled by internal disputes and was thus incapable of taking a clear position.

By May 1975, tension within the leadership of the CELU was so acute that it had practically ceased to function. Its turbulent meetings were marred by verbal quarrels, throwing of chairs, and fistfights among officials. Taking advantage of the situation on May 19, the PMAC ordered CELU headquarters closed on grounds that the confederation needed reorganizing. This may have been true, but it was also clear that the military government desired to control an organization that had become too autonomous and hostile. Although the closure was said to be temporary, the government indicated that henceforth workers would elect "their true leaders in line with the aims and objectives of Ethiopian socialism," a statement strongly implying it also intended to control the confederation in the future.[13] Furthermore, the government claimed that the CELU had functioned with the "financial, technical and moral support of certain countries which are opposed to the aims and objectives of socialism" and that the situation therefore needed correcting.[14]

In the following days, the state-controlled press mounted a campaign against the CELU. Not only its leaders, but also the principles of Western unionism, came under attack. The Amharic-language daily *Addis Zemen,* for example, dismissed the concept of collective bargaining as irrelevant to Ethiopian socialism.[15] However, because the workers reacted so hostilely to the government campaign, the *Derg* backed down by allowing the headquarters to be reopened and elections of new officers to be held. This ironically resulted in the election of a group of officials particularly hostile to the military and fairly radical in ideology. CELU's new chairman, Marcos Hagos, may have been more an opportunist than an intellectual radical, but as a long-time opponent of the previous leadership he rallied the more radical elements within the confederation.[16]

The final statement released after the elections on June 4 did not really clarify the CELU's conception of its role in the emerging socialist system.[17] It condemned the old leaders as reactionaries and noted that the elections had finally brought true progessives to power. Paradoxically, what the "progressives" wanted did not seem to be substantially different from the demand of the old "reactionary" leaders. They still wanted complete freedom to organize workers in nationalized and non-nationalized enterprises alike. They retained their view of the organization as one promoting workers' interests through collective bargaining and urged that salaries be raised to keep pace with increases in the cost of living. They demanded that enterprises still in private hands be nationalized, including bus and trucking companies, coffee and haricot bean exporting concerns, hotels, and even missionary-run hospitals. The workers' organization had to be strengthened and the employers prevented from organizing. Thus it asked that the federation of employers be immediately disbanded. It also said that the government should issue as soon as possible new labor legislation promised by the Endelkachew government after the general strike of March 1974.

The position of the CELU during this transitional period was obviously confused. Despite its lack of a coherent vision, the confederation assumed it would continue as an autonomous organization, and even enjoy the protection of the government against management. But since the government had now become the largest employer in the country, CELU's hopes were quite naive.

The Spread of Dissension

By the spring of 1975, the military government and civilian left were increasingly at odds with each other over a number of issues, notwithstanding implementation of land reform and nationalizations. A series of attempts by *zemacha* students to stir up trouble in Chilalo District to the south of Addis Ababa led to a number of arrests in June and July amidst government denunciations of their activities, including accusations that farmers' wives had been raped and their belongings pillaged. In August, students who were assigned to carry out a housing census in Addis Ababa held anti-government demonstrations on the campus of the university. Nearly a thousand were arrested and hauled away to a camp at Holetta, 20 miles outside the capital, for "reeducation."

Teachers, whose militancy had subsided with the announcement of salary increases and the postponement of educational reform in March 1974, were once again aroused. Their position is an interesting example of how a relatively conservative organization became part of the "leftist" opposition. Teachers had welcomed the advent of the PMAC, the deposition of the Emperor, and the arrest of former government officials. The Ethiopian Teachers' Association hailed the military takeover, and its statement was broadcast by the government-controlled radio as a proof of popular support.[18] Although the ETA warned that a true people's government had yet to be formed, the warning seemed perfunctory and was not repeated for months.

In the spring of 1975, however, it was rumored that the *Derg* would not only revive the Educational Sector Review, but would carry out even more radical educational reforms. The Ministry of Education had started setting up committees to work on a revision of curriculum and textbooks for primary and secondary schools. Alarmed anti-government members of the Teachers' Association began a campaign to keep teachers from taking part in the work of the committees and later accused the government of dictating educational policy without having consulted the teachers, just as the Haile Selassie government had done.[19] As a matter of fact, these committees dealt not so much with educational restructuring as seeing that references to the Emperor and his achievements were expurgated from textbooks and that the role of the Solomonic dynasty was played down in history texts. There were, it was true, some indications that more radical reforms were under debate—a new educational system that would stress basic education and vocational training, limit the role of the university, and strengthen the two-year colleges.[20] Yet no decisions were taken nor announcements made in this regard.

There was also more student discontent. Although older students were away on the *zemacha,* senior and junior high school students picked up the banner of dissent. What they wanted is difficult to say precisely: "people's government" and "down with the *Derg"* were their slogans, and disrupting schools their tactics. Long-term goals were obscure, if indeed they existed. Throughout the 1974–75 academic year, secondary schools operated only sporadically, and the government for a long time closed its eyes to the problem. But at the end of May, after a particularly bad period of turmoil, it warned that all students should report for class by June 2 or face punishment. On that day, large numbers refused, and the government responded by mass arrests. There was no violence. All day trucks moved back and forth between the schools and various army barracks carting off rebellious students. They were released the next day to wailing mothers and enraged fathers, who were made to sign declarations that they would henceforth take responsibility for their children's attendance and good behavior. Following this incidence, the rest of the school year was peaceful.

While high school students agitated, teachers stepped up their own campaign against any educational reform the *Derg* might attempt to impose. In meetings of the ETA in May and June, they expressed disagreement with the way the new curriculum was being prepared. Anti-government teachers claimed that those working on curriculum and textbook revisions were undemocratically elected and thus unrepresentative. Throughout this period, to the authors' best knowledge, the ETA did not seriously discuss in detail any educational reform or advance any concrete proposals. Teachers steadfastly refused to cooperate with the Ministry of Education. The annual in-service summer training program for teachers, for example, had to be cancelled in 1975 because the participants, at the instigation of the ETA, balked at attending. They claimed that the program had been devised in an authoritarian fashion and was thus irrelevant to the country's needs.

The ETA's opposition came into the open in late August when the association held its annual meeting in the provincial capital of Jimma. The lengthy document issued at the end of the congress, carrying the signatures of all the participants, spelled out the demand for teacher participation in the process of educational reform.[21] The new educational system, the ETA stated, should reflect the majority will and be geared to national needs. The old Educational Sector Review had proved unacceptable because it had been prepared without consulting teachers and students who best understood those needs. No concrete proposals for educational reform was advanced nor any indication given for what democratic process in curriculum revision meant.

There was only a vague statement that workers, farmers, and the Ethiopian Teachers' Association should all be allowed to participate.

Besides its overriding commitment to broad participatory democracy, the Jimma statement was noteworthy because it revealed the beginnings of a loose alliance with other civilian groups opposed to the *Derg*. It extolled in particular *zemacha* students who risked their lives to improve the conditions of the Ethiopian masses and to make them aware of their political rights. It asserted that the *Derg*, instead of supporting them, repeatedly took the side of reactionary landlords. The ETA therefore proposed that the *zemacha* program be run by students, peasants, and workers, and that democratic rights be guaranteed as a first step toward substantial change.

The ETA document contained another point that in retrospect is significant, namely the call for a "new democratic revolution." In a society wracked by intense class contradictions, the document stated in socialist terminology, it was important to distinguish the real enemies of the people from those elements which provided a basis for a people's alliance. Anti-feudal and anti-imperialist groups should band together to defeat reactionary forces. Such an alliance should include workers, farmers, the left-wing petty bourgeoisie, and "the like." The appeal for a "new democratic revolution" was nonetheless lost in the lengthy document and went virtually unnoticed at the time. It is doubtful that many teachers would have understood its Maoist origin or been aware of the great difference between the Western concept of democracy and the socialist vision of a "new democracy." Before long, however, the idea of "new democracy," understood or not, became the rallying cry of the civilian left.

Demise of the CELU

In the uneasy atmosphere of September 1975, the first anniversary of the deposition of Haile Selassie was celebrated as the official beginning of the revolution. The Emperor had died only a short time earlier, on August 27. Although ill, he had undergone surgery a few months before, at the age of 83. A rumor nonetheless arose that shortly before the celebration he had been murdered.[22] Just before September 12, the right-wing opposition released to the press in Europe and the United States statements alleging that the *Derg* also intended to execute all imprisoned members of the royal family, including children, before the anniversary.[23] Consequently, the occasion was greeted not by messages of congratulations from foreign governments, but by expressions of concern for the fate of princes and princesses.[24] The celebration itself, held in the presence of many foreign guests, was marred by incidents, as parading workers and students shouted anti-government slogans in front of the official podium. "Down with the Military," they cried, "People's Government," "Free the Political Prisoners," "Free the Students." This time, no one broke through police lines to embrace Mengistu, as had happened during the celebration of the land reform proclamation only six months earlier.

A few days later, the CELU held a general meeting in Addis Ababa. The resolutions passed at that gathering represented the boldest challenge yet that any civilian organization had posed to the military. The result, in late September, was an open and bloody confrontation. In these resolutions, the history of the revolution was amazingly described as an organized mass movement that had existed underground for many years only to surface in February 1974 to overthrow the feudal system by September.[25] The role of the military was not even referred to; only "the broad masses" merited mention. Indeed, the military was seen as distorter of the revolution's course who deprived the masses of political rights. Ethiopia had fallen into undemocratic hands, the resolutions continued; "office capitalists" controlled the country's wealth; the "broad masses" were not given their economic due; students were persecuted for trying to help the masses; unions were being destroyed; and civil sevants were prevented from organizing. The CELU reiterated the usual leftist demands for freedom of speech, the right to strike and organize, and the release of "progressive" prisoners. It asked that the *zemacha* be suspended unless put under the direction of "organizations representing the majority, i.e. CELU, Teachers' Association, Women's Associations, Farmers' Assocations." It demanded, as of old, price controls, minimum wage, free schools and health services, and the creation of more jobs in the cities.

The CELU resolutions argued that a developing country needed a period of transition before a socialist system could be created. A socialist revolution should be preceded by a "national democratic revolution," in which an anti-feudalist struggle was fought. In this period, the people should be given full democratic rights. The democratic revolution had necessarily both capitalist and socialist characteristics, but the former would "wither away." The revolution would be led by the "toiling masses" (apparently the urban working class) in partnership with the peasants, and all other oppressed groups would collaborate. Each class would have its own political party, but the working class party would lead the struggle to attain the ultimate goal of a socialist state and society. Only this working class party, freely formed by workers and progressives from among the educated, could carry out revolutionary goals. For this reason, the CELU rejected the validity of any political party organized by the military government. This latter point was an open rebuke to the *Derg* since, in his anniversary speech, Brig. Gen. Teferi Bante announced that the military council shortly intended to set up a political party. Clearly, the CELU of September 1975 had come a long way in its thinking from that of a year earlier. The socialist, even Maoist, language of its resolutions was unmistakable. American-trained leaders had been replaced by more radical ones who embraced a far different ideology and concept of unionism. But, as would become apparent later, the new leadership was far ahead of, and cut off from, the bulk of the confederation's own rank and file members.

The immediate effect of the CELU's radicalization was disastrous for the organization. Its stiff warning to the government of a general strike should any members of the executive committee be arrested, should the organization's headquarters be closed, or workers be prevented from freely distributing the resolutions provoked the *Derg*. On September 25, an employee of Ethiopian Airlines was caught distributing the resolutions among airport workers. Security guards attempted to arrest him, other workers tried to protect him, and in the ensuing struggle the police opened fire, killing four people and wounding twenty-two others, three of whom later died in the hospital. The incident created enormous tension in the capital. Having called all workers to strike, the CELU's frightened top leaders went underground without having had time to organize. The individual unions, more often the workers in each enterprise, were left with the decision to honor the call. Sufficient numbers did so that a violent government reaction was provoked. On September 30, a state of emergency was declared in Addis Ababa and the city was placed under martial law. "Our revolution will not be diverted because of the strikes taking place," the government warned in its emergency declaration. "If we have to shed blood, we will do so to protect the rights of the broad masses." A wave of arrests among suspect union officials, teachers, and students ensued, and more than 1,500 civilians were taken into custody during the month of October.

Not surprisingly, the attempted general strike fizzled before this show of military force. And significantly, participation was high only in white-collar organizations, as it had always tended to be. Employees of Ethiopian Airlines, the banks, the insurance companies, and the Board of Telecommunications joined the strike in large numbers; only a smattering of industrial workers did. Although individual unions survived, the confrontation with the military government brought about the permanent destruction of CELU's national organization. Its top leaders went into the clandestine Ethiopian People's Revolutionary Party (EPRP), whose existence, by no coincidence, became better known at this time. It was a transitional period for the civilian left, which had now moved from the pursuit of narrow corporate interests in early 1974 to broader political concerns.

In December 1975, the *Derg* issued a long-awaited Labor Proclamation which announced a union reorganization and eventually the formation of a new All-Ethiopia Trade Union (AETU).[26] This curious document, full of anomalies, once again bore witness to the rapid changes taking place in Ethiopia. From an earlier epoch, it carried over the concept of the workers' right to freely organize and to strike, while the newer socialist trend inspired the idea that the union's main function was that of educating the workers and increasing productivity. The preamble stated that "workers can better contribute their share in building socialism, participate effectively in the development of the country and attain political consciousness only when they are organized in trade unions and pursue their objectives systematically under the guidance of able and progressive leaders, in line with socialist principles."[27] In noting the objectives and functions of trade unions, it stressed the workers' responsibility to promote economic development and a high level of productivity and to participate in community affairs as well as educational and training programs. The proclamation did not spell out any specific management role for workers, even in the state sector. On the other hand, it dealt at length with the obviously non-socialist problem of collective bargaining in such matters as salaries and working conditions.[28]

The labor proclamation reflected the confused state in Ethiopian political thinking and the disarray of the country's institutions after more than a year of revolutionary upheaval. It was no longer a feudal empire moving toward capitalism; rather, a new nation tumbling into socialism, without either socialist ideology or socialist institutions. Neither the revolution's military leadership nor the civilian opposition had any precise notion of the kind of political institutions that should be established. The revolution had reached a political impasse because it had gone further and faster than anybody had anticipated while no one had pondered the means of building political institutions. Begun as a movement by the disenfranchised classes of the modern sector to gain representation in the political system, it could well have ended simply as a bourgeois revolution. Within a year, however, the military had enacted sweeping economic reforms and the civilian organizations were calling for a "new democratic revolution" and demanding representation for the "toiling masses." But neither the *Derg* nor the radical civilians had a clear idea of what political institutions should be created to consolidate the emerging socialist system. The military was mainly concerned with applying concrete economic reforms, suppressing the feudal opposition, and dealing with the secessionist movement in Eritrea. A new political system could wait. The civilian opposition had in mind an abstract model of a socialist political system, but it was too doctrinaire in its intellectual and emotional hatred of the military to accept the fact that this model did not fit the main political reality of the Ethiopian situation: revolution without the military was impossible. For its part, the *Derg* was adamant in its opposition to civilian participation in the decision-making process. The military viewed the civilian left with a mixture of disdain and fear and saw no reason to share power with it. Under these circumstances, the search for a way out of the political impasse proved exceedingly difficult.

8. The Attempt to Break the Impasse

In the fall of 1975, the *Derg* embarked upon a major, though unsuccessful, effort to break the political impasse that developed in its relations with the leftist civilian opposition. The campaign culminated in April 1976 with an appeal for all "progressive forces" to unite in a "National Revolutionary Front," an offer which was summarily rejected and led to a radical change in tactics on both sides. Terrorist activity in the urban areas began the following fall and by February 1977 had escalated into outright terror. These months were an extremely intense and important period with regard to the internal politics of the revolution. They marked the transformation of the *Derg* from a progressive military government bent on much-needed reforms into a repressive regime concerned chiefly with its own survival.

The second year of the revolution also saw the transformation of the civilian "left" from a relatively moderate opposition into a terrorist organization which attacked all institutions even remotely connected with the *Derg*. In a sense, the civilian left's claim that the *Derg* was no more than a "fascist dictatorship" became prophetic because the terrorism of the civilians eventually forced the military to respond in kind, so that, in Mengistu's own words, "terror and anarchy will vanish from the camp of the broad masses and reign in that of the reactionaries."[1]

Several reasons account for the total failure of reconciliation between the military and civilians. Success would have required the *Derg* to share power and the civilian opposition to accept less than the immediate demise of the military. But such compromise was foreign to Ethiopian politics. Another, more concrete factor in this period of deteriorating relations was the dramatic emergence of former student leaders on the Ethiopian political scene. Both the *Derg* and the leftist opposition turned to them for ideological inspiration and political leadership. There have been few, if any, countries where so many young and politically inexperienced intellectuals were catapulted so suddenly from student to national politics and to the highest positions of power. This had tragic consequences. Former student leaders were unprepared for the task at hand. In political discussions, they had dissected theoretical problems of socialism but not such practical ones as how to implement sweeping changes in feudal Ethiopia. As a result, they tended to continue debating theoretical issues that had also split the student movement, fighting the same old battles among themselves rather than discussing the new problems facing the country. Indeed, what was most striking in the Ethiopian revolution was not the factionalism of the leftist intellectuals *per se* or the acrimony of their debate, but the fact that they seemed largely disconnected from reality.

The Student Revolutionaries

The participants in the student movement were by and large an in-grown group, having been educated in a small number of high schools, primarily in Addis Ababa and Asmara. When they reached university age, they dispersed, some staying in Ethiopia to attend Haile Selassie I University while others received scholarships to attend foreign universities, particularly in the United States and Western Europe. Differences in the formal education they received had a considerable impact. Those at Haile Selassie I University were generally less well-read and more provincial in outlook.[2] They were less articulate and thus less inclined to debate ideological differences. Their meetings were reportedly chaotic. They compensated for a lack of discipline and debating skills with an enthusiasm and a sense of participatory democracy that verged on anarchy.

The students who went abroad tended to be much more intellectual, in part because many attended graduate schools. Inevitably, they were influenced not only by their own internal politics and ideological concerns but also by the characteristics of the student movement in the host country and the prevailing political atmosphere. As a result, differences developed between students studying in North America and those in Europe, although most activisits on both sides of the Atlantic declared themselves to be Marxists. Like the American New Left, students in North America endorsed a participatory and democratic concept of socialism, perhaps a romantic version of Maoism. Students in Europe, on the other hand, were closer to the more bureaucratic and disciplined Soviet concept of socialism that characterized the European Communist parties in the 1960's.

These trends were further accentuated in the early 1970's when the established leadership of the Ethiopian student movement in both the United States and Europe was challenged by younger students. Many of them had been at Haile Selassie I University at the time of the 1969 student confrontation with the imperial government, during which the top student association leader was assassinated in Addis Ababa and others were killed in an ensuing demonstration.[3] The challenge to the old leadership did not directly stem from ideological differences, although there were disagreements over the issue of Eritrean secessionism. Mostly, it stemmed from the younger students' impatience with what was considered the authoritarian rule of their seniors. In the United States, the revolt succeeded, and a new leadership took over the movement. In Europe, the attempt failed and the old leaders remained in control. Unbelievably, the position taken by individual students in the dispute became a crucial factor in 1975 in determining who would side with the *Derg* and the opposition. Generally, the old leaders lined up with the military, while the new ones took the opposing side. Within Ethiopia, too, the 1969 confrontation had a strong impact on the student movement. Many students became convinced it was time to move political action outside the university and into government offices and other organizations, the CELU in particular. However, by early 1974, no radical political organization existed outside the campus, and only a few radical individuals in government offices and civilian associations maintained close student contacts.

There were other divisions in the student movement, some simply the result of personality clashes and related power struggles, while others had more ideological origins. One heatedly debated issue on both sides of the Atlantic was whether it was possible to pass directly from feudalism to socialism or whether it was necessary to go through an interim period of capitalism and liberal democracy. This issue took on vital importance after the *Derg* came to power. Probably the most fundamental divisions, however, were ethnic. At Haile Selassie I University in particular, students tended to congregate according to ethnic group, which determined their living arrangements and friendships as well as political allegiance. Eritrean and Tigrean students were perhaps the most ethnically conscious, even refusing to speak Amharic because it was a "colonial" language, and most student meetings were conducted in English. These ethnic divisions were inevitably accentuated by the issue of Eritrean secessionism, over which students were deeply divided despite a surface allegiance they all gave to the Leninist concept of "the right of nations to self-determination." All these fissures in the student movement were transferred with a vengeance to national politics when many former student leaders became involved in the revolution.[4]

Creation of the Political Bureau

In the fall of 1975, the *Derg* started searching for civilian supporters to help form a party in order to enlarge its political base. In a speech on September 11, Brig. Gen. Teferi Bante announced the forthcoming formation of a political party:

> Peasant farmers and workers in urban centers are in the process of organizing themselves in associations with the aim of safeguarding their economic interests and preparing themselves to manage their own affairs. In view of this, the day is not far when peasant farmers, workers and progressive elements will be constituted under one progressive political party to assume the high responsibility of the state.[5]

Teferi's speech suggested that the promised political party would develop out of peasant and urban neighborhood associations, which would somehow be woven into a national organization. The task of forming such a party was entrusted to a secret "Political Bureau" appointed by the *Derg* in December. It is debatable whether there was any alternative to this approach, since the peasant and urban neighborhood associations were still being formed themselves and might not have provided a solid base for a party. But the decision to form a political party from the top created many problems, widening as it did the split already existing between self-governing associations and the centralized national government. In fact, it increased opposition to the *Derg* among civilians who conceived of the revolution as a spontaneous mass movement, not a series of reforms engineered by an elite.

Chairmanship of the Political Bureau was entrusted to Haile Fida, a French-educated Galla who had answered the *Derg*'s appeal for all educated Ethiopians to come home. He soon made himself known to the Addis Ababa public by opening a "Progressive Book Store" just off the university campus where the classics of Marxism-Lenism—and for a period Maoism—were for the first time made available to Ethiopians. The store, a dilapidated old house, was swamped by students, and each new shipment of books was immediately sold out. While selling books, Haile Fida was also getting himself involved in politics as his appointment testified.

It was typical of the secrecy in which the *Derg* cloaked its decisions that neither the creation of the Political Bureau nor the selection of Haile Fida to lead it were announced. Haile had been a leader of the student movement in Europe for many years, and his reputation was based less on ideological brilliance than on skillful political maneuvering. He had lived in France since the early 1960s, and was reportedly quite orthodox in his Marxist approach, closer to Moscow than to the New Left. His long residence abroad made him far more versed in student politics and abstract ideological debate than knowledgeable about concrete conditions at home, a common syndrome among returning students. Recruiting other members to the Political Bureau, however, proved a difficult task. The *Derg* hoped to enlist well-known radical intellectuals, but not all accepted, either for ideological reasons or because they had belonged to factions of the student movement opposed to Haile Fida. For example, one group of candidates refused to serve, explaining in a clandestine pamphlet that they could not accept appointment because they believed it was impossible to build a genuine political party from the top down:

> Organizations of the masses can only be strong and sound when they are established and sustained by active participation of the people; their democratic rights to discuss and organize without pressure being exerted on them must be respected. Organizations established by order of higher authority can only poorly serve the masses and become anti-people. The people who lack political awareness need support and direction, but should participate fully in the political activities of the country. Without this, the few intellectuals who are leaders will not improve the consciousness of the people.[6]

Some intellectuals approached nonetheless accepted positions on the Political Bureau, either out of ideological conviction or fear, or for reasons of political strategy.

The refusal of some intellectuals to join the Political Bureau often reflected more than personal protest: it was part of a deliberate strategy to relaunch the civilian leftist opposition to the *Derg*. While working to transform existing organizations like the CELU into opposition strongholds, the radicals also began organizing a political party of their own. By August 1975, a clandestine Ethiopian People's Revolutionary Party, or EPRP, emerged and circulated its program for the first time. It claimed the party had existed since 1972, and that the clandestine *Democracia,* its official publication, first appeared in early 1974. Though the idea of forming a political party had been under discussion in student circles for several years before the revolution, there are doubts that a "party" organization—as distinct from a small clique of pamphlet-producing intellectuals—existed before 1975. Whatever the exact date, August 1975 marked a turning point in the life of the EPRP, since the public now became aware of its existence and circulation of *Democracia* grew throughout the country.

Ideological Debate

Creation of the Political Bureau did nothing to ease military-civilian relations, since the civilian opposition, far from disappearing, moved from moribund corporate interest groups into the clandestine EPRP. This development split the country's radical forces in two, with the military and a few intellectuals on one side and the vast civilian majority on the other. An intolerable situation faced the revolutionary government. Consequently, the *Derg* attempted to reconcile its civilian opponents by proposing an alliance among it, the Political Bureau, and the EPRP in the general interest of the revolution. Yet, while an ideological affinity existed, it proved insufficient grounds for a reconciliation.

In order to pave the way for the rapprochement, the *Derg* initiated a period of surprisingly free political and ideological debate beginning in February 1976. The columns of the Amharic-language daily *Addis Zemen* were opened to a "revolutionary forum" in which the opinions of supporters and opponents of the *Derg* were freely expressed. Moreover, the government permitted the publication of an Amharic-language monthly, *Dawn,* which took an openly anti-government stance, going so far in its colums as to regularly dub the *Derg* "fascist." The clandestine *Democracia* was also allowed to circulate, apparently with tacit government approval, since it now became easily available. Initially, many tendencies were represented in the debate, even liberal democratic ideas favoring a multi-party system. However, the participants eventually divided into two main groups, one representing the position of the Political Bureau and the other that of the EPRP.

The fundamental choices that other countries in the throes of a socialist revolution have had to face were not part of the Ethiopian debate. The central issue was not whether socialism was possible or desirable; neither was it the question of what type of socialist system the country should have. There was no discussion of the possible alternative of either a highly participatory system based on self-management or a highly centralized system of state-run enterprises. Nor was there any debate about the virtue of peasant collectives versus state farms. And the question of the respective role of party and government in the revolution went unmentioned. Rather, the argument focused on whether the country could move immediately to socialism. The Fidaists asserted that a transition from feudalism to socialism could be forced by making use of military muscle to skip the stage of democratic reformism. Thus, an alliance with the *Derg* was both necessary and acceptable.[7] The military government was not yet "socialist," they believed, but it had taken "progressive" measures, such as land reform and nationalizations. While the arrest of union leaders and students was viewed as repressive, the *Derg*'s overall performance was sufficiently encouraging to justify an alliance. The Fidaists finally argued that by rejecting this strategy in favor of a grassroots mass struggle, the EPRP was taking an anarchist position which would eventually play into the hands of reactionaries.

The EPRP's position, by contrast, was that there was no shortcut to socialism since it could be ushered in only through a mass movement.[8] Such a movement required a transition period of "unlimited democracy" to allow all "anti-feudal" and "anti-imperialist" forces to organize. Such a popular movement had actually started in early 1974 and had gained momentum until it was ruthlessly suppressed by military intervention. In the EPRP's view, any government that crushed a popular uprising was "fascist," and the *Derg* was no exception, despite the progressive veneer it had acquired through economic reforms. The clearest evidence of its repressive tendency was that all reforms, particularly land reform, had in practice been sabotaged by the government. The state had deprived workers of all power in the newly nationalized enterprises and had prevented students from organizing the peasantry in a truly revolutionary manner. "When the peasants are organized, politicized, and armed," they claimed, "the government is afraid."[9] Any alliance with the "elite officers" of the *Derg* and their "running dogs" in the Political Bureau was thus out of the question. The only correct line was to continue the struggle for the formation of a true "provisional people's government," by which the EPRP specifically meant one formed by progressive civilian groups.

Curiously, though the EPRP and the Political Bureau published strikingly similar programs, both ignored the fact that many specific proposals had already been enacted.[10] A notable example was the statement in both documents that land and major industrial enterprises should be nationalized, a measure the *Derg* had taken months earlier. But the issue of whether these nationalized properties should be run by the state or the workers, a dispute still unresolved when the programs were published, received no attention from either group.

Likewise, both programs spelled out virtually identical social and economic goals. Both pledged equality of rights to all religious and tribal groups, equality of the sexes, and the eradication of illiteracy, poverty, and disease. Both promised job opportunities, higher salaries, pension rights, free medical care, and paid annual leave to all workers. Both proposed the nationalization of land and all foreign and other large enterprises, but agreed that small private businesses should be protected. Both programs pledged to free Ethiopia from foreign interference and eliminate foreign bases, by which they meant the American communications station in Asmara.

Despite the many similarities between the Political Bureau and the EPRP, they differed substantially over the role of the military and the type of government that should rule during the transitional period. The EPRP categorically opposed any cooperation with the military and insisted upon the immediate establishment of a "provisional people's government." The Fidaists accepted an alliance with the military as a temporary measure and called in Leninist terms for the formation of a "revolutionary provisional government," which they otherwise named a "national dictatorship."

A difference in revolutionary tactics and theory underlay these conflicting positions. The EPRP conceived of revolution in terms of a mass movement from the bottom up. No such movement ever existed in Ethiopia, however, and the EPRP implicitly recognized this historical fact in drafting its plans for a people's government. Its proposed alliance of workers, peasants, progressive intellectuals, and progressive elements of the petty bourgeoisie was to be implemented through direct interest-group representation. It demanded participation in the government for specific organizations such as the teachers' association, the students' union, the labor confederation, and even ethnic movements such as the Afar Liberation Front and the Tigrean People's Liberation Front. Herein lay a basic ambiguity in the EPRP position: radical in revolutionary orientation, its provisional people's government nonetheless encompassed moderate, sometimes frankly reactionary, groups.

The position of the Political Bureau was probably more coherent, though less democratic. It saw revolution as a process imposed from the top, and thus it accepted, at least temporarily, cooperation with the military and refused any suggestion of interest-group representation in its "national dictatorship." While it agreed with the EPRP that a transitional government should be based on an alliance of workers, peasants, progressive intellectuals and the progressive petty bourgeoisie, it argued that only selected revolutionary elements from these groups should be admitted to a "provisional revolutionary government." The Fidaist government, then, would be made up of individuals rather than groups.[11]

For most Ethiopians, even educated ones, the debate that unfurled in the columns of *Addis Zemen* and in clandestine and official literature was their first exposure to any kind of open political discussion. While many became highly politicized, many others became confused. The theoreticians of the EPRP and the Political Bureau all wrote with lofty disregard for the common level of political education. They talked in terms of fine ideological points taken from the Soviet and Chinese revolutions, a language more appropriate to scholarly debate than to general public discussion. Those who had not been involved in the student movement were unlikely to understand the different choices implicit in the political slogans. For months there was an unreal quality about the whole debate, as if intellectuals played revolutionary games and imagined themselves as modern-day Maos, Lenins, and Marxes. The Political Bureau ideologues came to view themselves as the revolution's "Bolsheviks" and denigrated their EPRP opponents as "Mensheviks." The EPRP leaders, however, saw themselves not as Mensheviks but as Maoists.

Despite such ideological name-calling, a great deal of duplication occurred in slogans and theories. An outside observer saw no profound and clear differences. But theoreticians on both sides proved deadly serious about their beliefs, to the point of being ready to kill and die for them. The entire Ethiopian intelligentsia was forced to immerse itself in Marxism-Leninism, whether individuals believed in it or not. The authors met Ethiopian university professors who were wholly confused by political arguments and had to ransack the classics in search of enlightenment. Third and fourth year university students would provide us with excellent literal translations of articles in *Addis Zemen* and of underground pamphlets and then confess they had little idea what the arguments were really about. Even those in charge of translations at the Ethiopian News Agency admitted that they could not always grasp the meaning of the more theoretical government statements emanating from the Political Bureau.

Inevitably, the confusion over ideological arguments engendered simplistic ad hoc interpretations of the differences between the EPRP and the Political Bureau. The most prevalent one was that the split represented ethnic, not ideological, differences. The Political Bureau and its supporters were the "Galla faction," and the EPRP and its backers were Amharas and Tigreans reacting against the rise to power of the Gallas. Even among those who interpreted the split ideologically, the subtleties were often lost, and they tended to explain the differences in terms of a "democratic" EPRP versus a "fascist" Political Bureau.

The National Democratic Revolution

After three months of public debate, the *Derg* made its grand bid for a reconciliation of all progressive elements in the country. Major Mengistu appeared on television on April 20, 1976, to announce the launching of a "national democratic revolution" that would pave the way for "scientific socialism" and a "people's democratic republic." The vanguard of the revolution was to be a "party of the working class" whose "unrestricted democratic rights" would be guaranteed. In his speech, Major Mengistu called for the creation of a "national revolutionary front" to implement the national democratic revolution's program and to "take the broad masses to the point where they can run their own affairs." The main aims of the program were:

... complete elimination of feudalism, bureaucratic capitalism and imperialism from the country, to build a new people's Ethiopia on solid foundations through the concerted collaboration among anti-feudalist and anti-imperialist forces and to pave the way for a transition toward socialism. To this end, a People's Democratic Republic will be established in Ethiopia under the leadership of the proletariat in close collaboration with the farmers, the support of the petty bourgeois, anti-feudalist and anti-imperialist forces to guarantee to the Ethiopian people their right to freedom, equality, unity, peace and prosperity as well as self-administration at various levels and unrestricted human and democratic rights.[12]

The task of educating the masses was to be entrusted to a People's Organizing Provisional Office.[13] This organization was supposed to create a nation-wide network of cadres in preparation for the establishment of a political party. A fifteen-member Political Bureau, called the Supreme Organizing Committee, was to head the Organizing Office, but would remain under the control of the head of state or, de facto, the *Derg.*

The national democratic revolution program included practically all the EPRP's demands: a Marxist ideology, a working class party, unlimited democratic rights, and the creation of a united front. In fact, the call for a national democratic revolution was taken from the EPRP program. The term was originally used by Mao Tse-Tung to indicate an alliance of all anti-feudal and anti-imperialist forces necessary as a preliminary step toward a socialist revolution at the time of Japan's invasion of China. The idea of such a revolution in Ethiopia had been propounded both by the Political Bureau in its program and by the EPRP in the resolutions passed by the CELU and the Ethiopian Teachers' Association, as well as in the party's clandestine publications. Since the two civilian leftist factions advocated a national democratic revolution, the *Derg* undoubtedly thought that it would prove a sound and acceptable ideological basis for a reconciliation between the government and its opponents.

But the proclamation of the revolution and the call for a national revolutionary front did not rally the EPRP to the *Derg*'s side. The party's answer, circulated in an issue of *Democracia* a few weeks after Mengistu's speech, stated that a "national democratic revolution" could be accepted in principle. However, the EPRP set such stringent preconditions that cooperation in practice was impossible.[14] Despite a similarity in verbiage, the EPRP's reply continued to betray profound conceptual differences. *Democracia* proclaimed, like the *Derg,* that the revolution should be carried out through the formation of a united front consisting of "the vanguard of the proletariat, the peasantry, the petty bourgeoisie and other oppressed people."[15] But in listing "anti-feudal" and "anti-imperialist" groups that should belong to the front, the EPRP enumerated every opposition group and deliberately excluded the *Derg.*[16] Its front would comprise virtually all ethnic "liberation" groups, including some very obscure ones, and organizations such as the CELU, the student union, peasant associations, and the women's association organized by *zemacha* students. It made no mention of the new Organizing Office or the already existing Political Bureau, clearly excluding any organization supporting the military. Furthermore, it demanded the immediate establishment of a "provisional people's government."

As a result of the EPRP's intransigence, the proclamation of a "national democratic revolution" led not to a reconciliation between the military and the civilian leftist factions but to a split within the opposition's ranks. The *Derg* retained only the support of the Political Bureau, and even this relationship eventually proved double-edged. It became clear that on one hand not all *Derg* members could accept an alliance with the Political Bureau, and on the other, that the Political Bureau was evidently hoping to use the alliance as a tactical step toward eliminating the *Derg* and instituting civilian rule under its authority. Many *Derg* members suspected the alliance with the Political Bureau as an attempt by Mengistu to extend his personal power base beyond the *Derg,* and by doing so, to bolster his dominant position within it. The fact that he alone, rather than the council's chairman, General Teferi, or a group of *Derg* members presented the idea of a national democratic revolution on television suggested strongly that not all of the ruling officers supported an opening toward the civilian left and that Mengistu and his supporters had pushed this strategy through.[17]

A second serious problem in the *Derg*-Political Bureau alliance was that each had differing views on the role of the party. The Fidaists intended the party to become quickly the most powerful revolutionary institution; the *Derg* was extremely ambiguous on this crucial point, showing great reluctance to hand over any real power to the Organizing Office. In fact, the proclamation begged the question by stating that the Office was a "provisional" institution under the *Derg*'s control. There was no indication what the future relationship between the military council and the party would be. On this issue, the Political Bureau and the *Derg* were soon at loggerheads. In their official capacity as members of the Political Bureau, the Fidaists quickly set up cells of the Organizing Office throughout the country, and in less than a year, a skeleton of a party existed in all *woredas* and *awrajas.* Unofficially, they were also busy setting up their own party. The All Ethiopian Socialist Movement (Me'ei Sone, or MEISON), which they obviously intended to become eventually socialist Ethiopia's ruling institution. As a result, the allegiance of the Organizing Office was very dubious. Its cadres were trained at an ideological school in Addis Ababa supported by the *Derg* but staffed mostly by MEISON elements. Some of the Office's cells were pro-military, but the majority was part of MEISON, which, like the *Derg,* preferred to work behind the scenes. Its membership remained between twelve and fifteen, its composition changing somewhat over time as new members were admitted and old ones defected or were killed. The complete membership list was never made public, and until Haile Fida was officially mentioned as chairman of the Political Bureau in April 1977, the only published names were those of assassinated victims of the EPRP.[18] In addition to Haile Fida, two other French-educated intellectuals, both Amharas, played key roles. They were Negede Gobeze and Fikre Merid, who as vice-chairman became widely regarded as the group's leading theoretician until gunned down by EPRP terrorists in October 1976. His place was then taken by Senay Likie, an American-educated Galla, whom Mengistu apparently used as a counterforce to Haile Fida before he, too, was killed.

Another important clique, consisting of Wondwossen Haile, Mesfin Kassu, and Tamrat Kebede, was made up of American-trained Amharas who had been working in the Ministry of Land Reform before the revolution. Tamrat Kebede left Political Bureau circles after a few months to become head of the state farm section in the Ministry of Agriculture.

The Political Bureau has been characterized as dominated by Gallas, by intellectuals trained in Western Europe, or by both. None of these descriptions is accurate. While Haile Fida himself was both Galla and French-educated, no more than half the membership was Galla and most were American-trained. When weighed against the traditional government predominance of Amharas and Tigreans, however, the number of Gallas is significant. One common characteristic among all members was their many years' experience abroad—in fact, almost none had received his higher education inside Ethiopia. They were also exceptionally young. Few had worked for long, and some had never even held a regular job. More importantly, none had any experience in politics or organizing outside the student movement.

The Political Bureau members played a risky game, and with an arrogance, typical of so many in the Ethiopian elite, that they would prevail over their adversaries because of an inherent superiority. A parallel exists here between their attitude toward the military and that earlier of the Ethiopian aristocracy: both misjudged the strength of the *Derg,* the aristocrats because its members were mostly lowly sergeants and corporals and the Fidaists because they were so ideologically unsophisticated.

The Political Bureau worked closely with Mengistu in the belief that he could be easily manipulated. As it turned out, Mengistu was a cunning politician despite a scant formal education and lack of political experience. Nevertheless, the Political Bureau's relationship with him contributed to splitting the *Derg* and succeeded in forcing the government to harden its position toward the EPRP. Bureau members' hatred for their former fellow students, amply reciprocated, was the kind found only among once-close allies who have fallen out. This visceral hatred between "enemy brothers" gave the period of terror and counterterror its particularly vicious character.

The EPRP

The 1976 ideological debate unintentionally increased the importance and popularity of the Ethiopian People's Revolutionary Party. The debate gave it exposure it had never before enjoyed and a chance to explain party ideas and demands to those who did not normally read underground political tracts. Consequently, the EPRP grew overnight into a prominent national organization with cells in all the major towns and cities as well as in a few rural areas. It still operated as a clandestine party, and although generally known in student circles, the names of its leaders were kept secret. Despite its rapid growth, new recruits probably all did not understand or share the ideological position of the EPRP. Party converts came from nearly all sectors. Their only common element was an intense dislike of military rule. Many conservatives, for example, declared their support for the EPRP in the hope that it would engineer the downfall of the *Derg* and open the way for a more moderate civilian regime.

Despite its soft outer shell, the EPRP had a large hard core of followers organized in an extensive network of cells which were located in most high schools and institutions of higher learning, in many ministries and other large government agencies in Addis Ababa, in some military units (notably in the Air Force), and in most unions, particularly those of white collar or technical workers. The support of high school students was a great asset, since it gave the EPRP a presence in smaller towns like Jimma, Dessie, or Dire Dawa where it might not have existed otherwise. Equally crucial for the party was the support it enjoyed at the highest levels of government, including inside the *Derg*. Despite its anti-military statements, the EPRP was known to have a faction of supporters in the *Derg*, including officers who favored a return to civilian rule and those who saw the EPRP as a possible ally against Mengistu and the Political Bureau.

The EPRP had its weaknesses too. Its influence in the countryside was very limited. Its foothold in the Chilalo District was due to the presence of EPRP members inside the Chilalo Agricultural Development Unit (CADU). It also had some influence among the agricultural extension agents of EPID, but little if any among peasant associations. Another major weakness of the party related to its petty bourgeois social base. In the labor unions, for instance, its support was concentrated among white collar and technical workers. Calls for strikes and anti-government demonstrations were almost always answered in greatest number by the well-paid employees of Ethiopian Airlines, banks, insurance companies, and the Board of Telecommunications. Such a narrow social base later made the EPRP vulnerable to accusations that it represented the "reactionary petty bourgeoisie."

Although much EPRP support may have come from middle-class moderates, its leaders were dedicated socialists, but no more radical than those of the Political Bureau. Leaders of the two factions came from the same educational background. American-trained student leaders were in both, although those educated in Western Europe tended to side with the Political Bureau. In some cases, leaders of the Political Bureau and the EPRP were close personal friends who agonized together over which group to join and remained in close contact at least until the onset of terrorism. Like those who joined the Political Bureau, many EPRP leaders had been offered and had accepted positions in the government when the *Derg* came to power. A number of *awraja* and *woreda* administrators and land reform officials appointed in March 1975 were EPRP members, some of whom were later removed from their posts for having abetted the activities of the most radical *zemacha* students. The administrator of Soddo *woreda,* Melaku Gebre Egziahber, a well-known former student activist at Haile Selassie I University, was arrested for encouraging peasants and the urban lumpenproletariat to turn against "exploiters" in the town of Soddo. Gebru Mersha, another prominent student leader at the university in the 1960's who had been plucked from an obscure position in the Ministry of Transportation and made the administrator of Zwai *awraja,* abandoned this post and went to Tigre Province where he took up arms against the goverment. In some cases, EPRP leaders chose to flee the country altogether. Such was the case of Henock Kifle, an American-trained economist whom the *Derg* had made executive director of CADU and then permanent secretary of the Ministry of Agriculture. While on a government mission to Scandinavia in the spring of 1976, he resigned his job and left for the United States.

After mid-1976, EPRP leaders started abandoning their government jobs in increasing numbers and went underground. Some stayed in Addis Ababa, where they organized the party's terrorist network. Others drifted to Tigre Province, where the party set up an Ethiopian People's Revolutionary Army (EPRA) and opened a small "front." The organization's *maquis* was first located in Tigre because it depended on supplies from the Eritrean Popular Liberation Forces. The locale helped to confirm the public belief that the EPRP was a Tigrean-Amhara ethnic front which opposed the Galla-dominated Political Bureau. As the EPRP came under increasing government pressure, exigencies of survival pushed it to form alliances of a dubious ideological nature with other opposition groups. It not only became allied to the EPLF and the TPLF, with which it shared common ideological beliefs, but also dealt with the Afar Liberation Front, Sultan Ali Mirah's reactionary group, with which it had nothing in common except opposition to the *Derg.*

From National Democratic Revolution to Terrorism

The era of "the hundred flowers" waned rapidly after Mengistu's speech in April and the EPRP's unequivocal refusal to cooperate with the military. The EPRP and the Political Bureau from that time on devoted energies to strengthening their positions vis-a-vis each other and the *Derg.* The Political Bureau had an enormous advantage over its civilian rival since it was authorized to establish branches of the Organizing Offices in all *awrajas* and *woredas.* It also ran the party's ideological school; it organized bi-weekly political sessions or "workers' forums" in government offices, factories, and army units; and it had an official voice in making government policy.[19] Such opportunities were used as much to strengthen MEISON as to create wider support for the *Derg.* In order to build up their own party, the Fidaists created a core of supporters within each ministry who carried out directives, and identified and eliminated EPRP members. They effectively undermined lines of command in most ministries and government offices and created an atmosphere of suspicion and uncertainty. The Political Bureau also made a major effort to establish a hold over the media, and although never completely succeeding, it acquired enormous influence, particularly in the radio and television services.

A turning point in the three-way contest involving the *Derg,* the Political Bureau, and the EPRP occurred in July 1976 when the power struggle within the *Derg* led to the arrest and execution of one of its most prominent members, Captain Sisay Habte, head of the Political Affairs Committee.[20] Sisay had been regarded as hostile to the Political Bureau and sympathetic to the EPRP. Mengistu and the Political Bureau denounced him for leading a "counterrevolutionary plot." The government statement insinuated that he had ties with the Central Intelligence Agency, and it drew a parallel between Chile and Ethiopia, both victims of "destabilization" campaigns. It was not long before the EPRP was also denounced in the state-controlled press as a machination of the CIA, an accusation that did more harm to Ethiopian-American relations than to the EPRP itself.

After its rejection of the national democratic revolution, the EPRP had returned underground. It continued to publish *Democracia* and other pamphlets, but a less tolerant attitude of the *Derg* and the Political Bureau made distribution more difficult. The public's interest in ideological debates began to wane, and street boys peddling magazines complained that *Revolutionary Ethiopia,* the official publication of the Organizing Office, and *Dawn,* the unofficial monthly of the EPRP, no longer found a ready market. However, this lessening of public interest did not reflect an intense but quiet preparation for street combat and terror. Once again, the civilian left chose to time a new offensive against the *Derg* with the anniversary of the revolution. Aware of this, the government acted first and arrested a number of student and labor union activists. As a result, the second anniversary celebrations on September 12 passed without a major incident, despite an EPRP attempt to get all workers to boycott the parade. Only unions representing Ethiopian Airlines, the banks and insurance companies, the Ethiopian Electric Light and Power Company and the Board of Telecommunications heeded the boycott call. The enthusiasm shown by many paraders, particularly by blue collar workers, suggested that the *Derg* had gained new supporters.

The EPRP soon stepped up its activities. It instigated a work slowdown in the telecommunications offices, suspiciously frequent electric power failures, and unexplained interruptions in the water supply. Then on September 22, it tried to organize a general strike to protest, of all things, the issuing of new banknotes without the face of Haile Selassie on them. The measure penalized exclusively those wealthy Ethiopians who had withdrawn money from the banks out of a fear that their accounts would be frozen. Only bills of large denomination were exchanged at less than par value.[21] But the EPRP decided to use the occasion to turn public discontent into open protest. Once again, only workers in the banks, insurance companies, the electric power company, and the telecommunications offices responded, and their participation failed to cripple any of these public services.

The EPRP now resorted to a new tactic of protest, urban terrorism or "armed struggle." On the night of September 23, an attempt was made to ambush Major Mengistu in the center of Addis Ababa. He was barely grazed by a bullet, although several bodyguards were wounded and his jeep badly damaged. It was a daring opening shot in its new campaign of terrorism, one that boomeranged in favor of Mengistu and the *Derg*. The government staged massive demonstrations in the following days to show its wide support and the impossibility for assassination to reverse the course of the revolution. Meanwhile, a new wave of arrests began. Suspected EPRP members and sympathizers were indiscriminately picked up in the streets and bars in Addis Ababa and sometimes executed on the spot without formalities. The EPRP reacted by stepping up its own terrorism, sending murder squads around the city to eliminate supporters of the Political Bureau. At least several hundred were slain during this terrible period. People were gunned down in streets and bars, and mutilated bodies were retrieved from under bridges and shallow graves. The EPRP hit important targets, such as the second-ranking man in the Political Bureau, Fikre Merid, who was killed in downtown Addis Ababa on October 2. If security officers managed to arrest or kill prominent EPRP leaders, they did not announce it, and the public was impressed by the apparent strength of the clandestine opposition.

The wave of terrorism also revealed the strained relations between the Political Bureau and the *Derg*. Anti-Mengistu military council members felt that the campaign against the EPRP only served Political Bureau interests. They argued that the real quarrel was not between the EPRP and the *Derg*, but between the EPRP and the Political Bureau. For a while, their views prevailed and attacks against the EPRP in the mass media, which had started in the summer, practically ceased in late October. The most strident accusations against the CIA and Western imperialism also disappeared from the press. The *Derg* began breaking up Fidaist cliques in government offices, and from October 1976 to February 1977, the fortunes of the Political Bureau were on the wane.

9.   The *Derg*

When the *Derg* was first mentioned in the summer of 1974, a joke circulating in Addis Ababa went, "Who is this *Leul* (Prince) *Derg*? We never knew the Emperor had a son by this name." The mysteries of the *Derg* and the myths surrounding it were always among its most striking characteristics. Partly, this was fostered by an Ethiopian love of mystery, plot, and intrigue—the more convoluted, the better. But it is also true that the atmosphere was deliberately cultivated by the *Derg*. It never officially announced the names of its members, their number, or the posts they occupied. The *Derg*'s secrecy gave it a flexibility in changing internal structures and appointments without having to explain them to the public, thereby preserving its image of unity. Thus, information about the *Derg* always came indirectly—a passing reference in the newspapers to a committee chairman giving a speech in some small town, the name of a new committee buried inside an article, the name of a new officer mentioned as carrying out a mission abroad or in the countryside. There may be few Ethiopians who today still regard the *Derg* as a bastard child of the Emperor, but its mysteries still abound.

One of the most persistent myths about the *Derg* was that it would not last long. Foreign diplomats from East and West vied in predicting the date of its downfall, some timing it to the next rainy season, others to the end of the harvest; some to an EDU offensive, others to an offensive by the EPRP. Although the *Derg* lasted for years, it acted with a sense of urgency that suggested it, too, believed in its imminent overthrow. "Stop arguing and get going," Major Mengistu was once reported as reprimanding one of his lieutenants, "tomorrow we may not be here." Whether or not the quote is authentic, the *Derg* always acted with a sense of urgency, apparently oblivious to the problems a hasty decision taken today might cause tomorrow. There is no understanding the rush of revolutionary measures of 1975 without taking into account this atmosphere of impending doom; the *Derg* felt it had an historic mission to carry out and little time to do it.

The *Derg* came increasingly to see itself as part of a socialist revolutionary tradition rather than a localized Ethiopian movement. Although in July 1974 it had declared, "the culture and history of Ethiopia are unique, and so is the nature and course of this movement,"[1] by 1977 it saw itself as a link in the revolutionary network ranging from the Soviet Union to Cuba, from China to Vietnam. "The Ethiopian Revolution is not only an event of national and continental scope and consequence in the Horn of Africa, it is part and stage of a world socialist revolution in a war against the international conspiracy and coalition of the imperialists and reactionaries in the contemporary world as a whole."[2] Ethiopia, like Cuba, was a revolutionary island surrounded by reactionaries.[3] The "white terror" of the royalists was matched by the "red terror" of the revolution, as in the Soviet Union,[4] just as the "white army" of the EDU would be crushed by the "red army" of the *Derg*.[5] The former slogan *Ethiopia Tikdem* gave way to the cry of "Revolutionary Motherland or Death."[6]

Like other revolutionaries before them, *Derg* officers discovered that revolution was no "tea party," to cite Mao's famous comment, and that it tended to devour its own children. The illusion that there could be such a thing as revolution without bloodshed vanished before the determination of the opposition, the vindictiveness of the revolutionaries, and the power struggle within their ranks. It became clear that only force could prevail over the revolution's enemies. Externally, the country was surrounded by hostile neighbors seeking the overthrow of the *Derg* and backing elements opposed to the revolution. Internally, various conservative opposition groups grew in size and fighting ability, and mounting nationalism threatened to tear the former empire asunder. The *Derg* came under increasing pressure from the left from both its own civilian allies in the Political Bureau and its opponents in the EPRP to carry out new and more radical reforms. These conflicts and pressures served to fuel the power struggle among *Derg* officers. There was a series of crises—attempted coups and countercoups—in which the most radical faction always emerged victorious. Consequently, the general tendency of revolutions to undergo a period of extreme radicalism, even terror, and the specifics of the power struggle within the *Derg* helped to push Ethiopia ever further leftward. Like the French, the Ethiopian revolution had its Jacobin era, and Mengistu was its Robespierre.

This radicalization took place in three stages. The first began with the military's seizure of power in June 1974 and ended with the execution of General Aman, the *Derg*'s first chairman, in November. It was a period of moderation, caution, and reformism, which created a split between the radical and moderate factions. The second stage lasted from Aman's death until the announcement of the "national democratic revolution" in April 1976. This was the period during which the revolution quickened and the radical faction consolidated itself by pushing through a series of far-reaching economic and political reforms. Despite continuing tensions between moderates and radicals, the military council maintained a degree of unity, or at least a facade of unity. The third stage, from the beginning of the national democratic revolution until Mengistu's "coup" of February 3, 1977, was marked by a violent struggle for power among the radicals, the death of many prominent members of the *Derg,* and the concentration of power in the hands of one man. It was the end of collegiality as the *Derg*'s guiding principle of government. The power struggle that led to Mengistu's victory did not remain an internal affair but involved an increasing number of civilians—the Political Bureau, the EPRP, the peasant militia, urban defense squads, trade unions, and even high schools. By spring, the entire country was caught up in the struggle for or against the revolution, or in one of the ethnic nationalist movements tearing at the fabric of the nation.

Internal Tensions and External Issues

It is impossible to explain the power struggle that shook the *Derg* periodically or the peculiar behavior of this awkward ruling body without understanding some basic tensions within it. The PMAC was initially a very large committee with no formal structure or rules. It had a mixed membership in terms of level of education, professional training, and ethnic background. It included illiterate peasants along with men who held law and business degrees; commissioned officers from the elite Harar Military Academy were mixed with noncommissioned officers of the Holetta (Guenet) Military School; and Galla NCO's found themselves working with Amhara and Tigrean officers.

Perhaps the most important problem involved transforming an inchoate body of more than 100 men into a structured organization capable of making decisions on a daily basis. From the beginning, there were proposals to disband the military council and form instead a small junta of twelve to fifteen officers. General Aman had pushed this idea, with dire consequences. After half a century of centralized and authoritarian rule under Haile Selassie, there was strong sentiment in favor of broad collegial rule within the *Derg,* particularly among lower-ranking officers who feared they would be easily cast aside. The concept of the *Derg* as a body representing all units of the armed forces required of necessity a large membership. Nevertheless, if the *Derg* were to reach necessary and important decisions, some form of internal hierarchy had to exist in order to avoid debate by the full body on every issue. This meant setting up committees and electing chairmen, thus making some *Derg* members more powerful than other. Inevitably, an inner group of committee chairmen emerged within the *Derg* to make routine decisions, and even some very important ones. Within this group the *Derg*'s two vice-chairmen constantly violated the principle of collegiality and tried to concentrate power in their own hands. The trend toward elitism periodically stirred reaction from rank-and-file members of the *Derg.* So strong were these revolts that Mengistu and Atnafu would at times disappear from the public eye for long periods of time and rumors flew about Addis Ababa that they had been placed under house arrest by their colleagues. Whether either of them was at any time is not known for certain. But it was certainly true that their reins were periodically pulled in. For example, from the fall of 1975 until April 1976,

Mengistu kept a very low profile, and only resurfaced when he announced the national democratic revolution.

Conflict between lower and upper *Derg* echelons was compounded by a wide difference in rank and education. The majority of them were NCOs and graduates of the less prestigious Holetta Military School near Addis Ababa,[7] but committee chairmen tended to be commissioned officers with degrees from the elite Harar Military Academy, Haile Selassie I University, or foreign academies. Two major exceptions were Majors Mengistu and Atnafu, both graduates of Holetta; this less prestigious background gave them greater strength within the *Derg*. In fact, it was widely believed among Western military attachés that there existed a kind of vendetta between Holetta graduates and Harar alumni, led by Mengistu. Whether or not such a vendetta existed, after February 1977 there were hardly any Harar graduates left among the officers holding high positions in the *Derg*.

The *Derg* also suffered from ethnic conflicts, which overlapped to some extent differences in education and rank. This was because there were always more Amharas and Tigreans attending Harar, while Holetta was more of a "Galla school." This, in turn, reflected the educational system which favored Amharas and Tigreans while discriminating against Gallas. Relations among even the *Derg*'s top officers were often given an ethnic interpretation by Ethiopians. For example, the conflict between Mengistu and Atnafu was seen as part of the struggle between Gallas and Amharas. Atnafu was an Amhara from Gojjam, while Mengistu was regarded as a Galla. At one point, a large number of committee chairmen were Gojjames, and rumors circulated that a "Gojjame cabal" would take control.[8]

The importance of the ethnic factor within the *Derg* was illustrated by the case of Brigadier General Teferi Bante. Just after being named chairman, he changed the spelling of this name slightly to strengthen the impression that he was of Amhara rather than Galla origin.[9] His exact origins remain unclear, but he chose to identify with the Amhara camp. Perhaps the clearest example of the importance attached to ethnic background was Major Mengistu. To Amharas and Tigreans he was a *baria*—a black-skinned slave from the deep south. Much of the dislike for him among many Addis Ababans was based on his physical characteristics—his dark skin and large lips immediately identified him as one of the empire's conquered subjects and thus an upstart by definition. Major Atnafu was also regarded as an upstart because of his low social origins, but at least he was an Amhara.

Another underlying tension within the *Derg* stemmed from its relation with units of the armed forces. Originally, members of the *Derg* had been haphazardly elected by the various military units to be *their* representatives to the Coordinating Committee of the Armed Forces, Police, and Territorial Army. When the committee became the Provisional Military Administrative Council, the relation between *Derg* members and their respective units changed. They were no longer representatives with a limited mandate, but members of a new self-appointed body arrogating to itself the right to rule the country. Not all units were willing to accept such a transformation, particularly since it occurred without new elections. After the Emperor's overthrow, some units within the Air Force, the Army Corps of Engineers, and the Army Aviation dissented openly by joining with civilians' demands for a people's government. Although it was soon abandoned by most military units, the demand was periodically reiterated by some elements of the Air Force.

With time, ties between military units and the *Derg* became increasingly loose. The military was never called upon again to reelect its representatives, and some *Derg* members, including Mengistu himself, refused to be called back by their respective units, arguing that they were no longer merely representatives of a unit but leaders of a revolutionary movement. In effect, it was the transformation from a concept of government based on interest-group representation to that of a "provisional revolutionary government," albeit a purely military one. As we have argued, the *Derg* did cease to represent only the interests of the military, as it was clearly demonstrated in the case of land reform, when it overruled petitions submitted by units of the Second and Third Divisions to increase the size of the maximum holding. It would be an exaggeration, however, to state that the PMAC had lost all contact with, or the support of, units in the field after the first few months. It is true that some units were chronically dissatisfied, particularly the Second Division, which was stationed in Eritrea and demoralized by the deteriorating situation. The Third Division, too, was a center of discontent because it was living in terrible conditions in the Ogaden and facing an escalating guerrilla war from Somali-backed insurgents. But such dissatisfaction was handled through petitions and visits from delegations to the *Derg*'s headquarters in Addis Ababa, and in no instance was the government threatened with mutiny as in early 1974. Considering how easily the Second Division could have seized the radio in Asmara and publicly challenged the *Derg*, the fact that this never happened was one proof of the success of the conciliatory tactics worked out by the officers. It was also true, however, that most military units were so internally divided by the revolution that it was difficult for them to act against the *Derg*.

Another reason why the *Derg* succeeded in avoiding a military revolt was that dissatisfied units invariably found spokesmen within its membership. When the Second Division sent delegations to Addis Ababa to demand either substantial reinforcements or negotiations to end the civil war in Eritrea, as did periodically occur, their position was always supported by a *Derg* faction. Similarly, when elements in the Air Force became mutinous in June 1976 over the issue of establishing a people's government, they found backing for their demands at the highest level of the council. Issues that could have provoked an open conflict between the *Derg* and military units and led to a coup were internalized and transformed into a conflict among the *Derg*'s various factions. Consequently, the plots that occasionally shook the *Derg* were hatched by insiders, not outsiders. Its very size and the lack of consensus on key issues among its members prevented the spread of private quarrels beyond the confines of the Council. This meant, however, that as the *Derg* was reduced to a smaller and somewhat more homogeneous group as a result of internal power struggles, it also became much more open to the danger of a coup by outside elements. Thus, the smaller, more coherent *Derg* led by Mengistu after the showdown of February 1977 was much more vulnerable than the conflict-ridden assembly of 120 officers that had governed the country in the fall of 1974.

There were also disagreements about some of the major policy choices the country faced, which helped to fuel the power struggle. Nonetheless, they were not always a major factor in the various attempts at coups and counter-coups as might have been expected. For example, dissension over the *Derg*'s Eritrean policy was constant during the first three years of the revolution. There was always a faction that favored a military solution and another pushing for a negotiated settlement. This sometimes caused the *Derg* to follow the two policies simultaneously, such as in the spring of 1976 when it offered a nine-point program for a peaceful resolution of the Eritrean conflict, while at the same time organizing a peasant "red march" to eliminate the guerrillas. Yet in three years of ever-worsening conflict in the northern province, the *Derg* was never split apart by this issue. Another issue with great potential for conflict within the *Derg* was the reversal of Ethiopia's traditional foreign alliances, from the West to the East, and specifically from the United States to the Soviet Union. The switch involved the extremely delicate problem of changing the military's supply of arms and ammunitions at a time when the country was in mid-war. Yet it did not lead to an open break in the *Derg*'s ranks.

These issues, major as they were, did not prove explosive because they did not affect the balance of power among leading officers of the *Derg* but the survival of them all. The most divisive issues proved to be precisely those that threatened this balance. When one faction or individual stood clearly to gain from a particular decision, such as how to deal with the civilian left or whether or not to arm urban defense squads—particularly in Addis Ababa where the *Derg* had its headquarters—there could be no compromise. Those favoring an opening to the EPRP were immediately suspected by their opponents of seeking to establish a power base; those who tried to arm urban defense squads were resisted by others for fear they would use this militia for their own purposes.

First Organization of the *Derg*

When the formation of the PMAC was first announced, no information whatsoever was disclosed about its structure, and there was even some confusion about whether General Aman Michael Andom was its "chairman" or its "spokesman." Only the volume of traffic passing through the gates of the old Menelik Palace compound revealed that the *Derg* maintained its offices there. The existence of first and second vice-chairmen became known only indirectly much later, although the name of Major Mengistu surfaced early as a key figure in the council.

The secrecy with which the *Derg* hid its operations partly stemmed from internal disagreements, and there is every indication that the organization of its various offices and committees was a slow and delicate process, involving an enormous number of meetings and long discussions among its more than 100 members. The fact that the council turned twice to an outsider to fill the post of chairman suggests just how sensitive the officers were to the idea that one of them would be raised above the others. Suspicions about the power of the chairman increased after the *Derg*'s experience with General Aman, who tried to use the position to destroy the organization. This led to the choice of Brigadier General Teferi Bante, an individual with no apparent personal ambitions, as the *Derg*'s second chairman. Nonetheless, suspicion among lower ranking members about the top leadership burst out in periodic revolts.

During the first two years, the *Derg*'s structure consisted of a chairman, a first vice-chairman, a second vice-chairman, subordinate committees and subcommittees, and a general assembly which included the entire membership. The committee heads, numbering from eight to twelve, formed a de facto executive council, though it would be two years before it was formally constituted. Ad hoc committees were occasionally set up, such as those established for the *zemacha* and the first peasant march. Key permanent standing committees included political and foreign affairs, administration, legal affairs, social and economic affairs, defense, information and public affairs and public security.[10] The officers who headed these seven committees constituted, with the chairman and two vice-chairmen, the *Derg*'s inner core. Because of their power, a number of these personalities should be discussed in greater detail.

Brigadier General Teferi Bante. Born near Addis Ababa in 1921, he was generally considered a Galla, although he implicitly denied such an origin by changing his name to a more Amharic spelling. He joined the army when he was twenty, graduated from the Holetta (Guenet) Military School, and served in various posts in the Second, Third, and Fourth Divisions as well as in the central ground forces command. He was commanding the Second Division in Asmara when appointed chairman of the PMAC in November 1974. He was considered a model career officer, and Mengistu himself praised him for being "untainted with selfish interest" throughout his long career in the armed forces.[11] At first a neutral and powerless figure, Teferi was eventually built up to become the *Derg*'s central leader by Mengistu's opponents. To the end, he was too colorless, soft-spoken, and undemonstrative to be the figurehead of the revolution. He primarily supported the nationalist rather than the socialist strain in the *Derg*.

Major Mengistu Haile Mariam (lieutenant colonel after November 1976). There are conflicting reports about his origins, including his birthdate. He is variously reported born in 1940 or in 1942. He is often, though incorrectly, called a Galla. His mother apparently belonged to the Konso tribe of southern Gemu—Gofa Province. His father, probably an Amhara, was reportedly first a sergeant in the army, and then a *zabanya,* or house guard, for the well-known family of *Dejazmatch* Kebede in Addis Ababa. Mengistu thus grew up partly in army camps around the country and party within the compound of an aristocratic family. He attended the Holetta Military School and went twice to the United States for ordnance training, his specialty. He was serving as chief ordnance officer for the Third Division based in Harar in 1974. According to an officer who served under him, he was a good commander but was given to bouts of drinking and disorderly conduct. He was once reportedly accused of irregularities in the handling of spare parts and even court-martialed, but later pardoned by the division's commander, General Nega Tegegne, who would later become the EDU's top military strategist. Although Mengistu has little formal education, probably not even a high school degree, he has repeatedly impressed foreigners as intelligent and capable of understanding complicated matters. Some Ethiopians have attributed his success to a capacity to take decisive action while his opponents hesitated, a quality that also played a role in Emperor Haile Selassie's rise to power. There is little doubt about his personal ambition, natural cunning, and ruthlessness. More than any other top ranking *Derg* officer, Mengistu seemed to symbolize the revolution. He was the *baria,* the slave who overthrew the master, the member of a conquered tribe who got even with the conquerors, the poorly educated son of a servant who rose against the intellectual elite.

Major Atnafu Abate (lieutenant colonel after April 1975). A symbol of the rebellion of a conservative, nationalistic, and religious peasantry against the corruption and abuses of the aristocracy, Atnafu was born near Bichena in Gojjam Province in the late 1930s. He early projected the image of the officer devoted to the traditional values of motherland, flag, and church. Shortly after the revolution, he kept close ties with the church and even probably prevented the arrest of the Patriarch, *Abuna* Tewoflos, in the fall of 1974. He belonged to the Fourth Division based in the capital, but relatively little else has been published about his military career. He obviously had some unusual qualities which enabled him to establish himself so early as one of the *Derg*'s leading figures. One of these was an organizing ability, which led him to play a key role in the initial establishment of the *Derg* in June 1974 and later in the formation of the peasant militia. He was regarded for a time as the revolution's hangman, but this ruthless image later passed to Mengistu. The relationship between the two vice-chairmen was always slightly mysterious. The two were rumored to be bitter enemies from the beginning, to the point of pulling guns on each other in meetings. Yet, Atnafu seemed always to be on Mengistu's side at times of major crisis within the *Derg*. In terms of their ethnic background and public appeal, they complemented each other, and both probably realized this.

Captain Sisay Hapte (major after April 1975). An Amhara air force officer, he came to lead the key political and foreign affairs committee, and thus was one of the leading contenders for power. Extremely well educated, he was a graduate of Haile Selassie I University and held a Master of Science degree in electrical engineering from an American university. He had a reputation for being an eloquent speaker and a good mediator in internal *Derg* disputes, and was reputed to be one of its leading theoreticians. He was involved in the very first air force uprising at the Debre Zeit base and remained close to air force officers who asked for a "people's government." Sisay came to be regarded as a relatively moderate, "pro-Western" member of the *Derg*. It was known that he had made contacts with Israeli officials, despite the absence of diplomatic relations between Ethiopia and Israel, to arrange for the training of the special "Flame Brigade" formed in 1976. He was also suspected of having used his Israeli contacts to make liaisons with the United States, unbeknownst to the rest of the military council. Since the entire air force depended on American aircraft and was American-trained, it seems likely that he at least favored a continuing relationship with the United States.

Captain Alemayehu Haile. Another Amhara, he was head of the administrative committee and came from the police force. A graduate of the Abba Dina Police College in Addis Ababa and of Haile Selassie I University, he was part of the *Derg*'s "educated elite," and this may have been a factor in his feud with Mengistu. He was certainly no moderate and was remembered by his university professors as a very articulate, argumentative student who believed in radical policies as the only means to bring even moderate change to a feudal country such as Ethiopia. Alemayehu was a key *Derg* organizer and worked his way up to become the executive secretary before being killed in February 1977. Theretofore, he had attracted relatively little public attention, suggesting he was an agile behind-the-scenes operator.

Although these men were undoubtedly the important figures in the *Derg*, power was by no means concentrated solely in their hands, nor in the informal inner executive council. The key committees, or the executive council, took some decisions on their own, but their authority was never clearly delineated and always subject to challenge by the *Derg*'s rank and file. Not only were all major decisions put before the full body, but other issues could be forced before it whenever sufficient interest or protest was expressed. The size of the full body of the *Derg* was always kept a secret. It is uncertain that there were ever 120 members, as was first reported.[12] Between twenty and thirty members were killed or defected in the first three years. Estimates of its size varied from sixty to ninety members.[13]

One problem in trying to determine the total membership was that some *Derg* members were always outside the capital, either on missions abroad or in training, or else travelling inside the country explaining government policies to the peasants. In addition, some officers were very close to the council without being full members; such as Major Kiros Alemayehu, who was head of the *zemacha* office, and a large number of officers who acted as "eyes and ears" of the *Derg* in various ministries. Whatever the full size of the *Derg*, it maintained a degree of moral authority that could successfully hold in check the top leadership.

The decision-making process within the *Derg* always involved a number of formal and informal civilian groups and individuals. A council of ministers met under the chairman, but it was an inconspicuous and powerless body. The council received directives from the *Derg* and discussed means of implementation. It did not make decisions. The *Derg* never abolished the civilian council, nor did it appoint its own members as ministers. It apparently wished to maintain the fiction that a civilian government still existed. The Political Bureau was by far the most important civilian advisory body, although officially it had no other role than organizing the party. It was particularly influential in ideological matters and in making foreign policy. Individual members such as Haile Fida and Senay Likie served as special advisors to top *Derg* members. There was also an official civilian advisory board that was formed in October 1974, whose only known contribution to policy-making was to fix a calendar of official holidays. Thanks to this board three Moslem feast days became state holidays.

Many other informal civilian groups were appointed by the *Derg* to carry out specific studies, prepare proclamations, or draw up alternative policies. For instance, the Labor Proclamation of December 1975 was initially formulated by a working group whose members came mostly from the Ministry of Labor and Social Affairs. Innumerable ministries, groups, and individuals also submitted projects or memoranda on the land reform bill. A project for administrative decentralization was studied and drawn up by personnel from the Ministry of Interior and by university professors. There were also official individual advisors, such as Michael Imru, who had been prime minister at the time the Emperor was deposed and was still serving in an advisory role in the chairman's office three years later.

A good deal of technical advice came to the *Derg* through informal contact with personnel in the ministries. According to one ministry official who tried at times to influence the *Derg* on specific issues, such advice was more likely to be heeded if it seemed to originate from a variety of sources rather than from a single proponent. The more generalized and impersonal, the more effective the advice was likely to be.

While little publicity was given to the positive role civilians played in government, the military council tended to hold them responsible for most problems, regardless of who was to blame. The existence of a separate civilian council of ministers made this possible, and this may have been one reason the *Derg* deliberately kept itself out of government. For example, the Minister of National Resources and several other officials from that ministry were arrested in May 1976 and blamed for the failure of the National Grain Board to purchase planned amounts of grain from state farms and peasant associations. In this case, as in many others, civilians involved in the matter were accused of "sabotaging the economy." In fact, the government alleged that EPRP sympathizers in the Ministries of Agriculture and Natural Resources were responsible for about eighty million Ethiopian dollars worth of damage to crops and agricultural machinery on the state farms in 1976.[14]

While at times bureaucrats opposed to the military council may have deliberately attempted to worsen the economic situation, the official explanation linking failure with sabotage had an extremely demoralizing effect on the civilian administration. Failures were often the result of incompetence, lack of experience, or even contradictory instructions issued by the *Derg*. For example, one reason the Grain Board failed to reach its target was that it was outbid for grain by the government's own Relief and Rehabilitation Commission, which was making purchases from state farms to feed drought victims. Another related to a truck shortage which occurred when the *Derg* commandeered hundreds of trucks to transport peasants and their provisions to the north for the abortive march on Eritrea in May 1976. Moreover, state farm managers had also received contradictory government instructions. On the one hand, they were told to sell their crop to the Grain Board, while on the other they were urged to maximize profits, which meant selling to private merchants rather than to the government.[15]

Power Struggles

The *Derg* was constantly plagued by bitter struggles between its leading and most ambitious members over the top positions. Until February 1977 no single officer was undisputed leader, and the authority of Mengistu and Atnafu was continuously challenged. A revolutionary situation existed within the *Derg* itself, in the sense that there, too, no power was necessarily recognized as legitimate. One's authority depended to a large degree on the consensus of his colleagues, and if this was questioned, so his position was jeopardized. In conditions of such unlimited democracy, top-ranking officers like Mengistu could conceivably be put under house arrest for misbehavior and yet reemerge on top. The struggle for power was nonetheless a fairly democratic process in which contenders sought to rally a majority within the *Derg*. There were few examples of hidden conspiracies until February 1977, and the ebb and tide of each contender's power became well known publicly.

After the defeat and subsequent arrest of Major Tafara Tekleab in July 1974,[16] and the rise and fall of General Aman the same year, there followed a period of relative peace. This was facilitated by General Teferi's acceptance of a figurehead role and the general consensus within the *Derg* that the war in Eritrea should be intensified and that the country should be launched on its socialist course. Peace was broken in March 1975 when land reform measures caused discontent in certain military circles, especially the Second and Third Divisions. A group of officers, some in the *Derg*'s own security force, some from the disgruntled divisions, tried to organize a plot to free Haile Selassie, get rid of Mengistu and Atnafu, and replace them with more moderate leaders. About twenty officers, including the head of the council's security force, Lieutenant Colonel Negussie Haile, were arrested on April 20–21, and the rebellion was effectively quashed. The *Derg* publicly denied the existence of a plot and dismissed reports circulating in the capital as "fabricated lies," but there was too much evidence to the contrary to make their statements believable. Again, in July 1975, some kind of conspiracy was organized from within the police force, but this, too, was quietly quashed before it developed into a real threat. Both plots originated on the margins of the *Derg* and did not shake its power structure. They nonetheless indicated the existence of discontent within the military.

The origins of a second shake-up within the *Derg* went back to the issue of how to deal with the civilian left. The conflict started in the fall of 1975, at the time the Political Bureau was being organized and the first mass arrests of civilian leftists were taking place. Two conflicting approaches were expressed within the *Derg* over the question of civilian opposition: reconciliation or repression. After the wave of arrests in the fall, a conciliatory attitude prevailed during the following six months. It produced the ideological debate in the media and the offer of an alliance with progressive forces in April 1976. The offer, however, was accompanied by an open bid for power by Major Mengistu. During his nationally televised speech, it was widely noticed that he repeatedly said "I" instead of "the *Derg*" in presenting the national democratic program. Since Mengistu had been out of the public eye for five months, his speech had the earmarks of a grand reentry. He might have consolidated his power at this time if the EPRP had accepted the alliance offer. Its refusal reopened within the military council the bitter controversy over how to deal with the civilian left. Since Mengistu sided with the Political Bureau and favored a tough stand against the EPRP, his opponents were forced to take the opposite point of view. In any case, a number of Mengistu's rivals in the *Derg* were known to favor the "people's government" idea and were sympathetic to the EPRP. Chief among them was Major Sisay Habte, the chairman of the powerful political and foreign affairs committee.

The *Derg* might have been able to resolve this dispute had it been the only one. However, it simultaneously faced the more difficult problem of Eritrea, where the military situation was slowly deteriorating. Over this the *Derg* was split: whether to negotiate or to escalate. By early May 1976, the war faction was recruiting and arming tens of thousands of peasants and sending them by truck convoy north toward the Eritrean border, from where they were to move into the province to supplement the war-weary soldiers of the regular army.[17] The entire operation was under the command of Atnafu. But just at this point, *Derg* chairman Teferi Bante announced on May 16 a new nine-point government policy aimed at settling the conflict through political negotiations with the more Marxist wing of the Eritrean nationalist movement, the Eritrean People's Liberation Forces (EPLF). The two obviously contradictory policies revealed a deep cleavage within the military council, and numerous stories floated about Addis Ababa at the time as to which *Derg* officers favored which policy. In light of subsequent events, it appears that both Mengistu and Atnafu supported the peasant march, while Captain Sisay and Captain Alemayehu Haile, chairman of the administrative committee, and Captain Mogus Wolde-Michael, chairman of the economic affairs committee, led the group favoring a negotiated solution.

When the peasant march aborted with heavy losses to government forces, Mengistu and Atnafu seemed to share most of the blame and Sisay's popularity rose considerably, particularly since he led a special commission which was set up to negotiate with the Eritreans. There was intense speculation in the capital that he would replace Mengistu and Atnafu as the *Derg*'s top officer. Sisay was believed particularly powerful because of his support from the air force, which had been a center of dissension throughout the revolution, many of its officers and technicians having long supported the idea of a "people's government." It was not entirely coincidental that a new wave of unrest swept through the air force base at Debre Zeit in May and June, just at the height of this confrontation. Nor was it a coincidence that both Mengistu and Sisay made personal appearances at the base, presumably to rally support for their respective views.

The conflict came to a head in early July. As chairman of the *Derg*'s political and foreign affairs committee, Sisay accompanied Teferi Bante to the Organization of African Unity's annual summit conference being held that year on the island of Mauritius. Shortly after their return, Sisay was arrested and accused of being involved in an "anti-revolutionary plot" together with the commander-in-chief of all armed forces in Eritrea, Brigadier General Getachew Nadew, and seventeen other civilians and military officers, including two other *Derg* members.

Sisay was tried and found guilty on five counts, according to the official communique issued July 13 which announced his execution.[18] He had used his office, the document said, to make contacts with unnamed "agents of the imperialists;" he had organized an "anti-revolutionary mafia" within the air force in an attempt to divide it; he had used government funds allocated for the Eritrean negotiations to finance "anti-revolutionary activities;" he had refused to lead a high-level delegation on an "urgent mission" to the Soviet Union; and he had headed "an anti-revolutionary conspiracy along with right-wing anti-revolutionaries." The communique asserted that his lack of revolutionary fervor had been manifested in a wavering attitude toward land reform, nationalization of urban land, the program of national democratic revolution, and establishment of the People's Organizing Provisional Office. Sisay was executed with eighteen others; the two *Derg* members fled to Gondar Province, where they were later hunted down and killed. Another prominent officer, Captain Kiros Alemayehu, head of the *zemacha* campaign, was killed or committed suicide while undergoing investigation in prison.

What did Sisay and his faction really stand for? Was he conservative, as the *Derg* alleged, or was he a leftist allied with the EPRP civilian opposition? Was he involved in an attempt to "destabilize" the revolutionary regime similar to that undertaken against the government of President Salvador Allende in Chile, as the *Derg* charged in its communique?[19] Much remains unclear. What can be said about Sisay is that he was no doctrinaire leftist and was generally willing to compromise in solutions to the problems of the revolution. He had no doubt taken steps, as would others after him, to strengthen his personal position. It was known that with the *Derg*'s approval, he had had secret contacts with Israel, and he may well have had secret contacts with the United States on his own initiative, as Mengistu would later have with Cuba and the Soviet Union. He was regarded as being hostile to the Political

Bureau, and it is thus possible that he had also had contacts with the EPRP. In any case, shortly after his elimination the *Derg* opened its campaign against the clandestine party.

The execution of Sisay did not result in the immediate consolidation of Mengistu's power, as might have been expected. To the contrary, it seemed that more than ever before the majority of *Derg* members wanted to reassert the principle of collegiality. To this end, the council undertook during the summer and fall the delicate task of reorganizing itself internally to create a system of checks and balances. The results were finally announced on December 29, 1976, although the new system had been functioning since the beginning of that month.[20] The *Derg* was restructured into a three-tier system: at the base was a Congress composed of all council members, but no fixed number was given; in the middle, a forty-member Central Committee whose members were elected by the Congress; and at the top, a seventeen-man Standing Committee, also elected by the full body. The new PMAC was intentionally patterned after the Soviet system, except that the Congress was not composed of party representatives but military officers. The congress was invested with powers to establish broad outlines of the government's policies, the Central Committee was empowered to see to their implementation and the Standing Committee acted as the executive body with collective responsibility. Within the Standing Committee, the four key positions were chairman, first and second vice-chairman, and secretary general. The powers of each were closely delineated. The chairman was invested with broad authority, acting as head of state and commander-in-chief of the armed forces, and presiding over meetings of the Standing Committee, Central Committee, and Congress, as well as those of the defense and security councils. He was charged with overall supervision and implementation of decisions taken by all these bodies and by the council of ministers.

The powers of the first and second vice-chairmen were far less extensive. In addition to replacing the chairman in his absence, the first vice-chairman served as head of the council of ministers and saw to it that the PMAC's decisions were implemented; in other words, he became a sort of prime minister to an executive body subordinated to the Standing Committee. The second vice-chairman took charge of politicization, organization, and arming of the people's militia. The secretary general funneled all matters presented to the PMAC to the appropriate body and ensured that all decisions taken by the Congress, Central Committee, or Standing Committee were transmitted to the responsible government agencies. As a result, the secretary general became more powerful than the first or second vice-chairman, although in theory he remained subordinate to both. By and large, power was widely and deliberately diffused among the four top positions. And, for the first time, the powers of each office were carefully spelled out to prevent abuse.

With its usual secrecy, the PMAC never announced the names of the members of the Congress, the Central Committee, the Standing Committee, or that elections were held at the beginning of December. Teferi Bante, Mengistu, and Atnafu were reconfirmed in their respective positions as chairman, first vice-chairman, and second vice-chairman. The new key position of secretary general went to Alemayehu Haile, head of the administrative committee, who together with Mogus Wolde-Michael, head of the economic affairs committee, had been the architect of the new system.[21] Teferi Bante emerged from the reorganization with powers so extensive that he could no longer be considered a figurehead. Atnafu had been relegated to a highly specialized, though important, position as organizer of the militia and appeared to have been shoved out of direct competition for power.

Mengistu and Alemayehu were now openly pitted against one another. It was known by this time that Alemayehu and Mogus were leading a campaign to squeeze out Mengistu through legal means and that the reorganization was part of their scheme. The desire among members to counterbalance powers invested in top officials played into their hands. Ironically, the rank and file membership, where Mengistu normally drew his strength, appeared to have turned against him in this instance and to have favored Teferi Bante as the more neutral figure. Immediately after the reorganization, reports circulated in Addis Ababa that Mengistu was highly dissatisfied with his minor role as chairman of the Council of Ministers and in protest was refusing to call meetings of that body. The rumor was well founded, it subsequently turned out, but Mengistu did not react to his humiliation by pouting. Within two months, he organized his own coup within the *Derg* and emerged as its chairman and strongman.

The "Counterrevolutionary Plot" of February

The hour-long shoot-out that took place within the compound of the old palace of Emperor Menelik on February 3, 1977 was the culmination of tensions and feuds that had been building up within the *Derg* since the proclamation of the national democratic revolution and its rejection by the EPRP nearly a year before. By this time, the power struggle between the Mengistu and the Teferi-Alemayehu factions had become thoroughly entangled with the increasingly pressing problems of urban terrorism and national unity. In early February, the lines had been sharply drawn between two conflicting concepts of the revolution—how to organize it and how to defend it and Ethiopia against outside enemies. The key issue continued to be the formation of a grand alliance of progressive Ethiopian forces, including the EPRP, as a means to thwart internal and foreign counterrevolutionary efforts.

At a mass gathering in Revolution Square on January 30, called to rally the nation in defense of the motherland, General Teferi put the case for reconciliation before the public for the last time. He declared that all revolutionaries must set aside personal and ideological quarrels in the national interest. There might be "differences of opinion" among various Ethiopian groups, he said, but these merely reflected "international intramural differences" among revolutionaries and should not be allowed to hinder the defense of the nation and the revolution:[22]

In times of revolutionary ferment, differences are bound to be more pronounced for reasons that have to do with power struggle. We have seen and heard that this is a universal phenomenon. . . . Such differences should in no way be allowed to provide an opportunity for either external enemies or the exposed reactionaries who have been uprooted.

When we so frequently refer to unity, we mean that various classes or interest groups should get together and form an all-encompassing party which will spearhead all progressive forces in the task of defending our country and leading the popular revolution to the ultimate cherished objective. . . .

In the absence of a party, it is difficult to channel the energy of progressive forces in a single direction and to hold the reins of government. Had this been sufficiently realized during the last two-and-a-half years, we would have had a national party by now. . . .

The appeal I make to all progressive Ethiopians at this particular moment from this square is that you unite, establish a party and form a common front. As long as this is not done, our revolution will continue to be on the verge of disaster.

Alemayehu and Mogus stood behind Teferi. The absence of Mengistu and Atnafu eloquently testified to their violent disagreement.

Precisely how the shoot-out began and which side took the initiative remains a typical *Derg* mystery. Given the high toll suffered by the Teferi-Alemayehu faction, it seems probable that the initiative was taken by the other side. When the shooting ended, eight top *Derg* officers were dead. Seven belonged to the anti-Mengistu faction: Brigadier General Teferi Bante, Captain Alemayehu Haile, Captain Mogus Wolde-Michael, Lieutenant Colonel Asrat Desta, Lieutenant Colonel Hiruy Haile Selassie, Captain Tefera Deneke, and Corporal Haile Belai. The chairman and secretary general of the PMAC, in addition to the chairmen of three of its most important committees, had been eliminated.[23] The only *Derg* officer of the Mengistu faction to die in the clash was Lieutenant Colonel Daniel Asfaw, head of its security force. Two of his aides also died. The only civilian casualty was Senay Likie, apparently an unintended victim.[24]

Mengistu succeeded in taking his opponents unawares, it was said at the time, by calling a meeting of the Standing Committee and slipping out with his allies, allowing Daniel and his men to carry out the mass execution. The losing faction was subsequently accused of attempting a "fascist coup d'etat in the capital identical to what had taken place in Chile" and of plotting the liquidation of progressives, including *Derg* members.[25] Its leaders were called EDU and EPRP "fifth columnists" and accused of preventing the "politicizing, organizing and arming of the broad masses." The course of the revolution had been halted for the past four months, the official government statement said, because of machinations of the officers against whom the "ultimate revolutionary measure" had finally been taken. Mengistu in particular blamed his slain colleagues for the PMAC's failure to take more decisive measures to halt the EPRP terrorist campaign:

It is by no means hidden from you that these internal reactionaries (EDU, EPRP and ELF) supported by collaborators within the PMAC and imperialists who have generously extended to them moral and material help and assistance have inflicted severe damage against our revolution. . . .

We can only say that it is only the various households that can keep full record of the number of those murdered over the past four months by bullets of hired assassins during which time they were encouraged and aided by internal reactionaries and the government was incapacitated from taking the proper measures by the same internal reactionary elements.[26]

Mengistu now became undisputed leader of the *Derg*. Of the initial group of top military council officers, only two were still alive in addition to him— Colonel Atnafu and Major Berhanu Bayeh, chairman of the legal and administrative affairs committee and of the special commission on Eritrea. Atnafu had been out of town at the time of the shoot-out, presenting a flag to a militia unit that had just completed its training. Berhanu had apparently sided with Mengistu. As for Atnafu, theretofore regarded as Mengistu's number one rival, he quickly sided with the winner in the aftermath.

On February 11, the *Derg* was again reorganized. Three signficant changes had been made to the December organization. There was now only one vice-chairman, who was in charge of the peasant militia, arming of revolutionary urban defense squads, and modernization of the armed forces; the PMAC chairman added the chairmanship of the council of ministers to his other duties; the Standing Committee was reduced to sixteen members and the Central Committee to thirty-two.[27] These changes had obviously been made to fit the new roles Mengistu envisaged for himself and Atnafu and to take account of the smaller size of the *Derg*.

With the confrontation of February 1977, the internal power struggle within the *Derg* reached its logical conclusion. One of the 120 officers had finally emerged as supreme leader. For the first time since the overthrow of the Emperor, Ethiopia was again dominated by a strongman. Ironically, however, the *Derg* unified under a supreme leader was probably now in a weaker position in the face of external opposition than the conflict-ridden *Derg* had been before. The internal divisions of the military council had facilitated the absorption of discontent from the armed forces. But once one individual emerged as supreme leader, imposing policies and eliminating internal divisions, it inevitably became more difficult for the *Derg* to internalize dissension from without. Similarly, one source of Mengistu's personal strength in the past was undermined by his victory: whereas previously he received support from the lowest ranking officers who had identified with him against the "elite" of the *Derg*, he now was the elite, and discontented rank-and-file members could easily be turned against him. The *Derg*'s transformation from a conflict-ridden collegial body to a more homogeneous one dominated by a single, strong leader may have marked the end of the period of internal struggles and plotting, but it also may have opened new possibilities of external coup attempts.

The Period of High Terror

Having dealt with his enemies and rivals within the *Derg*, Mengistu turned to his civilian opposition, intent upon applying the same uncompromising logic. He completely abandoned the concept of broad participation by all progressives in a national democratic revolution and turned his back on Teferi's nationalist plea for unity. Instead, he set out to crush the civilian leftist opposition, the EPRP in particular. His strategy for achieving this was to arm the *Derg*'s civilian supporters and employ them in order to eliminate its opponents. But this tactic opened up a Pandora's box of urban violence and led to the first confrontation between the Political Bureau and the *Derg*. The episode demonstrated all too clearly how thin the line was between the *Derg*'s friends and foes since by arming the masses, the military unwittingly provided weapons to both.

In his "victory speech" before a mass rally on February 4, Mengistu announced that henceforth "comrades of the broad masses" would be armed and that the revolution would pass from "the defensive to the offensive position" with a vengeance:[28]

> As a result of the determined and decisive step taken Thursday by the Provisional Military Administrative Council against the internal collaborators and supporters of the EPRP, EDU and ELF, our Revolution has, in keeping with the demands of the broad masses, advanced from the defensive to the offensive position. Henceforth, we will tackle enemies that come face to face with us and we will not be stabbed from behind by internal foes. . . .
>
> To this end, we will arm the allies and comrades of the broad masses without giving respite to reactionaries and avenge the blood of our comrades double and triple-fold. . . .
>
> In order to enable the broad masses—guardians of the nation and defenders of the revolution—to participate fully in the revolutionary process, the motto and clarion call of "Arms and Democracy to the Broad Masses" will be implemented.

The policy of arming civilians—which had begun in rural areas in mid-1976 when the first peasant militias were organized—was now extended to the cities, particularly Addis Ababa. A month after Mengistu's speech, the first 600 arms were distributed to defense squads formed by urban neighborhood associations, or *kebeles,* or by the workers in factories and government offices. Contrary to expectations these squads did not all side with the *Derg* or heed its call to track down "reactionaries" and "anarchists." Rather, many followed their own whim and law, in accordance with the political faction that controlled each *kebele* or factory. Not only had numerous defense squads been infiltrated by the EPRP, but also those controlled by the Political Bureau were often bent on furthering the interests of MEISON rather than the *Derg*.

Toward the end of March, the *Derg* launched a search operation in Addis Ababa. The Political Bureau had long clamored for such an operation in order to root out EPRP terrorists who had slain scores of its officials and supporters in the party, the labor unions, government offices, factories, neighborhood associations, and schools. The situation had reached the point by February that no Political Bureau partisan was safe in the streets or even in his office. Two top trade union leaders had been gunned down inside the AETU headquarters; several permanent secretaries—the second highest-ranking official in each ministry—had been slain on their way to work; some thirty *kebele* officials had been assassinated in their homes or offices; and dozens of students had been beaten—and several lynched—inside the high schools.[29]

The week of March 22 marked the height of the "red terror" in the capital. By then, the *Derg* and the Political Bureau felt that they had armed a sufficiently large number of defense squads to permit a house-by-house search for EPRP members, arms, and printing equipment. Defense squads in each neighborhood set up roadblocks and began visiting homes. The operation, however, was carried out in an anarchical manner, each squad a law unto itself. Some looked only for arms, but others confiscated food supplies, building materials, and gasoline; some considered cameras as espionage equipment, and others regarded typewriters as highly dangerous. While house searches led to relatively few incidents, the city was tense, and by nightfall an orgy of shooting broke out which continued into the early hours of the morning. Long before the official curfew hour of 10 p.m., anyone moving about the streets became a target for the defense squads. People were taken from their homes in the middle of the night and often families did not know whether they had been abducted by defense squads or the EPRP. No one will ever know how many died during that one week, but the toll was certainly high.[30] Few top leaders of the EPRP were among the dead, however. The government announced the liquidation of Tesfay Debessai, head of the EPRP's domestic and political affairs department, Marcos Hagos, the former leader of the CELU, and a few minor officials of the clandestine party. The defense squads also seized about 1,600 small arms and a few duplicating machines, but the booty was too insignificant to suggest that the EPRP had been seriously crippled. Meanwhile the *Derg* decided that matters had gotten out of hand. On the fourth day, it warned that the "revolution should distinguish between friend and foe" and hinted that it might call off the searches.[31] But the Political Bureau urged it be continued, arguing that excesses were inevitable and that in a revolutionary situation the ends justified the means.

A particularly ugly incident persuaded the *Derg* to end the searches at the end of the first week. Members of the Berhanena Selam Printing Press defense squad denounced a dozen co-workers as EPRP members. At first, this was not thought unusual, since throughout the city workers were busy "uncovering the reactionaries" in their midst. The suspect Berhanena Selam workers were turned over to the police, who investigated the matter and then released them for lack of evidence. But to the horror of the city, nine of them, including a woman in an advanced stage of pregnancy, were found slain the next morning, March 26.

The "executions," it was learned, had been carried out by the defense squad of the *kebele* where the printing press was located, led by a certain Girma Kebede, the neighborhood association chairman. The *kebele* population was enraged and sent a delegation to the *Derg* to protest the killings. A solicitous *Derg* member met the delegation at the gates of Menelik Palace, heard their complaint, and announced that the culprits had been found and would be punished. Then, in a surprise statement, he informed the group that Girma and his accomplices had been appointees of the Political Bureau and had been acting under its orders. In the following days, it was discovered that Girma was the Political Bureau's chief executioner; he had already murdered twenty-four persons and had a list of over two hundred others he was supposed to liquidate.[32] On April 2, he and five accomplices were taken to the top of Entoto Mountains overlooking the city and executed as counterrevolutionaries in front of the assembled residents of his *kebele.* Despite solid evidence against him, the Political Bureau tried to prevent Girma's execution on the grounds that every revolution has its excesses and that Girma was at most guilty of an excess of zeal.

The Berhanena Selam Printing Press incident was not the only indication that the Political Bureau was working undercover to establish its authority separately from the *Derg*'s. On the night of March 25, it trucked into the city some 600 peasant militiamen from areas nearby under its control. They were ostensibly brought in to reinforce the defense squads in search operations, but without the *Derg*'s knowledge or approval, and it is possible that the Fidaists had other plans for them. In fact, some Fidaists had talked openly at *kebele* meetings and in factories of forming a civilian government in the near future. The *Derg* at any rate regarded the presence of the militiamen as a direct threat to its authority and ordered them out of the capital after a shooting incident occurred between them and army troops.

An unintended result of this week of high terror was that a new relation between the Political Bureau and the *Derg* was established. Fidaists had defied the military council and had hinted only too clearly at their future intentions. Because the *Derg* had the military strength on its side, they had been forced to back down. The PMAC, for its part, had checked the Political Bureau's autonomy and authority but had not taken measures against its members. Implicitly, both sides acknowledged they could not yet afford a break.

The Fidaists nonetheless refused to retract their demand for a complete purge, and in early May the *Derg* decided to resume the search for "reactionaries" and "anarchists." This time they brought in peasant militia reinforcements and kept closer control over the operation. On the eve of May Day celebrations, however, the Political Bureau committed a major blunder that probably led to its final break with the *Derg.* Taking as a pretext an anti-government student demonstration, which according to some reports it had organized, the Bureau ordered the *kebeles* to arrest any young person suspected of being an EPRP sympathizer. Hundreds were arrested, taken to three different sites on the outskirts of Addis Ababa, and executed en masse. Scores of others were simply gunned down in the streets by the *Derg*'s "permanent secretaries," the jeeps mounted with machine guns constantly patrolling the streets of Addis Ababa. The death toll may have been as high as one thousand. It was the largest mass execution of the revolution and marked the triumph of "red terror" in Ethiopia. Subsequently, the *Derg* disowned the outrage, blaming it on the Political Bureau with which it now broke completely. This was made official on July 14, 1977, when a new proclamation placed the Provisional Office for Mass Organizational Affairs and the Political School directly under the *Derg*'s Standing Committee. All members of the Political Bureau were in effect suspended from their offices, and in late August Haile Fide and a group of his supporters attempted to flee the capital, but were caught and imprisoned. It was now the turn of the fidaists to be hunted down.

10. External Influences and Internal Wars

When the young military officers toppled Emperor Haile Selassie in September 1974, they set loose a process that threatened the empire's unity. Ethiopia had been held together for half a century by the "divine right to rule" of the Emperor and the whole network of personal relations he had woven between himself and the provincial notables. Haile Selassie's efforts to establish the structures of a modern administration had not really altered this basic reality. With his removal, the whole political fabric of the empire began to unravel. What remained was a physical entity known as Ethiopia seeking a new ideological justification for its existence and trying to establish the political-administrative structures of a modern nation-state.

With its conglomeration of tribes, languages, and cultures, Ethiopia was not a modern nation, and the very strength of its ancient cultures made nation-building that much more difficult. Nor was Ethiopia a modern polity: its inhabitants had been mere "subjects," not "citizens" with recognized political rights and some control over the government. Ethiopia was barely even a state in the sense of having an administrative apparatus organized throughout the country. Independent for thousands of years, Ethiopia was paradoxically further from being a nation-state than most of the fragile, newly independent countries of black Africa. One of the main tasks of the revolution, then, was to transform Ethiopia from an empire in which one ethnic group dominated the conquered "subjects" into a country in which all enjoyed equal rights. In the Leninist language that was officially adopted by the *Derg*, this became known as solving "the problem of the nationalities."

It took the PMAC well over a year to realize that the revolutionary forces unleashed by its own policies could easily provoke the disintegration of the empire. Although a nationalist movement was already under way in Eritrea Province when the military came to power, the *Derg* initially regarded it as a special, isolated problem that could be either settled by negotiation or crushed militarily. However, it soon discovered that there were other dormant nationalisms in the country, specifically among the unassimilated Gallas of southern Ethiopia and the Somalis of the southeast. Somali nationalism, fanned by the government in Mogadishu, quickly became as serious a problem as Eritrean secessionism. The PMAC found itself fighting major wars in the north and the southeast and faced with the danger of losing vast tracts of land and four to six million people. It was not until April 1976 that the military council proposed an overall policy to try to bring about the reintegration of the old empire on an entirely new basis: it proclaimed the principle of the equality of all ethnic groups, or "nationalities," and the right of each one to "self-determination" within the context of Ethiopian unity. But by this time, the Eritreans conceived of self-determination only as total independence and the Somalis as outright annexation of their territory to Somalia. As a result, the adoption of the Soviet doctrine of the "rights of nationalities" was to prove a total failure.

The already difficult task of finding a new framework for the reintegration of the old empire was further complicated by the extremely complex international situation in which the revolution was unfolding. Ethiopia's image under the Emperor had been one of a conservative, pro-Western, and militantly Christian country surrounded by hostile Moslem Arab states; it was an image he had carefully cultivated to secure Western sympathy and backing in general, and from the United States in particular. He had closely tied Ethiopia to America by a series of 25-year treaties signed between the two countries in 1953 giving the U.S. military-base rights in the Eritrean capital of Asmara. In return, the United States agreed to equip and train virtually all the Ethiopian armed forces. By 1974, more than 2,000 officers had received at least some training in the United States, and the Ethiopian Army, Air Force, and Navy was totally dependent on American arms. The American commitment to Ethiopia took on even more meaning after the Soviet Union became involved in Somalia in the early 1970s, signing a twenty-year Treaty of Friendship and Cooperation with the government of President Mohamed Siad Barre and supplying that country with all its arms, just as the Unied States was doing for Ethiopia. In return, Somalia gave the Soviets naval and air facilities on the Indian Ocean. The commitment of the two superpowers to these two neighboring countries changed the nature of their border dispute over the Ogaden region, which was within Ethiopian frontiers but was claimed by Somalia, from a merely local dispute into an international one with cold war overtones.

Ethiopia's position as a pro-Western bastion in the area was enhanced even further by the fact that the Soviets had a presence not only in Somalia but also in the Sudan. Although their influence decreased considerably after a Communist-backed coup attempt against President Jaafar Numeiry in 1971, they were still probably the foreign power with the greatest influence in the Sudan. Moreover, Soviet bloc countries were showing some sympathy and giving some help to the Eritreans. When the *Derg* first came to power in 1974, Ethiopia was still an American client surrounded by Soviet-backed states and threatened by a liberation movement enjoying at least token Soviet support.

However, in the space of three years everything radically changed. Under the impact of the revolution in Ethiopia, the general deterioration in Soviet-Arab relations, and a far more aggressive foreign policy by Saudi Arabia, the system of superpower alliances in the Horn of Africa crumbled, leading to a situation of tremendous international tension and diplomatic turmoil. By mid-1977, the United States had been replaced by the Soviet Union as Ethiopia's main arms provider and foreign ally; Cuban advisers had replaced the Americans serving with the Ethiopian armed forces; all Soviet military advisers and half the Soviet embassy had been ordered out of the Sudan; and relations between Somalia and the Soviet Union had become extremely tense.

It was a staggering shift of friendships and alliances that had important repercussions for the unity of the old Ethiopian empire. The *Derg* ran an enormous risk in shifting alliances so radically in the midst of two major military conflicts. It had actively sought this change both to align its foreign policy with its newly proclaimed Marxist revolution and because the United States was becoming increasingly reluctant to continue providing the military assistance necessary for the PMAC to prosecute the war in Eritrea, deal with Somali insurgents in the Ogaden, and defend itself against the growing army of the Ethiopian Democratic Union. It was in effect both an ideological and pragmatic choice. But the radical change in Ethiopia's foreign policy raised the question of whether the *Derg* would lose the nation in order to save the revolution. The close alliance with the Soviet Union fueled opposition to the *Derg* from practically all of Ethiopia's neighbors, from the conservative Saudi Arabia and moderate Sudan to Marxist Somalia. Increasingly, these countries sought to further the territorial disintegration of the Ethiopian empire as well as the isolation of the Ethiopian revolution. Ethiopia was once again an isolated country, now pro-Soviet, radically revolutionary, and surrounded by hostile, pro-Western conservative states.

Eritrea

No other conflict had more importance for the PMAC and the revolution than the civil war in Eritrea. It was this unending war that first gave rise to assertions that the *Derg* was "fascist" rather than "revolutionary," and it was difficult for the officers ruling Ethiopia to prove otherwise so long as their troops committed massacres and assassinated civilians in Eritrea. Certainly the *Derg*'s policy of seeking to crush the Eritrean nationalist movement by force tarnished the image of both the military and the revolution. Moreover, this approach would prove highly counterproductive and even self-defeating. When the PMAC came to power in September 1974, a de facto cease-fire was in effect throughout the province as both sides waited to see how the other intended to act after the overthrow of the Emperor. For a while, there was at least a hope of reaching a peaceful solution to the then thirteen-year-old war that had already caused the deaths of tens of thousands of Eritreans, the destruction of hundreds of villages, and the flight to the neighboring Sudan of close to 100,000 civilians. At the time of this writing nearly three years later, not only was all hope dead but the Ethiopian army had lost control over all of the province except the capital of Asmara and the two Red Sea ports of Massawa and Assab. The strategy of using force to push through revolutionary reforms was probably both justifiable and unavoidable; but carrying over this same strategy when it came to dealing with a strong nationalist movement was highly questionable. It was a typical military establishment reaction to a basically political problem, all too reminiscent of the American response to the war in Vietnam.

The problem of Eritrea dates back to 1889, when the Italians in a belated attempt to join the scramble for Africa established a colony by that name on the Red Sea coast. The territory of the new Italian colony was composed of the highlands—inhabited mainly by Tigrinya-speaking Christians—which had been historically part of the Ethiopian empire; and the lowlands—peopled by a variety of Moslem nomadic tribes—which had been alternatively under Turkish, Egyptian, and Ethiopian suzerainty but were really controlled by no power in any meaningful sense. It has always been a matter of contention between the Eritrean nationalists and the central Ethiopian government whether Eritrea was historically part of the Ethiopian empire. In a sense, both claims are wrong, since both Ethiopia and Eritrea are political entities of very recent creation. There was never an Eritrea in its present boundaries before the Italian conquest, just as there was never an Ethiopia in its modern configuration before the conquests of Emperor Menelik at the turn of the century and before the federation between Ethiopia and Eritrea in 1952. But it is absurd to deny the historical ties between the Eritrean highlands and the central highlands of Ethiopia over a period of centuries and even of millenia.

Despite these historical ties, the recent histories of Eritrea and Ethiopia have been quite different, and this rather than their historical relations is the relevant background to the current conflict. Eritrea underwent the typical experience of other African colonies. It was exploited and its traditional cultures were suppressed, but it was also exposed to modern technology and education, endowed with a relatively good infrastructure of roads and communications, and generally brought into the modern world. It is not that Italian colonization was particularly benevolent. The development of Eritrea was quite definitely for the benefit of the colonizers, and Eritreans were discriminated against in schooling, jobs, and services available to them. Yet, compared with the rest of Ethiopia, literacy rates were higher, hospitals more numerous although segregated, the road network more extensive, agriculture more advanced, and above all the Eritrean population was more open to the idea of change and development. The brutal truth is that Eritrea stood far ahead of the rest of Ethiopia in practically every respect.

In 1941, Italy lost to the allies control over Eritrea and the rest of Ethiopia it had conquered in 1936. While Ethiopia soon reverted to its previous independent status under Emperor Haile Selassie, Eritrea was put under British military administration until the final disposition of the former Italian colonies was decided. Settling the fate of the two to three million people of

Eritrea was not easy, and the big powers were as divided as the Eritreans themselves. The Soviets pressed for the establishment of an independent Eritrean state; the United States backed the Emperor's claim to the former Italian colony; and the British suggested alternatively its partition between the Sudan and Ethiopia and federation with Ethiopia. Within Eritrea, the Unionist Party favored annexation to Ethiopia; its support came mostly from the Tigrinya-speaking Christians in the highlands. The Moslem League, which drew its strength from the lowland inhabitants, advocated independence. A third faction, the Independence Bloc, also favored independence and was backed by a coalition of Moslems, Christians, and Italians. Thus, the problem of ethnic and religious divisions, which was to plague the nationalist movement later, became evident in the immediate postwar period. By and large, Moslems wanted complete independence and Christians some kind of tie with Ethiopia.

The solution finally adopted by the United Nations in 1952 was to join Eritrea and Ethiopia in a federation. Ethiopia was given control over defense, foreign policy, finance, transport, and communications, while Eritrea was allowed to have its own government, with an elected legislature and executive, to deal with local affairs. In Eritrean schools, lessons were taught in Tigrinya and Arabic rather than Amharic, and newspapers were printed in the local languages. While tensions existed between the Moslems and the Christians, a degree of equilibrium was maintained by carefully balancing the number of each in the government. The major remaining problem was Eritrea's relationship to Ethiopia: there was a fundamental contradiction between the democratic political system and the internal autonomy enjoyed by Eritrea and the autocratic rule imposed by the Emperor on the rest of Ethiopia. The example of Eritrea was bound to encourage demands for liberalization and internal autonomy in other parts of the country, demands which the Emperor had little intention of meeting. Rather than accept the fact that Eritrea was fundamentally different from the rest of the country, Haile Selassie tried to "refeudalize" it, returning it to a centralized, autocratic, and Christian Amhara system. Playing on the region's ethnic and religious divisions, he skillfully manipulated the Eritrean parliament and obtained in 1962 a vote in favor of dissolution of the federation and Eritrea's outright annexation to Ethiopia. From then on, Eritrea was treated like the other thirteen provinces. Tigrinya was immediately eliminated from the schools and Arabic was progressively phased out. The parliament and political parties were disbanded and censorship imposed. Amharas took over top positions in the administration, while the principle of parity between Moslem and Christian officials was abandoned. Haile Selassie even appointed a symbol of the old order, *Ras* Asrate Kassa, to govern the province. It was an attempt to obliterate the modernizing effect of some fifty years of colonialism and ten years of British administration with a single stroke of the imperial pen. Inevitably, the attempt proved disastrous.

A nationalist movement, the Eritrean Liberation Front, was formed in 1960 in Cairo, once it was clear that the federation was headed for dissolution.

The first shots of the struggle were fired on September 1, 1961.¹ From the beginning, the Front was dedicated to Eritrea's total independence from Ethiopia. Initially a movement of the Moslem population, it received support from Arab countries, notably Syria and Iraq, and was guided by nationalist rather than Marxist revolutionary principles. Its principal leaders included Osman Saleh Sabbe, who had headed the pre-federation Moslem League; Idriss Mohamed Adam, the ELF's first president; and one Christian leader, Woldeab Woldemariam, a former labor-union leader. By the mid-1960s, however, the Front had also begun attracting Eritrean Christians, particularly from among the urban youth. It even managed to get the support of some prominent Christian leaders such as Tedla Bairu, a former leader of the Unionist Party and later the first chief executive of Eritrea under the federation. The Christian influx broadened the movement, but also created divisions within it because the urban Christians were far more radical in outlook than the rural Moslems.

As the nationalist movement grew, so did its internal fissures. There were divisions between Christians and Moslems, urban and rural elements, socialists and nationalists. Only the fact that these divisions crisscrossed to some extent kept the Front from completely disintegrating during the ensuing ten years. But there were bloody battles between Christian and Moslem guerrillas and reciprocal betrayals to the Ethiopian army, while periodic attempts at reconciliation proved futile. A publication of the Eritrean nationalists later described this period in the following terms: "Fascist methods: kidnappings, assassinations, terror among the people. Secretarianism, tribalism, regionlism. One step forward, two steps backward."² A split finally occurred in June 1970, with one faction under Osman Saleh Sabbe breaking away to establish the Eritrean People's Liberation Forces. Despite the leadership of a moderate Moslem like Osman, the EPLF initially tended to attract the urban, intellectual, and leftist Christian youth and made an effort to project a strong socialist as well as nationalist image.³ The infighting became particularly fierce between 1972 and 1974, with casualties on the two sides officially recognized as mounting to 1,200 during the two-year period and unofficially much higher.⁴ The EPLF, however, managed to survive and even to divide Arab support for the Eritrean cause, thanks largely to Osman's close ties with Iraq and the Palestinian Liberation Organization.

Emperor Haile Selassie established the policy of dealing with the Eritrean problem militarily rather than politically. The Second Division in Eritrea was strengthened, a unit of special police commandos trained with Israeli aid, and martial law was imposed on the province. At the same time, the Eritrean nationalists were belittled as mere *shiftas,* or bandits. To make matters worse, there were a number of massacres of civilians, such as the one near Keren in which hundreds of unarmed villagers were gunned down. This brutality did nothing to reconcile the civilian population to the central government. Still, by the onset of the revolution in 1974 the majority of Eritreans may still have favored some kind of federation providing ample local autonomy rather than outright independence.⁵ Despite increased guerrilla activity, the Ethiopian army still controlled all the towns and the main roads.

This was the situation inherited by the *Derg* when it took over the Eritrean problem from Haile Selassie in September 1974. Neither a political nor a military approach promised a ready solution. The difficulty of eradicating by force of arms the Eritrean guerrillas had already been made clear. But a political solution implied a decision by the *Derg* regarding not only the status of Eritrea but the new configuration of the whole of Ethiopia. The *Derg* no more than the Emperor could afford to have a totally different political and economic system in Eritrea. There could be no lasting federation, for example, between a capitalist Eritrea and a socialist Ethiopia, or between an Eritrea with a Western-style democracy and an Ethiopia under a people's democracy. The situation was complicated by the divisions within the *Derg* over how to deal with Eritrea and the power struggle with the first chairman, General Aman.

The *Derg*'s first short-lived attempt the solve the Eritrean problem focused on a political solution. This was largely at the personal initiative of General Aman, himself an Eritrean, and by all evidence not a Marxist socialist. Aman's peace offensive started even before the overthrow of the Emperor when the General, then serving as defense minister, toured the province for twelve days, returning to the capital on September 6. The theme of his speeches was that the problem of Eritrea simply resulted from the "divide and rule" policy of the old regime, which sought to heighten ethnic and religious divisions in order to impose more easily its own authority on a fragmented country. But a government dedicated to a policy of national unity and progress would soon restore peace and normality in Eritrea. He also promised to investigate the misdeeds and massacres committed in the past by the Ethiopian army and to punish the offenders. After his appointment as chairman on the PMAC, Aman continued his peace campaign by naming an Eritrean, Amanuel Amde Michael, as chief administrator of the province and by making other personal visits. Yet, Aman never really made any concrete proposals for the future political status of the region. It is not clear whether he was prevented from doing so by the opposition of other *Derg* members, or whether he thought that his personal prestige and a show of goodwill by the central government would be enough to put an end to a conflict that had already lasted for over ten years. He talked about "understanding, cooperation, and unity" and promoting Eritrea's general welfare, but he never spelled out whether he envisaged internal autonomy for the northern province, a return to the federation, or some other special status.[6] He seemed to imply, however, that a solution to the Eritrean problem would come as part of the process of establishing democratic rights for the Ethiopians and through the creation of an elected national government. In any case, the majority of the *Derg*'s members turned against him a few weeks after his second visit to the province, and on November 23 he was killed. Within hours of his death, an order was signed to send several thousand troops as reinforcements to the province.

The PMAC had decided to send additional troops to Eritrea not because it was planning a new offensive against the guerrillas, but because the ELF had been taking advantage of the de facto cease-fire in the province since the summer to consolidate its positions even on the outskirts of the provincial capital. In fact, Asmara was practically surrounded by ELF and EPLF guerrillas, who each night infiltrated the city to taunt the military. The two groups held unity meetings in broad daylight on the hills outside Asmara in open defiance of the army. Moreover, both recruited in and around Asmara, and the EPLF in particular met with enormous success among the youth, with thousands joining its ranks at this time. Still, the *Derg* hesitated to return to war, being uncertain of its general policies and even more so of its Eritrean stand. In December 1974 and the following January, it sent several peace delegations to Asmara and tried to get a dialogue going with the ELF and EPLF through the mediation of the city's elders. A delegation of 38 elders held separate talks with the two factions but found no basis for an agreement. The two movements gave their final reply on January 23, 1975 when they both began a series of attacks inside and around Asmara in a bold show of force that at first suggested they were trying to take over the city itself.[7] With the help of more reinforcements and the use of jet fighters, the army after about a month of almost daily fighting managed to clear guerrillas from their positions around the provincial capital and to reestablish its control over the city and main roads of the province.[8] But all hopes of a peaceful settlement were destroyed. The Eritrean nationalists, their ranks swollen with thousands of new recruits, had made it clear they were not interested in solutions that excluded independence. The *Derg*, for its part, had now made the Eritrean conflict its own. Worse yet, the army had reverted to using the same tactics which General Aman had just denounced and disowned. Dozens of villages, including many on the outskirts of Asmara, had been indiscriminately bombed, and the policy of randomly shooting down innocent civilians inside the city in retaliation for the slaying of officers by guerrilla commandos was once again in force. From the Eritrean point of view, there seemed to be no difference whatsoever between the PMAC's policy toward the province, or its style in warfare, and those of the Emperor. But the military position of the central government was far worse than it had been before. Although by the spring of 1975 there was a new stalemate in the fighting and the army still controlled all the cities and towns of the province, the roads were far less safe and much more of the countryside had become part of the "liberated zone" controlled by the guerrillas.

The escalation of the war in Eritrea did not bring to an end the *Derg*'s efforts to find a negotiated solution to the conflict. In the months following the renewed outbreak of warfare, one PMAC delegation followed another to the province, holding meetings with the population, visiting hospitals and orphanages, and cautiously trying to renew indirect contacts with the ntionalists. In September, the PMAC summed up in an official communique all the initiatives it had taken to bring peace to Eritrea:[9]

a. A message of goodwill was conveyed to the bandits [*sic*] to join hands with the Ethiopian masses in building the new Ethiopia.

b. The then chairman of the Provisional Military Administrative Council, Lt. Gen. Aman Michael Andom, was sent to brief the Eritrean people on the objectives of the government and its desire for a peaceful solution to the problem in the region.

c. Security forces in the region were ordered not to track down the bandits.

d. A competent Ethiopian from Eritrea was appointed chief administrator of the region for the first time.

e. A high-level government delegation consisting of members of the PMAC and the council of ministers was sent to Eritrea to explore ways for a peaceful settlement of the problem. Consequently, a deputation of elders elected by the delegation was made to convey the goodwill of the government to the bandits.[10]

f. The same delegation had visited some Arab countries who provide assistance to the bandits on religious grounds with a view to explain the sound and good intentions of the government. In particular, great efforts have been made to use the good offices of President Nimeri, leader of sisterly and neighborly Sudan, in finding a solution to the problem. Other similar government delegations sent to various Arab countries have also reaffirmed Ethiopia's desire for a peaceful settlement.[11]

g. Later, a deputation of elders from the capital headed by Abuna Philipos was sent to the region to stop unnecessary bloodshed among brothers. Members of the deputation returned here recently at the end of their four-month mission in the region.[12]

None of these moves, the communique stated, had met with any success. Rather, there had been a notable "lack of spirit of coopertion and goodwill on the part of some Eritreans and bandits."

The PMAC's lack of success was hardly surprising, considering that none of its initiatives had included a concrete proposal on the future status of the northern region. The PMAC, like Aman, seemed to assume that a political solution could emerge out of nothing more than a show of goodwill, a blind confidence in the new central government, and frequent reminders of the strength of the historical ties binding Eritrea to the rest of Ethiopia. Even a concept of how the future relations between Eritrea and the central government could be shaped had not yet been formulated. With the benefit of hindsight, it is easy to see that this absence of a clear concept or of concrete proposals was bound to doom the PMAC's efforts. But it would have been extremely difficult for the PMAC to set forth any concrete proposal in 1975, because the new economic and political reforms being implemented in Ethiopia had not yet been consolidated into an overall, coherent system into which a solution to the Eritrean conflict could be fitted. It was first necessary for the *Derg* to outline its new political organization for the entire country before any viable relationship between Eritrea and Ethiopia could be worked out. But by the time the PMAC did elaborate its political program for the new Ethiopia, the situation in Eritrea had deteriorated to what seemed to be the point of no return.

It was the proclamation of the national democratic revolution on April 20, 1976 which first provided the overall framework in which the PMAC hoped to work out the problem of Eritrea. This was the recognition of the "right of any nationality existing in Ethiopia to self-determination" and "the unity of Ethiopian nationalities . . . based on the common struggle against feudalism, bureaucratic capitalism, imperialism, and reactionary forces."[13] The proclamation went on to say:

> . . . under the prevailing conditions in Ethiopia, the problem of nationalities can only be solved when the nationalities are guaranteed regional autonomy. Accordingly, each nationality will have the right to decide on matters prevailing within its environs, be they administrative, political, economic, social or language, as well as elect its own leaders and administrators. The right of nationalities for local autonomy will be implemented in a democratic way.[14]

The proclamation was followed on May 16 by another statement on which the *Derg* stated its intention to:

> study each of the regions of the country, the history and interaction of the nationalities inhabiting them, their geographic position, economic structure and suitability for development and administration. After taking these into consideration, the government will at an appropriate time present to the people the format of the regions that can exist in the future. The entire Ethiopian people will then democratically discuss the issue at various levels and decide upon it themselves.[15]

In regard to Eritrea specifically, the statement, which was to become known as the "Nine-Point Policy," said that the military government was "prepared to discuss and exchange views with the progressive groups and organizations in Eritrea which are not in collusion with feudalists, reactionary forces in the neighborhood and imperialists."[16] But the policy made clear that the purpose of any negotiations was to "promote the unity of the oppressed classes of Ethiopia."[17] In addition, the statement announced a program to facilitate the return of Eritrean refugees from the Sudan, promised the release of Eritrean political prisoners and pledged itself to lifting the state of emergency as soon as the other steps were carried out. A "Special Commission on Eritrea" was set up to oversee the implementation of the program under the *Derg's* political affairs committee.[18]

For the first time, it became clear what the *Derg* had in mind for Eritrea: internal autonomy no greater than that to be granted to all other regions. Moreover, the proclamation left in doubt whether Eritrea would be maintained as a region in its present boundaries or carved up into its component "nationalities," following ethnic and linguistic criteria. The *Derg's* political tactics toward the Eritrean nationalists also became clear for the first time. By declaring that it was prepared to hold talks with "progressive groups and organizations in Eritrea," the PMAC was saying that it intended to deal with the EPLF only, trying to widen the split in the nationalists' ranks. The reason for this choice was that it regarded the EPLF to be more Marxist than nationalist and thus more amenable to an agreement. Already, Major Sisay, chairman of the *Derg*'s political affairs committee, and Haile Fida, the head of the Political Bureau, were seeking contacts with the EPLF. During the following year the PMAC never attacked the EPLF in its statements, reserving all its venom for the ELF. But the new policy on Eritrea did not pay off. This was partly because the nationalism of the EPLF proved stronger than its Marxism and partly because the *Derg* chose the very moment of its peace offer to launch a "peasant march" against Eritrean guerrillas. Only the existence of a deep division within the *Derg* explains how it could have simultaneously pursued a peace and a war policy.

The idea of a peasant march on Eritrea was probably first discussed in the confines of the Political Bureau in early 1976 as a way of meeting the pressure for reinforcements coming from the First and Second Divisions fighting in Eritrea. A new elite army unit, the Flame Brigade, was being trained, but it was clear that this would not be enough, with pressure mounting on the Somali border as well as in Eritrea. The *Derg* was deeply divided over the proposal. Mengistu and Atnafu almost certainly favored it, while the Sisay-Alemayehu faction opposed it. Instead of reaching a consensus on a single policy, each faction in effect pursued its own separate one, thus giving rise to absurd contradictions in the *Derg*'s stance toward Eritrea. While the political affairs committee under Sisay was shaping the new policy proclamation, Mengistu and Atnafu were preparing the march, with the latter officially in charge.

The idea behind the march was to raise an instant army of tens of thousands. of "peasant warriors" and then transport them to Eritrea to overwhelm the nationalist movement by sheer force of numbers. The use of untrained and self-armed peasants to fight wars was a time-honored Ethiopian tradition. It was just such an army that Emperor Menelik used to conquer the southern provinces, to defeat the Italians at Adwa in 1895 and gallantly to resist their advance in 1936. The *Derg* further appealed to tradition by giving the peasant march overtones of a Christian crusade against Moslem invaders in an obvious attempt to incite the peasants in the Amhara highlands against the Eritrean nationalists. The operation thus had from the beginning an extremely ambiguous character. It was a Christian march against the Moslems invading the country; it was another Amhara colonial campaign (there were rumors that the *Derg* had promised the peasants land and booty in Eritrea); and finally it was a "people's war" in the best Maoist tradition, one fought not by professional soldiers but by the true representatives of the people.

Although preparations started in March, the movement of peasants northward was postponed several times and did not start until mid-May. At this time, thousands of peasants—estimates varied between 10,000 and 40,000— were trucked north through both Tigre and Begemdir to the southern boundary of Eritrea, from where they were suppose to advance on foot. Most of the peasants came from the Amhara and Tigrean highlands and had been recruited through the peasant associations, each of which was given a quota to fill. It was perhaps the first large-scale demonstration that these organizations had really begun functioning in the conservative northern provinces where land reform had been resisted the most. Once the peasants arrived at the border, the campaign faltered for several reasons: the logistics for the march were in shambles, with hardly enough food available from day to day to feed the peasants; the *Derg* was too divided to take decisive action and apparently wanted to hold off pending the outcome of the new round of contacts with the EPLF; finally, there were international pressures, particularly from the *Derg*'s main arms supplier, the United States, to call off what was seen abroad as a "barbaric" march.

But the most crucial factors in the *Derg*'s decision to call off the march were two brief engagements in mid-June between the peasants and the Eritrean guerrillas that ended in total disaster for the central government. At Inticho and another site north of Adigrat, both in Trigre Province, guerrillas attacked the peasants during the night, killing hundreds and capturing nearly one thousand. Routed, the survivors fled southward spreading word of the disasters through rear base camps and convincing thousands of warrior-peasants to quit the march and go home. Ill-equipped, untrained, and poorly led, the peasant army had met with a debacle even before it had really begun to fight. The PMAC never admitted that the march had taken place and to cover up its defeat, it decided to make use of the thousands of armed peasants to establish the promised "people's militia." On June 20, the government announced that it had already organized a militia of nearly 500,000 peasants "to resist imperialism, to crush internal and external reactionaries and elements opposed to the national unity and territorial integrity of Ethiopia."[19]

By mid-1976, the war in Eritrea had definitely begun to turn against the central government. Although the army still held all the major urban centers, only heavily armed convoys could move between them. None of its attempts to launch a counteroffensive had met with any success. The peasant march had been routed at the outset. The new elite Flame Brigade, upon which the government was counting to break the stalemate, was proving a disappointment, less aggressive and tough than even the two war-weary divisions that had been carrying the brunt of the fighting. The guerrillas, on the other hand, were beginning to extend their control from the contryside, where they were now solidily implanted, to some of the army's smaller garrisons. They were now strong enough to begin attacking fixed army positions and even taking some of them. In fact, the two movements together now had more guerrillas in the field than the Ethiopian army had soldiers, with ELF forces estimated at around 20,000 and those of the EPLF at about 15,000. The PMAC, on the other hand, had only 20,000 to 25,000 men, taken from the First and Second Divisions, the police, and territorial army. However, the guerrillas were still hampered by the lack of sophisticated arms. Although various Arab countries were providing the nationalists with arms, money, and moral support, they were not willing to give them heavy weapons. The reasons why the Arab commitment was less than total are not altogether clear, but certainly the continuing divisions within the Eritrean nationalist movement was one of them. Even the Eritreans acknowledged this.[20] Unity was becoming essential both to obtain greater external support and to mount larger offensives against the towns and cities of the province, the next step in the "people's war."

Back in late 1974, the two factions had finally agreed to stop fighting each other under enormous pressure from both the population and their own rank-and-file guerrillas.[21] They agreed to cooperate in military operations while working on the long and arduous task of reaching a formal unity agreement. In September 1975, leaders of the ELF and EPLF met in Khartoum to discuss ways and means of unifying the two movements. The conference did not lead to immediate reunification, but only to issuing a joint statement of principle on the need for it. The two parties agreed that:

> The unity of our land . . . calls upon all national forces to uplift themselves from secondary differences and fights and face the real constraints that hinder the realization of national unity (e.g. religious fanaticism, tribalism, regionalism, etc.) and devote all their efforts to realize Freedom, Pride and Dignity.[22]

The two sides agreed to hold within six months a "unification conference of the Eritrean revolution," whose specific purpose would be to create "a single organization, with one leadership, and one liberation army in Eritrean land." The conference never took place. On the contrary, the pressures for unity brought into the open not only the continuing divisions between the ELF and the EPLF, but also the split that existed within the EPLF between its military leadership within Eritrea under the command of Issayas Afeworki and its foreign mission led by Woldeab Woldemariam and Osman Saleh Sabe. The EPLF's internal wing wholly rejected the agreement on the ground that their representatives had not been present at Khartoum and that Osman was not entitled to negotiate for the internal forces. The EPLF was suffering from the classical conflict affecting many national liberation movements, a split between fighters in the field and their representatives abroad. Osman had never been inside Eritrea leading troops, but always in foreign capitals soliciting funds for the movement. Furthermore, while the EPLF internal forces had been moving more steadily toward an increasingly Marxist position, Osman had remained first and foremost a moderate Arab nationalist. The unification effort as a result ended by creating a third faction, after Osman was expelled from the EPLF by the internal fighting forces under Issayas on March 25, 1976. Subsequently Osman set up his own organization, called the ELF-EPLF, which had only 2,000 to 3,000 guerrillas in its army but received considerable foreign support, particularly from Iraq, thanks to its leader's contacts.[23]

The efforts at unification also highlighted the changing nature of the divisions between the ELF and the EPLF. While in the beginning the fissures had been mostly due to leadership squabbles and ethnic and religious differences, there had developed later both a "pride of organization" and a different concept of how to wage a liberation war. The EPLF saw the war as a means not only of expelling Ethiopians, but also of restructuring Eritrean society. Thus it went to great lengths to set up administrative structures in liberated zones and to indoctrinate the population in its own Marxist-oriented ideology.[24] Socialism was almost more important for the EPLF than independence. The ELF on the other hand wanted independence first, and was willing to wait until later to decide what type of regime Eritrea would have. Ironically, they both pledged themselves to carry out a "national democratic revolution." Behind these shades of ideological differences, there were by 1976 vested interests in separate organizations, which made compromise all the more difficult. As the smaller but also faster growing of the two organizations, the EPLF was particularly jealous of its identity and afraid of being overwhelmed if an immediate and total merger took place, but confident that in the long run it would prevail over its rival. Despite the lack of progress toward unification, the ELF and EPLF both began achieving great military successes in late 1976. These were the result of the slow but steady strengthening of the two organizations and also of the changing overall situation in Northeast Africa, which suddenly turned the Eritrean conflict from an Ethiopian into an international problem, involving both the Arab countries and the big powers.

The Ogaden

The border conflict between Ethiopia and Somalia dates from the day the former colonies of British Somaliland and Italian Somalia were joined together in the new Republic of Somalia in 1960. The border between the new country and Ethiopia was typically colonial, a line arbitrarily drawn on the map without regard for ethnic, cultural, or economic factors.[25] It cut across a vast area, the Ogaden region, sparsely but uniformly inhabited by Somali tribesmen. The fact that Somalis were nomads, regularly crossing the border in search for water and pastures, did not help to establish separate identities between Somali and Ethiopian citizens. In fact, it would be very difficult to decide which of the nomads regularly crossing the border should be considered citizens of Somalia and which those of Ethiopia. Such a situation is of course far from unique in Africa, where many borders cut across regions inhabited by the same ethnic group. However, there was a difference in this case. As an independent state at the time the Somali-Ethiopian border had been established, Ethiopia was a participant in the negotiations. In other words, Ethiopia had not been a helpless victim of the dealings of European colonial powers, but a party to the conquest of the Horn of Africa: most of the Ogaden was annexed to Ethiopia only in the 1890s, and the contested borders were simply variants of those established in treaties between Ethiopia and Britain in 1897 and Ethiopia and Italy in 1908. The problem was further complicated by the fact that Somalia demanded not minor boundary adjustments but a drastic change, one which would have resulted in its annexation of about one-third of the present Ethiopian territory, including the major towns of Harar and Dire Dawa.[26]

Somali irredentism aimed at annexing not only part of Ethiopia but also the former French Territory of the Afars and the Issas (TFAI) and part of what used to be called Kenyan Northern Frontier District. Again the basis for its claims to these areas was the contention that they were inhabited by Somali-speaking people, an assertion which was basically correct with regard to northern Kenya, but only less than half so in the case of the French Territory, where perhaps 40 percent of the population was Afar. Somali claims to the TFAI were another direct source of conflict between Somalia and Ethiopia, since the port of Djibouti was the terminus of the Chemin de Fer Franco-Ethiopien, the only rail link between Addis Ababa and the Red Sea. The French presence in the TFAI had provided Ethiopia with a guarantee that it could use the port, but France was under compelling pressure in 1974 to grant the Territory its independence, and finally agreed to do so. Pressure came particularly from the Organization of African Unity, which was pressing for the complete decolonization of the continent. Then in July 1974, Somali President Mohamed Siad Barre became president of the Organization and mounted a campaign for the independence of Djibouti that was clearly not due exclusively to his commitment to the principle of decolonization. The Territory's independence was seen by Somalia simply as a first step toward its incorporation into a Greater Somalia.

The Somali-Ethiopian dispute was not merely verbal. The two countries fought a brief border war in 1964 in the Ogaden, in which the Ethiopian army had proven its superiority in a matter of days and had been kept from marching on Mogadishu only by international pressure led by the United States. Ever since that time, Somalia had planned a counteroffensive, building up an irregular guerrilla force, the Western Somalia Liberation Front, which was behind the unrest in Bale Province in the 1960s. After Siad Barre came to power in 1969 and struck an alliance with the Soviet Union, Somalia also started building up its regular armed forces, which quickly became better equipped than the Ethiopian army, although not as well trained. By the onset of the Ethiopian revolution, Somalia had a very respectable standing army of 22,000 men and a large irregular guerrilla force with which to press its irredentist claims.[27] Only the occasion to press its claims was lacking, and the Ethiopian revolution provided it by provoking opposition forces that weakened the central government and stretched the Ethiopian army thin. About half the regular army was bogged down in Eritrea alone after early 1975; there were armed insurrections of one kind or another in eight other provinces also requiring periodically the intervention of the military; and the *Derg* itself was perceived as being extremely unstable.

By mid-1975, according to the Ethiopian government, the Somalis decided the situation was ripe to launch an offensive in the Ogaden. In a document distributed to some African heads of state in January 1976, the PMAC claimed that the Somalis had "set in motion a process of hostile actions which . . . by a gradual process of escalation [can] be guided to a full scale war."[28] The memorandum continued:

While the ultimate objective is to recover by force what Somalia calls her "lost territories"—the Ogaden, the Territory of Djibouti, and the former Northern Frontier District of Kenya—by fomenting a war of subversion in Southern and Eastern Ethiopia, by helping to intensify the secessionist war in Eritrea, and finally by creating a situation of confrontation around the territory of Djibouti, the immediate objective is to force Ethiopian forces into being deployed thinly in many parts of the country, so that Somali forces in areas bordering Ethiopia would have the maximum freedom of action to make a move against Ethiopia at a time and place of their choosing.[29]

The document claimed that the first stage of Somalia's war was already being implemented and that "large groups of well armed and trained agents" were infiltrating Bale, Haraghe, and Sidamo provinces, while the security situation was rapidly deteriorating throughout the Ogaden and in southern Bale. In fact, there were plenty of indications that the Mogadishu government was not content simply to stir up Somali nationalism but was also encouraging the growth of Galla nationalism. Galla elements led by their old leader, Wako Gutu, were again operating under the aegis of the Western Somalia Liberation Front and were now far better armed than they had been in the 1960s. Just how Somalia intended to deal with the Galla population, if it did succeed in seizing control of all the territory it claimed inside Ethiopia, was not clear. Perhaps symptomatic of the embarrassment over this issue was the attitude of WSLF officials who in the summer of 1977 were assuring the authors, against all evidence, that Wako Gutu was a Somali. As the Ethiopian government claimed, "war clouds" were indeed gathering over the Horn of Africa, and the storm was beginning to involve not only Ethiopia and Somalia but also neighboring Arab states and the big powers.

The Arab Factor

Arab involvement in Ethiopia dates back for centuries. Moslems had invaded the Christian empire at various times in its early history; the Turkish empire had claimed suzerainty over the coastal region around Massawa; and Egypt had invaded and controlled parts of Ethiopia in the late 19th century. The Arab interest in Ethiopia in the mid-20th century no longer stemmed from the Moslem-Christian antagonism or from territorial expansionism. It was above all a strategic consideration—the need to dominate the Red Sea as part of the Arab effort to cut Israel off from its sea routes. Thus, ever since the birth of the Eritrean Liberation front, the Arab countries, radical and conservative alike, had been its main backers. For years, the ELF's external headquarters was in the Syrian capital of Damascus, and its other main offices were in Cairo, Beirut, Tripoli, and Baghdad. But Arab support for the Eritrean cause was always less than total because it was tempered by other considerations, at least until the onset of the revolution.

There had been a solidarity across religious lines between the conservative monarchs of Ethiopia and Saudi Arabia. Haile Selassie and Egypt's Gamel Abdel Nasser had respected each other, and the Emperor had held in check Sudanese support for the Eritrean guerrillas by helping President Jaafar Numeiry solve his own problem of secessionism in the southern Sudan. As a result of the Emperor's skillful foreign diplomacy, Eritreans had fought mostly with captured arms and had lacked the sophisticated weaponry such as the Arabs provided to the Palestinian Liberation Organization. The PMAC was far less successful than the Emperor in tempering the Arab commitment to the Eritrean cause. By definition, conservative Arab countries were against revolutionary Ethiopia. But moderates and most of the radicals also turned against it and stepped up their support for the Eritreans. The new military government succeeded in swaying only South Yemen and Libya away from their commitment to the Eritreans, but not before the latter country had made a final U.S. $4 million contribution to help finance the Eritrean assault on Asmara in January 1975.[30] The PMAC had to pay a high price for Libyan support: it agreed to allow Ethiopian territory to be used as a staging ground for an attempt by Colonel Muammar Qaddafi to overthrow Jaafar Numeiry in July 1976. This precipitated a series of changes in the fortunes of the Eritrean nationalists and the Ethiopian Democratic Union as well as in Ethiopia's international relations.

Until the coup attempt, President Numeiry had tried to serve as mediator between the PMAC and the Eritrean nationalists, just as the Emperor had done between himself and the Anyanya guerrillas of the southern Sudan, and as late as September 1975, the PMAC was publicly thanking him for his efforts.[31] It is not clear what drove the *Derg* to become involved in a plot to overthrow Numeiry by a conservative religious group like the Ansars. The apparent explanation is that this was the price Qaddafi asked for his change of policy toward the Eritreans and that the PMAC was becoming increasingly desperate in its efforts to curb the guerrillas' steady military progress. It may also have been related to the military council's efforts to establish an opening toward the East, the Soviet Union in particular, and to obtain a source of arms other than the United States.[32] In any case, the *Derg* agreed to help the Libyans train some of the 5,000 Ansar refugees living in northwest Ethiopia near Gondar and to allow them to infiltrate back into the Sudan in the months before the July 5 coup attempt. Unfortunately for the PMAC, the coup failed and Numeiry became furious upon discovering the Ethiopian involvement. He then decided to throw his wholehearted support not only behind the Eritreans but the EDU as well. In this manner, he hoped to create a buffer zone controlled by elements hostile to the Ethiopian military government along the extensive Ethiopian-Sudanese border in order to prevent further Ansar infiltrations.

Beginning in September of 1976, the fortunes of the EDU, and shortly thereafter of the ELF, dramatically changed. EDU forces were given arms and were trained in camps outside Gedaref near the border of Begemdir Province, and the ELF and EPLF were given complete freedom of movement in Sudanese territory as well as official Sudanese military and diplomatic backing. By December, Numeiry was openly attacking the *Derg* for its involvement in the July coup attempt, and by January 1977 he was publicly declaring his full support for the Eritrean cause. Moreover, he enlisted Egypt and Saudi Arabia in his anti-Ethiopian campaign, appealing to these two nations' interest in completing Arab control of the Red Sea by assuring an Eritrean victory.

The new interest of pro-Western conservative and moderate Arab countries in the Eritrean cause fit into their larger diplomatic game of combating Soviet influence throughout the Middle East and of building closer ties to the United States, despite its backing of Israel. Saudi Arabia encouraged Numeiry to make a final break with the Soviet Union, offering him $200 million to buy arms from the West to replace outdated Soviet weapons and large-scale economic aid in addition. It was the same policy the Saudis had successfully pursued in Egypt and were attempting in Somalia. There, Saudi Arabia was again offering hundreds of millions of dollars in economic and financial assistance to entice the Somalis away from the Soviet Union. As the independence of Eritrea became more likely, the Saudis also took a greater interest in the conflict because of their desire to prevent a radical, Marxist regime from being established on the other side of the Red Sea and to pull the new state into its own conservative orbit.

The United States and the Soviet Union

The Ethiopian revolution presented the United States with the dilemma of whether to continue supporting Ethiopia despite the increasingly radical policies pursued by the new government or to rethink its entire position in the Horn of Africa. Ever since the November 1974 executions, the United States had questioned whether Ethiopia's strategic value remained sufficient to justify continuing American backing for such a radical military government. Already, the American perception of Ethiopia's importance as a link in the worldwide U.S. communications and defense system was waning. The Kagnew base in Asmara had been transformed from a sprawling installation with 3,000 military and civilian employees into a residual radio communications center with only a few hundred personnel by the onset of the revolution. An unusually steep request for $500 million in military assistance made by the Emperor in 1973 had in effect been turned down, although officially it remained "under review." Still, the United States was committed by various treaties with Ethiopia to continue providing military assistance until 1978, and whatever might happen the country was by far the most populous and central in the Horn of Africa. The policy adopted after an official "reconsideration" in December 1974 reflected an ambivalence toward the new Ethiopia and Washington's incapacity to reach a clear decision. It was in effect to keep a low profile, continue selling arms and offering economic aid, and wait and see. In the meantime, it continued "phasing down" its Kagnew communications center, spurred on in this by the numerous kidnappings of American personnel there by Eritrean guerrillas.

The Ethiopian attitude toward the United States was equally ambivalent. A continuing close alliance with Washington hardly fitted in with the increasingly radical policies of the *Derg*, nor the Marxist image it tried to project after April 1976. On the other hand, the Ethiopian armed forces were totally dependent upon American arms, and their modernization through the purchase of more than $200 million worth of new weapons, including M-60 tanks and F-5E jets, was already under way. Furthermore, there was no ready alternative supplier, since the Soviet Union was backing Ethiopia's principal enemy, Somalia.

Still, the PMAC began in early 1976 sounding out the Soviets on the possibility of obtaining arms, but the results of these first contacts were not encouraging. When Major Mengistu went in June 1976 to talk to disgruntled leftist elements at the Debre Zeit Air Force Base, who asked why the *Derg* was still buying its arms from the United States, he is reported to have told them, "What else can we do, the Soviets will not provide them."[33] Initially, Yugoslavia was the only Communist country willing to provide arms, albeit only small ones.[34] The Soviet Union, on the other hand, had presented the PMAC with a stark choice: in order to get Soviet arms and backing, it would have to commit itself to a clear break with the United States. The choice, as could have been expected, was a difficult one, and what made it even more difficult was its entanglement in the power struggle under way inside the military council.

The opening to the Soviet Union and the break with the United States was almost certainly engineered by Mengistu with the strong support of the Political Bureau's Marxist ideologues. The American embassy in Addis Ababa had reports that Mengistu bore a grudge against the United States that stemmed from a racial incident that had occurred during one of his training stints there. Certainly he kept his distance from American officials, for none ever saw him after he came to power as the *Derg*'s first vice-chairman. Mengistu's problem was to convince a majority of his colleagues of the wisdom of a sharp swing toward the Soviet Union and away from the West, the United States in particular. In this task, he was greatly facilitated by the attitude of American officialdom that was slow to respond to the military council's emergency requests for $25–27 million of ammunition in the spring of 1975 following the Eritrean nationalists' assault on Asmara.[35] In effect, Washington was showing that it could not be counted upon to meet the *Derg*'s military needs, even though it was the country's main arms supplier.

Mengistu had to find another source of military aid. The search began in early 1976 with a series of official delegations visiting the Eastern bloc countries, China and Vietnam. The latter country was of particular interest to the PMAC since it had vast quantities of captured American arms. Other military delegations were sent on secret missions to China during the summer and to the Soviet Union in December 1976. China made a goodwill gesture, providing 200 tons of small arms for the peasant militia in January 1977, but refused to make a larger commitment. The Soviet Union, however, signed an agreement for some initial military assistance and declared itself ready to become Ethiopia's main arms supplier on the condition that the PMAC sever its military relationship with the United States. By the end of the year, Mengistu and the Political Bureau must have felt they had sufficient commitment from the Soviet Union and its allies to make such a military break feasible. This growing confidence was first reflected in the increasingly venomous attacks in the media against the United States and in particular the C.I.A.

The exact role of the Soviet Union and is allies, Cuba in particular, in Mengistu's seizure of power in early February 1977 remains unclear. In retrospect, there seems to be little doubt that he had made secret contacts with Soviet and Cuban diplomats in Addis Ababa and had received assurances of immediate recognition if he took power and eliminated his adversaries within the PMAC. Less than twenty-four hours after his takeover, Mengistu received a personal message of congratulations from Fidel Castro and met with the Soviet ambassador to Ethiopia, Anatoli P. Ratanov, who assured him of Soviet backing. Such quick recognition strongly suggests that these two Communist countries were aware of Mengistu's plan ahead of time.

Following the Soviet lead, all Eastern bloc countries sent messages of support to Mengistu in the first days after his takeover in a well-orchestrated show of support. China, on the other hand, only affirmed its continuing approval of Ethiopia's national democratic revolution and its admiration for the "men in uniform" without singling out Mengistu for special praise or congratulating him on his success. In mid-February, a large delegation from the German Democratic Republic paid a visit to Ethiopia with much fanfare, while the Soviet Union apparently pledged to send heavy arms, and Cuba promised military advisers to replace the Americans.

In early March, thirty Soviet tanks arrived from South Yemen, providing the first public evidence of the new Soviet commitment to supply more than $100 million in arms to Ethiopia. By mid-April, more than 100 tanks and armored personnel carriers had arrived directly from the Soviet Union. On April 23, Mengistu was ready to make his formal break with the United States, encouraged no doubt by the fact that he had been informed a few days earlier that Washington would reduce by more than half its forty-six man Military Advisory Assistance Group and was planning to close its communications center in Asmara by September. Taking the initiative away from the Americans, he ordered the expulsion of the entire MAAG and the closure of the U.S. communications center and consulate in Asmara, the United States Information Service, and the Naval Medical Research Unit in Addis Ababa. On May 3, Mengistu went to the Soviet Union on a week-long state visit and signed an agreement establishing the framework for future Soviet-Ethiopian cooperation in various fields. The American connection was finally broken and the Soviet one established. In the following six months, the Soviet Union was to provide well over $500 million in arms to Ethiopia after having already sent more than $1 billion worth to Somalia.

The Soviet Gamble

The new Soviet policy toward Ethiopia involved a huge gamble. It directly jeopardized the Soviet position in Somalia which had been one of the keystones of its overall diplomacy toward black Africa, and risked a total break with the Sudan. Having been summarily ousted from Egypt in 1973 with the cancellation of the Soviet-Egyptian treaty of Friendship and Cooperation, the Soviet Union stood a good chance of losing its foothold at the other end of the Suez Canal-Red Sea waterway as well. Furthermore, the new Soviet tilt toward Ethiopia provided the cement for consolidating all of the PMAC's enemies and for building an alliance of moderate and conservative countries in the region against Ethiopia. The question is why the Soviet Union felt it worthwhile to back an unstable regime of uncertain duration that was fighting wars simultaneously on three different fronts.

There were both strategic and ideological considerations behind the gamble. Like the Americans, the Soviets fully realized that Ethiopia, with its large territory and population, was in the long run the real power of the Horn of Africa. Furthermore, it was strategically located—provided Eritrea did not become independent. Ethiopia fitted nicely into the Soviet regional policies, one regarding the Arab world and the other the strategic waterways of the Indian Ocean and the Red Sea. In the Arab world, the Soviet Union in the 1975–77 period was backing radical Libya against the pro-Western moderate and conservative Arab states, namely Egypt, Saudi Arabia, and the Sudan. Ethiopia had already shown its willingness to ally itself with Libya's Colonel Qaddafi in his quarrel with Sudanese President Numeiry and was increasingly bitter about conservative Arab support for the Eritreans. Thus, there was a basis for an Ethiopian-Libyan axis that could serve Soviet designs aimed at undermining President Anwar Sadat of Egypt and his Arab allies.

In the Red Sea region, only Ethiopia could keep this waterway from becoming an "Arab Lake" dominated by conservative and moderate Arab countries hostile to the Soviet Union. It is true that supporting Ethiopia entailed the risk of losing Somalia and thus the western approaches to the Red Sea, but Soviet strategists apparently calculated that Somalia was far too dependent on Moscow militarily and too ideologically committed to the socialist camp to break entirely away from it. They also thought that they could get Ethiopia and Somalia to overcome their nationalist conflicts in the name of socialism and to unite in a federation that would also include Marxist South Yemen on the eastern side of the Straits of Bab-el-Mandeb. Such a solution would have tremendously strengthened the Soviet position both in the Red Sea and the Indian Ocean, giving it naval and air facilities in three and possibly four countries, if Djibouti could be included in the federation once it became independent. There was also an ideological rationale for backing the PMAC. By the spring of 1976, Ethiopia was a self-declared Marxist state that had carried out undisputably sweeping reforms and was desperately trying to free itself from its dependence on the United States. The Soviet Union simply could not turn its back. Furthermore, many Soviet diplomats in the region had come to the conclusion that the Ethiopian military were carrying out a revolution very similar to the Soviet one, with its overthrow of a feudal monarch, its bypassing of a bourgeois revolution to plunge headlong into a socialist one, and with a real element of class struggle that was lacking in Somalia. One Soviet diplomat explained to an Arab colleague in Mogadishu that his government had decided to back the Ethiopian military government even at the risk of losing Somalia because "we feel the Ethiopian revolution is more genuine."[36]

At the time of this writing, the odds against the Soviet gamble paying off seemed great indeed, since nationalism was proving to be a much greater force than Marxism throughout the Horn of Africa. Far from accepting the imposition of the Soviet policy of federation, Somalia rejected it flatly and regarded the shipment of Soviet arms to Ethiopia as a betrayal of the Soviet-Somali Treaty of Friendship and Cooperation signed in 1974. The new Soviet policy even served to stimulate Somali nationalism, inciting the Somali government to step up the activities of the Western Somali Liberation Front throughout southeast Ethiopia. Not even the personal intervention of Fidel Castro could convince Ethiopia and Somalia to bury their differences and join together in a federation. During his visit to the Horn of Africa in mid-March, Castro forced a confrontation between Mengistu and Somali President Siad Barre in the South Yemen capital of Aden that backfired, adding to the wave of anti-Soviet sentiment sweeping over Somalia.

The Soviets tried to resolve the Eritrean conflict in a similar manner, proposing a federation between Eritrea and Ethiopia that would have given the province a status analogous to Belorussia in the Union of Soviet Socialist Republics. But the reaction of the Eritrean nationalists was just as negative as that of the Somalis and the proposal summarily rejected. Furthermore, the Eritreans were enraged that the Soviet Union and Cuba, which had supported them during their long years of struggle against the Emperor, had now turned against them and were even forcing them into the orbit of moderate and conservative pro-Western Arab countries. Paradoxically, by 1977 even the more moderate ELF was drawing its main ideological inspiration from Marx, Lenin, and Castro, while the vagaries of international politics had pitted the Eritrean nationalists against the Soviet Union and put them increasingly under obligation to the conservative Arab countries.

The Arab reaction to the new Soviet presence in Ethiopia was just as strong. Sudanese support for both the ELF and the EDU became quite open, and by mid-April Sudanese artillery and tanks were providing ground fire for the latter group's successful assault on the Ethiopian border town of Metemma. Moreover, in early March, the Sudan became part of the joint military command that had been formed earlier between Syria and Egypt. The new tripartite alliance, which had strong Saudi backing, was aimed partly against Libya and partly against Ethiopia, with Arab control of the Red Sea one of its main preoccupations. Far from solving any of the conflicts facing the *Derg,* Soviet intervention in Ethiopia had the opposite effect of worsening them, escalating the wars in Eritrea, the Ogaden, and northwest Ethiopia. All of the PMAC's enemies scrambled to score decisive victories before the impact of new Soviet arms could be felt or before Cuba sent troops to bolster the military government, an eventuality that neither Eritreans nor Somalis excluded. In short, Soviet intervention in Ethiopia touched off what Mengistu called a "race against time" to bring down the *Derg* and dismantle the old empire "within the next three months."[37]

The Unravelling of the Empire

Beginning in early January, the military situation for the central government began taking a decisive turn for the worse on all fronts. In Eritrea, the army first lost its major border garrisons at Kerora, Om Hagger, and Tessenei and then began losing major towns deep inside the province such as Nakfa, Elaberet, and Afabet.[38] Finally, in early July it lost the three major towns of Keren, Agordat, and Decamhare, leaving only the ports of Massawa and Assab and the provincial capital of Asmara still in the hands of the central government.[39] In the northwest province of Begemdir, the EDU captured Humera, then Abderafe, and finally Metemma along the Sudanese border, while its forces began penetrating Ethiopia to within a few miles of the provincial capital of Gondar. By early 1977, the "white army" of the EDU had grown into a force of some 6,000 men and was armed with bazookas and light artillery, much of it Soviet equipment given earlier to the Sudan.[40] The Union, moreover, attracted more and more support, as anti-Marxist and anti-Soviet elements in Ethiopian society rallied to its side and against the "red" *Derg*. In the Ogaden, the Western Somalia Liberation Front seized all the small villages and towns and then the larger centers of Gode and Degahabur, and by late July engaged the Ethiopian army in major battles for the towns of Dire Dawa and Harar.[41] The PMAC claimed that regular Somali army officers, troops, tanks, and airplanes were involved in the fighting. The Somali government denied any direct involvement, but proudly proclaimed tht two-thirds of the territory to which it lay claim were now in the hands of the Western Somalia Liberation Front.

Faced with the possible loss of over half the land mass belonging to the old empire, the PMAC resorted to the tactic Emperor Menelik had used in the late 19th century to conquer the same territory, the levy of a huge army of peasant-warriors. But there was an ironic historic twist to the whole venture: the bulk of the soldiers for this new peasant army came this time from Galla territories conquered by Menelik in the south; it was the subjected who were now fighting to hold the empire together. Aware that its own survival, national unity, and perhaps the fate of the revolution were at stake, the PMAC went to great lengths to avoid the same mistakes made a year earlier in the organization of its peasant march on Eritrea. This time, the 100,000 recruits were given six weeks training, with the help of twenty to thirty Cuban military advisers, and armed with new automatic rifles provided by the Soviet Union and East Germany. It was a formidable looking "people's army" that paraded through Revolution Square on June 25. Whether it would prove itself equally formid-able on the battlefield and stem the unravelling of the empire remained to be seen.

11. The New Ethiopia

In mid-1977, many unknowns hung over the future of Ethiopia. Would Eritrea finally become indepndent as seemed more and more likely? Would Somalia succeed in annexing the Ogaden region and possibly much more? Would the Soviet Union and Cuba increase their commitment to the Mengistu government to turn the course of the various wars under way in its favor? Would they continue supporting the PMAC if these wars were lost and Ethiopia became a landlocked country of marginal strategic value? Finally, would Mengistu survive if the empire crumbled and what changes would his demise bring? None of these questions could be answered with any certainty. However, one thing was quite clear: a revolution had taken place in Ethiopia, and no matter what happened to the nation or Mengistu, there would be no returning to the *ancien régime*. The three pillars of the old order—monarchy, church, and landed aristocracy—had been swept away in a torrent of reforms. There was no chance whatsoever that another emperor would rule Ethiopia with absolute powers, and even the likelihood of a constitutional monarchy was remote, as the Ethiopian Democratic Union itself had come to recognize.

The Orthodox Christian Church had ceased to play any role in national politics and was struggling simply to survive after the loss of all its land and of its influence with the country's rulers. In February 1976, the *Derg* had finally deposed the patriarch, Abuna Tewoflos, with no opposition, accusing him of corruption, abuse of power, and embezzlement. In June, the church for the first time in its history held elections for a new head, selecting a barefoot monk by the name of Melaku Wolde-Michael, who had no interest in politics and apparently not even in church reform. Under his guidance, the Ethiopian Orthodox Church appeared destined to remain a marginal institution at the national level, completely out of step with the rapidly changing times.

The landed aristocracy appeared to be going through its death throes in scattered revolts throughout the country. Even the EDU, which was providing arms and encouragement to rebel landlords, was trying hard to convince the public that it was not just the party of the fallen aristocracy and that it did not favor a restoration of the old order. There was every indication that the days of the *rases* and *dejazmatches* were over, although it was still conceivable that a new class of "kulaks" and agricultural entrepreneurs might arise to take their place.

Although a profound social and political revolution had taken place in Ethiopia, it was still unclear in mid-1977 what kind of society and polity would emerge. The Soviets and Cubans had seen the revolution's potential for development toward a socialist system. The Chinese recognized this, too, although they were somewhat more reserved in their support because Mengistu had chosen Moscow over Peking. In the West, the prevailing judgment of the revolution was negative, and the PMAC was generally denounced as a "fascist military dictatorship" by the left and a "Communist regime" by the right.[1] Within Ethiopia, the educated civilian elite by and large supported the contention that the *Derg* was "fascist" rather than socialist, meaning that it was authoritarian and repressive rather than democratic. In the midst of these sharply conflicting views about the Ethiopian revolution, where did the truth lie? To some extent, the problem was one of semantics, depending on one's definition of the terms "fascism" and "socialism." If the word "fascism" is taken in its historical meaning, an authoritarian government collaborating with capitalist interests as in Italy under Mussolini or Spain under General Franco, then it should be clear by now that the *Derg* was hardly "fascist." But if the term is interpreted to mean more loosely any system that suppresses individual liberties in the name of a common interest as defined by the government, then it was fascist, but no more so than Fidel Castro's Cuba or Mao's China. In other words, this concept of fascism is far too broad to be meaningful. Conservative regimes have no monopoly on authoritarianism. The term "socialism" is also open to many interpretations. If the word is understood in a strict historical sense, that is, to denote the political-economic system existing in countries such as the Soviet Union and China, then the PMAC was certainly heading toward the establishment of some variant of this kind of government and economy. On the other hand, if socialism is taken in the utopian sense of a system which combines perfect participatory democracy with economic equality and complete respect for individual liberties, then Ethiopia is not socialist, any more than are China, Vietnam or Cuba. Whatever the classical meanings of such terms, the conclusion of the authors is that Ethiopia is moving toward some form of socialism, despite the undeniable authoritarianism of the *Derg,* its brutal attempt to crush the EPRP, and its lack of respect for individual liberties.

What kind of socialism will the Ethiopian revolution produce? Will it be state socialism of the Soviet variety, characterized by centralization and bureaucratic management, as suggested by the growing Soviet influence? Will it be Chinese-style socialism, combining some decentralized, local democracy in communes with the centralizing rule of a party, as suggested by the emphasis on peasant associations? Might it become a form of Yugoslav socialism, based on worker self-management of enterprises and farms and incorporating some features of a market economy? Or will the final outcome be some version of "soft" African socialism, more humanitarian than Marxist in its ideology, one in which an authoritarian but weak central government tries with limited success to bring about national social and economic changes, such as in Tanzania or Zambia?

If the radicals in the *Derg* and the ideologues of the Political Bureau have any model in mind, it is probably the Chinese one. The peasant associations and urban *kebeles* are institutions favoring a democratic, decentralized system, one which creates a powerful "contradiction" to the central administration and bureaucracy. Also, the plan for creating autonomous regions for each of the country's "nationalities" would seem to point toward a highly decentralized system. On the other hand, there are powerful centralizing forces in the military, the central bureaucracy, and the embryonic party. Beginning in early 1977, the *Derg* sought to use its newly created institutions, particularly the *kebeles* and peasant associations, to crush internal opposition and to fight its wars in Eritrea and the Ogaden. It was trying to employ these institutions of local democracy to extend the military council's control over the country. Yet the central government remained relatively weak and risked becoming far weaker if the PMAC lost the wars in Eritrea and the Ogaden. There was the possibility that the government, far from imposing excessive control over the new institutions, would not even be strong enough to offer sufficient guidance and assistance to prevent them from drifting aimlessly. The conflict between centralizing and decentralizing forces could be seen at work in all of Ethiopia's institutions, old and new, in the first half of 1977. In a parody of the famous Marxist prediction, one Western economist working in Ethiopia observed that there was a real danger of the "premature withering away of the Ethiopian state."

The Central Administration

The central administration in Ethiopia remained, throughout the first three years after the overthrow of the Emperor, the civilian institution with the most authoritarian tendencies. For all the newspaper articles by ideologues of the Political Bureau on the need to fight "bureaucratic capitalism" and "petty bourgeois" inclinations among nearly 100,000 civil servants, the central administration was never subjected to an overall reform or a systematic purge. The lack of alternative personnel with sufficient education was probably the main reason for this. There were not enough socialist-minded cadres to form and staff a new administration.

The *Derg* first tried to deal with this problem by appointing army officers to serve as its "eyes and ears" in every ministry and by trying to recruit *zemacha* students into the administration. But the PMAC's appointees in the ministries spent most of their time dealing with left-wing "counterrevolutionaries" rather than conservatives in civil service ranks, and the *zemacha* graduates were inexperienced and often anti-military. The *Derg* then adopted another approach: reeducation of as many senior civil servants and political appointees as possible. It sent hundreds of them to special indoctrination sessions at the ideological school in Addis Ababa and hundreds of others, including many *Derg* members, to Eastern Europe and China. this process certainly succeeded in politicizing the top echelons of the various ministries. Lower echelons of the administration nevertheless remained essentially the same as they had been under the Emperor, staffed by conservative and cautious civil servants unlikely to oppose reform openly but inclined to slow it down through inaction and indecision. Their passive resistance was undoubtedly encouraged by the atmosphere of fear engendered by the PMAC's tendency to blame civilians for everything that went wrong.

Around this passive inner administrative core was a fringe of activists— supporters of the Political Bureau and the EPRP, or even of the ELF and EDU. These activists engaged in furious debates in the "workers' forums" held on Monday and Friday afternoon in all government offices and enterprises; they later tried to eliminate each other through assassinations and mutual denunciations. Their activities served only to divide and further paralyze the administration. They also diverted attention from policy to politics, from carrying out reforms to jockeying for positions of power or simply worrying about survival. To be sure, there were some reform-minded civil servants in each ministry sincerely trying to tackle the economic and social problems at hand. But they were consistently opposed by the administration's conservative inner core.

At the heart of the struggle between reformers and conservatives was the issue of whether to maintain the old, centralized system of administration, where the central government made all decisions, collected all taxes, and delivered all services, or to establish a new decentralized form of government, in which peasant associations and *kebeles* would be given considerable autonomy, the power of taxation, and the responsibility for providing most local services. For example, a group of reformers in the Ministry of Education was preparing in mid-1976 a new "basic education" program emphasizing control of the schools by the peasant associations in accordance with policy guidelines approved by the *Derg*. Suddenly, they were ordered to stop their work by a high official in the ministry who opposed the principle of relinquishing central control to the associations. Finally, the minister himself had to intervene on behalf of the reformers.[2] Another example of contradictory policies followed simultaneously was the Awash Valley Authority's resettlement of nomads. In 1976, reformers in the Authority prepared a project for a "minimum mechanization" settlement in the valley aimed at making nomads into independent farmers within a few growing seasons rather than keeping them under the tutelage of the AVA, as previous programs had done. This approach was in agreement with the new official government policy on nomad settlement. While the new approach was being tested in a pilot project, another department of the AVA undertook a large-scale settlement scheme on the basis of the old, heavily criticized bureaucratic model. Afar nomads were again settled around Assaita in the Awash Delta, where they would have no other future except as dependents of the AVA. Even worse, they were allowed to hire highland migrants to do their work in open defiance of both the spirit and letter of land reform.

The struggle between reformers and conservatives also involved the Ministry of Agriculture. After land reform was announced in March 1975, radicals in the ministry broke up many of the large nationalized farms and distributed the land among neighboring peasant associations in an attempt to combat the tendency toward centralization and bureaucratic state management inherent in government-run enterprises. At the same time, another faction within the ministry pushed for the maintenance of large farms as state-run operations and even the creation of many new ones as the government's main answer to the problem of supplying the urban centers with sufficient food. This faction also drew up plans for the establishment of a third, heavily mechanized sugar plantation without even taking into consideration the possibility of encouraging peasant associations to grow cane themselves with a much smaller capital outlay. The ministry remained divided over whether to expand agricultural production by providing services to peasant assocations or establishing state farms it could control directly.

The tendency toward state socialism and centralized control was strongest and most evident in the industrial sector. There, the government simply appointed managers of its own choosing to run the some 200 nationalized agricultural and industrial enterprises and placed most of them under a new Ministry of National Resources Development. The result was not only a large, over-centralized bureaucracy but also a tremendous amount of strife between the workers and the state-appointed managers. In the spring of 1976, this labor-management conflict reached the point where over two dozen state managers were "locked out" of their offices by the workers. The government's response was to send in the police, and in some cases regular army troops, to quell the workers' revolts and to uphold the existing state manager. The ministry was eventually dismantled and the various state farms, industries, and commercial enterprises were divided up among four different ministries.[3] Still, all the nationalized companies remained under state management, and the government never seemed to consider seriously an alternative management model that would give a direct role to the workers in running their own enterprises. This predominant tendency toward state socialism in the industrial sector stood in sharp contrast to the policy of direct participation and decentralization prevailing in the agricultural sector of the economy with the creation of the peasant associations.

On balance, it was the centralizing tendency that dominated the central administration. In the provinces, or "regions" as they were called after 1975, the situation was quite different. Land reform had abolished the lower echelons of the provincial administration, the *balabbats* and *chika shums* who had run the villages. There had also been a systematic purge of *woreda* and *awraja* administrators at the time of land reform, and the new appointees were not only younger and more dynamic but also much more progressive. In fact, well-known student activists were given posts. It was not only the different character of the new administrators but also the structural weakness of the provincial administration that helped check any centralizing, authoritarian tendency there. Local administrators under the *Derg* still had very little to work with, having only a tiny staff and a budget that covered little more than salaries.

While the provincial administration remained about as weak as it had been under Emperor Haile Selassie, it now had to deal with peasant associations that quickly grew in strength and militancy. With the help of *zemacha* campaigners, the balance of forces in the countryside was soon swinging away from the administrators and toward the associations. There were reports of *woredas* where the administrator had virtually ceased to exercise any power and was paralyzed by the conflicting pressures brought to bear upon him by the Ministry of Interior in Addis Ababa, the peasant associations, the police, the town *kebeles,* and the local officials of the Provincial Office for Mass Organizational Affairs (POMOA). The successful administrator became simply a good arbitrator among the conflicting political forces at work in his area. It was he, for example, who mediated between the Ethiopian Road Authority wanting to build a coherent network of rural roads and the peasant association willing to give land and labor only for a road leading to *its* market. Or it was he who succeeded in resolving the conflict between the associations that wanted all children immediately to attend school and the single teacher sent by the Ministry of Education who balked at the impossible task of educating them all at once. In sum, the prevailing tendency in the regions was toward the diffusion and decentralization of power, rather than its centralization. As for a bureaucracy, there was scarcely any since the Ministry of Interior still had a very limited presence in the countryside. Its influence waned even further as peasant associations and urban *kebeles* were strengthened by new decrees.

The Peasant Assocations

The peasant associations were a powerful countervailing force to all centralizing trends. If anything, they contained the potential for creating extreme, and even excessive, decentralization of power and administration throughout the country. The rural land reform proclamation of March 1975 had left many unresolved issues concerning the role and power of the peasant associations, particularly whether they were to become units of self-government or merely local land reform offices staffed by peasants. The answer to this question came when the "Peasant Association Organization and Consolidation Proclamation" was issued in December 1975.[4] This lengthy proclamation both broadened and precisely defined the functions of the associations and even sought to establish the missing links between them and the central government. First, it empowered the associations to carry out the following:[5]

1. To enable peasants to secure and safeguard their political, economic and social rights

2. To enable the peasantry to administer itself

3. To enable the peasantry to participate in the struggle against feudalism and imperialism by building its consciousness in line with *Hebrettesebawinet*

4. To establish co-operative societies, women's associations, peasant defence squads and any other associations that may be necessary for the fulfillment of its goals and aims

5. To enable the peasantry to work collectively and to speed up social development by improving the quality of the instruments of production and the level of productivity.

6. To sue and be sued

7. To issue and implement its internal regulations in order to achieve its goals and aims

If there had been any doubts earlier about the government's intentions regarding the peasant associations, they were now dispelled. It was clear that they were supposed to become self-governing political units, channels through which rural development would henceforth be implemented.

Their economic and political role was further spelled out in provisions regarding the formation of cooperative societies. Two types of cooperatives were envisaged: service cooperatives and "agricultural producers' cooperative societies."[6] The former had strictly economic functions, namely to provide their members with extension services, loans, storage facilities, and marketing services. They were also meant to encourage savings, distribute basic consumer goods, and establish flour mills and small cottage industries. The agricultural producers' cooperatives, on the other hand, had essentially political objectives and seemed to open the way for the establishment of communes. They would control directly the "main instruments of production" of their members, their officials would be drawn only from among poor and middle peasants, and their main tasks would be the abolition of exploitation and the political indoctrination of the peasantry. Membership in both types of cooperatives was open to peasant associations but not to individual farmers, thus strengthening the collective aspect of these bodies. In addition, the proclamation gave the associations the power to set up women's associations and defense squads or militias, the latter which would replace the old rural police forces. At the same time, it broadened the powers of the judiciary committee so that they could deal not only with land reform issues and disputes but also with a large variety of local civil and criminal cases where the penalties involved jail sentences up to three months.

The proclamation simultaneously established *woreda, awraja,* and regional "revolutionary administrative and development committees" which were to be the links between the elected peasant association officials and appointed local, district, and regional administrators.[7] These committees were regarded as temporary until a new law on local self-administration was promulgated. They were to be composed of both appointed officials and peasant association representatives, with the former in the majority, particularly at the regional level. There, the peasants had no representation at all, leaving only the *zemacha* coordinator for the region and a *zemacha* student representative to counter-balance a long list of government officials.

With the end of the *zemacha* in June 1976, only bureaucrats remained on the regional revolutionary committees. The main intent of the PMAC in setting up these bodies was obviously to establish some government control over the associations and to integrate them into an overall administrative structure, one far more extensive than had ever existed before. But the associations seemed to have had as much impact on the government bureaucracy as bureaucrats had on peasants. By the fall of 1976, officials in the Ministry of Interior were reporting that splits were developing within the revolutionary committees, with the peasant association representatives, and the more progressive government officials on one side and the more conservative bureaucrats and police officers on the other.[8] The most divisive issues were reported to be those regarding the application of land reform, particularly the distribution of plots belonging to the state farms. It would probably be grossly exaggerated to state that the revolutionary committees brought about drastic changes in regional administration. However, they did introduce a new element of challenge to the established bureaucracy which had not previously existed. Moreover, they served their main purpose by finally linking Addis Ababa to the far-flung peasant associations.

The proclamation empowered peasant associations to form women's associations and defense squads, or people's militias. The formation of women's associations proved difficult, and, in fact, in the months following the proclamation, their number apparently dwindled rather than increased.[9] This failure may be related to the withdrawal from the countryside of *zemacha* students who had been the dynamic force behind the drive to organize the women and had succeeded in forming 3,240 associations with roughly 324,000 members.[10] The attitude of students on the question of women's liberation and their insistence in pushing for an immediate, radical change in this regard in the countryside became a major irritant in the campaigners' relations with the peasants. It even led in some instances to demands for students to be withdrawn immediately from the peasant associations. The lack of receptivity among the peasantry to the idea of women's emancipation was further confirmed by the prompt collapse of many of their associations as soon as the *zemacha* was terminated.

The *Derg* met with few obstacles, on the other hand, in organizing peasant defense squads. The idea of forming such militias had first been set forth by *zemacha* students and radicals in both the Political Bureau and EPRP who saw it as a means to help peasants stand up to those landlords who resisted implementation of land reform. It was undoubtedly the influence of these radical intellectuals that was responsible for the provisions regarding the formation of peasant militias in the December 1975 proclamation. What caused the *Derg* to embark on a major drive to form the militias, however, was something completely different.

The decision to call off the peasant march on Eritrea in June 1976 had left the *Derg* with many thousands of armed and discontented peasants on its hands. The problem was solved by organizing rural defense squads and integrating into them the peasants returning from the aborted campaign. The peasant militias rapidly increased in size, for there was no shortage of men wanting to be trained and armed. They were provided with rather old guns and given one to three month's training and political indoctrination. Then they were sent to track down, alone or with the help of the army and police, dissident landlords. In Bale Province, they were extensively used to help fight the guerrillas of the Western Somalia Liberation Front. The government claimed in June 1976 that there were already 500,000 militia men and women, and that any army of six million peasants could easily be raised.[11] By the authors' own reckoning, the size of the peasant militia in early 1977 was closer to 200,000, still a very large number.[12] This force remained under the control of the associations. When the *Derg* in mid-1977 organized a new peasant army of 100,000 men to fight in Eritrea and the Ogaden, it recruited and trained new elements, leaving the old militias to protect their home territories. The creation of the defense squads greatly strengthened the associations, giving them the means to oppose not only "counterrevolutionary" landlords but potentially also the central government.

During 1976, the government made further efforts to consolidate the peasant associations and to integrate them into the national administrative structure. In January, it issued a decree setting the amount of land taxes to be paid by the peasants and giving the associations the responsibility of collecting them.[13] The associations were allowed to keep only 2 percent of the taxes collected as payment for their services. Because of this, the proclamation was interpreted by some radical critics as a sign that the government was out to destroy the autonomy of the peasant associations, reducing them to the role of simple tax collectors rather than allowing them to become self-governing units with their own taxation powers.

However, such criticism seemed to be completely unfounded. The land tax imposed by the government was extremely low, amounting to only Eth.$3.00 (US$1.50) a year for most peasant families.[14] There was nothing to prevent the associations from imposing additional taxes on their members to raise funds for local projects. Indeed, the tax was so low that it showed the government did not intend to extract revenue for development from the peasantry. The Ministry of Finance even had trouble collecting the small land tax it had imposed. The truth of the matter was that by the time the land tax proclamation was issued there already existed strong pressure on the *Derg* to make a radical departure from the centralized, bureaucratic concept of the state as an agency entrusted with monopolistic powers to collect revenues and provide public services.

Ideologues and pragmatists in and around the *Derg* promoted the idea that peasant associations should become increasingly responsible for financing and delivering services to their members. For example, plans already existed in the Ministry of Education to put schools under the control of the associations and to decentralize the production of textbooks and other teaching material to the provincial level so as to make it possible to introduce instruction in the local languages, rather than only in Amharic. In this way, education would be tailored to the cultural and economic needs of each region, and the right of all "nationalities" would be respected. There were even proposals that each peasant association should become responsible for the hiring and paying of teachers and the building of schools. The Ministry of Public Health, similarly, considered switching the emphasis in health care from doctors and hospitals to rural clinics and "barefoot doctors," both of which would work under the peasant associations. In fact, most government agencies studied programs whose implementation relied heavily on the peasant associations rather than the central government, although the idea was still opposed by many conservative civil servants.

This new approach was not dictated by ideology alone, but was also influenced by financial and political considerations. If the central government was not going to extract high taxes from the peasantry, then the associations themselves would have to shoulder the cost of most local services. There was no other way the government could fulfill its promise and satisfy the general public expectation for universal education, medical care, and greater opportunity for local development. As a political ploy, decentralization offered a perfect means of breaking down some interest groups which had proven hotbeds of opposition to the PMAC.

The first area in which the peasant associations and urban *kebeles* were given a direct role was in education. The Ethiopian Teachers' Association was from the beginning of the revolution a center of resistance to the military government and a stronghold of the EPRP. Furthermore, students and teachers together had participated in strikes against the government throughout much of the 1975–76 academic year. In fact, the government was trying to forestall yet another strike by the teachers when it announced in September 1976 its decision to give the peasant associations and urban *kebeles* a large voice in running the schools in the areas under their jurisdiction.[15] The effect of this reform was first to prevent the planned strike by teachers and then to undermine the Ethiopian Teachers' Association, bringing to bear upon it the counterpressure of the associations and *kebeles* whose main concern was to keep the schools functioning.

The creation of peasant associations remains one of the most revolutionary reforms instituted by the PMAC. It gave concrete meaning to the claim that the Ethiopian revolution was "anti-bureaucratic," and substance to the promise of a "people's government" contained in the national democratic revolution program, albeit only at the local level. It also produced a powerful force for decentralization which would have to be reckoned with by any future government, civilian or military, conservative or radical. By February 1977, there were 24,707 peasant associations with a membership of 6.7 million. Some observers wondered whether the government by continuously strenghening these bodies was not creating 24,000 "independent republics."[16] To be sure, the functioning of these associations varied greatly. Some were in the hands of rich peasants; in some local priests had a large say; and in others elected officials were beginning to act like *balabbats*. Some radical critics found the associations more "petty bourgeois" than socialist in orientation, and their members more interested in private ownership of land than fired by a new spirit of collectivity. The associations certainly were not Chinese-style people's communes, but the legal framework had been provided so that they could evolve in that direction. There were even scattered experiments throughout the country in collective farming. What was missing, particularly after the end of the *zemacha* campaign, was any clear guidance from the government which would steer the associations toward socialism. In fact, as the problem of national unity became more acute, the PMAC's primary interest in the associations became their ability to help wage war in Eritrea and the Ogaden. In April 1977, the PMAC converted the revolutionary administration and development committees into "revolution and development committees," whose main purpose was to mobilize the population, raise funds for the government, and stabilize agricultural production while many men were away fighting.[17]

Whatever political direction the peasant associations might take in the future, there can be no doubt that land reform had brought about a significant, and sometimes dramatic, improvement in the standard of living enjoyed by millions of Ethiopian peasants. They were now allowed to keep the entire harvest, and the prices set by the government for grains were much higher, giving them more food and money than they had ever had before. In coffee producing areas of the country, like Kaffa Province, peasants even became relatively wealthy almost overnight. Many associations in these areas transported their own coffee beans to the capital, thereby eliminating middlemen. They also began "playing the market" in capitalist fashion, holding back deliveries to force prices up during the worldwide coffee shortage in 1975–77.

The sudden national shortage of basic consumer goods, such as sugar, shoes, and textiles, and the building boom among peasants in the Rift Valley, making use for the first time of corrugated iron roofs and wood-framed windows, were clear indications that the buying power of the Ethiopian peasantry had soared enormously after land reform. In fact, a major danger in this sudden rural prosperity was that the peasantry would become redivided between rich and poor peasant associations, creating a new class structure. Nevertheless, it provided eloquent testimony to the enormous success of land reform measures.

The Kebeles

As with peasant associations, the PMAC sought to devolve more and more power and responsibility on urban neighborhood associations. The outcome, however, was different because the *kebeles* became engulfed in the political struggle between the *Derg*, the Political Bureau, and the EPRP. This forced the PMAC to curtain their autonomy, to involve itself deeply in who controlled them, and finally to use them to mobilize and control the urban population in its own behalf. Particularly in Addis Ababa the *kebeles* became more instruments of control by the government over the people than by the people over the government.

A first effort to make the *kebeles* into extensions of the central administration occurred immediately after their creation in August 1975. The Ministry of Public Works and Housing, under whose authority they fell, wanted to turn them into administrative instruments, in effect minor cogs in the central bureaucracy. A project was studied within the ministry that would have entrusted the organization of the *kebeles* to administrative experts, working with the help of a computer, who were primarily interested in creating a well-planned bureaucratic structure. Mengistu himself ordered this plan scrapped and demanded that elections be immediately held, so as to create a popular political force to check the landlords opposing the recently decreed urban land reform. Nevertheless, the first round of elections in September 1975 did not produce a uniformly radical leadership in the *kebeles*. In fact, it appeared that a majority of the positions on the executive committees were filled by representatives of the urban petty bourgeoisie, such as schoolteachers, accountants, and civil servants, whose political views varied from conservative to radical.[18] On the whole, the political weight of the *kebeles* during their first year of existence was rather limited.

On October 9, 1976, the PMAC issued a proclamation on the organization and consolidation of the *kebeles* that paralleled in many respects the one strengthening the peasant associations.[19] However, it went further in integrating the new elected bodies into the central administration and created a multi-tier system of urban government that would eventually replace the existing municipal administrations. Provisions broadening the legal authority of the *kebeles,* strengthening judicial committees, allowing the establishment of women's associations, defense squads, and cooperatives were virtually indentical to those of the decree consolidating the peasant associations.

The most innovative feature of the new proclamation involved the creation of a three-tier *kebele* system. At the base would be a neighborhood association with a fifteen-member executive management committee; above them, a "higher" association with committees of twenty-six to thirty members; and finally in the larger towns and cities there would be a "central" *kebele,* also with an executive committee of twenty-six to thirty persons. The highest level town *kebeles* would be equal to city councils, and in chartered municipalities they would elect a major. While the new decree established elected local governments throughout the country for the first time, it still did not give them any means for funding their own projects or paying full-time personnel. Nor did it define clearly the respective areas of competence between the central administration and the associations. Thus, conflict between the two continued, particularly over housing matters. Two weeks after the publication of the new decree, the 291 *kebeles* of Addis Ababa were called upon to reelect representatives to their management committees and then another two weeks after that those to the twenty-five new "higher" associations.[20]

The elections brought the national struggle between the Political Bureau and the EPRP into the center of neighborhood *kebele* organizations, undermining their autonomy and making them into tools used by rival factions. Both the Political Bureau and the EPRP immeditely tried to gain control of the nomination process. While later events suggest that both parties managed to get some of their candidates elected, the Political Bureau gained the upper hand. In any case, soon after the elections, the EPRP extended its urban terrorist campaign to the neighborhood associations, killing scores of pro-*Derg* and pro-Political Bureau officials. By the spring of 1977, the *kebeles* had been turned into veritable battlefields, with almost daily assassinations of their officials and even fights between neighboring associations of opposite political tendencies.

The climate of insecurity for the pro-government *kebele* officials was one factor behind the creation of urban defense squads in March 1977. But far from enhancing security for anybody, these urban militias worsened it. Despite careful screening, the militias were not uniformly on the side of the *Derg*: some were infiltrated by EPRP members and some fell under the control of MEISON supporters who tried to use them against the military government. Finally, some defense squad members became little more than mercenaries at the service of the highest bidder, willing to assassinate anyone for as little as Eth.$50.

Despite infighting and reciprocal killings, the *kebeles* became extremely successful in mobilizing the population of Addis Ababa for demonstrations in support of the *Derg*. Beginning in early 1977, they repeatedly turned out crowds of 200,000 or more at a few hours notice. It is true that the *kebeles* sometimes used coercion, threatening to deprive those who did not participate of their allocation of *teff* or sugar, fining them, or even publicly denouncing them as enemies of the revolution or EPRP sympathizers. Still, as instruments of mass mobilization they quickly proved their effectiveness and value to the PMAC. Yet the heavy-handed use of the *kebeles* by all contending political factions for their own ends was a serious threat to their successful functioning as democratic institutions and to public confidence in them. In particular, the mass executions of youths and students in late April 1977 dealt a severe blow to the prestige of neighborhood associations, since they had allowed themselves to be based by MEISON to commit what the Addis Ababa public came to regard as a massacre with no possible political justification.[21] In July, the *kebeles* were openly pleading for public forgiveness. It remained to be seen whether they could recover from over-politicization and regain the confidence of the population.

The All-Ethiopian Trade Union

During 1976, the *Derg* not only continued to devolve new powers on grassroots organizations like the peasant associations and the *kebeles* but also sought at the same time to create centralizing institutions such as a new trade union and a party. The PMAC's attitude toward the labor union was unambiguous: it was simply to be an institution under its command, whose main purpose would be to control the labor force in the modern sector. Whatever doubts the labor proclamation of December 1975 had left about the military's concept of unionism—whether there would be free trade unions capable of bargaining with employers as in the West or government-controlled trade unions as in socialist countries—was dispelled as soon as the *Derg* started forming the new All-Ethiopian Trade Union. The fact that the old CELU had become a stronghold of the EPRP made it even more imperative for the PMAC to become closely involved in the reorganization of the labor movement, so as to prevent it from becoming a new center of opposition. The process proved to be long and arduous, lasting throughout 1976 and well into 1977. The EPRP heatedly contested the government for control of the new locals as well as of the nine national unions set up to represent the major sector of the economy. In some cases, the government had first to purge individual enterprises of EPRP sympathizers before it could form a pro-government local.

In early January 1977, the government was finally able to establish formally the national executive of the All-Ethiopian Trade Union (AETU) with Tewolde Bekele as its chairman. By this time, the union had 1,341 local chapters, called "workers' associations," with a total membership of 287,000.[22] The new labor union was thus more than twice as large as the CELU had ever been, in large part because the new labor code allowed locals to be formed in enterprises employing as few as twenty workers whereas fifty were necessary under the old labor law.

The process of reorganization neatly revealed the political tensions and conflicts within the labor movement. It showed clearly that the old division between white and blue collar workers still persisted and that the former constituted the main center of opposition to the military government. The first and most easily organized national unions were those of blue collar workers in the manufacturing industries, although even in this sector reorganization was marked by struggles with the EPRP. On the other hand, the government had great difficulty in organizing the white collar and technical workers in banks, insurance companies, and Ethiopian Airlines, the old stronghold of the CELU and later of the EPRP. In fact, when the AETU national executive was set up, the planned national union for workers in the financial institutions (banks and insurance companies) was still not in existence. And as late as April 1977, the government was still "reorganizing" the union representing Ethiopian Airlines employees in an effort to establish control over them.

By early 1977, the PMAC had succeeded in breaking the EPRP's control of or influence over most labor unions. The AETU was becoming one institution it could count upon to combat "counterrevolutinaries" of all kinds, but the EPRP in particular. The defense squads set up in many factories beginning in March 1977 proved extremely effective in eliminating leftist opposition, although with heavy cost in lives. Many EPRP sympathizers were killed, and in retaliation the clandestine party assassinated a number of labor union leaders, including the AETU chairman, Tewolde Bekele. The *Derg* created one additional problem for itself, however, in the process of purging the labor movement: it allowed MEISON to replace the EPRP as the dominant political force within the AETU. However, after the assassination of many union officials and the break between MEISON and the PMAC, the trade union showed little interest in allowing itself to be used once again by a civilian faction against the military. Indeed, its remaining leaders' main concern appeared to be bare survival.

Having established a pro-government trade union, the PMAC was left with several outstanding issues. The first was what would the role of AETU be? Would it be only an instrument of control over the work force? Would it be used to give the workers a voice in management or even to promote self-management? Finally, what would be the relationship between the union, with its mass membership of 280,000 representing the "proletariat," and the party being formed, which was supposed to be placed under "the leadership of the working class?" Regarding the first point, there was still much pressure from the rank and file for the AETU to play an independent role, defending the economic interests of the workers against the state as well as against the remaining private enterprises. This basically nonpolitical pressure was exerted above all by the lowest-paid workers, the guards and cleaners, who tried to take advantage of the new recognition given them by the labor proclamation to press claims for overtime pay, higher wages, and even new uniforms and shoes. For example, in the midst of killings by pro-and anti-government students, a major revision of the curriculum, and a discussion on the fate of higher education in Ethiopia, the highest officials of the university had to devote most of their time in the spring of 1977 to discussing the demands of these laborers, who were besieging their offices.

The issue of the unions' role also existed on a more political level. There remained considerable conflict between workers and state managers, since the former were no longer satisfied with simply taking orders. While there was no articulated demand for the establishment of a self-management system, there were numerous revolts against state managers which clearly showed the desire for direct worker participation in the running of state enterprises. Concerning the relationship between the embryonic state party and the trade union, no open discussion occurred nor were articulated theories advanced. Yet, within the Political Bureau the issue of whether the AETU should provide the basis for a mass party had been raised and some union officials were pushing for this. But as of mid-1977 no clear move had been made to use the unions as the foundation of the party, and the apparent demise of the Fidaists made such a development increasingly unlikely.

The Party

The missing keystone of the new Ethiopia was undoubtedly an all-embracing political party. Without it, the decentralized system of government the PMAC was creating through peasant associations and urban *kebeles* risked plunging the country into anarchy. Without a party, there was no national integrating institution to hold together the promised autonomous regions of the various "nationalities" and to prevent them from becoming virtually independent entities following different policies. Without a party, there was no way of making the transition from military regime to promised "people's democratic republic." Finally, without a party, there was no assurance that the final outcome of the revolution would be socialism in any of its historical forms. Yet creating a genuine political party in Ethiopia proved extremely difficult, because of the endless splintering of the political elite. In mid-1977, there were five more or less pro-government factions aspiring to party leadership, plus a number of anti-government underground movements of which the EPRP was the most important. These pro-government parties were as follows:

1. The All Ethiopian Socialist Movement (MEISON). Organized by Haile Fida in early 1976, it provided most Political Bureau members and formed the basis for the official Provisional Office for Mass Organizational Affairs (POMOA) established after the proclamation of the national democratic revolution.[23] MEISON never became identical with the POMOA, but tried to staff the POMOA with its own men. This attempt was facilitated by the fact that MEISON leaders were responsible for setting up the ideological school and were able for a long time to control this institution. When the PMAC became aware that MEISON was making a bid for power, it removed the school from its control.[24] By that time, however, the school had already produced about 4,200 cadres. Although the graduates were divided in their allegiances, a large number of them were undoubtedly pro-MEISON. There is also little doubt that MEISON had a strong ethnic base among Gallas from Wollega Province, Haile Fida's home area. MEISON initially supported Mengistu and received his support, but by the spring of 1977, as has been already seen, it began competing openly with the military for power, seeking control of the *kebeles,* the AETU, and the ministries, and even trying to use the defense squads for its own purposes. This induced the military, and even Mengistu, to turn against MEISON, which was beginning to look and act as much like an opposition movement as the EPRP. The formal fallout came in late August when Haile Fida attempted to flee the capital to Wollega Province with a group of his followers but was arrested. Subsequently, the military turned to eradicating MEISON members just as they were those belonging to the EPRP.

2. Revolutionary Flame (*Abiotawi Seded*). This party was created by the military as a counterforce to MEISON in early 1977. Never officially acknowledged, the party was headed by Master Sergeant Legesse Asfaw, one of the sixteen members of the standing committee of the PMAC and chairman of its "provisional committee for the arming of the masses." He was regarded as a strong supporter of Mengistu. By mid-1977, *Seded* was actively working to regain control of the *kebeles* from MEISON and even resorting to the assassination of its cadres when necessary. There was every indication the military intended to establish *Seded* as the dominant political organization

before the POMOA was formally transformed into the party. With this purpose in mind, the PMAC started sending officers to the Soviet Union, East Germany, and Cuba for up to two months of ideological training. By July, some 600 military cadres had thus been formed. *Seded* had support not only within the military but increasingly among high-level civil servants who felt threatened by MEISON, had links of one kind or another to individual *Derg* members, or were simply tired of political infighting and supported the military faction in the hope it would reestablish peace. Its civilian supporters were above all older professionals who had not been involved in student politics and who saw themselves as technocrats rather than politicians.

3. Labor League (*Wez Ader*). This civilian party was established by Senay Likie, the first vice-chairman of the Political Bureau who was slain in February 1977 during Mengistu's seizure of power. It was also set up to counter MEISON and Haile Fida, but, unlike *Seded,* it was not based in the military. After Senay's death, its importance declined.

4. The Marxist-Leninist Revolutionary Organization (Ma. Le. Ri. De.). This was a small faction within the Political Bureau variously described as a splinter group of MEISON or as a youth wing of this organization. The authors were unable to establish the leadership of this group or how it differed from MEISON. In the spring of 1977, the MLRO was very active in distributing leaflets on the campus of Addis Ababa University.

5. The Ethiopian Oppressed Revolutionary Struggle (I.Ch. A.T.). Another small faction within the Political Bureau led by Baru Tumsa, who had been initially a close friend of Haile Fida and was also a Galla. Like the Labor League and the Marxist-Leninist Revolutionary Organization, it was probably more a personality clique than a political party in any meaningful sense.

These five factions all claimed to be socialist and Marxist-Leninist in orientation. The main difference among them appeared to be their attitude toward military rule and the personalities who led them. Of the five, only *Wez Ader* and *Seded* were pro-military in the sense of accepting the necessity of military rule. Of the five, only MEISON and *Seded* were forces to be reckoned with as of mid-1977. In February 1977, the five factions had signed a joint communique in which they pledged to form eventually a united front that would provide the leadership for the party, which would presumably take over the POMOA organization. But within a few months, it appeared extremely unlikely that the five groups would ever unite, since MEISON and *Seded* were fighting each other for control of every position from POMOA provincial offices to high government posts in Addis Ababa.

One effect of this struggle was that an increasing number of positions, particularly in the regional administration, were being filled by either retired or active army officers. In effect, the military was being pushed to take direct control of the government and the party, since even the civilians who had originally supported it had subsequently been exposed as false friends. The infighting among supposedly pro-government factions left the POMOA in a strange position. In terms of organization, it grew rapidly, with cells from the *woreda* level up, with control of the ideological school and perhaps 4,000 cadres—a good nucleus for a party in a country like Ethiopia. But instead of being a political force of its own, it had become a veritable battleground for contending civilian and miltiary factions and was thus extremely fragmented. As of mid-1977, it was impossible to say whether the POMOA was more pro- or anti-military. Apparently, Mengistu had the same doubts. After promising the Soviets during his visit to Moscow in May that he would immediately set up a party upon his return to Ethiopia, he failed to do so, and as of August there was still no party.

In fact, it was doubtful that the PMAC would ever be able to overcome the fragmentation of the political elite and the civilian-military antagonism in order to build a solid political party. Nor did it appear that the conflict between civilians and military was abating. If anything, it was becoming more bitter as the time for setting up the party neared. The alliance between Mengistu and MEISON was over, and the creation and rapid growth of *Seded* suggested that the party, when established, would be essentially a military-dominated organization.

This trend toward militarization could be seen in other areas as well. There was a growing number of officers in the regional administration and military representatives could be found in all ministries, even though the minister himself might be a civilian. Moreover, the important Ministry of Interior and Ministry of Foreign Affairs were already under officers, and a third, the Ministry of Information and National Guidance, was being run directly by the *Derg* without a minister. The deteriorating security situation in many of the fourteen provinces was one factor explaining the slow militarization of the government. In Eritrea, in the southern provinces where the Somali threat was serious, in Begemdir where the EDU was most active, military administrators were particularly numerous. But the worsening conflict between the *Derg* and MEISON was without question the main cause of this trend, for if the military could not trust those who proclaimed themselves its allies, then how could it trust any civilians? The radicals' claim that the PMAC was nothing but a "military dictatorship" risked becoming true, thanks to their own scheming and maneuvering.

The Ethiopian revolution was a very unfinished one in mid-1977. There were strong centralizing tendencies at work in the country and just as strong decentralizing ones. No balance had been struck between the two yet to give the revolution a measure of stability. The institution needed to reconcile the centralizing and the decentralizing tendencies of the revolution, the party, was still missing.

In mid-1977 it was hard to see how a party capable of performing an integrating role could be established given the prevailing political circum-stances of bitter civilian-military struggle and rampant factionalism within the civilian political elite. It appeared that only the military could somehow hold the country together, but even their ability to do this might well be destroyed if they lost the wars in Eritrea and the Ogaden. How could a defeated army still rule the country?

Building a new nation on the ruins of an empire remained an unfinished task. Fifteen months after the proclamation of the right of nationalities to self-administration, no steps had been taken to implement this policy, and it was difficult to see how it could be done in the midst of an intensive drive by the Eritreans to achieve independence and of the Somali government to annex a large part of Ethiopia.

The severity of the problems still facing the country, however, should not obscure the enormous accomplishments of the revolution. If there was a threat of 24,000 "independent republics" it was because the peasants, who as recently as 1973 had been allowed to starve to death by the tens of thousands, had now been given land and guns and were finally asserting themselves. There was convincing evidence that millions of peasants were economically far better off than they had been under Haile Selassie. The urban population had undoubtedly suffered, landlords as well as lumpenproletariat, since both were affected by the sharp rise in food prices and growing shortages. Thousands had been killed in the cities in spiraling political violence for which civilians bore even more responsibility than the military, and a sense of insecurity affected the entire urban population.

The Ethiopian revolution had produced its share of horrors, but it had also destroyed feudalism and liberated the peasantry from conditions of centuries-old servitude. There was no guarantee that in the long run the new Ethiopia would not be ruled by another authoritarian, repressive government, but enough democratic institutions had been put into place to make this difficult. Once the peasants were given arms and land, they were not likely to surrender them to any government, at least not without a violent and long struggle.

As a process of destruction of an antiquated and oppressive system, the Ethiopian revolution had met its goal. As a process of reconstruction, it had also achieved much, though much still remained to be done. Still, by virtue of the magnitude of the changes already brought about and of the radical alteration in the economic, social and political relations between classes, it had the potential for becoming Africa's first real revolution.

Notes

Chapter 2
Notes

1.   The controversy over the use of the term "feudal" as applied to Ethiopia is discussed in John Cohen, "Ethiopia: A Survey on the Existence of a Feudal Peasantry," in *Journal of Modern African Studies,* XII, 4 (1974): 665–672. See also, Frederick Gamst, "Peasantries and Elites without Urbanism: The Civilization of Ethiopia," *Comparative Studies in Society and History,* XII, 4 (1970): 373–392; and Allan Hoben, "Social Stratification in Traditional Amhara Society," in Arthur Tuden and Leonard Plotnicov, eds., *Social Stratification in Africa* (New York: Free Press, 1970).

2.   The best single summary of the land tenure system in Ethiopia is found in John Cohen and Dov Weintraub, *Land and Peasants in Imperial Ethiopia. The Social Background to a Revolution* (Assen, The Netherlands: Van Gorcum and Co., B. U., 1975). The book contains ample bibliography on studies of land tenure in different parts of the country.

3.   Ibid., p. 52. In Begemdir, 9 percent of the peasants were tenants and 6 percent part owners and part tenants; in Tigre, the figures were respectively 7 percent and 18 percent; in Gojjam 13 percent and 7 percent. Like most Ethiopian statistics, these figures, derived from a government study, should be considered estimates.

4.   For a detailed explanation of the communal land tenure system in one part of Gojjam, see Allan Hoben, *Land Tenure Among the Amhara of Ethiopia* (Chicago: University of Chicago Press, 1973).

5.   Allan Hoben, "Social Stratification in Traditional Amhara Society" in Arthur Tuden and Leonard Plotnicov, *Social Stratification in Africa* (New York: Free Press, 1970), 172f.

6.   Cohen and Weintraub, *Land and Peasants,* 32.

7.   Ibid., 40, 51. One of the problems in determining how much land was held by absentee landlords is the large amount of unmeasured lands. Although many studies bravely attempt to estimate what percentage of unmeasured land belonged to absentee owners, such figures are very imprecise by definition.

8.   Cohen and Weintraub, p. 51, put the tenant population of the south at 5.6 million, with an additional 1.1 million peasants who rented some land in addition to what they owned. Given the estimated average size of rural Ethiopian families of 6 members this would mean around one million families. Patrick Gilkes calculates the number of tenant families at just under 1,500,000 and adds to this about 450,000 landless peasant families. The trouble with both these estimates is that they are based on government figures that almost certainly underestimate the total rural population. See Gilkes, *The Dying Lion, Feudalism and Modernization in Ethiopia* (London: Julian Friedmann Publishers Ltd., 1975), 115.

9.   Cohen and Weintraub, *Land and Peasants*, 53.

10.   For a summary of the development of the Awash Valley, see John W. Harbeson, "Nomads and Rural Development in Ethiopia: The Development of the Awash Valley" (Awash Valley Authority, Addis Ababa, July 1975), mimeo, ch. V.

11.   International Bank for Reconstruction and Development, "Current Position and Prospects of Ethiopia," 1965.

12.   For a summary view based on the studies carried out in the mid 1960s, see Bengt Nekby, *CADU: An Ethiopian Experiment* (Stockholm: Prisma Publishers, 1971), 16 ff.

13.   Raymond Borton, et al., "A Development Program for the Ada District, Based on a Socio-Economic Survey." Stanford Research Institute, Project 6350, Report #14. Menlo Park, California, 1969.

14.   Unpublished figures obtained from bank officials. See also Institute for Agricultural Research, "Report of the Survey Mission on the Agricultural Development of Setit-Humera," Addis Ababa, 1967.

15.   Harbeson, "Nomads and Rural Development," p. V-4. See also, Awash Valley Authority, Feasibility Study of the Lower Awash Valley, Final Report, Part I, Annex 3, *The Afar People, Land Tenure and Institutions* (1975), 36.

16.   In 1970, Ellis found 2,500 hectares of land under tractor cultivation in Ada *woreda*, all of it developed in the previous three years. Mechanization spread at a very rapid pace. See Gene Ellis, *Men or Machine, Beast or Burden: A Case Study of the Economics of Agricultural Mechanization in Ada District, Ethiopia* (unpublished Ph.D. dissertation, University of Tennessee, 1972), 113. See also J. A. Castella and W. A. Eshetu, "Report on Mechanized Farming in Hararghe Province and Yerer and Kerayu Awraja of Shoa Province," Addis Ababa, Ministry of National Community Development and Social Affairs, 1975.

17.   International Bank for Reconstruction and Development, "Agricultural Sector Brief, Ethiopia," May 1972, Map 5 gives a fair overview of the distribution of mechanized farms.

18.   The figures are our own conclusions on the basis of often conflicting information derived from a variety of sources. Even after the nationalization of land, no official figures have been issued.

19.   Imperial Ethiopian Government, Ministry of Agriculture, "The Ada Agricultural Development Project" (Addis Ababa, 1970), 37.

20.   The problem of social versus economic incentives for mechanization is discussed very well in Ellis, 113 ff.

21.   For a discussion of the government's agricultural loans policy, see Gerry Gill, "The Agricultural Sector" (Addis Ababa University, Institute for Development Research, December 1975, mimeo), 76–81.

22.   Ibid., 81.

23.   One of the few studies available is on migration to the Rift Valley town of Shashamanne, an area where tenants were being expelled in large numbers. It did not find the immigration of displaced tenants to be a significant factor in the growth of the town. See Gunilla Bjeren, "Migration to Shashamanne" (Discussion paper, University of Stockholm, Department of Sociology, December 1975, mimeo), 9.

24.   Henock Kifle, "Investigation on Mechanized Farming and Its Effect on Peasant Agriculture," CADU publication no. 74, 1972.

25.   Ellis, *Men or Machine*, ch. 6. Cohen and Weintraub, *Land and Peasants*, 53.

26.   Ellis, *Men or Machine*, 115.

27.   One estimate of the number of workers on modern farms in 1965 is between 21,000 and 22,000. Given the rapid growth in the number of farms between 1965 and 1970, it seems likely there were more than 30,000 by the latter date. However, our figure is an estimate. See *Area Handbook for Ethiopia* (Washington, D.C.; American University, 1971), 388.

28.   Throughout most of March 1974 there were scattered clashes between peasants and

landlords throughout the Rift Valley between Meki and Arba Minch. Galla tenant farmers attacked their Amhara landlords and even some foreign farmers, burned crops, cut down fruit trees, and destroyed farm houses. One report on March 18 said 30 persons were killed and another on March 30 spoke of 15 others killed, including ten landlords hacked to death with knives and spears and three cut into pieces and thrown down wells. It seems that the peasants were incited by leaflets calling for the land to be returned to them, but relatively little is known about this Rift Valley uprising or what was behind it. *Reuters* carried reports on it March 18, 22, 30, and 31.

29.   Cohen and Weintraub, *Land and Peasants,* 39. Detailed information concerning two districts in Yerer and Kereyu Awraja is given in John Markakis, *Ethiopia: Analysis of a Traditional Polity* (London: Oxford University Press, 1974), 132–33. Gildas Nicholas presents some information on Bale in "Peasant Rebellions and Socio-Political Context of Today's Ethiopia," paper presented to the 15th Annual Meeting of the African Studies Association, 1972.

30.   Cohen and Weintraub, *Land and Peasants,* 39 f.

31.   See Markakis, *Ethiopia,* 369 ff. for an interpretation of revolts in Gojjam and Bale; Gildas Nicholas for an interpretation of the Bale revolt. Nega Ayele, "Centralization v. Regionalism in Ethiopia, The Case of Gojjam 1932–1969" (senior thesis, Haile Selassie University, Department of Political Science, June 1970); and Peter Schwab, "Rebellion in Gojjam Province, Ethiopia," *The Canadian Journal of African Studies* (spring 1970). Also see, Patrick Gilkes, *The Dying Lion* (London: Julian Friedmann Publishers, 1975), 204 ff.

32.   In discussing reasons why the 1789 revolution was supported by peasants in parts of France but not in the Vendée, Alexis de Tocqueville singles out the fact that the Vendée aristocracy was not an absentee class but still residing on the land and that they had historically resisted the authority of the king, refusing to spend time at court and to "fulfill the duties of the king." On the other hand, in other parts of France, feudalism had to a large extent broken down, creating a very unstable situation. "For even after it had ceased to be a political institution, the feudal system remained basic to the economic organization of France. In this restricted form it was far more hated than in the heyday of feudalism." There seems to be some parallel between France and Ethiopia in this regard. The *rist* areas, particularly Gojjam Province, proved to be the Vendées of the Ethiopian revolution. In the south, feudalism was a hated economic leftover of a sociopolitical system that no longer existed. See De Tocqueville, *The Old Regime and the French Revolution* (Garden City, N.Y.: Doubleday, 1955), 122 and 31.

33.   The spontaneous takeover of land was suppressed by the military government, apparently because no consensus had yet been reached inside the *Derg* on what kind of land reform should be implemented. Nonetheless, many tenants refused to harvest the crops and hand them over to the landlords.

34.   Estimates of Ethiopia's total population, urban population, and modern labor force vary considerably. The figure given here for the urban population is taken from the *Statistical Abstract of Ethiopia, 1975* (Addis Ababa: Central Statistical Office, 1976?), 24. The estimate of the modern sector labor force results from the following figures: number of government employees, 100,000; armed forces and police, 80,000; government estimate in 1976 of the number of workers who could be enrolled in unions, excluding government employees, military, and police, 270,000. This gives a rough total of 450,000. There are no government figures on the size of the labor force.

35.   "Advance Report on the 1972–73 Rural Survey of Cottage and Handicraft Industries" (Central Statistical Office, Addis Ababa, April 1975). The few efforts made to develop cottage industries seem to have been made by foreign missionaries and charities usually employing handicapped people.

36.   Even private foreign investment in Ethiopia was relatively small. The U.S. Embassy in Addis Ababa estimated in 1974 that the total was about US$300 million of which Italian investment accounted for two-thirds. U.S. investment amounted to about US$22 million.

37.   Imperial Ethiopian Government, Ministry of Commerce and Industry, *Economic Progress of Ethiopia* (Addis Ababa, 1955).

38.   Imperial Ethiopian Government, Second Five Year Plan (Addis Ababa, 1962), 77.

39.   Gerry Gill, ed., *Readings on the Ethiopian Economy* (Haile Selassie I University, Institute for Development Research, 1974), 1.

40.   Central Statistical Office, *Statistical Abstract of Ethiopia, 1975* (Addis Ababa, 1976?), 58.

41.   Gill, ed., *Readings on the Ethiopian Economy,* 120.

42.   For the early history of the CELU, see Seyoum Gebre Egziahber, "The Development of Some Institutions Concerned with Labor Relations in Ethiopia" (Addis Ababa University, Department of Public Administration, 1969); and Arnold Zack, "Trade Unionism Develops in Ethiopia," in Jeffrey Butler and A. A. Castagno, eds., *Transition in African Politics* (New York: Praeger, 1967).

43.   By December 1974, the CELU was claiming a membership growth from 83,000 to 120,000. See the *Ethiopian Herald,* December 31, 1974.

44.   Markakis, *Ethiopia,* 182. Between 1969–70 and 1972–73, the Haile Selassie University issued decrees and diplomas to an average of 1,300 students a year. Of this number, only about 500 were awarded degrees for finishing all four years. The others were given diplomas for short special programs. This means the number of graduates from the university in Addis Ababa, the country's main one, between 1970 and 1974 was around 2,000. In addition, in 1972 there were 2,575 students abroad, but there are no figures on the number graduating from foreign universities each year. See Ministry of Education, *School Census for Ethiopia, 1969–70 and 1972–73,* vol. I, 102–111.

45.   This is the authors' rought estimate. In addition to 9,000 to 10,000 university graduates, we have included the large number of high school graduates who qualify as part of the educated elite by virtue of the jobs they hold and general outlook. For example, there are many high-level bank employees and officers holding only high school diplomas. The same is true among higher echelon civil servants.

46.   For a discussion of this problem, see Donald Levine, "Class Consciousness and Class Solidarity in the New Ethiopian Elite," in Peter Lloyd, ed., *The New Elites of Tropical Africa* (London: Oxford University Press, 1966).

47.   Central Statistical Office, "Employment and Pattern of Income Distribution Among Central Government Employees in Addis Ababa Between 1969 and 1974," Staff Report no. 8 (January 1975), 3. This minimum salary paid to university graduates by the government is in sharp contrast to what was paid to other employees. The same study shows that in 1974, 19.5 percent of government employees in Addis Ababa received less than Eth$50 a month, and 34.3 percent less than Eth$100. At the other end of the spectrum, 15 percent of government employees in Addis got 50 percent of the total paid out in government salaries.

48.   See Markakis, *Ethiopia,* 186 f; Levine, *Wax and Gold,* 183 ff; and Christopher Clapham, *Haile Sellassie's Government* (New York: Praeger, 1969),87 f.

49.   Levine, *Wax and Gold,* 111.

50.   The major student publication, *Struggle,* contains many examples of this position. A blatant one appears in the first issue of the paper in March 1967: "The future of the old country that still refuses to convince itself that its past glory is merely history now lies in his (the student's) hands. He is at the head of a march and his choice is either to consolidate the constituents of this march from scattered, unequal individuals into a whole united body, or to exploit this situation and become as prosperous and fat as many Ethiopians have already become."

51.   See in particular Siegfried Pausewang, "Students in a Developing Society," (Haile Selassie University, Department of Sociology, 1968, mimeo). Also David Korten, *Planned Change in a Traditional Society* (New York: Praeger, 1972), 255 ff.

52.   "Miscellaneous Papers from the Seminar on the Sociology of Development in Ethiopia," (Haile Selassie I University, Department of Sociology and Anthropology, 1968–69, mimeo).

53. "Report to the Student Activity Committee at Haile Selassie University," (summer 1968, mimeo). The report's conclusions were based on interviews of students by a foreign faculty member with a radical reputation, and thus rather close to students.

54. Pausewang, "Students in a Developing Society."

55. Margery Perham's, *The Government of Ethiopia* (Evanston: Northwestern University Press, 1969), first published in 1947, provides an excellent measure of the depth of change since Ethiopia's liberation from Italian wartime rule.

Chapter 3
Notes

1. His words, as told to the authors, came from a high-level government official who was a personal friend of the close associate in question.

2. Christopher Clapham, *Haile-Selassie's Government* (New York: Praeger, 1969), 65–71.

3. The view that Asrate Kassa was the major power behind the prime minister has been expressed to the authors by various Ethiopian sources, including one key minister in the Endelkachew cabinet. The liberals anxious to institute serious political reforms regarded Asrate as the major obstacle.

4. *Ras* Imru and his family are curious figures in recent Ethiopian history. The *Ras* himself, who was still alive in 1976, had been raised with Haile Selassie and remained very close to him until the Emperor's death in 1975. Yet, he showed throughout his life a concern for social justice that was most unusual among the nobility. He even distributed land to his tenant farmers. Because of his progressive ideas, he was the choice of the organizers of the abortive 1960 coup for prime. minister. Nevertheless, he remained a close confidant of the Emperor.

5. On the views of Asrate Kassa see Colin Legum, *The Fall of Haile Selassie's Empire* (New York: Africana Publishing Co., 1975), 30 f. Legum says the information came directly from *Ras* Asrate.

6. Those who could be considered part of this bourgeois reformist faction included Dr. Aklilu Habte, president of the university; Worku Teferra, Abraham Demoz, and Haile Wolde-Michael, all professors at the Haile Selassie I University; Tafarra Deguefe, then head of the Ethiopian Commercial Bank. There were also a few members of the Endelkachew cabinet, such as Belay Abaye, land reform minister, and Takalign Gedamu, first planning and then communications minister, regarded as reformists although without much influence.

7. Conversations with members of the Christian Relief Committee, the Addis Ababa based umbrella organization of church groups involved in drought relief operations.

8. Interview with an ETA official in the *Ethiopian Herald,* March 17, 1974.

9. Ministry of Education and Fine Arts, *Education: A Challenge to the Nation,* 1973, Draft Revised Edition, Parts A and B. See particularly chapter IV for details of several alternative plans suggested and the one finally adopted. The document is known as the Educational Sector Review.

10. Ibid., 40 ff.

11. Teachers' Education Panel, "Materials for a Proposed National Basic Education Programme in Ethiopia," Addis Ababa, November 1975, Section VI.

12. Ibid., 49 ff.

13. See *Africa* (May 1974), 18. A CELU spokesman stressed much the same point in an interview with one of the authors during the strike.

14. "Resolutions of the General Council of CELU," mimeo, February 28–March 1, 1974. See also the *Ethiopian Herald,* March 7, 1974.

15. Interview with a top CELU spokesman during the strike.

16. Agreement between the Imperial Ethiopian Government and the Ethiopian Confederation of Labor Unions, March 10, 1976, mimeo. See also the *Ethiopian Herald,* March 12, 1974.

17. On April 30, Endelkachew also declared that employees of all public utilities could neither strike nor form unions until new legislation concerning their status had been approved by Parliament.

18. Ministry of Education, *School Census for Ethiopia, 1969/70–1972/73,* vol. I, 48–49. The 1971/72 school enrollment figures show 16,080 students in government high schools in Addis Ababa and 2,443 in nongovernmental ones. The number was probably only slightly higher by the 1973/74 school year.

19. Personal observations of the authors and news agency estimates.

20. Reports reaching the capital at the time mentioned pamphlets being distributed among the peasants that called for land reform and the return of Galla lands confiscated by Amhara landlords. These pamphlets were believed to be the work of students.

21. For other accounts of these confusing events, see Blair Thompson, *Ethiopia: The Country that Cut Off Its Head* (London: Robson Books Ltd., 1975), 56–62 and Legum, *The Fall of Haile Selassie's Empire,* 42–43.

22. *Addis Zemen,* Miazia 20, 1966 (April 27, 1974), unofficial translation.

23. For details on the relationship between the coordinating committee and the National Security Commission, see chapter 4.

24. See Seleshi Sisaye, "The Confederation of Ethiopian Labor Unions and the March 1974 General Strike." Paper presented to the Conference of the New York African Studies Association, Cornell University, Ithaca, New York, May 1, 1976.

25. Conversation between the authors and the former student leader who was in prison in 1976.

26. Other assertions of its authority included charges brought by the lower house of deputies against four provincial governors, those of Kaffa, Arussi, Gemu Gofa, and Illubabor, of embezzling public funds; accusations that Information Minister Ahadu Saboure had misappropriated Eth$114,000 in government funds while ambassador to Somalia and a demand that he be dismissed; and the rejection of Endelkachew's choice of persons for the seven-member commission on inquiry into government corruption.

27. The *Ethiopian Herald,* March 14, 1974.

28. Officially, there was only one representative of the Orthodox Christian Church heirarchy, Melake-Selam Tekeste-Berhan Wolde Jesus, but he was joined in the committee's deliberations by an unofficial delegation of five church officials. In addition, the church had strong support from several lay members of the committee. Altogether, the Church put up a strong fight against separation of church and state.

29. Interviews by authors with members of the constitutional committee.

30. A long summary of the proposed constitution appeared in the *Ethiopian Herald,* August 10, 1974.

31. Ministry of Information, "Policy Statement of the New Council of Ministers," official translation, Addis Ababa, n.d.

32. One of the most significant passages is the statement of the government's policy regarding political matters. It spells out the following objectives: "The strengthening of the country's unity, the safeguarding of its borders, the enriching of the cultural heritage a united people have handed to us; the strengthening of the country's diverse traditions as pillars of national culture; the further consolidation of Ethiopian nationalism and cultural heritage without regard to ethnic affiliation, religion or sex." No mention was made of the need for reforms. ibid., 3.

33. See *Africa* (May 1974), 18.

34. The *Ethiopian Herald,* March 17, 1974.

Chapter 4
Notes

1. *Area Handbook for Ethiopia* (Washington, D.C.: U.S. Government Printing Office, 1971), 487.

2. Among the groups indicating sympathy or support for the Asmara revolt were the Fourth and Third Division, the Air Force, the Navy, the Signals Corps, the Engineering Corps, the Army Aviation, and even the Musicians Corps. The only major units not to send messages, as far as the authors have been able to determine, were the Imperial Bodyguard and the Airborne Company (Paratroopers). In no case is it clear whether the entire unit or just a section of it was supporting the Second Division revolt.

3. The second salary hike increased the minimum monthly pay for privates to Eth$112.00, including Eth$22.00 for rations, and set a ceiling of Eth$150.00. Their pensions were increased from Eth$30.00 to Eth$50.00.

4. Private conversation with the authors.

5. The Air Force later denied these allegations in a statement issued July 4, 1974, after the military Coordinating Committee had taken over the radio station in Addis Ababa.

6. Reuters, March 28, 1974, and Blair Thompson, *Ethiopia, The Country that Cut Off Its Head,* 52–54.

7. The *Ethiopian Herald,* August 11, 1974.

8. The Provisional Military Administrative Council, *The Ethiopian Revolution* (Addis Ababa, September 1975), 12.

9. Sources for the authors' version of the formation of the June Coordinating Committee include both military and civilians. None of the military was a member of the committee but several had close contacts with those involved in the operation. All asked that their names not be disclosed.

10. This part of the committee's history is told in PMAC, *The Ethiopian Revolution,* but no date is given. "The previously constituted provisional committee of the Armed Forces, seated at the headquarters of the Fourth Division of the Army, began to send out its representatives to various units of the Armed Forces and the Police stationed in and around Addis Ababa to explain to them in detail the need for change and to consolidate their support for the movement." Ibid., 8.

11. A serious clash occurred June 20 at the base between paratroopers and Air Force officers in which two military were killed and 20 wounded.

12. According to the authors' sources, there was a sharp competition for leadership of the committee between Atnafu, Mengistu, and Tafara. Mengistu's success was the result of his popularity among the lowest ranking rebel officers and NCOs, many of whom were Gallas, as he himself is partly. Tafara lost out because the elections were held when he was absent from the capital. Upon his return, he did not submit readily to the *fait accompli*: he is reported to have screamed to the assembled committee members, "You have snatched history from my hands," and to have pulled a machin gun on his colleagues. He was overwhelmed by force and taken to the Bodyguard prison, where he was still being held at the time of this writing.

13. PMAC, *The Ethiopian Revolution,* 12.

14. Ibid., 10.

15. See *infra,* 137.

16. A student pamphlet issued shortly after Michael's appointment bitterly criticized the *Derg.* Under the title "Government by Aristocrats: For How Long," the pamphlet said the military's choice "has disappointed the peasants and the working class who have now realized that the promises made by the Coordinating Committee are false. . . . The Ethiopian people are tired of aristocratic rule and want their freedom now. . . . They declare that Michael, his relatives like Princess Tenagne Work, are no different from those detained."

17. The Crown Council, composed of about 12 members, was the most powerful consultative body to the Emperor and the real center of palace politics. The *chilot* was the highest court, with the Emperor acting as sole judge and dispensing justice according to his personal whim.

18. *Addis Zemen,* Nehassie 10, 1966.

19. Ibid., Nehassie 11, 1966.

20. Interview with Sergeant Bekele Anassimo on Radio Ethiopia, August 17, 1974.

21. *Ethiopia,* Nehassie 16, 1966.

22. The special commission of inquiry investigating the misdeeds of former government officials revealed on August 28 that Wollo Governor Mamo Seyoum had warned the Emperor about the drought situation as early as 1970, three years before the famine hit its peak, but that the Emperor had taken no action.

23. PMAC, *The Ethiopian Revolution,* 16.

24. Proclamation No. 1 of 1974, *Negarit Gazeta,* September 15, 1974.

25. *Kedem Ethiopia Tikdem* means literally "Ethiopia First, With Blood." The original full motto of the *Derg* had been *Kalemenim Dem, Ethiopia Tikdem,* or "Ethiopia First, Without Blood." After the November 23 executions, the *"Kalemenim Dem"* was dropped from the official motto and many Ethiopians replaced it with *"Kedem".*

26. See chapter 6.

27. The creation of the courts was first announced October 19, but the official proclamation establishing them was not published until a month later. See Proclamation Number 7 of 1974, *Negarit Gazeta,* November 16, 1974. The decree provided for a Special General Court-Martial of five officers based in Addis Ababa and Special District Courts-Martial having three officers and empowered to sit anywhere in the country. The five officers of the high court were named October 29, two weeks before the proclamation was issued.

28. Proclamation Number 8 of 1974, *Negarit Gazeta,* November 16, 1974.

29. General Aman wanted to march the Third Division into Somalia and despite an order from the Emperor began attacking into enemy territory. Aman was a kind of General McArthur of the Ethiopian army and became a direct challenge to the Emperor.

30. The Provisional Military Council issued a statement November 26 charging Aman with the following crimes: 1) working against the philosophy of *Ethiopia Tikdem;* 2) plotting against the movement in order to consolidate his power; 3) creating divisions within the armed forces; 4) blocking the implementation of decisions reached by majority vote inside the council; 5) seeking to divide members of the council and 6) failing to remain at his post and being absent from office for eight days. In fact, there were numerous rumors that Aman aspired to become the first president of an Ethiopian republic.

31. When General Aman was made chairman of the PMAC on September 12, Major Mengistu, who had been chairman, became the first vice-chairman and Major Atnafu became the second vice-chairman. Atnafu's title and position did not become clear until mid-December.

32. The decision to execute the political prisoners the same night as Aman's death appears to have been taken in extreme haste. There are at least two versions as to how the decision was reached. According to one, the entire *Derg* voted only on the principle of execution and on the categories for which capital punishment would be imposed—the Wollo famine cover-up, gross abuse of authority, and plotting against the military reform movement. But the actual choice of individuals was left to a committee of seven officers, presumably headed by Major Mengistu and Major Atnafu. According to the second version, those *Derg* members present in the capital at the time, about 107 out of the 120, all voted on each individual to be executed.

33. Aman had led the Third Division and had gone to Harrar in mid-November to get its support. He was also popular with the Second Division because of its efforts to put an end to the fighting in Eritrea. These two divisions, together with the officers serving at the Harrar Military Academy, were thought at the time to be siding with Aman.

Chapter 5
Notes

1. "Ethiopia *Tikdem:* The Origins and Future Direction of the Movement," official English translation, December 20, 1974, mimeo.

2. There were many such reports in the fall of 1974, emanating mainly from the south. The authors were personally told of several, including a large farm near Holeta in Shoa Province, where workers burned the crop to keep the landlord from getting it. Around Ambo, many crops were harvested but not threshed because peasants did not want to pay rent to the landlord.

3. The *Ethiopian Herald,* September 25, 1974.

4. There were many exposés allegedly beginning in August 1974 in the Ethiopian media of how the royal family pocketed profits of state companies, regarding them as private property. See also, Patrick Gilkes, *The Dying Lion* (London: Julian Freedman, 1975), 137 ff.

5. The *Ethiopian Herald,* February 4, 1975, gives the complete list.

6. Provisional Military Government, "Declaration on Economic Policy of Socialist Ethiopia" (Addis Ababa, February 7, 1975), 3.

7. Ibid., 9.

8. The *Ethiopian Herald,* February 6, 1975. The statement released by the PMAC accused five officials in the Ministry of Commerce, the Grain Board, and the Livestock and Meat Board of "intentionally committing economic sabotage against the country's popular movement."

9. "Declaration on Economic Policy of Socialist Ethiopia," 4.

10. See chapter 7.

11. A moderate bill regulating landlord-tenant relations had been submitted to Parliament since 1968 without ever being passed. The Endelkachew government, in its White Paper, proposed regulation of tenancy coupled with an unspecified limit on the size of holdings. Virtually all foreign agencies and embassies had recommended and pushed for similar measures under the Emperor. Even the Ministry of Land Reform in August 1972 had proposed the same measures in a lengthy study of the problem entitled "Draft Policy of the Imperial Ethiopian Government on Agricultural Land Tenure." See also Gilkes, *The Dying Lion,* 133 f.

12. The estimate of 35,000 was obtained by the authors from unofficial military sources. A report of the Ministry of Land Reform states that by 1971 the government had distributed about 45,000 *gashas* under the "patronage grant system" but does not specify how much of this went to military personnel and how much to civil servants who were also entitled to land grants. The same report states that only 35 percent of land granted was actually cultivated, and only about 10 percent of the beneficiaries of the grants cultivated the land themselves. Many grants were sold. See "Draft Policy of the Imperial Ethiopian Government on Agricultural Land Tenure," 30 f.

13. Proclamation No. 31 of 1975. "A Proclamation to Provide for the Public Ownership of Rural Lands," March 4, 1975. *Negarit Gazeta,* April 29, 1975.

14. At the time of the land reform announcement, many observers expected that it would disappoint the peasants, since they had been expecting ownership of land and had instead only been given possession. Actually, the very concept of freehold property is a very recent development in Ethiopia; traditionally, people had rights to use the land, or rights of taxation over it, but it was not ownership in the modern, Western sense. Small holders in the *rist* areas did not have ownership of the land, but only possession, since ultimate rights belonged to the entire descent group. For more on the meaning of *rist,* see Allan Hoben, *Land Tenure among the Amhara.*

15. *Negarit Gazeta,* April 29, 1975, 96–97.

16. Ethiopia is divided into 14 provinces, 102 *awrajas,* and 556 *woredas.* (The official new names of these divisions are respectively regions, provinces, and districts.) The Ministry of

Interior appoints paid administrators to all these local government units. Below the *woreda* level, there have never been paid officials. Before land reform, a variety of traditional officials were compensated for their services either by being allowed to keep a small percentage of the central government taxes they collected or by extracting various fees in cash and kind from the population under their jurisdiction.

17. In one nomadic area, the lower Awash Valley near the border of the French Territory of the Afars and the Issas, Sultan Ali Mirah had for years been collecting payments from the Afars in lieu of land taxes, and had declared himself ready to turn the amount over to the government, if it would recognize that the land in that area belonged to the Afar people rather than to the state. At the same time, he and the *balabbats,* the local nobles, also received payments that could be considered the equivalent of land rent.

18. Interviews with personnel in the Ministry of Interior. The new appointees were generally much better educated than the old administrators, many of whom had no education other than what they had received in church schools. On the other hand, many of the new appointees had no administrative experience.

19. Initially, the objectives of the *zemecha* were defined as 1) teaching the peasants and learning from them; 2) helping launch local development projects; 3) collecting data essential for development purposes; and 4) participating in drought relief efforts.

20. Statement issued on December 21, 1974, by the Development through Cooperation headquarters, mimeo.

21. Private conversation with the authors.

22. In early May 1975, there were four refugee camps in Gojjam along the main road between Debre Markos and Finote Salam housing several thousand Moslem tenants. Most had been expelled from Metekele *awraja* after their homes were burned and their cattle confiscated.

23. See chapter 6.

24. For more details on the initial phase of land reform, see Marina Ottaway, "Land Reform and Peasant Associations in Ethiopia: A Preliminary Analysis," *Rural African* (fall 1975), 39–54.

25. See Johan Holmberg, "Pricing Strategies for Agricultural Produce in a Changing Society: Rural-Urban Contradictions in Ethiopia," unpublished paper presented to the 19th annual meeting of the African Studies Association, Boston, November 3–6, 1976.

26. In late May, students there incited the peasants against landlords and "exploiters," namely merchants and shopkeepers. One hotel owner was lynched and many other townspeople beaten; some of those responsible for the incident were later executed.

27. Throughout March and much of May, there were *Derg* delegations touring all the provinces to explain land reform. In some cases where there were real problems, they stayed for weeks. The reform was applied by force particularly in the lower Awash Valley, where Sultan Ali Mirah was expelled by troops and fled to Djibouti.

28. The authors met one student near Mojo, south of Addis Ababa, who explained how the campaigners were keeping daily work charts and planned to distribute the crop according to the number of hours each peasant worked.

29. The "commune" was at Ethaya, a small town near Assela in Arussi Province. The entire *zemecha* camp was finally closed down by force. Other closings occurred elsewhere in the province.

30. Befekadu Degefe and Clement Cottingham, "Rural Transformation in the Countryside: A Preliminary Analysis of the Emergence of the Peasant Associations," Addis Ababa University, Institute for Development Research, Occasional Paper Number 10, 1976.

31. These conclusions are based on numerous firsthand reports by individuals who had occasion to work in rural areas and talk to both peasants and students.

32. Information obtained from *zemecha* officials and "Development through Cooperation Campaigns Summary Report 1967/68 E.C.," volume I, Addis Ababa, Sene 30, 1968 E.C.

33. Information obtained from *zemecha* officials.

34. Harvest estimates in Ethiopia are very approximate. The only report available on the 1975/76 crop estimated an increase of roughly 10 percent over the previous year when the harvest had been good. See John Dalton, "Report on Prospects of the Ethiopian Harvest of 1968 E.C. (1975/76 G.C.)," prepared for the Relief and Rehabilitation Commission of the Government of Ethiopia and the United Nations Development Program, Addis Ababa, December 23, 1975.

35. Membership figures issued in the fall by the Ministry of Land Reform, with the warning that they are not precise, are as follows:

Arussi 213,000 (1972 population estimate 853,000)
Shoa 1,013,000 (population excluding Addis Ababa 5,369,000)
Wollega 273,000 (population 1,269,000)
Kaffa 372,000 (population 1,693,000)
Wollo 371,000 (population 2,450,000)
Gemu Gofa 83,000 (population 698,000)
Bale 90,000 (population 708,000)
Gojjam 62,000 (population 1,750,000)
Tigre 311,000 (population 1,828,000)
Hararghe 340,000 (population 3,359,000)
Begemdir 145,000 (population 1,353,000)
Sidamo 1,113,000 (population 2,480,000)
Illubabor 159,000 (population 688,000)

36. Ethiopia imported a total of about 125,000 tons of grain during 1976. Of this amount, 50,000 tons went to the Relief and Rehabilitation Commission for distribution in drought-stricken rural areas, mostly the Ogaden. The rest was destined for the urban market. The amount imported was higher than in past years but not unprecedented. In 1970, Ethiopia imported 71,000 tons and in 1971, 45,000. These imports had always been destined for the urban areas where the demand for wheat was growing fast.

37. Holmberg estimated the probable increase in on-farm consumption at between 150,000 and 200,000 tons, while Dalton estimated it at over 200,000.

38. For a detailed discussion of these bottlenecks, see Holmberg, "Pricing Strategies," particularly 12 f.

39. Dalton, "Report on . . . the Ethiopian Harvest," 7.

40. Figures released by the Ministry of National Resources Development indicated that the ministry had taken over 130,000 hectares of commercial farm land and then distributed 39,000 hectares to peasant associations. Altogether, it was farming 91,957 hectares and employing 54,329 seasonal and permanent laborers. Not all commercial farms went under the ministry's control, however. The most notable exception was the Setit-Humera area, which was de facto exempted from the land reform. Many of the smaller commercial farms are believed to have gone directly to the peasant associations, but there are no available figures. See the *Ethiopian Herald,* July 30, 1975, and August 17, 1975.

41. Holmberg claims that the government was reluctant to accept the suggestions of foreign experts that grain prices be set high enough to provide an incentive to farmers to sell more of their crop. This policy was finally adopted, but within a few months retail prices skyrocketed above the government's minimum. See Holmberg, "Pricing Strategies," 7 f.

42. Proclamation No. 47 of 1975, "A Proclamation to Provide for Government Ownership of Urban Lands and Extra Urban Houses," *Negarit Gazeta,* July 26, 1975.

43. See the *Ethiopian Herald,* December 30, 1975.

Chapter 6
Notes

1. The Bichena incident took place in August 1975, when a *Derg* delegation was in the region trying to explain the meaning of land reform to a hostile peasantry. When a meeting was disrupted, nervous soldiers opened fire on the crowd; later artillery and planes were summoned to quell what the government feared would become a major disturbance. Reports of the death toll vary from one hundred to one thousand. The other massacre took place northwest of Dessie in October 1976, when troops fired into a large crowd of peasants marching on the provincial capital at the instigation of local landlords. Again reports of the death toll vary widely, from several hundred to nearly a thousand.

2. Ethiopian Democratic Union, *E.D.U.: What Does It Stand For? Who Is Behind It? What After the Derg?* (London, September 1976), 4.

3. *Declaration of The Ethiopian Democratic Union* (London, March 1975), 4.

4. *E.D.U.: What Does It Stand For?*, 3.

5. Ibid., 4.

6. Ibid., 4.

7. See chapter 10.

8. See pp. 134–135 for more on Mengistu.

9. For a more detailed analysis on this early Galla movement, see John Markakis, *Ethiopia: Anatomy of a Traditional Polity,* (Oxford: Clarendon Press, 1974), 178 ff.

10. The most detailed account of the Bale revolt during the 1960s is found in Aberra Ketsele, "The Rebellion in Bale 1963–70," unpublished B.A. thesis, Haile Selassie I University, 1971. See also Patrick Gilkes, *The Dying Lion,* (London: Friedman, 1975), 204 ff. and Markakis, *Ethiopia,* 368 ff.

11. Aberra Ketsele, "Rebellion in Bale," 15–16.

12. Ibid., 13.

13. Ibid., 9.

14. Ibid., 17.

15. In Delo *awraja,* the one most affected by the rebellion, the Ministry of Land Reform found that 36.5 percent of measured land had been confiscated and redistributed. See Markakis, *Ethiopia,* 370.

16. From *Warraaqa,* n.d., mimeo, unofficial translation.

17. See chapter 10.

18. Scholarly estimates of the Afar population vary, but none put the total number above 250,000. Moreover, the sultan did not control the entire Afar population, only the semi-settled clans of the Awash Delta. Ali Mirah's own estimate of three million is fantastical.

Chapter 7
Notes

1. See especially Allan Hoben, *Land Tenure among the Amhara of Ethiopia* (Chicago: The University of Chicago Press, 1973), and his "Social Stratification in Traditional Amhara Society," in A. Tuden and L. Plotnikov, eds., *Social Stratification in Africa* (New York: The Free Press, 1970), 187–224. Also see Donald Levine, *Wax and Gold* (Chicago: The University of Chicago Press, 1965).

2. Margery Perham, *The Government of Ethiopia* (Evanston, Ill.: Northwestern University Press, 1969), 270.

3. By late July, the CELU claimed a membership of 125,000. See the *Ethiopian Herald,* July 25, 1974. More reliable estimates put the membership at around 115,000 at this time, still a considerable increase from 85,000 members in early 1974.

4, The *Voice of Labour,* vol. 11, no. 6, August 1974, editorial.

5. Proclamation no. 1 of 1974 and Proclamation no. 2 of 1974, *Negarit Gazeta,* September 15, 1974.

6. "Resolutions Passed by the General Assembly of the Confederation of Ethiopian Labor Unions," September 16, 1974, mimeo, unofficial translation.

7. Ibid.

8. The *Ethiopian Herald,* September 24, 1974.

9. The Chilalo Agricultural Development Unit (CADU) and the Wollamo Agricultural Development Unit (WADU) were projects set up with foreign aid to develop peasant agriculture. They were not peasant cooperatives in any real sense of the term, and staff members were outside professionals.

10. The *Ethiopian Herald,* October 26, 1974.

11. The *Voice of Labour,* vol. 12, no. 7, April 1975.

12. Statement issued by the Confederation of Ethiopian Labor Unions, June 4, 1975, mimeo.

13. The *Ethiopian Herald,* May 20, 1975.

14. Ibid.

15. Quoted in the *Ethiopian Herald,* May 28, 1975.

16. Marcos Hagos had a dubious reputation. He had been dismissed from one insurance company for embezzling funds and then somehow found a position in another, his record notwithstanding. Before the onset of the revolution, he had no reputation in labor circles as a radical.

17. Statement issued by the Confederation of Ethiopian Labor Unions, June 4, 1975, mimeo.

18. See the *Ethiopian Herald,* September 20, 1974, for the text of the ETA statement.

19. See "A Resolution passed by the Ethiopian Teachers' Assocation in its 11th General Meeting at Jimma," August 31 to September 10, 1975, mimeo, unofficial translation.

20. A document containing proposals along this line circulated in university circles in mid-1975. The *Ethiopian Herald* later published the outline of a radically revised system of education without specifying whether it was the official government proposal. See the *Ethiopian Herald,* August 17, 1975. As of this writing, no overall educational reform has been announced, although there was some experimentation taking place at the local level within peasant associations.

21. "A Resolution passed by the Ethiopian Teachers' Association in its 11th General Meeting at Jimma," August 31 to September 10, 1975, mimeo, unofficial translation.

22. The rumor stemmed largely from the clumsy official communique announcing the Emperor's death. It indicated that he had died following a relapse without having received medical attention because his personal physician could not be found. While it is not known what actually happened, there are strong indications that no efforts were made to save him. It is unlikely he was actually killed. Such rumors were bound to arise no matter what happened, given the atmosphere of suspicion and distrust prevailing in Addis Ababa at the time.

23. These allegations were made following the government's decision to move the royal family from the palace of the Duke of Harar to the Akaki central prison, where the executions of the previous November had taken place. Government sources told the authors the move was made because several prisoners had gone on a rampage inside the palace, destroying some of the furnishings.

24. Appeals to the military government to spare the lives of members of the royal family came

first from the British government and then from the Common Market, acting at the behest of the British. On Sept. 12, the PMAC issued a statement denying it had ever intended to execute any member of the royal family.

25. "Resolutions Passed by the Special Session of the General Assembly of the CELU," held September 19–23, 1975, mimeo, unofficial translation.

26. Proclamation no. 64 of 1975, "Labour Proclamation," *Negarit Gazeta,* December 6, 1975.

27, Ibid. 55.

28. Ibid. 72 f.

Chapter 8
Notes

1. Mengistu's speech of February 4; see the *Ethiopian Herald,* February 5, 1977.

2. These characterizations are based on conversations with a large number of Ethiopians who studied at Haile Selassie University and abroad.

3. See John Markakis, *Ethiopia: Anatomy of a Traditional Polity* (Oxford: Clarendon Press, 1974), 359 ff.

4. The close link between student and national politics is reflected in the surprising attention still paid to statements issued by Ethiopian students abroad. For example, as late as December 1976, both *Addis Zemen* and the *Ethiopian Herald* dedicated long columns to refute a statement issued by the Ethiopian Student Union in North America. See the *Ethiopian Herald,* December 7 and 8, 1976.

5. "Speech addressed to the Nation by Brig. Gen. Teferi Bante, Chairman of the PMAC, on the Occasion of the Ethiopian New Year, the First Anniversary of the Revolution and the Reunion of Eritrea with the Motherland," Ethiopian News Agency mimeo, official translation, September 11, 1975.

6. The pamphlet was signed by Assefa Medhane, Eshatu Chole, Melese Ayelu, Yonas Admassu, Wondwossen Hailu. All of them except Eshatu Chole were prevailed upon to join the Political Bureau. Eshatu remained firm in his position, and was arrested after a time. Yonas Admassu later defected from the Political Bureau to join the TPLF.

7. No single document clearly spells out the Fidaist position. Our analysis is based mostly on the debate in *Addis Zemen,* various issues of the semi-clandestine *Voices of the Masses,* and innumerable conversations with Ethiopians of both factions. The Fidaists also published another underground sheet called *Wez* ("Sweat") directed toward the workers.

8. Sources for this interpretation include the debate in *Addis Zemen,* numerous issues of *Democracia,* and conversations with EPRP members and sympathizers. The EPRP also published *Lab Ader* ("Toiling Masses") and "Revolutionary Youth."

9. Statement made to the authors by a pro-EPRP intellectual.

10. Both programs, including that of the Political Bureau, circulated as clandestine pamphlets. Thus, even the Political Bureau's program was not an official government document, and it is far from sure it had the explicit approval of the *Derg.* In fact, it was published as a special issue of the *Voice of the Masses.*

11. On the ideological debate, see also Marina Ottaway, "Democracy and New Democracy: The Ideological Debate in the Ethiopian Revolution," paper presented at the Annual Meeting of the African Studies Association, Boston, November 3–6, 1976.

12. See the *Ethiopian Herald,* April 21, 1976.

13. Proclamation No . . . [*sic*], "A Proclamation to Establish a People's Organizing Provisional Office," the *Ethiopian Herald,* April 21, 1976. The name of the organization was later changed to Provisional Office for Mass Organizational Affairs (POMOA).

14. *Democracia,* vol. 3, no. 3, n.d., unofficial translation.

15. Ibid.

16. The only mention of military representation was a reference to "military forces movements," which probably meant those soldiers and officers favorable to the EPRP and a return to civilian rule.

17. See chapter 9.

18. An unofficial list of Political Bureau members in March 1977 reads as follows: Haile Fida, Oromo, French educated; Negede Gobeze, Amhara, French educated; Mesfin Kassu, Amhara, educated in France and U.S.A.; Assefa Medhane, Eritrean, educated in U.S.A.; Wondwossen Hailu, Amhara, educated in U.S.A.; Melesse Ayelew, Amhara/Oromo, educated in U.S.A.; Bezabeh Kenbatu, unknown origin; Negiste Gebre-Mariam, female, educated in U.S.S.R.; Kadir Mohamed, Oromo, head of the Provisional Office in Illubabor; Baro Tumsa, Oromo, educated in U.S.A. There were at least two others members, but it is not cetain who they were.

19. These "workers' forums" were established in April 1976. Participants were supposed to discuss papers submitted to them by the Political Bureau. However, in many offices and enterprises they became for several months arenas of anti-government agitation. The workers often refused to discuss the official papers, or tried to turn the meetings into grievance sessions against managers and the government. After a few months, the Political Bureau managed to establish control over these meetings, after many of the workers who had led the anti-government campaign were arrested. The meetings were discontinued in early 1977.

20. See chapter 9.

21. The new banking and currency proclamation also sought to finance the cost of issuing the new currency. In order to exchange old banknotes for the new ones, everyone was forced to deposit the money into an account. Moreover, 50- and 100-Ethiopian dollar notes were exchanged at an 8 percent discount. See the *Ethiopian Herald,* September 21, 1976.

Chapter 9
Notes

1. From the statement of the Coordinating Committee of the Armed Forces on July 9, 1974, the *Ethiopian Herald,* July 10, 1974.

2. From "*Abiot* Forum," the *Ethiopian Herald,* April 12, 1977.

3. See, as one of many examples, Mengistu's speech of February 4, 1977, the *Ethiopian Herald,* February 5, 1977.

4. See the *Ethiopian Herald,* March 12, 1977.

5. "*Abiot* Forum," the *Ethiopian Herald,* April 27, 1977.

6. Mengistu's speech of February 4, 1977, the *Ethiopian Herald,* February 5, 1977.

7. The Holetta (Guenet) Military School offered specialized training to soldiers and NCOs who did not have high school degrees. In the Ethiopian armed forces, there was always a distinction between its graduates and those of the Harar Military Academy, which only took the best high school graduates.

8. To understand the meaning of these rumors, one must realize that the Amhara officers in the army had always been divided between Shoans and Gojjames, and that under Emperor Haile Selassie the top positions tended to go to Shoan officers.

9. Teferi's name was originally transliterated as Teferi Benti; this spelling was later changed to Teferi Bante, and the change was regarded as extremely significant by Ethiopians.

10. The chairmen of these committees until July 1976 were as follows: political and foreign affairs—Captain Sisay Hapte; administrative affairs—Captain Alemayehu Haile; legal affairs—Captain Berhanu Bayeh; social and economic affairs—Captain Mogus Wolde-Michael; information and public affairs—Major Asrat Desta; defense—Captain Haddis Tedla; and public security Majors Daniel Asfaw or Teka Tula. Most of these officers were promoted to the next highest rank in April 1975.

11. The *Ethiopian Herald,* November 29, 1974.

12. According to sources close to the *Derg,* the figure of 120 was an invention of foreign journalists that the council decided not to dispute so as to avoid revealing the real number.

13. The highest number of *Derg* members the authors were ever able to identify from newspaper reports was 65, but there were almost certainly more.

14. The *Ethiopian Herald,* September 16, 1976.

15. See Johan Holmberg, "Pricing Strategies for Agricultural Produce in a Changing Society; Rural Urban Contradictions in Ethiopia," unpublished paper presented to the 19th annual meeting of the African Studies Association, Boston, November 3–6, 1976.

16. See p. 000n.

17. For details on the peasant march, see chapter 10.

18. Official PMAC communique of July 13, 1976, mimeo.

19. Among those executed at the same time as Sisay were several merchants accused of hoarding food. While it seems highly unlikely that Sisay was in league with them, linking the two fit nicely into the Chilean analogy the government was propounding.

20. The *Ethiopian Herald,* December 30, 1976.

21. In addition to Alemayehu and Mogus, there was a third officer widely regarded as part of the group that engineered the reorganization. He was Petty Officer Michael Asgedom, who became vice-chairman of the political affairs committee under Mogus in the reorganization of December 1976. Michael Asgedom was killed in Asmara in early January 1977 in an "accident" widely believed to be part of Mengistu's vendetta: he was shot by *Derg* security officers, purportedly by accident.

22. The *Ethiopian Herald,* February 1, 1977.

23. At the time, Mogus Wolde-Michael was head of the political affairs committee, Asrat Desta was head of the information and public affairs committee, and Hiruy Haile Selassie was head of either the security affairs or the defense committee.

24. Senay was reportedly working in his office in Menelik Palace when the shooting started. He was killed by a stray bullet when he stepped out to see what was happening.

25. Government statement on the attempted coup, the *Ethiopian Herald,* February 5, 1977.

26. Mengistu's speech of February 4, the *Ethiopian Herald,* February 5, 1977.

27. The *Ethiopian Herald,* February 12, 1977.

28. Mengistu's speech of February 4, the *Ethiopian Herald,* February 5, 1977.

29. The permanent secretary of the Ministry of Labor and Social Affairs, Guetenet Zewde, was killed on November 8, 1976. The permanent secretary of the Ministry of Culture, Sports, and Youth Affairs, Tsegaye Debalke, was assassinated on February 2, 1977. The chairman of the All-Ethiopian Trade Union was assassinated on February 25, 1977. The AETU deputy secretary, Bekele Legesse, was seriously wounded in the same incident.

30. The government announced it had "flushed out" several hundred "counterrevolutionaries," but gave no further details. See the *Ethiopian Herald,* March 29, 1977.

31. Government statement read on the radio on March 25, 1977.

32. The *Ethiopian Herald,* April 3, 1977 carried the official communique regarding Girma's misdeeds and his execution.

Chapter 10
Notes

1. A chronology of the Eritrean independence movement appears in *Erythrée en Lutte,* Bulletin d'Information du Front de Libération de l'Erythrée (September-October 1975), 5. The Front credits a certain Hamid Idriss Awate with launching the armed struggle with thirteen companions and nine old-fashioned guns.

2. Ibid.

3. The same EPLF publication describes the ideological position of the EPLF as "revolutionary patriotism," while that of the ELF is qualified as "nationalist." Ibid., 5.

4. Ibid. for the official figure. ELF officials told the authors that the number of deaths stood at more than two thousand.

5. This is the conclusion the authors reached after a tour of Eritrea in September and October 1974. A surprisingly large number of Eritreans interviewed still seemed willing to accept a federal solution short of total independence.

6. The *Ethiopian Herald,* October 11, 1974.

7. The ELF and the EPLF had started sending in commandos in late December, and there were numerous isolated incidents during January before the launching of the major attack.

8. The guerrillas took heavy losses in the fighting. A statement of the PMAC issued on February 22 gave the following statistics on the fighting over the previous month: 2,321 Eritrean guerrillas killed, and 374 other wounded or captured. It claimed that only 83 government soldiers were killed and 188 others wounded, but this is certainly a gross underestimate. It is also likely the figure of 2,321 dead included civilians as well as guerrillas. The Eritrean nationalists for their part claimed they killed 16,000 Ethiopian troops—out of 20,000 troops in the province at that time— between January 15 and the end of March 1975. See *Erythrée en Lutte* (January-April 1976), 16–17. See also the *Ethiopian Herald,* February 23, 1975.

9. The *Ethiopian Herald,* September 3, 1975.

10. The delegation was led by Lij Michael Imru, former prime minister and then adviser to the *Derg,* and toured Eritrea in December 1974 and January 1975.

11. The Imru delegation visited Sudan, Egypt, Syria, and Iraq in January 1975.

12. The delegation of elders visited Eritrea during the summer of 1975.

13. The *Ethiopian Herald,* April 21, 1976.

14. Ibid.

15. The *Ethiopian Herald,* May 18, 1976, Nine-point Policy, Point 2.

16. Ibid., Point 3.

17. Ibid., Point 4.

18. In effect there were two special commissions, one inside the *Derg* and one in the province itself. The *Derg* commission was headed first by Major Sisay Hapte and after his death by Major Berhanu Bayeh. The official Special Commission on Eritrea was set up only on October 20, 1976.

19. The *Ethiopian Herald,* June 20, 1976.

20. In the "Unification Agreement" signed by the ELF and the EPLF in September 1975 it

was stated the movement's internal divisions had "decreased material and moral aid from sisterly Arab countries."

21. The greatest pressure for unity came when both the ELF and the EPLF moved in around Asmara in the fall of 1974. Reportedly there were scenes where civilians placed themselves bodily between the positions of the two factions so as to stop them from fighting. Also, some guerrillas on both sides refused to fight against the opposite nationalist faction and were court-martialed by their leaders for insubordination, but later pardoned.

22. "Unification Agreement Between the Eritrean Liberation Front and the People's Liberation Forces," informal English translation, mimeo, n.d. The conference was held in early September 1975.

23. The two organizations popularly known as ELF and EPLF were formally called ELF-Revolutionary Command and ELF-People's Liberation Forces. When Osman was expelled, he continued to use the name ELF-People's Liberation Forces. The main faction of the old EPLF maintained the acronym unchanged, but changed the formal name to Eritrean People's Liberation Front. See Resolutions and Recommendations of the First Organizational Congress of the EPLF, held January 23–31, 1977," in *Vanguard,* vol. II, no. 1 (February-March 1977).

24. The EPLF never officially described itself as Marxist. At its first Congress of January 1977, it adopted an eleven-point "National Democratic Program," which called for the establishment of a "democratic people's government and the building of a planned, self-sufficient economy, based on collective ownership by the broad masses." However, the basic texts used for political education were the classics of Marxism-Leninism and the works of Mao and Castro.

25. For a brief account of the historical background to the conflict between Somalia and Ethiopia, see Tom J. Farer, *War Clouds on the Horn of Africa* (New York: Carnegie Endowment for International Peace, 1976). For an Ethiopian viewpoint, see Mesfin Wolde-Mariam, *The Ethio-Somalia Boundary Dispute* (Addis Ababa: Haile Selassie I University, 1964).

26. Somali claims to Ethiopian territory included by mid-1977 four entire provinces, Hararghe, Bale, Sidamo, and Arussi, according to the leaders of the Western Somalia Liberation Front. This meant in effect that Somalia was also laying claims to vast territories not inhabited by Somalia tribesmen but by Galla peasants. Moreover, while the Ogaden is a semi-desert region, the larger, more recent Somali claims included some of Ethiopia's best and most well-developed agricultural land.

27. The size of this irregular force has been put at 40,000 men by the Ethiopians, 30,000 by the Western Somalia Liberation Front, and 6,000 to 8,000 by outside observers.

28. "War Clouds on the Horn of Africa," memorandum of the Provisional Military Administrative Council, January 1976.

29. Ibid.

30. Interview given by Osman Saleh Sabbe to the South African weekly *To the Point* (March 14, 1975), 24.

31. The *Ethiopian Herald,* September 3, 1975.

32. Ethiopia did later obtain some Soviet arms through Libya, before the Soviet Union started giving direct military aid.

33. Personal communication with an officer present at the meeting with Mengistu.

34. Yugoslavia sent a shipment of small arms and ammunitions in the spring of 1975.

35. The United States government took months to reach a decision on the Ethiopian request and finally responded in the fall of 1975 by offering to provide $11.6 million worth of ammunition, less than half the requested amount.

36. Personal communication.

37. The *Ethiopian Herald,* April 12, 1977.

38. Kerora, Om Hager, and Tessenei all fell during the first three weeks of January. Nakfa fell March 22, Afabet April 6, and Elaberet a few days later.

39. Keren and Decamhare fell July 8, and Agordat shortly afterward.

40. The exact size of the EDU army remains unclear and even its leaders were uncertain. By June 1977 it had less than 2,000 regularly trained troops. The rest of the army consisted of untrained peasants, many of them operating within Ethiopia under the command of local landlords, like *Dejazmacth* Berhane Meskal in Wollo and Semineh Desta in Gojjam. Altogether the EDU army may have been more than 10,000, but it was not operating as a single force under a unified command.

41. By the end of July, the Western Somalia Liberation Front claimed that it had "annihi-lated" 5,266 Ethiopian soldiers, shot down 23 Ethiopian planes, and destroyed 32 Ethiopian tanks. It listed 65 towns "where the WSLF flag had been hoisted" inside Ethiopia. From the Somali News Agency Bulletin, July 28, 1977.

Chapter 11
Notes

1. This included American liberals who were very upset about the state of human rights in Ethiopia and the French and Italian Communist parties that had long supported the Eritrean Liberation Front and tended to accept its interpretation of the PMAC as being "fascist."

2. The plan advanced by this particular group had not been adopted as of this writing, although the principle that peasant associations and *kebeles* should take major responsibility for schooling was generally accepted.

3. The Ministry of National Resources Development was established in January 1975, a month before the issuing of the decree nationalizing 72 industries and commercial enterprises and giving the state a majority share in 29 others. All state farms were also put under its authority. The ministry became eventually responsible for about 200 enterprises and assets of US$500 million before the government decided it had become too unwieldy and dismantled it in September 1976. At that point, the state enterprises were divided between the Ministry of Commerce, the Ministry of Communications, the Ministry of Agriculture, and the new Ministry of Industry. See the *Ethiopian Herald,* February 3, 1977.

4. "Peasant Association Organization and Consolidation Proclamation," Proclamation No. 71 of 1975, *Negarit Gazeta,* No. 15, December 14, 1975. For a detailed discussion of this decree, see John M. Cohen and Peter H. Koehn, "Rural and Urban Land Reform in Ethiopia," *African Law Studies* 14 (1977), 3–61.

5. Ibid., Preamble.

6. Ibid., Articles 5, 6, and 7.

7. Ibid., Articles 42–54.

8. Personal communication.

9. This impression is based on still unpublished data gathered in Hararghe and Arussi provinces by Zenabework Tadesse, who was carrying out research for the Swedish International Development Agency. Her information has been confirmed by *zemacha* officials in private conversations with the authors.

10. "Development Through Cooperation Campaign's Summary Report 1967/68 E.C.," Vol. I, Addis Ababa, Sene 30, 1968 E.C., p. 93.

11. The *Ethiopian Herald,* June 20, 1976.

12. This total was reached by adding together the figures for the size of the militia in each province, published by the press each time a unit was formally established.

13. "Rural Land Fee and Agricultural Activities Income Tax Proclamation," No. 77 of 1976, *Negarit Gazeta,* No. 19, January 4, 1976.

14. Ibid. Peasants earning up to Eth$600 were to pay Eth$3.00, and those with incomes of

Eth$600 to Eth$900, Eth$4.50. The overwhelming majority of peasants in Ethiopia earn under Eth$600 annually.

15. The reform was not as far-reaching as some radicals had proposed. The schools still remained under the Ministry of Education, which continued to provide and pay the teachers, establish the curriculum and provide textbooks. However, the *kebeles* and associations were empowered to set up committees to oversee the general running of the schools and to enforce discipline among both teachers and students.

16. On the second anniversary of land reform, the government released the following statistics on the number of peasant associations and the size of their membership: Shoa Province, 5,498 associations with 1.9 million members; Gojjam, 2,476 associations with 678,000 members; Wollega, 2,264 associations with 432,000 members; Begemdir, 2,040 associations with 294,000 members; Wolo, 1,974 associations with 699,000 members; Kaffa, 1,581 associations with 396,161 members; Sidamo, 1,529 associations with 660,000 members; Tigre, 1,394 associations with 449,000 members; Hararghe, 1063 associations with 676,000 members; Gemu-Gofa, 740 associations with 298,000 members; Eritrea, 12 associations with 5,000 members; Bale, 1,132 associations with 207,000 members; and Illubabor, 985 associations with 193,000 members. See the *Ethiopian Herald,* March 2, 1977. No figures were given for Arussi Province.

17. These committees were officially created on April 21, 1977. For a detailed description of their powers and purposes, see the *Ethiopian Herald,* April 22, 1977. In brief, they were the old revolutionary administration and development committees with the added responsibility of raising funds and mobilizing the population for the war effort.

18. No systematic study was ever done to the author's knowledge on the social composition of those elected to the first executive committees. Our conclusions are based on our personal knowledge of some *kebeles* and on conversations with government officials who helped organize and supervise the elections.

19. "Urban Dwellers' Associations Consolidation and Municipalities Proclamation," Proclamation No. 104 of 1976, *Negarit Gazeta,* No. 5, October 9, 1976.

20. The elections for new lower *kebele* officials were held in Addis Ababa on October 24 and in 63 other cities and towns throughout the country on December 3, 1976. Those for the higher *kebeles* were held in Addis Ababa on November 7. As of this writing, no central *kebeles* had been formed anywhere in the country.

21. See p. 147.

22. "The Ethiopian Worker—Years of Stuggle Bear Fruit: From CELU to AETU," the *Ethiopian Herald,* April 27, 1977.

23. Originally the POMOA was known as the People's Organizing Provisional Office (POPO).

24. MASON's control over the ideological school began to slip when the school's director, Terefe Wolde-Tsadik, was named Minister of Education in March 1977. Then in July, the school was formally placed under the control of the PMAC.

Appendix A

PROGRAMME OF THE NATIONAL DEMOCRATIC REVOLUTION OF ETHIOPIA

Introduction

In order to advance the revolution of the broad masses of Ethiopia and guide it towards it ultimate goal, it is necessary to start from a correct understanding of Ethiopia's current reality. The character of the revolution at this stage and its future course must be known. The class enemies and class friends of the revolution must also be correctly distinguished. The nature of the Ethiopian society is semi-feudal and semi-capitalist and as such its basic problems originate from feudalism, imperialism and bureaucratic capitalism, the product of these twin forces. These three determine the nature of the present Ethiopian society and its various manifestations.

The Ethiopian people have waged a continuous struggle against their class enemies for a long time. This struggle attained a new and radical form in February 1974. Since then, it has been proceeding at a great momentum. Yet, it cannot be said that contradictions between the peasantry and the feudal class, between the working class and the bourgeoisie, between Ethiopia's broad masses and imperialism has been resolved. In addition, contradictions among nationalities, religions, sexes, etc., though of a secondary nature with respect to class contradictions, also await solution.

The proper resolution of these contradictions will begin with the national democratic revolution and will attain its consummation through the subsequent socialist revolution. The objective of the national democratic revolution is to liberate Ethiopia from the yokes of feudalism and imperialism and to lay the foundations for the transition to socialism. But it is necessary to make a proper class analysis of Ethiopian society which is semi-feudal and semi-capitalist and determine the real friends and the real enemies of the national democratic revolution.

In general, the national democratic revolution is a struggle between two broad fronts. On one side, there is the front of the counter-revolution. This front comprises of the feudal class, the comprador bourgeoisie and the bureaucratic bourgeoisie. Imperialism is a partner and supporter of this front. On the other side, the broad front of revolutionary forces is based on the worker-peasant alliance. The petty bourgeoisie is a close friend and ally of this latter front. In addition, there are other oppressed strata of society and progressive and patriotic individuals who have transcended their class and are ready to stand on the side of the revolution. The lumpen proletariat will immensely gain from the revolution. But by its class character, it is possible that it can become an instrument of reactionary forces. Therefore, the revolution should handle the lumpen proletariat with care and caution. As one of the basic features of the national democratic revolution is that it is anti-feudal, its aim is to unite all anti-feudal forces in a struggle for the attainment of genuine democracy for all oppressed classes. And as the national democratic revolution is also anti-imperialist, it also establishes a broad front of all anti-imperialist forces and strives towards the establishment of a society with an independent economic, political and social order. This is why the present stage of our revolution is characterized as the national democratic revolution. Uniting and leading the broad masses through the national democratic revolution is the only road to the transition to socialism.

In the short span of time since February 1974, the revolutionary movement of the Ethiopian people has attained several major victories. On the economic front, all rural land has been nationalized; urban land and extra houses have been put under government control; banks, industries and insurance companies have become public property through various proclamations. These measures have shaken the feudo-capitalist system at its base. On the political front, the major victory is not only the removal of the emperor from power, but also the dealing of death blows to feudal lackeys and thereby the heralding of the complete abolition of the archaic autocratic monarchical rule which has remained the mainstay of feudal Ethiopia. This has also resulted in the awakening of the masses. Socialism has also been declared as the guiding principle of the revolution. And this has opened the way for the public propagation of the socialist world-outlook.

In order to consolidate and give these victories a lasting premise and increase popular participation in the overall revolutionary process, it is imperative that the broad masses be politicized, organized and armed. The Provisional Military Government of Ethiopia, on various occasions, has declared its clear intention to transfer state power to the broad masses. Therefore, in order to enable all anti-feudal and anti-imperialist forces to organize freely, and in order to establish a united front under the leadership of the working class party which can establish a people's democratic state, the following programme has been issued.

PROGRAMME OF THE NATIONAL DEMOCRATIC REVOLUTION OF ETHIOPIA

SECTION I

Aim of the Programme

1. To completely abolish feudalism, imperialism and bureaucratic capitalism from Ethiopia and with the united effort of all anti-feudal and anti-imperialist forces build a new Ethiopia and lay a strong foundation for the transition to socialism.

2. Towards this end, under the leadership of the working class and on the basis of the worker-peasant alliance and in collaboration with the petty bourgeoisie and other anti-feudal and anti-imperialist forces, establish a people's democratic republic in which the freedom, equality, unity and prosperity of the Ethiopian peoples is ensured, in which self-government at different levels is exercised and which allows for the unconditional exercise of human and democratic rights.

SECTION II

Contents of the Programme

3. To release the country's productive forces from all feudal and imperialist production relations; to accelerate the economic development of the country in order to raise the standard of living of the broad masses. Since the building of a strong and an independent national economy is possible only through the balanced development of the industrial and agricultural sectors of the national economy, it is necessary to have a centralized national plan based on socialist principles. Such a plan must take agriculture as the foundation of the country's economy and proceed towards establishing light industry that serve the immediate needs of the broad masses. At the same time emphasis will also be given to the establishment of heavy industries which will be primarily based on utilizing the country's natural resources. It is a known fact that heavy industry is a prerequisite for a strong national economy. Towards this end, it is necessary:

a) to fully implement the revolutionary proclamation that nationalized all rural lands. The government shall ensure the rights of individually owning farmers and at the same time it encourages and shall provide the necessary moral and material support to all cooperative endeavours of the peasant masses. In order to increase the total agricultural output of the country, the government will also establish large-scale state farms in different places.

b) to strengthen the major industries, banks and insurance companies already under government control and make them more beneficial to the broad masses. And to free the country from imperialist domination, major transport and foreign trade organizations have to be placed under state control.

c) to give the necessary incentive to local businessmen and industrialists and to all those citizens engaged in individual enterprizes useful for the society. Within the guidelines of the national plan, these groups will be provided with the opportunities to benefit for themselves while contributing to the overall development of the national economy.

4. The enhancement of the welfare of the broad masses of Ethiopia and the entire development of the country depends on the determined effort of the people themselves. It is the determination and the effort of the masses that will pave the future course of the country. But in order to mobilize the energy of the masses for the purpose of increasing production, the following steps need to be undertaken.

a) There will be an educational programme that will provide free education, step by step, to the broad masses. Such a programme will aim at intensifying the struggle against feudalism, imperialism and bureaucratic capitalism. All necessary measures to eliminate illiteracy will be undertaken. All necessary encouragement will be given for the development of science, technology, the arts and literature. All the necessary effort will be made to free the diversified cultures of imperialist cultural domination from their own reactionary characteristics. Opportunities will be provided to allow them to develop, advance and grow with the aid of modern means and resources.

b) To ensure full and meaningful life for the broad masses, all the necessary effort will be undertaken to provide adequate health services.

c) Better jobs and employment opportunities will be provided for the jobless and for those employed as servants and housemaids by private persons. Every necessary effort will be undertaken to allow women to participate fully in productive labour and thereby eliminate prostitution.

d) All the necessary effort to ensure the welfare of patriots, citizens who have no supporters, and other individuals who have served the society with distinction in diverse ways will be made. Orphans, abandoned children, and the disabled will be given adequate care. Relief shall be provided to help those groups affected by natural disasters such as drought, flood, earthquake, etc.

5. The right to self-determination of all nationalities will be recognized and fully respected. No nationality will dominate another one since the history, culture, language and religion of each nationality will have equal recognition in accordance with the spirit of socialism. The unity of Ethiopia's nationalities will be based on their common struggle against feudalism, imperialism, bureaucratic capitalism and all reactionary forces. This united struggle is based on the desire to construct a new life and a new society based on equality, brotherhood and mutual respect.

Nationalities on border areas and those scattered over various regions have been subjected to special subjugation for a long time. Special attention will be made to raise the political, economic and cultural life of these nationalities. All necessary steps to equalize these nationalities with the other nationalities of Ethiopia will be undertaken.

Given Ethiopia's existing situation, the problem of nationalities can be resolved if each nationality is accorded full right to self-government. This means that each nationality will have regional autonomy to decide on matters concerning its internal affairs. Within its environs, it has the right to determine the contents of its political, economic and social life, use its own language and elect its own leaders and administrators to head its internal organs.

This right of self-government of nationalities will be implemented in accordance with all democratic procedures and principles.

6. There will not be any sort of discrimination among religions and sexes. No citizen will be accorded special privilege in his or her political, economic and social undertaking on the basis of religion and sex.

7. The role of Ethiopia's armed forces and police is to safeguard Ethiopia's territorial integrity, unity and peace. They will be given all the necessary socialist education that will enable them to fulfil these tasks and protect the welfare of Ethiopia's broad masses. Steps will be taken that during peace time, side by side with the masses, they take active part in production and development areas.

Ethiopia's national interest, unity and integrity ultimately depends on the energy of its broad masses. It is this energy that can ultimately deter all external and domestic enemies. Therefore all the necessary steps to arm and train the masses will be undertaken.

8. All effort will be made to ensure that the rights of Ethiopian nationals living in foreign lands are fully respected. The rights of expatriates legally residing in Ethiopia will also be properly respected and protected.

9. The foreign policy of the country will be guided by the well-known principles of non-aligned nations. These are:
a) respect for peace, justice and equality
b) non-alignment
c) national independance, national unity and non-interference in the internal affairs of other countries.

Therefore, close and strong collaboration will be established with the sister countries of Africa, Asia and Latin America, and with all national liberation movements and other progressive organizations dedicated to the struggle against imperialism, neo-colonialism and racism.

The principles of the charters of the United Nations and of the Organization of African Unity will be respected. All measures to strengthen ties and collaboration with sister African states, in particular with neighbouring ones, will be undertaken. No effort shall be spared to foster the spirit of good neighbourliness and mutual respect among states.

SECTION III

Immediate Tasks

To attain the above objectives and taking into full account the objective conditions of the country, the broad masses of Ethiopia, united and free from any form of coersion, must be provided with all opportunities to construct a new society. Feudalism, imperialism and bureaucratic capitalism should be defeated as soon as possible. In short, all reactionary forces must be liquidated. Hence, the following steps require immediate implementation.

1. The revolution can advance forward only if the popular masses are made politically conscious, and are organized and armed. But in order to do all these, all sectors of the oppressed classes must be furnished with the opportunity to learn, to teach, to organize and be organized. For all these, it is imperative to put into practice an unrestricted exercise of democratic rights for all anti-feudal, anti-imperialist and anti-bureaucratic capitalist forces. These forces will be immediately accorded full freedom to speak, to write, to assemble, to demonstrate peacefully, to organize and be organized.

2. The national democratic revolution of Ethiopia will be assured of victory if all anti-feudal and anti-imperialist forces unite in a broad revolutionary front. Therefore, all progressive forces will be accorded the freedom to organize and be organized in political parties and in mass organizations as a step towards establishing such a united front. But since final victory by such a united front is only assured when a true proletarian party is organized, strengthened and assumes the full-leadership of the front, the government will extend unceasing assistance to revolutionary groups and individuals struggling to establish such a vanguard party. The necessary moral and material help will be given to all democratic parties, mass organizations and other progressive forces engaged in the anti-feudal and anti-imperialist struggle so as to make such groups contribute to the general struggle of Ethiopia's broad masses.

3. All strata of the broad masses must be organized and become part of the popular revolutionary front. Hence, the need to raise the political awareness of the masses and to organize and arm them. Also, the effort to eliminate the enemies of the masses must inexorably proceed. During this process, the government has the duty to make sure that secondary contradictions that may arise among progressive elements are not taken advantage of by reactionary forces. Otherwise, counter-revolutionary forces will have the chance to do all they can to retard the revolution of Ethiopia's broad masses. Therefore, the government will stand by the side of all progressive elements and will take all the necessary measures against direct or

indirect attempts by reactionary forces to obstruct the achievements of Ethiopia's revolution. No one will be given the chance to sabotage the revolutionary procla- mations and especially those that made rural land the collective property of the Ethiopian people and ended monarchical and feudal rule in Ethiopia.

SECTION IV

Conclusion

As soon as the masses are properly organized and a popular revolutionary front is formed, an assembly which will assume state power will be established. Such an assembly will consist of representatives of parties and popular organizations that have participated in the front. Members of the assembly will be elected demo- cratically and through secret ballot. In accordance with the constitution that such an assembly will approve the people's republic of Ethiopia, under the leadership of the working class party will be declared.

To facilitate these steps, to coordinate the dissemination of the principles of scientific socialism, to aid the anti-feudal, anti-imperialist and anti-bureaucratic capitalist struggle of the broad masses of Ethiopia, and in general to help all efforts of the masses to be organized in order to form a popular revolutionary front, to find ways of advancing the revolutionary front, to find ways of advancing the revolu- tion, a Provisional Office For People's Organizational affairs is hereby established.

Appendix B

A PROCLAMATION TO PROVIDE FOR THE ORGANIZATION AND CONSOLIDATION OF PEASANT ASSOCIATIONS

"ETHIOPIA TIKDEM"

WHEREAS, the oppressed peasantry, the beneficiary of the Public Ownership of Rural Lands Proclamation, is constantly organizing itself in every area into associations and gaining increasing consciousness and it is necessary that the broad masses in Socialist Ethiopia administer their own affairs, solve their own local problems and participate directly in the political, economic and social movement;

WHEREAS, it is necessary to make the peasant associations already formed or to be formed more conscious and organized, so as to make sure that the Revolution will achieve its ultimate goal and to give proper revolutionary guidance to the public agencies which the Revolution has already created or will create by co-ordinating their activities and organization;

WHEREAS, it is necessary predicate the activities of Government and its agencies upon the problems and needs of the broad masses and the co-ordination of the activities of same into a common programme of work at all levels will minimize the intricacies of the bureaucracy;

WHEREAS, it is necessary to organize and develop co-operatives in all places and at all levels in order to lay down the foundation for socialist agriculture so that the peasantry may benefit from joint labour;

WHEREAS, it is necessary to give legal personality to peasant associations already formed or to be formed in the future at all levels and to define by proclamations and regulations the powers and duties of judicial tribunals, co-operative societies, women's associations and the like;

NOW, THEREFORE, in accordance with Article 6 of the Definition of Powers of the Provisional Military Administration Council and its Chairman Proclamation No. 2/1974, it is hereby proclaimed as follows:

CHAPTER 1
General

1. *Short Title*:

   This Proclamation may be cited as the "Peasant Associations Organization and Consolidation Proclamation No. 71/1975."

2. *Definitions*

In this Proclamation, unless the context otherwise requires:

1/ "Rural Lands Proclamation" shall mean the Public Ownership of Rural Lands Proclamation No. 31/1975;

2/ "peasant association" shall mean an association established or to be established in accordance with the Rural Lands Proclamation;

3/ "rural land" shall mean all lands outside the boundaries of a muncipality or town;

4/ "locality" shall mean the area delimited pursuant to Art. 8 of the Rural Lands Proclamation.

3. *Scope of Application*:

This Proclamation shall apply only to rural lands.

CHAPTER 2
Peasant Associations in General

4. *Legal Personality of Peasant Associations*

Peasant associations which are established or are to be established at all levels under the Rural Lands Proclamation shall have legal personality.

5. *Powers and Duties of Peasant Associations*

In addition to those specified in the Rural Lands Proclamation, a peasant association shall have the following powers and duties:

1/ to enable peasants to secure and safeguard their political, economic and social rights;

2/ to enable the peasantry to administer itself;

3/ to enable the peasantry to participate in the struggle against feudalism and imperialism by building its consciousness in lines with *Hebrettesebawinet*;

4/ to establish co-operative societies, women's associations, peasant defence squads and any other associations that may be necessary for the fulfillment of its goals and aims;

5/ to enable the peasantry to work collectively and to speed up social development by improving the quality of the instruments of production and the level of productivity;

6/ to sue and be sued;

7/ to issue and implement its internal regulations in order to achieve its goals and aims.

6. *Organization and Membership of Service Co-operative Societies*

1/ Unless the number of the members is otherwise determined by law, not less than three and not more than ten peasant associations may form a service co-operative society without affecting the legal personality of each association.

2 /Service co-operative societies may establish one service co-operative society at Woreda level and where necessary, higher service co-operative societies as may be prescribed by law.

3/ Woreda peasant associations shall supervise all service co-operative societies established in the Woreda at any level. However, the peasant association shall not interfere with the day to day activities of service co-operative societies.

7. *Objectives, Powers and Duties of Service Co-operative Societies*

The objectives, powers and duties of a service co-operative society shall include the following:

1/ to procure crop expansion services;

2/ to market the produce of members at fair prices;

3/ to give loans at fair interest rates;

4/ to give storage and savings services;

5/ to supply consumer goods to the members according to their needs;

6/ to give education in socialist philosophy and co-operative work in order to enhance the political consciousness of the peasantry;

7/ to supply improved agricultural implements and provide tractor services;

8/ to collect contributions;

9/ to give flour mills services;

10/ to organize craftsmen in order to promote cottage industry;

11/ to provide political education with a view to establishing agricultural producers' co-operative societies by forming, promoting and consolidating mutual aid teams like *debo*;

12/ to sue and be sued;

13/ to draw up its internal regulations.

8. *Objectives, Powers and Duties of Agricultural Producers Co-operative Society:*

An agricultural produers' co-operative society is a society that is established voluntarily by peasants associations; it shall have the following objectives, powers and duties:

1/ to put the main instruments of production under the control of, and when necessary to gradually transfer their ownership to, the society;

2/ to divide members into working groups to enable them to work collectively for the society especially by organizing members with special abilities in order to obtain mutual benefits;

3/ to give priority to the interests of poor and middle peasants and to ensure that the leadership of the association is drawn from such peasants;

4/ to raise production and to gradually improve the instruments of production;

5/ to pay the members according to the quality and quantity of their work;

6/ to assign a special fund for the welfare and security of the members;

7/ to struggle for continuous improvement, democratic rights and unity;

8/ to struggle for the gradual abolition of exploitation from the rural areas and to refraim from any kind of exploitation;

9/ to engage in continuous political movement in order to enhance the political consciousness of its members;

10/ to sue and be sued;

11/ to draw up its internal regulations.

9. *Proclamation of Co-operative Societies*

The organization and administration of co-operative societies shall be governed by another proclamation.

10. *Objectives, Powers and Duties of Women's Association:*

The objectives, powers and aims of a women's association shall be the following:

1/ to do every thing necessary to secure the rights of its members;

2/ to establish mobile teams which will closely follow the political, economic and social problems of its members;

3/ to establish professional associations;

4/ to sue and be sued; to enter into contract and to acquire property;

5/ to draw up its internal regulations.

11. *Powers and Duties of Defence Squad:*

The peasant defence squad shall have the following powers and duties:

1/ to hand over to the appropriate authorities persons arrested in *flagrante delicto*;

2/ to produce wanted persons upon order, in accordance with the law of the executive committee or judicial tribunal of a peasant association;

3/ to execute decisions and orders given by the judicial tribunal;

4. to safeguard forests, mines, bridges, crops and other such properties which need safeguarding from time to time;

5. to carry on the necessary security and defence activities according to the decision of the government;

6/ to institute criminal cases that are under the jurisdiction of the judicial tribunal.

12. *Defense Squad Members and Term of Service*

1/ the defence squad shall have:

a) a leader of the squad who shall be elected by the general assembly of the peasant association and who shall be a member of the executive committee; and

b) other members elected by the executive committee which shall decide their numbers as may be necessary.

2/ The members of the defence squad shall be elected for a term of two years. However, the executive committee may, when it deems it necessary, suspend any such member at any time.

13. *Criteria for Membership*

A member of the defence squad must be a person who is:

1/ from the broad masses of peasants and stands for their interest;

2/ in good health;

3/ not addicted to alcohol or other dangerous drugs;

4/ esteemed for his wisdom by the local people;

5/ not convicted for theft;

6/ responsible; and

7/ over 21 years old

14. *Registration of Peasant Associations*

Every peasant association shall be registered by the Ministry of Lands and Settlement as soon as such association is formed.

CHAPTER 3
Judicial Tribunal of Peasant Associations

1/ The number of the members of the judicial tribunal shall not be less than three and not more than five.

2/ The term of service of the members of the judicial tribunal shall be one year.

16. *Election Procedure*

1/ The members of the local judicial tribunal shall be elected by the general assembly of the local peasant association.

2/ The members of the Woreda judicial tribunal shall be elected by the general assembly of the Woreda peasant association.

3/ The members of the Awraja judicial tribunal shall be elected by the general assembly of the Awraja peasant association.

17. *Working Procedure of the Tribunal*

1/ The judicial tribunal shall register:

a) the charges and evidence brought against the defendant; and

b) the defence and reasons produced by the defendant; and shall give an equitable decision.

2/ All decisions of the tribunal shall be given by majority vote.

18. *Places Where Judicial Tribunals are not established*

The ordinary courts shall assume the civil and criminal jurisdiction of judicial tribunals hereunder and apply the ordinary procedures in places where, upon the effective date of this Proclamation, no judicial tribunals are established to enforce this Proclamation. However, such court shall, as of the date on which the Minister of Lands and Settlement notifies it of the establishment of a judicial tribunal, only settle the cases pending before it and shall not hear cases which come under the jurisdiction of the judicial tribunal.

19. *Cases Instituted before the Promulgation of this Proclamation*

Cases instituted in the ordinary courts before the promulgation of this Proclamation, even if they are within the jurisdiction of the judicial tribunal, shall be finalized by the ordinary courts.

20. *Civil Jurisdiction of the Local Judicial Tribunal*

The local judicial tribunal shall, in addition to those provided in the Rural Lands Proclamation, have the power to hear and decide:

1/ disputes involving up to $[Eth]100.00;

2/ disputes involving garden plots or succession cases involving private properties situated within the locality;

3/ disputes involving division of common property of spouses within the locality;

4/ disputes involving fees for collective use of places or instruments;

5/ disputes involving not more than $[Eth]500.00 arising between the local peasant association and the inhabitants of the locality;

6/ disputes arising between the peasant association and its members involving payment of loans advanced through the association.

21. *Criminal Jurisdiction of the Judicial Tribunal*

The local judicial tribunal shall have jurisdiction to hear and decide the following:

1/ violations of regulations relating to rural areas which are specified in the Code of Petty Offences of the Penal Code;

2/ intimidation;

3/ offences against the privacy of domicile;

4/ contempt of local judicial tribunal or refusal to carry out orders;

5/ violation of internal regulations issued by the peasant association concerning the property, security and welfare of the locality.

22. *Scope of Jurisdiction*

The local judicial tribunal shall have the jurisdiction specified in Articles 20 and 21 of this Proclamation:

1/ where the parties are residents or associations of the locality;

2/ where the source of the dispute is situated or the offence is committed within the locality.

23. *Power to impose Penalty*:

Where the local judicial tribunal finds the defendant guilty in cases it hears in accordance with Article 21 of this Proclamation, it may impose, according to the gravity of the offence, any one of the following penalties:

1/ to warn the offender;

2/ to order the offender to give public apology to the offended person or association;

3/ to order the offender to confess publicly that his act was shameful;

4/ to impose fines ranging from $[Eth]1.00 to $[Eth]300.00 or imprisonment up to 3 months;

5/ to impose compulsory labour not exceeding 15 days;

6/ to order the offender to compensate the offended party.

24. *Repeated offenses*

The tribunal may impose more than one of the penalties referred to in Article 23 on any offender who is proved to be guilty of committing:

1/ repeated or

2/ concurrent criminal offences.

25. *Transfer to an Ordinary Court*

1/ The tribunal shall transfer the cases presented to it to the prosecution office to be referred to the ordinary courts where:

a) the accused brought before the judicial tribunal has a case pending in the ordinary courts;

b) the tribunal, in the course of its session, realizes that it lacks jurisdiction to entertain the case.

2/ ordinary court to which the case is referred pursuant to sub-article (1) of this Article shall also decide on the charge which is triable by the judicial tribunal.

26. *Non-Compliance*

If a person who is ordered to perform compulsory labour fails to comply with such order, the tribunal may convert the compulsory labour into imprisonment not exceeding three months or into a fine not exceeding 300 [Eth] dollars.

27. *Evidence*

1/ The tribunal may hear witnesses and examine documents which are necessary for the decision of the case at hand.

2/ Any person or organization summoned pursuant to sub-art. (1) of this Article shall appear in person and produce the required documents in time.

28. *Time and Place of Hearing*

The tribunal may sit in any convenient place and at any time as it may deem fit. However, the time shall, as much as possible, be outside working hours.

29. *Appeal*

1/ Any party may appeal within 15 days from the date of decision by the tribunal;

2. The tribunal shall give a copy of the judgement and evidence to the party appealing; in cases where this is not possible, the chairman of the tribunal or his delegate must appear in person and explain the matter orally to the appellate tribunal.

30. *Option Not to Entertain Case*

The tribunal shall have the option not to entertain the case or give decision thereon when the following conditions occur:

1/ the defendant, in good faith, pleads guilty and apologises before the tribunal and, through his own initiative, makes good the damage he caused; or

2/ the plantiff withdraws the case.

31. *Execution of Decision*

The tribunal shall execute its decision through the local peasant defence squad or the Woreda police.

32. *Opposition to the Members of the Tribunal*

1/ Any party to a proceeding before a judicial tribunal may, where he has sufficient cause, object that one or more members of such tribunal should not hear his case.

2/ The tribunal shall decide on such objection.

3/ The member of the tribunal against whom a valid objection is made shall be replaced by another member and the hearing shall proceed.

33. *Jurisdiction of Woreda Judicial Tribunal*

The Woreda judicial tribunal shall, in addition to those provided in the Rural Lands Proclamation, have the power to hear and decide:

1/ appeals relating to land disputes which were heard at the local judicial tribunal in the first instance;

2/ appeals relating to criminal and civil cases which were heard by the local judicial tribunal in the first instance;

3/ in the first instance land disputes arising between the local peasant associations of the Woreda;

4/ in the first instance
   a) disputes arising between service co-operative societies and peasant associations;
   b) disputes arising between service co-operative societies;
   c) disputes arising between service co-operative societies and Woreda service co-operative societies;
   d) non-criminal disputes arising between service co-operative societies and its employees.

34. *Procedure of Appeal*

The Woreda judicial tribunal may confirm, amend or remand the case with guidelines to the local judicial tribunal.

35. *Additional Evidence*

The Woreda judicial tribunal may, when necessary, hear evidence during appeal.

36. *Finality of Decision*

Decisions given on appeal by the Woreda judicial tribunal shall be final.

37. *Jurisdiction of the Awraja Judicial Tribunal*

The Awraja judicial tribunal shall, in addition to those provided in the Rural Lands Proclamation, have the following jurisdiction:

1/ to hear and decide on appeal cases which were heard by the Woreda judicial tribunal in the first instance;

2/ to hear in the first instance and decide cases arising between Woreda peasant associations or Woreda service co-operative societies within the Awraja.

38. *Procedure of Appeal*

The Awraja judicial tribunal may reverse, confirm, amend or remand the case with guidelines to the Woreda tribunal.

39. *Additional Evidence*

The Awraja judicial tribunal may, when necessary, admit additional evidence during the appeal.

40. *Finality of Decision*

Decision given by the Awraja judicial tribunal shall be final.

CHAPTER 4
Woreda, Awraja, and Provincial Revolutionary
Administrative and Development Committees

41. *Scope of Application*

This chapter shall be effective only until the local self-administration law is issued.

42. *Establishment of Revolutionary Administrative and Development Committee*

There is hereby established a revolutionary administrative and development committee at Woreda, Awraja and provincial levels with the objectives, powers and duties provided for in this chapter.

43. *Objectives of the Committee*

The committee shall have the following objectives:

1/ to see that the various government organizations that are established for the development and growth of the country serve the people in a co-ordinated manner;

2/ to enable peasants to participate in the political, social and economic movement through peasant associations with a view to help the broad masses administer their own affairs.

44. *Working Procedure*

1/ The majority of the members of the committee shall constitute the quorum.

2/ All decisions shall be given by majority vote. However, when there is a tie the chairman shall have a casting vote.

3/ The chairman shall have the duty to execute all decisions made by the committee.

45. *Jurisdiction of the Committee*

The committee shall not interfere with technical matters of government offices. It may, however, express its protest on any such matter to a higher committee.

46. *Members of Woreda Revolutionary Administrative and Development Committee*

1/ The Committee shall have the following members:
   a) the Woreda Administrator . . . . Chairman
   b) the Woreda Azmatch . . . . Vice Chairman
   c) the co-ordinator of the Woreda Zemecha . . . . Member
   d) two Campaign participants . . . .   ''
   e) three members of the executive committee of the Woreda peasant
      association . . . .   ''
   f) a representative of the Ministry of Lands and Settlement . . . .   ''
   g) a representative of the Ministry of Agriculture and Forestry. . . . .   ''
   h) the Woreda Police Chief. . . . .   ''

2/ The representatives of the Ministries of Education and Health shall be members of the committee in cases where those specified in sub-article (1), (b), (c) and (d) are not available.

3/ When matters under discussion by the Committee concern other Government offices, such offices shall send a representative as member and explainer.

4/ In the absence of the Woreda Administrator, the Woreda administration shall be represented by one person as a member only.

47. *Powers and Duties of the Committee:*

The Committee shall have the following powers and duties:

1/ to enforce and execute relevant laws and government policies;

2/ to co-ordinate the exploitation of the natural resources of the Woreda taking into consideration the interests of the inhabitants and the country;

3/ to submit reports and information to the Awraja Revolutionary Administrative and Development Committee concerning development activities carried out from time to time;

4/ to co-ordinate and supervise the activites of government offices, peasant associations and any association established by such associations within the Woreda;

5/ to examine any person or evidence in connection with any decision it may give;

6/ to cause appropriate action to be taken against any person who opposes or fails to perform its order or decision;

7/ to draw up its internal regulations.

48. *Members of the Awraja Revolutionary Administrative and Development Committee:*

1/ The Committee shall have the following members:
   a) the Awraja Administrator...Chairman
   b) the Awraja Azmatch ....Vice-Chairman
   c) the co-ordinator of the Awraja Zemetcha ....Member
   d) two Campaign participants...................................... ”
   e) three members of the executive committee of the Awraja peasant association ... ”
   f) a representative of the Ministry of Lands and Settlement .... ”
   g) a representative of the Ministry of Agriculture and Forestry................ ”
   h) the Awraja Police Chief... ”

2/ In cases where those specified in sub-article 1 (b), (c) and (d) are not available the representatives of the Ministries of Education and Health shall be members.

3/ When the matter being decided by the Committee concerns other Government offices, such offices shall send one representative as a member and explainer.

49. *Powers and Duties of the Committee*

The Awraja Revolutionary Administrative and Development Committee shall:

1/ co-ordinate and supervise the activities of the Woreda Revolutionary Administrative and Development Committees specified under Art. 47 of this Proclamation.

2/ distribute to the Woredas within it and execute development and other programmes that are issued by the Provincial Revolutionary Administrative and Development Committee;

3/ collect and dispatch to the Provincial Revolutionary Administrative and Development Committee the reports and information that are sent from each Woreda;

4/ draw up its internal regulations.

50. *Members of the Provincial Revolutionary Administrative and Development Committee*

1/ The Committee shall have the following members:
   a) the Provincial Administrator or his Deputy ....Chairman
   b) the Provincial Azmatch......................................Vice-Chairman
   c) a representative of Campaign participants in the Province ....Member
   d) the Zemetcha co-ordinator of the Province............................... ”
   e) the Provincial Police Chief.. ”
   f) a representative of the Ministry of Lands and Settlement .... ”
   g) a representative of the Ministry of Agriculture and Forestry................ ”
   h) a representative of the Planning Commission .... ”
   i) a representative of the Ministry of Finance............................. ”
   j) a representative of the Ministry of Education .... ”
   k) a representative of the Ministry of Health.............................. ”

2/ When the matter being decided by the Committee concerns other Government offices, such offices shall send one representative as a member and explainer.

51. *Powers and Duties of the Committee*

The Provincial Revolutionary Administrative and Development committee shall:

1/ co-ordinate and supervise the activities specified under Article 49, of the Awraja Revolutionary Administrative and Development Committees in the Province;

2/ distribute to the Awrajas within it and execute development programmes that are sent by various Government offices;

3/ co-ordinate and dispatch the information and reports that are sent by the different Awrajas within it;

4/ draw up its internal regulations.

CHAPTER 5
Permanent Committee

52. *Establishment of a Permanent Central Committee*

1/ There is hereby established a Permanent Central Committee with the following powers and duties; the Committee shall have the following members:
   a) the Minister of Interior . . . . Chairman
   b) the Minister of Lands and Settlement . . . . Vice-Chairman
   c) the Minister of Agriculture and Forestry. . . . . Member
   d) the Chairman of Development Through Co-operation, Enlightenment and
      Work Campaign Headquarters. . . . . ,,
   e) the Planning Commissioner . . . . ,,

2/ When the matter being decided by the Committee concerns other government offices, such offices shall send one representative as a member and explainer.

53. *Objectives, Powers and Duties of the Permanent Committee*

The Committee shall have the following objectives, powers and duties:

1/ to implement this Proclamation and issue policies which are necessary for its implementation;

2/ to co-ordinate and execute policies issued by the Government concerning the rural sector;

3/ to submit to the Government recommendations relating to rural development and growth;

4/ to decide on matters submitted by Provincial Revolutionary Administrative and Development Committees;

5/ to co-ordinate and supervise, when found necessary, various provincial programmes.

54. *Working Procedure*

1/ The majority of the members shall constitute the quorum.

2/ Decisions shall be made by majority vote. However, in case of a tie, the Chairman, shall have a casting vote.

3/ The Chairman shall have the duty to execute all the decisions made by the committee.

4/ The office of the Permanent Committee shall be the Ministry of Lands and Settlement.

CHAPTER 6
General Provisions

55. *Conflict with Other Laws*

No law, regulation, practice or procedure written or customary in so far as it is inconsistent with the provisions of this Proclamation shall have force or effect in respect of situations provided for by this Proclamation.

56. *Offences*

Any person who obstructs the implementation of this Proclamation or who violates the provisions of this Proclamation shall be punished in accordance with the Penal Code.

57. *Power to Issue Regulations*

The Minister of Lands and Settlement shall, in consultation with the Permanent Committee, issue regulations which are necessary for the implementation of this Proclamation.

58. *Effective Date*

This Proclamation shall come into force as of the 14th day of December, 1975.

Done at Addis Ababa, this 14th day of December, 1975

THE PROVISIONAL MILITARY
ADMINISTRATION COUNCIL

Appendix C

PROCLAMATION NO. 104 of 1976

URBAN DWELLERS' ASSOCIATIONS CONSOLIDATION AND MUNICIPALITIES PROCLAMATION

"ETHIOPIA TIKDEM"

WHEREAS, it is necessary to consolidate the foundations laid by the Government Owner-ship of Urban Lands and Extra Urban Houses Proclamation providing for urban dwellers to get organized in *kebele*, Higher, and Central Associations and run their own affairs, solve their own problems, and directly participate in political, economic and social activities;

WHEREAS, to make the urban dwellers' associations already formed or to be formed more conscious and organized and to make sure that the Revolution will achieve its ultimate goal, it is necessary to give proper revolutionary guidance to the mass organizations which the revolution has already created or will create by co-ordinanting their activities and organization;

WHEREAS, it is believed that the organization of the broad masses of urban dwellers in *kebele*, Higher and Central Associations enabling them to directly take over the municipal administration of urban centers will not only enhance the organizational set-up of the people but will also improve their due participation in development projects;

WHEREAS, urban dwellers' associations formed or to be formed in each *kebele* have direct contact with the broad masses of urban dwellers and form the basis for their organizational set-up; and accordingtly, the *kebele* associations have primary responsibility to organize the people and encourage their participation in both association and government initiated development projects so that their socialist political consciousness will be raised;

WHEREAS, further, this type of set-up will enable the people to run their own affairs and prevent wastage of their time by removing the involved bureaucratic red-tape and further facilitate the direct involvement of the people in the revolutionary process thereby gaining revolutionary experience;

WHEREAS, accordingly, it has been found necessary to consolidate the organizational set-up of urban dwellers' associations formed at every level and to define by proclamation and regulations their powers and duties;

NOW, THEREFORE, in accordance with article 6 of the Definition of Powers of the Provisional Military Administration Council and its Chairman Proclamation No. 2/1974, it is hereby proclaimed as follows:

CHAPTER 1
General

1. *Short Title*

This Proclamation may be cited as the "Urban Dwellers' Associations Consolidation and Municipalities Proclamation No. 104/1976".

2. *Definitions*

In this Proclamation, unless the context otherwise requires:

(1) "Government Ownership of Urban Lands and Extra Houses Proclamation" shall mean the Government Ownership of Urban Lands and Extra Houses Proclamation No. 47/1976;

(2) "urban dwellers' association" shall mean any cooperative society of urban dwellers formed or to be formed at every level under the Government Ownership of Urban Lands and Extra Houses Proclamation;

(3) "*kebele* association" shall mean any cooperative society of urban dwellers formed or to be formed at the first level under the Government Ownership of Urban Lands and Extra Houses Proclamation;

(4) "higher urban dwellers' association" shall mean any association to be formed in accordance with article 25 of the Government Ownership of Urban Lands and Extra Houses Proclamation;

(5) "central urban dwellers' association" shall mean any association to be formed in accordance with Article 26 of the Government Ownership of Urban Lands and Extra Houses Proclamation;

(6) "council" shall mean the assembly of members of Higher Urban Dwellers' Associations representing the Policy Committee of every *kebele* association pursuant to the Government Ownership of Urban Lands and Extra Houses Proclamation and this Proclamation;

(7) "congress" shall mean the assembly of members of Central Urban Dwellers' Associations representing the council of Higher Urban Dwellers' Associations established under the Government Ownership of Urban Lands and Extra Houses Proclamation and this Proclamation;

(8) "policy committee" shall mean a committee composed of persons elected to serve as leaders of urban dwellers' associations formed at every level and constituted of members of executive, judicial, public safety and financial inspection committees in accordance with the internal regulations of such associations;

(9) "Minister" or "Ministry" shall mean the Minister or Ministry of Urban Development and Housing;

(10) "urban center" shall mean any place in which a municipality has already been established or which is designated as an urban center by the Minister in consultation with concerned Government offices;

(11) "charter" shall mean a delegation of power to a muncipality to administer the urban center in which it is established being directly responsible to the Central Government;

(12) "Mayor" shall mean the official nominated by the Congress and appointed by the Government in accordance with Chapter 5 of this Proclamation to head the administrative branch of Municipalities;

(13) "stray animal or lost property" shall mean any animal or property not under the charge of any person. The phrase "stray animal" shall also include animals under the charge of any person but wandering at large in public places designated as such by municipalities;

(14) "private tree" shall mean any tree located within the area alloted in private possession to a family, individual or organization in accordance with Article 5 of the Government Ownership of Urban Lands and Extra Houses Proclamation.

CHAPTER 2
Urban Dwellers' Associations:
Common Provisions

3. *Legal Personality*

Urban dwellers' associations formed or to be formed at every level shall have legal personality of their own.

4. *Qualifications for Election*

(1) Any Ethiopian to be elected to the Policy Committee of any urban dwellers' association established under the Government Ownership of urban Lands and Extra Houses Proclamation and this Proclamation shall satisfy the following requirements:
    (a) that he is of the broad masses and accepts the Ethiopian National Democratic Revolution Programme;
    (b) that he is esteemed by nearby dwellers for his integrity and hardwork; that he gives precedence to the interests of the broad masses over his private interests;
    (c) that he is not serving a sentence of imprisonment or has not been convicted of misuse or waste of public property or breach of trust;
    (d) that he has not been deprived of his civil rights by a court of law;
    (e) that he has no mental disease; and that he is not addicted to alcohol and dangerous drugs;
    (f) that he is not less than 21 years of age.

(2) The General Assembly, Congress or Council of urban dwellers' associations formed or to be formed under the Government Ownership of Urban Lands and Extra Houses Proclamation and this Proclamation shall carefully examine that persons it elects to serve the association as officials satisfy the provisions of sub-article (1) above.

(3) Any Ethiopian, to be eligible to elect members of the Policy Committee of urban dwellers' associations to be formed under the Government Ownership of Urban Lands and Extra Houses Proclamation and this Proclamation, shall satisfy the following requirements:
    (a) that he has attained 18 years of age at the time of election;
    (b) that he has no mental disease;
    (c) that he is not serving a sentence of imprisonment;
    (d) that he has not been deprived of his civil rights by a court of law.

5. *Term of Office of Association Leaders and Conditions for their Removal*

(1) The term of office of leaders of urban dwellers' associations elected at every level shall be fixed in accordance with the model internal regulations issued by the Minister.

(2) Leaders elected by the association shall, before they are removed from office, be informed in detail of the faults they have committed and shall be afforded enough time and opportunity to present their defence. Members shall, as far as possible, be always guided by the principle of criticism and self-criticism.

(3) The procedure for the removal from office of association leaders shall be as laid down in the model internal regulations issued by the Minister.

6. *Powers and Duties Common to Associations*

Subject to the provisions of Chapters 3, 4 and 5 of this Proclamation, urban dwellers' associations shall, in addition to their powers and duties under the Government Ownership of Urban Lands and Extra Houses Proclamation, have the following powers and duties:

(1) to enable the broad masses of urban dwellers to administer their own affairs;

(2) to develop the ideology of the broad masses in line with the philosophy of *Hebrettese-bawinet* with a view to enabling them to struggle against feudalism, imperialism and bureaucratic capitalism and their influence;

(3) to assist and encourage the formation of women's and other associations necessary for the effective accomplishment of its objectives;

(4) to enhance the development of the community by making the people participate in the activities of the associations and government initiated projects;

(5) to establish, in cooperation with the concerned institutions, people's shops and other services, and encourage and give the necessary assistance for the establishment of cottage industries and other cooperative societies by mobilising the community;

(6) to rent and construct houses in accordance with the master-plan and housing policy issued by the Ministry or any office or organization delegated by the Ministry;

(7) to encourage dwellers who want to build their own houses by getting organized in associations;

(8) to assist in the drafting of articles of associations for associations established to accomplish its objectives and ratify and enforce the same in accordance with powers conferred on it.

7. *Mode of Operation*

(1) As *kebele*, Higher and Central Urban Dwellers' Associations are, in their organizational set-up, broad mass organizations, they shall follow the principle of democratic centralism. The associations shall, therefore, ensure that in their operations, power flows properly from lower to higher and from higher to lower bodies in accordance with the philosophy of *Hebrettesebawinet*. The following shall be the principal directives:

(a) the members who run the various activities of associations at all levels shall be elected by the general assembly of the association;

(b) associations at every level shall have the duty to submit from time to time their work programmes and report of their activities from lower to higher and from higher to lower bodies. Lower bodies shall, moreover, have the duty to observe and enforce the decisions given by higher bodies of the association;

(c) every decision of associations shall be given by majority vote. The number of votes required to constitute a majority shall be determined by the internal regulations of the association.

(2) The *kebele*, Higher and Central Urban Dwellers' associations shall follow economical, simple, efficient, trustworthy and public service oriented revolutionary method of work. It shall be the revolutionary duty of association leaders and members to curb the practice of bribery, undue advantage and influence and strictly control and expose them with a view to making them condemned by the society.

(3) No salary or allowance or any other payment may be paid to association officials, except for those who work full time as Mayors, Heads of Urban Centres or members of standing committees of Central Urban Dwellers' Associations as the case may be.

CHAPTER 3
Kebele Urban Dwellers' Associations

8. *Number of Members of Policy Committee*

The number of members of every *Kebele* Policy Committee shall be not less than fifteen (15).

9. *Powers and Duties*

Every urban dwellers' association formed at *kebele* level shall, in addition to those specified in Article 6 of this Proclamation, have the following capacity, powers and duties:

(1) to collect in accordance with the Government Ownership of Urban Lands and Extra Houses Proclamation on its own responsibility with receipts prepared by the Agency for the Administration of Rented Houses and expend on *kebele* activities the rent of urban

land and houses within its jurisdiction and run the general administration and maintenance of such houses;

(2) to open an account in the Housing and Savings Bank and deposit therein, or where there is no Housing and Savings Bank, deposit in trust in any other bank designated by the Housing and Savings Bank, or, where there is no such other bank, in Municipalities or, where there are no Municipalities, in Government treasuries, the rent and other contributions and revenue the association collects;

(3) to pay living allowance to those dwellers within its boundaries who, in accordance with Article 21, sub-articles (2), (3) and (4) of the Government Ownership of Urban Lands and Extra Houses Proclamation, are entitled thereto; provided that where any dwellers entitled to living allowance have from among the houses they have handed over to the Government, any house the (monthly rental) value of which exceeds One Hundred (100) Birr the association shall:
  (a) pay the whole of the required living allowance from the accounts of the Agency for the Administration of Rented Houses; or
  (b) pay the living allowance from the rent it has already collected and demand reimbursement from the Agency for the Administration of Rented Houses;

(4) to establish and co-ordinate, in co-operation with the Higher Urban Dwellers' Association, and in accordance with the directives issued by it, such educational, health, market, recreational, road construction and other similar facilities as are necessary for the community;

(5) to construct, in cooperation with the Higher Urban Dwellers' Association and in accordance with the directives issued to it, low cost houses to the community; and organize activities with a view to improving the living conditions of the community;

(6) to preserve and maintain non-private trees and forests within the jurisdiction of the *kebele*; fell, mow and sell trees and grass in accordance with directives issued by the Central Urban Dwellers' Association except, demarcated trees, forests and grass, and expend the proceeds therefrom for the purposes of the activities of the association;

(7) to develop forest resources, protect the soil from erosion and beautify the urban centre:
  (a) carry on afforestation to replace felled trees, in unutilized areas, along street sides and around residential areas;
  (b) encourage the observance by private possessors of the directives specified in (a) above, and give any assistance where necessary;

(8) to protect any public or Government property within its jurisdiction;

(9) to conduct educational activities on hygiene and cleanliness; and take the necessary measures to ensure the cleanliness of the *kebele*;

(10) to eradicate illiteracy within the *kebele*;

(11) to prevent the placing of undue obstacles on roads within the boundary of the Kebele and immediately remove same where they have been placed;

(12) to keep a proper register of houses located within the *kebele*;

(13) to keep a proper register of the number of residents living within the *kebele*;

(14) to keep a register of births, marriages and deaths within the *kebele*;

(15) to cooperate with the Ministry of Commerce and Tourism on matters pertaining to price control;

(16) to assist, in cooperation with the Postal Service Authority, the extension of postal service to the people;

(17) to cooperate with the concerned office in matters relating to the collection of Government taxes, fees and other revenue;

(18) to contribute to the Higher Urban Dwellers' Association at least fifteen percent of the fund it retains after paying living allowances to persons entitled thereto; the amount of such contribution shall be determined by the Higher Association having regard to the income from rents of the association;

(19) to establish a judicial tribunal of three members;

(20) to establish a public welfare committee in order to fulfill its duties under the Government Ownership of Urban Lands and Extra Houses Proclamation and this Proclamation; and to ensure and protect effectively the welfare of the community. The *kebele* association may mobilize the community for this purpose.

10. *Powers and Duties of the Public Safety Committee*

(1) The members of the public safety committee shall jointly or severally have the following powers and duties:

   (a) to submit to the appropriate authority in cooperation with nearby dwellers any criminal held in *flagrante delicto*;

   (b) to produce wanted persons in accordance with orders legally issued by the executive committee or judicial tribunal of urban dwellers' associations;

   (c) to enforce the decisions and orders of the judicial tribunal;

   (d) to protect public and government property within its boundary;

   (e) to carry on guarding and security activities in accordance with directives issued by the Ministry of Interior;

(2) Members of the executive committee of associations jointly or severally or residents of the *kebele* delegated in writing by such committee may exercise the duties specified under sub-article (1) of this Article.

11. *Powers and Duties of Judicial Tribunal*

Judicial tribunals of *kebele* dwellers' associations shall, in addition to those specified in the Government Ownership of Urban Lands and Extra Houses Proclamation, have jurisdiction to hear and decide the following:

(1) Civil Jurisdiction:

With the exception of cases falling under Article 15 (2) of the Civil Procedure Code and the Labour Proclamation No. 64/1975 and disputes to which the Central Government is one of the parties:

   (a) any disputes involving pecuniary claims of up to Five Hundred (500) Birr or any disputes on property of a value of up to Five Hundred (500) Birr;

   (b) disputes involving claims of rents and service charges on houses and lands within the boundary of the *kebele*;

   (c) suits based on Articles 1212, 1218, 1219, 1220, 1221, 1225, 1226, 1245 and 1246 of the Civil Code;

   (d) any civil cases where the parties to the dispute give their consent to its jurisdiction.

(2) Criminal Jurisdiction:

Without prejudice to the provisions of sub-article (1) of Article 33 hereof as to the penalty:

   (a) offences under Articles 471, 543, 544, 548, 552, 571, 583, 608, 625, 626, 649, 650, 652, 653, 661; of the Penal Code;

   (b) any offence under Article 439 of the Penal Code where the offence specified therein is committed against it;

   (c) offences under the code of Petty Offences of the Penal Code excluding traffic violations and offences under Articles 733, 738–743 inclusive, 746–756 inclusive, 758, 759, 765, 767, 776, 783, 786, 787, 789–791 inclusive, 817–820 inclusive;

   (d) any offences under the code of Petty Offences specifically enumerated under Sub-article (2) (c) of this Article where the complainant Government Office refers the case to the judicial tribunal;

(3) in addition:

   (a) the judicial tribunal of the *kebele* association may examine in detail the means of livelihood of the person who submits any application to get any kind of free services in court or Government offices and grant certificate thereto;

   (b) the judicial tribunal of *kebele* associations shall cooperate to serve court summons to parties to a dispute and witnesses through the *kebele* association of which the persons so summoned are residents.

12. *Scope of Jurisdiction*

The Judicial Tribunal of *kebele* associations shall have the powers specified in Article 11 of this Proclamation where:

(1) the parties to the disputes are residents of the *kebele* or associations within the *kebele*; or

(2) the property, the matter or the offence which is the cause of the dispute is located or committed within the *kebele*; or

(3) the defendant is a resident of the *kebele*.

CHAPTER 4
Higher Urban Dwellers' Associations

13. *Establishment of Association*

(1) More than one *kebele* associations located in an area defined by guidelines issued by the Ministry shall together form Higher Urban Dwellers' Association.

(2) In urban centers where Higher Urban Dwellers' Associations cannot be formed, *kebele* associations shall additionally perform the duties of such associations.

(3) In urban centers where a *kebele* association performs the duties of Higher Urban Dwellers' Association, the general assembly of such association shall elect a Special Judicial Tribunal of from three to five members to hear appeals against decisions given by the *kebele* Judicial Tribunal. Decisions given by judicial tribunals thus established shall be final. Members of the Special Judicial Tribunals may not serve as members in any other functions of Policy Committees.

14. *Membership Mandatory*

Kelebe associations located within areas demarcated for the establishment of Higher Urban Dwellers' Associations have the duty to become members of such Higher Associations.

15. *Number and Election of the Members of Councils*

(1) The Policy Committee of every *kebele* association shall elect at least one of its members to represent it in the Higher Association. The number of representatives shall be based on the number of *kebele* associations which are members of the Higher Association.

(2) Where *kebele* associations perform duties of Higher and Central Urban Dwellers' Associations or where Higher Associations perform duties of Central Urban Dwellers' Associations, as the case may be, a representative of the Ministry may participate as member of the Policy Committee, or of the Council.

16. *Operations of the Association*

The association shall carry out its activities through its Council and Policy Committee.

(1) *Council*:

The number of members of the Council of the association may not be less than 26. The Council shall:

(a) elect and discharge members of the Policy Committee of the association, and establish the judicial tribunal of the association. The members of the judicial tribunal of the association shall be not less than three and not more than five;

(b) examine and approve the budget of the association and supervise its accounts;

(c) elect from among its members at least two members to represent it at the Central Urban Dwellers' Association;

(d) elect from among its members from three to five members and establish a Special Judicial Tribunal to hear appeals against decisions of the judicial tribunal of the association in urban centers where Central Urban Dwellers Associations are not established. Members of the Special Judicial Tribunal may not be members of the Policy Committee of the association;

(e) supervise the proper implementation of the powers and duties conferred on the association under this proclamation.

(2) *Policy Committee*

The number of members of the Policy Committee of the association and their detailed duties shall be prescribed in its internal regulations.

17. *Powers and Duties of Higher Urban Dwellers' Assocation*

The association shall, in addition to those specified in Article 6 of Chapter 2 of this Proclamation, have the following powers and duties:

(1) to ensure, in co-operation with the Central Urban Dwellers' Association, that associations within its boundary have as far as possible equal holdings and adequate income;

(2) to give the necessary assistance, in consultation and collaboration with the Ministry, when any family, individual or organization having no urban land applies to the Ministry for such land for the construction of dwelling or business houses;

(3) to study and implement methods with a view to giving better services to the community by coordinating the financial and manpower resources of the *kebele* associations within its boundary;

(4) to coordinate the activities of the public safety committee within its boundary and within neighbouring associations;

(5) to assist *kebele* associations to give better service to the community by coordinating their activities with respect to the collection of rent and maintenance of houses;

(6) to establish and supervise places where stray animals and lost property may be kept;

(7) to designate and supervise, in consultation with the Central Urban Dwellers' Association, livestock marketing centers within its boundary;

(8) to study and implement methods with the view of establishing cooperative societies, people's shops and the like and giving better services to the community by coordinating the *kebele* associations in the vicinity;

(9) to subsidize the activities of *kebele* associations within its boundaries from the fund it acquires from the Central Urban Dwellers' Association and from contributions it collects;

(10) to operate and coordinate, in cooperation with Central Urban Dwellers' Associations, social service programmes;

(11) to contribute to the Central Urban Dwellers' Association one-third (1/3) of the fund it acquires pursuant to sub-article 18 of Article 9 hereof.

18. *Judicial Tribunal of Higher Urban Dwellers' Association*

The judicial tribunals established by Higher Urban Dwellers' Associations shall have the following jurisdiction:

(1) to hear appeals against decisions of judicial tribunals of *kebele* associations, which decisions thus rendered shall be final.

(2) to hear and decide on first instance, disputes between *kebele* associations and between *kebele* associations and dwellers relating to urban lands and houses, subject to the provisions of Article 11 hereof.

CHAPTER 5
Central Urban Dwellers' Associations

19. *Establishment of Association*

(1) Where more than one Higher Urban Dwellers' Associations are formed within the

boundary of any urban center they shall establish a Central Urban Dwellers' Association and take over the administration of the urban center.

(2) In urban centers where Central Urban Dwellers' Associations are not established, the Higher Urban Dwellers' Association shall perform the duties of such Central Urban Dwellers' Association.

(3) In all urban centres where Higher Urban Dwellers' Associations are not established, the *Kebele* Association shall perform the duties of Central Urban Dwellers' Associations.

20. *Membership Mandatory*

In urban centers where Central Urban Dwellers' Associations are to be formed, Higher Urban Dwellers' Associations are obliged to be members of such Central Urban Dwellers' Associations.

21. *Number and Election of Members of Congress*

(1) Every Higher Association shall elect at least two members from among members of its Council to represent it at Central Urban Dwellers' Associations. The number of representatives shall be based on the number of Higher Associations which are members of such Central Associations, provided that their number may not, in any urban centre, be less than 30.

(2) In chartered urban centres, the concerned Ministries and offices shall delegate one member to the Congress.

(3) In non-chartered urban centers, the representatives of the Ministry and the Ministry of Interior shall participate in the Congress as members; other Ministries and offices shall participate in the Congress when necessary.

(4) In chartered urban centers, representatives of each Ministry shall only participate in the meetings of the Congress but shall not have the right to vote or to be elected as officials of the administration.

22. *Operations of the Association*

The association shall carry on its activities through the Congress, the Standing Committee and the Administrative Section of the urban center.

(1) *The Congress*

The congress of the urban center shall be the assembly of members represented in accordance with Article 21 hereof.
The Congress shall:
(a) supervise the effective implementation of the powers and duties conferred on Central Urban Dwellers' Associations under Article 23 hereof;
(b) give recommendations to the Government on matters relating to the development and expansion of urban centers;
(c) determine the schedule for the meetings of the Congress provided that regular meetings of the Congress may not exceed four times annually;
(d) elect the members of the Standing Committees of the central Association; the number of Standing Committees may not exceed the number of Higher Associations;
(e) submit to the Government for appointment as mayor or head of the urban center a list of three nominees from among its members; the Government shall appoint one of the nominees as mayor or head of the urban center and dismiss the same;
(f) define the job descriptions of all higher officials; dismiss same from their jobs; provided that where dismissal of the mayor or the head of the urban center is involved, it shall submit its recommendations to the Government;
(g) establish a judicial tribunal of from three to five members;
(h) approve the budget of the urban center and supervise its implementation;
(i) appoint auditors and approve or reject their reports;
(j) submit through the Ministry for determination by the Government land rents and service charges, taxes, charges and fees in chartered urban centers;

(k) have the power in chartered urban centers to issue and amend laws pertaining to, the administration of the urban centre, the maintenance of the property of municipalities, and security and public health;

(l) issue regulations for the effective implementation of its powers and duties;

(m) the mayor or head of the urban center shall be chairman of the Congress.

(2) *Powers and Duties of the Standing Committee*

The Standing Committee of the Central Association shall when the Congress is not in session, supervise the proper implementation of the powers of the Congress under sub-article (1) of Article 22 hereof.

(3) *The Administrative Section*

(a) The mayor or the head of the urban center shall run the Administrative section of the urban center as the head thereof. The mayor or the head shall be responsible to the Congress and the Standing Committee;

(b) The mayor or the head of the urban centre shall submit to the Council for appointment the higher officials of municipalities;

(c) The mayor or head of the urban center shall have the power to hire and dismiss any employee other than those higher officials appointed by the Congress.

(d) The conditions for the employment, dismissal and promotion of the employees of the municipalities shall be prescribed in laws or regulations issued by the Congress in consultation with the Government.

23. *Powers and Duties of the Association*

Central Urban Dwellers' Associations shall, in addition to those specified in Chapter 2 hereof, have the following powers and duties:

(1) to collect and allocate charges and rents which, in accordance with the various legislations previously in force, and regulations to be issued under this Proclamation, are due to Municipalities, and collect taxes in accordance with the policy of the Government relating to taxes;

(2) to lay out, close and maintain main streets, squares, bridges, resorts, parks and public gardens;

(3) to insure that sewerage systems and houses are built properly and according to plan;

(4) to organize and prepare for public use water and electric supplies, grand market places, cemeteries, abattoirs, drainages, public baths, theatres, and public halls;

(5) to provide, in cooperation with the concerned Government offices, adequate transport services throughout the urban center;

(6) to organize and supervise fire brigades, ambulance services, and garbage trucks;

(7) to take the necessary measures to ensure public health and hygiene in urban centers;

(8) to perform, in accordance with directives issued by the Ministry works relating to large scale maintenance and demolition activities; to decide the width, propriety and construction of any new road; and generally to supervise that any work done by or under private individual is not contrary to the requirements of public health and safety;

(9) to operate and coordinate social service programmes in collaboration with the concerned Government offices and agencies;

(10) to demarcate, in consultation with the Ministry of Agriculture and Settlement, large forests located within the boundary of urban centers and supervise their proper up-keep; and also to issue, the necessary directives concerning undemarcated trees in accordance with sub-article (7) of Article 9;

(11) to put into effect all the powers and duties conferred on municipalities by various laws and regulations previously in force to the extent that they do not generally contravene this Proclamation and the Government Ownership of Urban Lands and Extra Houses Proclamation, and also to perform the duties expected of municipalities;

(12) to insure, in consultation with the Ministry, that the Higher Associations in Urban Centers have equal holdings;

(13) to coordinate the development projects operated by Higher Urban Dwellers' Associations.

(14) to give the necessary financial support from the revenue of municipalities, to development projects run by Higher and *kebele* assocations;

(15) to protect, in collaboration with the Ministry of Mines, Energy and Water Resources, minerals like quarries and sand within the boundaries of urban centers, and to insure that the same are used to the development and expansion of urban centers.

24. *Judicial Tribunal of Central Urban Dwellers' Association*

Judicial tribunals of Central Urban Dwellers' Associations shall have the following powers and duties:

(1) to hear and decide appeals against decisions of Higher Urban Dwellers' Associations given on first instance;

(2) the decisions on appeals of the judicial tribunal of Central Urban Dwellers' Associations shall be final.

CHAPTER 6
Provisions and Procedure
Common to Judicial Tribunals

25. *Scope of Application*

(1) The provisions of this chapter shall apply *mutatis mutandis* to all judicial tribunals established under this Proclamation.

(2) Judicial tribunals are public tribunals; therefore, any dweller of the *kebele* who is present at the hearing has the right to comment and forward his views on the case at hand, provided however, that the judicial tribunal shall have the power and responsibility to render its own independent judgement based on law and justice.

(3) Judicial tribunals established at every level shall only follow the procedures laid down in this Proclamation.

26. *Time and Place of Hearing*

Any judicial tribunal may hold hearings in the office of the association or in any other place and time which it deems suitable for holding hearings; provided that the time of hearing shall, as far as possible, be after working hours.

27. *Procedure*

(1) With the exception of cases on appeal, judicial tribunals established at every level shall have jurisdiction to hear a case only where such case has been examined in advance and referred to it by the executive committee of the association. All decisions or orders shall be given in the name of the association.

(2) No member of judicial tribunals may hear on appeal any case which he has previously heard at the first instance.

(3) The tribunal may hold hearings when more than half the members thereof are present.

(4) Where a case cannot be decided by majority because of lack of quorum of the Tribunal, the Chairman of the association may co-opt one of the members of the Executive Committee to hear the case.

28. *Production of Evidence*

(1) Any judicial tribunal may require evidence to be produced before it and examine witnesses as may be necessary for the determination of the case.

(2) Any person, office or organization shall have the duty to appear before the tribunal and produce the required evidence on time when summoned pursuant to sub-article (1) of this Article.

29. *Option not to entertain Case*

Any judicial tribunal shall have the option not to entertain or decide a case where the following conditions obtain:

   (1) the defendant in good faith, pleads guilty and apologises before the tribunal or the association and on his own intiative makes good the damage he caused; or

   (2) the plaintiff or the appellant has withdrawn his charge or appeal.

30. *Change of Venue*

Where in accordance with sub-articles (2) and (3) of Article 12, the places where the defendant resides and where the offence was committed do not concide and where the judicial tribunal finds the *kebele* in which the defendant resides more convenient for the enforcement of the punishment and it is ascertained that it would not delay the determination of the case, it may transfer the case to the judicial tribunal of the *kebele* in which the defendant resides.

31. *Transfer to Regular Courts and Concurrent Offences*

   (1) Where in the course of first instance or appeal proceedings any judicial tribunal finds that it has no jurisdiction to hear the case, it shall order the transfer of the case to a regular court having jurisdiction. The court to which any case have been thus transferred shall have jurisdiction to hear and decide such case.

   (2) The court to which the case has been transferred in accordance with sub-article (1) of this Article, shall, adhering to the penal provisions prescribed in this Proclamation, give decisions including on the charges against the defendant before the tribunal.

   (3) Where any regular court gives decisions pursuant to sub-article (2) of this Article and where it deems that its decision will be better executed through *kebele* Associations, it shall transfer the execution of its decision to the Judicial Tribunal of the *kebele* Association of which the defendant is a resident.

   (4) Where the offences committed fall within the jurisdiction partly of the judicial tribunal and partly of the regular court, the regular court shall have jurisdiction to hear all of the offences together.

32. *Giving of Judgement*

Any judicial tribunal shall register:
   (a) the charge and supporting evidence against the defendant; and
   (b) the defences produced by the defendant; and shall give judgement thereon.

33. *Power to Impose Penalties and Give Rulings*

   (1) Where any judicial tribunal finds the defendant guilty in cases it hears under this Proclamation it may impose, according to the gravity of the offence, any one of the following penalties:
      (a) warn the offender;
      (b) order the offender to make a public apology to the injured person or association;
      (c) publicize the offender's shameful act;
      (d) impose fines of up to Three Hundred (300) Birr;
      (e) impose a sentence of imprisonment of up to three (3) months;
      (f) impose a sentence of hard labour of up to fifteen (15) days;
      (g) order the offender to compensate the injured party.

   (2) In civil suits under this Proclamation:
      (a) where the defendant is found guilty, the tribunal may order him to make an immediate payment of the fine imposed, or to effect payment within a fixed period of time or to do or to refrain from doing a certain act;
      (b) where the tribunal is certain that the plaintiff instituted the suit with intent to cause undue inconvenience to the defendant, it may order the plaintiff to pay damage to the defendant.

34. *Repeated Offences*

The tribunal may impose more than one of the penalties referred to in Article 33 (1) on any offender who is proved to be guilty of committing:
(a) repeated, or
(b) concurrent
offences.

35. *Non-compliance*

Where any person ordered to perform compulsory labour by a tribunal fails to comply with such order, the tribunal may impose a sentence of up to three (3) months imprisonment or a fine of up to Three Hundred (300) Birr.

36. *Execution of Decision*

Tribunals shall execute their decisions through the *kebele* Public Safety Committee or the local police.

37. *Appeal*

(1) Any party may appeal within fifteen (15) days from the date of decision by the tribunal;
(2) The tribunal shall give a copy of its judgement and the evidence to the party appealing; and in cases where this is not possible, the chairman of the tribunal or a member he delegates must appear in person and explain the matter to the appellate tribunal.

38. *Decisions on Appeal*

The Higher or Central judicial tribunal may reverse, confirm, vary or remand the case with guidelines to the *kebele* or Higher Judicial Tribunal, as the case may be.

39. *Additional Evidence*

The Higher or Central Judicial Tribunal may, where it finds it necessary, admit additional evidence during the appeal, provided that where any party to the dispute intentionally or negligently failed to produce any evidence during the hearing at the first instance, such party may not produce at the appeal stage any additional evidence he did not produce initially.

Chapter 7
Special Provisions

40. *Transitory Period*

(1) Powers of the Minister
  (a) Subject to the provisions of this Proclamation, the Minister shall have the power to issue regulations regarding the establishment of Higher and Central Urban Dwellers' Associations.
  (b) Until the issuance of a Proclamation enabling self-administration to municipalities in non-chartered urban centers, the Minister, being subrogated to the powers conferred on the Ministry of Interior by various laws and regulations previously in force, shall have the powers to supervise municipalities as the head thereof.
  (c) In urban centers where Higher and Central Urban Dwellers' Associations cannot be formed, the Minister shall issue directives regarding the conditions whereby *kebele* associations may take-over the administration of municipalities.
  (d) The Minister shall study ways and means by which urban centers become self-sufficient; and where, considering their population and economic activity he finds that they are competent to administer themselves, he shall propose to the Government that they be chartered.
  (e) The Minister shall prepare model articles of association to Associations formed or to be formed under this Proclamation and the Government Ownership of Urban Lands and Extra Houses Proclamation.

(f) Where the Minister ascertains that members of policy committees and especially of Judicial Tribunals of Urban Dwellers' Associations formed or to be formed at any level cannot conduct their duties in their extra time only, he shall, taking into the consideration the load of work of the associations, allow the members to suspend their regular work and work for the association instead for not more than eight (8) working hours a week. Any Government Office, organization or employer receiving notice from the Minister in accordance with this, has the duty to comply with the order.

(g) Powers and duties conferred on the Minister and the Ministry of Public Works and Housing by the Government Ownership of Urban Lands and Extra Houses Proclamation and other laws are conferred on the Minister and the Ministry by this Proclamation.

(2) Chartered Urban Centers

All urban centers which had charters prior to the promulgation of this Proclamation shall be deemed to have been granted Charters upon the establishment of congresses in accordance with chapter 5 of this Proclamation.

(3) Right to elect and be elected

The following urban dwellers shall neither have the right to elect or be elected for a period of one year from the date of issuance of this Proclamation, as members of the policy committee, the council, or the congress of urban dwellers' associations formed or to be formed under this Proclamation and the Government Ownership of Urban Lands and Extra Houses Proclamation:

(a) any person or husband and wife who, before the promulgation of the Government Ownership of urban Lands and Extra Houses Proclamation, had a monthly income from house rent of more than Fifty (50) Birr or any person who, having no income of his own from work, is dependent on such persons;

(b) any person or husband and wife who, before the promulgation of the Public Ownership of Rural Lands Proclamation, had more than ten (10) hectares (¼ of a *gasha*) of land or any person who having no income of his own from work is dependent on such persons;

(c) subject to sub-article 3 (a) and (b) above, any person or husband and wife whose property has been nationalized in accordance with the various Proclamations, Directives and Orders issued by the Provisional Military Government or any person who, having no income of his own from work is dependent on such persons.

41. *Conflict with other Laws*

(1) No law, regulation, practice or procedure written on customary, in so far as it is inconsistent with the provisions of this Proclamation shall have force or effect in respect of situations provided for by this Proclamation.

(2) In respect of urban dwellers' associations only, the following Articles of the Urban Lands Rent and Urban Houses Tax Proclamation No. 80/1976 are hereby repealed or amended:

(a) Article 5 and Article 13 which provides for the obligation of the Ministry of Public Works and Housing;

(b) Article 14 (2) is deleted and replaced by the following Article 14 (2):

14. (2) "Dwelling houses whose estimated annual rental value is up to Three Hundred (300) Birr are exempt from tax for a period of one year from the effective date of this proclamation. After one year, however, the conditions of tax payment shall be determined in accordance with Urban Dwellers' Associations Consolidation and Municipalities Proclamation No. 104/ 1969".

42. *Offences*

Any person who contravenes or obstructs the implementation of this Proclamation or regulations issued under this Proclamation or who violates this Proclamation shall be punished in accordance with the Penal Code.

43. *Jurisdiction of Regular Courts*

(1) Subject to sub-article (3) of this Article no regular count shall, as of the effective date of this Proclamation, have jurisdiction to entertain any suits which fall within the jurisdiction of the Judicial tribunal of Urban Dwellers' Associations under this Proclamation.

(2) A case instituted in a regular court before the effective date of this Proclamation shall, even if it falls within the jurisdiction of the judicial tribunals of Urban Dwellers' Associations under this Proclamation, be decided by the regular court handling the case.

(3) In urban centres where *kebele* judicial tribunals are not established, civil and criminal cases falling within the jurisdiction of judicial tribunals under this Proclamation shall be heard by the regular courts and the regular procedure shall apply; provided that as of the date of notification to the court by the Minister of the establishment of the judicial tribunal, such court shall only decide cases already instituted and shall cease to entertain cases falling under the jurisdiction of the judicial tribunal.

44. *Effective Date*

This Proclamation shall come into force as of the 9th day of October, 1976.

Done at Addis Ababa, this 9th day of October, 1976

THE PROVISIONAL MILITARY
ADMINISTRATION COUNCIL

Index